The Second Language Curriculum

THE CAMBRIDGE APPLIED LINGUISTICS SERIES
Series editors: Michael H. Long and Jack C. Richards

This new series presents the findings of recent work in applied linguistics which are of direct relevance to language teaching and learning and of particular interest to applied linguists, researchers, language teachers, and teacher trainers.

In this series:

The Second Language Curriculum

Edited by

Robert Keith Johnson

University of Hong Kong

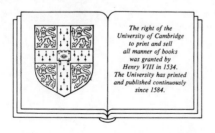

The right of the
University of Cambridge
to print and sell
all manner of books
was granted by
Henry VIII in 1534.
The University has printed
and published continuously
since 1584.

Cambridge University Press
Cambridge
New York   Port Chester
Melbourne   Sydney

Published by the Press Syndicate of the University of Cambridge
The Pitt Building, Trumpington Street, Cambridge CB2 1RP
40 West 20th Street, New York, NY 10011, USA
10 Stamford Road, Oakleigh, Melbourne 3166, Australia

First published 1989
Reprinted 1990

Printed in Great Britain
at the University Press, Cambridge

Library of Congress cataloguing in publication data

The second language curriculum / edited by Robert Keith Johnson.
        p.   cm. – (The Cambridge applied linguistics series)
Bibliography.
Includes index.
ISBN 0 521 36156 7   ISBN 0 521 36961 4 (pbk.)
1. Language and languages – Study and teaching. 2. Curriculum
planning.   I. Johnson, Robert Keith.   II. Series.
P53.295.S44 1989
418'.007–dc19   88-23433

British Library cataloguing in publication data

The second language curriculum.
(Cambridge applied linguistics).
1. Non-English speaking students.
Education. Curriculum subjects: English
language. Curriculum. Development.
I. Johnson, Robert Keith, 1936–
428.2'4'07

ISBN 0 521 36156 7 hard covers
ISBN 0 521 36961 4 paperback

Contents

Contributors

Lyle F. Bachman, University of Illinois at Urbana-Champaign, USA
Richard Berwick, Kobe University of Commerce, Kobe, Japan
Michael Breen, University of Lancaster, Lancaster, England
Geoffrey Brindley, Adult Migrant Education Service, Sydney, Australia
James Dean Brown, University of Hawaii, Honolulu, USA
Chris Candlin, Macquarie University, North Ryde, Australia
Leni Dam, Education Authority, Greve, Denmark
Warwick B. Elley, University of Canterbury, Christchurch, New Zealand
Gerd Gabrielsen, Danmarks Laererhøjskole, Copenhagen, Denmark
Peter Hargreaves, University of Cambridge Local Examinations
   Syndicate, Cambridge, England
Thom Hudson, University of California at Los Angeles, USA
Robert Keith Johnson, University of Hong Kong, Hong Kong
Andrew Littlejohn, University of Lancaster, Lancaster, England
Graham Low, University of York, York, England
David Nunan, National Curriculum Resource Centre, Adelaide,
   Australia
Martha C. Pennington, University of Hawaii, Honolulu, USA
Theodore S. Rodgers, University of Hawaii, Honolulu, USA
H. H. Stern, formerly Ontario Institute of Studies in Education, Ontario,
   Canada
John Swales, The University of Michigan, Ann Arbor, USA
Scott Windeatt, University of Lancaster, Lancaster, England

Series editors' preface

This book in the Cambridge Applied Linguistics series presents an overview of the scope and dimension of language curriculum development and also demonstrates how many of its leading practitioners apply curriculum theory and practice to language teaching. Publication of this collection of mainly original papers is a healthy sign that, in the last few years, language curriculum practitioners have moved away from a narrow view of their work, one which focused largely on issues of content and methodology, to a more comprehensive, and at the same time, complex understanding of curriculum. This is one which encompasses policy making, needs assessment, instructional design and development, teacher preparation and development, as well as programme management and evaluation. This is a far cry from the days of 'syllabus design'.

The value of this collection of papers which Keith Johnson has assembled lies in the many different perspectives it offers on the language curriculum. Both macro and micro issues are presented, and curriculum development is seen to be a dynamic process that must be understood in its entirety if the particulars are to work with any degree of efficiency. Throughout, the emphasis is thus on systematicity and interrelatedness of elements. The message the book delivers is that if we wish to improve the effectiveness of language teaching programmes, we need to examine in more depth the hidden dimensions of language programmes. Educational institutions need to assume a greater degree of responsibility in the planning, implementation and evaluation of their own programmes and instructional materials. This book will serve as a valuable resource in this process, allowing practitioners in the field of language curriculum development to have a comprehensive introduction to theory and practice in this growing field.

Michael H. Long
Jack C. Richards

Acknowledgements

The authors and publishers would like to thank the following for permission to reproduce copyright material:

Norman Whitney and Oxford University Press, *Checkpoint 1* (1984: p. 69) on p. 157; Andrew Littlejohn and Cambridge University Press, *Company to Company* (1988: p. 82) on p. 158; A. J. Thomson and A. V. Martinet and Oxford University Press, *A Practical English Grammar* (4th edn., 1986: p. 197) on pp. 159–60; Sylvia Chalker and Macmillan Publishers Ltd, *Current English Grammar* (1984) on p. 160; Leo Jones and Cambridge University Press, *Functions of English* (1981: p. 16) on pp. 160–1; Jon Blundell and Oxford University Press, *English Visa* (1984: pp. 40, 1) on pp. 166 and 173; Alice Lester and Alan McLean and Longman Group UK Ltd, *Dilmun: English for Bahrain* (pilot edition) on p. 167; B. Abbs, C. Candlin, C. Edelhoff, T. Moston, and M. Sexton and Longman Group UK Ltd, *Challenges* (1978: Introduction) on p. 168; Ann Brumfit and Scott Windeatt and ELTA/OUP SARL, *Communicative Grammar 1* (1983: p. 58) on p. 170; B. Abbs and I. Freebairn and Longman Group UK Ltd, *Discoveries 2* (1986: p. 43) on p. 172. Chapter 13, *Seeing the wood* AND *the trees: some thoughts on language teaching analysis*, by H. H. Stern, appeared in its original form on pp. 319–44 of M. Heid (Ed.) *Kommunikation im Klassenzimmer: Protokall eines Werkstattgesprächs des Goethe House New York im September 1982*. New York and Munich: Goethe House, New York, Goethe Institut München, 1983. Chapter 15, *The development and use of criterion-referenced tests of language ability in language program evaluation*, by Lyle F. Bachman, appeared originally as 'The development and use of criterion-referenced tests of language proficiency in language program evaluation' in A. Wangsotorn, K. Prapphal, A. Maurice, and B. Kenny (Eds.) *Trends in Language Programme Evaluation*. Bangkok: Chulalongkorn University Language Institute.

Overview

The aim of this collection is to present 'state of the art' papers in language curriculum studies by writers who have been actively involved in shaping theory in this field and who, between them, have applied that theory in almost every part of the world and in a variety of contexts.

The idea of a 'coherent language curriculum' summarises the range of the papers included and the theme which unites them. 'Curriculum' is used in the British sense to include all the factors which contribute to the teaching and learning situation, while the term 'coherence' emphasises the interdependence of these factors and the need for mutually consistent and complementary decision making throughout the processes of development and evaluation.

To set this publication within the context of developments in language curriculum studies over the past twenty-five to thirty years, I would like to propose that applied linguistics, the theoretical arm of language teaching, has passed through two major phases in its brief history, and is now entering a third. The first phase was that of the communicative revolution when it was inspired by new ideas and iconoclastic zeal. Its main achievement was to demonstrate the inadequacies in theory and practice of the *'ancien régime'*, but much that was valuable fell into disrepute or neglect through a form of guilt by association. The first revolutionary phase came to an end with applied linguistics focused upon the new linguistic sciences, psycholinguistics and sociolinguistics, divorced from its structuralist/behaviourist past, and distanced, if not estranged from the mainstream of educational theory.

The second phase was one of piecemeal reconstruction, epitomised by the flowering of a thousand methods. Work worthy of greater respect was carried out on particular aspects of the language curriculum to bring it more closely into line with our new and broader understanding of the nature of communicative competence and the processes of language acquisition and use. These aspects included needs analysis, the syllabus, materials design, the roles of the teacher and the learner and the nature of classroom interaction. The insights were genuine and the progress real, but there was little interaction between or integration of the different areas.

A third phase seems to me to have been initiated during the 1980s with a growing interest in the curriculum process as a whole, attempts to put language teaching back in touch with educational theory in general and curriculum studies in particular (Stern, 1983) and to impose order on the chaos into which at least fringe communicative methodology had fallen (Richards and Rodgers, 1986). This third phase is one of consolidation and integration, with a new sense of realism replacing the ideological fervour and speculative utopeanism that were all too characteristic of the revolutionary and post revolutionary phases.

This publication contributes to the 'new realism' and to a view of the language curriculum in which a discussion of any part must take account of the aims of and constraints upon the whole. The first paper, an overview, provides a framework for the seventeen papers which follow and a rationale for the sections into which the collection is divided: curriculum planning; ends/means specification; programme implementation (teacher training and materials writing); implementation in the classroom; and evaluation. The main focus of each paper is indicated in a short introduction to each section and in the overview. As would be expected from writers with such broad and diverse experience, their approach is constructive and lacks the proselytising zeal and factionalism which have done little for language teaching and learning and less for the reputation of applied linguistics as a discipline. In sum, the papers provide a major review of developments in language curriculum studies, and identify the problems that we currently face and the directions in which we need to move.

I would like to thank Jack Richards for proposing the collection, and for his consistent help throughout. Peter Donovan of Cambridge University Press and the contributors have had to put up with an editor who was not only learning his trade but travelling through China, England, Canada and Australia while doing so. Their tolerance and helpfulness have been greatly appreciated. I owe special thanks and appreciation to my wife, Anne, for her work on the bibliography and for her assistance in many other ways.

The book is organised in the following way:

Part I: Curriculum planning

In the first paper, in Part I, I describe language curriculum development, in the broadest sense, as a decision-making process. The framework I propose has three dimensions: that of policy, the aims of the curriculum, or what it seems desirable to achieve; pragmatics, the constraints on what it is possible to achieve; and finally the participants in the decision-making process, whose task it is to reconcile policy and pragmatics. Four stages of decision making are identified: curriculum planning, ends/ means specification, programme implementation, and implementation in the classroom. These stages provide the headings for the first four sections of this book. The heading for the fifth section, 'evaluation', is not seen as a stage in itself, but as a necessary and integral part of each and all of the stages already mentioned. I argue that these stages are ordered, but that the curriculum process overall must be interactive, so that decision making is fully informed; the coherence of the curriculum is more important than the 'perfection' of any or all of its separate parts.

A coherent curriculum is one in which decision outcomes from the various stages of development are mutually consistent and complementary, and learning outcomes reflect curricular aims. The achievement of coherence is said to depend crucially in most educational contexts upon the formalisation of decision-making processes and products. This formalisation facilitates consensus amongst those involved and is a prerequisite for effective evaluation and subsequent renewal. Decision making is therefore a continuing and cyclical process of development, revision, maintenance and renewal which needs to continue throughout the life of the curriculum.

In the second paper, Ted Rodgers considers the problems of curriculum planners, whose task is to set out a policy which is capable of being implemented. He maintains that failure in curriculum projects results more often from poor planning than from inadequacies in design and implementation *per se*. He develops this argument by examining three levels of programme planning: syllabus design, curriculum development and polity determination. In the same way that curriculum development may be regarded as a contextually enlarged view of syllabus design, polity determination is a contextually enlarged view of curriculum development, involving all the factors which need to be taken into account in general in educational planning, and in particular in determining the level and types of resources which will be required to implement a curriculum successfully. To assist in this process, and as a means to increase curriculum planners' awareness of the problems that are involved, Rodgers proposes a 'polity planning framework', a set of factor scales designed to assist planners in assessing the relative difficulty and 'cost' of implementing a particular curriculum change or innovation in a particular 'polito-pedagogical' context.

Peter Hargreaves's perspective is that of the evaluator and he argues that decisions relating to evaluation need to be taken during and as part of the curriculum planning process, and not, as is so often the case, as an afterthought to implementation. He presents and illustrates in use a checklist covering twelve major factors which need to be taken into account if evaluation is to be planned successfully: target audience, purpose, focus, criteria, method, means/instruments, agents, resources, time factors, findings, presentation of results and follow-up. These factors are interdependent since decisions in relation to one affect other decisions. The importance of integrating the various aspects of the curriculum in the planning stage is expressed concisely, if not euphoniously, in the term 'Des-impl-evalu-ign' which, at my urging (Ed.) was promoted from the text to the title. Hargreaves proposes a logo, derived from it, which might be awarded to projects which meet the required criteria in curriculum design. Experience suggests that the logo might not be awarded very often.

Part II: Ends/means specification

Part II deals with that stage in the decision-making process in which policy is made educationally explicit; the stage most often discussed under the headings of needs analysis and syllabus construction. On the theoretical level, discussion has concentrated upon the questions: 'whose needs?' and 'how can these needs best be assessed?' For practitioners the main problem often lies in moving beyond the findings of a needs analysis to the development of a teaching and learning programme. The three papers in this section offer different perspectives on the theoretical issues and practical problems involved: Berwick, that of a Japanese steel company; Brindley, adult migrant education in Australia; and Swales, academic service English programmes at university level.

Richard Berwick describes the general theory from which needs analysis derives, the problems in applying that theory, and the major stages to be followed through from the decision that a needs analysis is necessary to the transformation of data into a set of aims (ends specifications) and a language teaching programme. He distinguishes different approaches to design and notes that many philosophies of planning, and mixtures of them, find their means of expression in different forms of needs-based syllabuses, depending upon how the notion of need is defined and who defines it. Berwick distinguishes between the 'felt' needs of the learner and the 'perceived' needs of authority, and describes a range of data-gathering techniques under the general headings of inductive (category-generating) and deductive (category-dependent) methods of achieving a needs profile. He shows that language curriculum projects based on needs analyses require the continuing commitment and co-operation of all those involved and all those affected, over a considerable period of time. Berwick illustrates the problems that occur when theory and practice collide, and discusses approaches most likely to achieve a successful outcome in a commercial environment. He concludes that needs analyses should be designed to serve an established policy and not as a policy-making, least of all as a policy-seeking exercise.

Geoff Brindley states as axiomatic the importance of sensitivity to learners' needs in learner-centred approaches to curriculum design, and of needs analysis itself as a prerequisite for the specification of language learning objectives in curriculum design in general. The two axioms nevertheless reveal a considerable potential for disagreement over the definition of 'needs' and what 'needs analysis' should entail. Brindley identifies and attempts to reconcile two major orientations within the discussion: a 'narrow' or 'product-oriented' interpretation which focuses upon the learners' current and future uses for the language; and a 'broad' or 'process-oriented' interpretation which focuses upon the needs of the student as a learner, with the latter view requiring 'means specification' to take account of affective and cognitive variables such as attitudes, motivation, personality and learning style. Brindley discusses the feasibility of fruitful negotiation between teachers and learners in a learner-centred approach and illuminates this controversial area by proposing that needs analyses cannot be effective if conducted only at the curriculum planning stage, since learners cannot make valid choices amongst 'methods' until they have experienced the available options. The investigation of the learners' felt needs must therefore be a process which continues throughout the life of the curriculum. In this sense, needs analysis should be seen as an aspect of formative evaluation.

John Swales considers what 'counts as' a paper on programme design and its potential value. He then develops and explores the notion that an educational programme, and in particular a 'service' programme, forms part of an ecosystem within which the various participants and interest groups co-exist symbiotically in an often precarious state of balance; one in which 'all the competing but interdependent elements need to survive if the ecosystem is not to suffer damage'. The concept of 'opportunity cost', borrowed from economics, is then applied to curriculum development. 'Opportunity' represents the gains that might be obtained by successful implementation of a new or revised policy while estimates of costs must take account of the damage the ecosystem might sustain. A parasitic (no disrespect intended) service organisation would need to be particularly alert to the possible consequences of annoying or damaging the host body. Not surprisingly, the ecological approach Swales advocates is one of 'cautious gradualism', and the costs to be taken into account when assessing opportunities for curricular innovation are seen as going far beyond the human and material resources directly required for implementing an ends/means specification. The identification of appropriate ends and means therefore depends as much and perhaps more upon factors external to the curriculum (cf. Rodgers's discussion in Part I of 'polity determination') as it does upon factors controlled directly by participants in the curriculum process.

Part III: Programme implementation

Part III deals with programme implementation: the stage at which ends and means are realised as a teaching and learning programme ready for use in the classroom. It has two related aspects, the training of teachers and the preparation of teaching and learning resources. The first paper discusses the relationship between staff training and programme implementation, maintenance and renewal; the second describes the development of a teacher-training programme, or rather curriculum, since policy and ends and means all change as the programme develops; the third and fourth papers deal with the writing, organisation and evaluation of resources within a programme.

Martha Pennington argues that 'the heart of every educational enterprise, the force driving the whole enterprise towards its educational aims, is the teaching faculty' and deals with this crucial issue of faculty development under three broad headings. In the first, *The education and training of language teachers*, she outlines areas of broad agreement as well as differences of approach (holistic versus competency-based), emphasis (knowledge, attitudes, skills), perspective (optimistic, pessimistic) and conceptualisation of the teaching act (magic, art, profession, craft, science). In the second section, *Organizing a language program faculty*, she discusses the extent to which administrative constraints predetermine other aspects of the curricular decision-making process. The third section, *The evolution and growth of a language program faculty*, maps out a programme for the professional development of teachers, showing how the assignment of teachers' responsibilities within the curriculum should reflect this development, and also the complex role which evaluation needs to play in this very sensitive area.

The second paper, by Mike Breen, Chris Candlin, Leni Dam and Gerd Gabrielsen, describes the evolution of a series of teacher-training workshops conducted by the authors in Denmark since 1978. The initial aim was to stimulate interest among teachers in new methods and techniques based on communicative approaches to language teaching, but the account of the development of these workshops is less about the achievement of that aim than about achieving a meeting of minds between teachers and teacher trainers. In the first stage (transmission), the target methodology was presented by the trainers on the assumption that it would then be applied. In the process of discovering that 'transmission' was largely ineffective, the second stage (problem solving) evolved, whereby the target methodology was offered in response to problems raised by the teachers. Difficulties with this approach led to the third stage in which the workshop has focused upon classroom decision making and investigation. Thus the emphasis has moved from the trainers to the teachers to the learners, and the role of the teacher trainers as they perceived it changed from 'expert' to problem solver to problem investigator.

Graham Low discusses the advantages and disadvantages of different approaches to the organisation and structuring of language teaching materials. In addition to the traditional concerns with presentation of new material, practice designed to give mastery of that material and opportunities for integrating what has been mastered into the learners' established communicative competence, he focuses upon the patterns of organisation within and between course units, discussing past and current approaches, proposing alternatives, and introducing the terms 'feeding' and 'bleeding' to describe relationships which enhance or detract from learning opportunities. Low points out that in many courses in the past there have either been no obvious relationships or else highly contrived ones between units and between the elements within units. Writers have tended to establish sequences of activities which are then followed inflexibly regardless of changes in objectives, topics etc.

Materials of the kind Low criticises have been particularly prevalent in third world countries where the teachers' own English language proficiency and professional training have been weak. The high level of predictability of this approach makes these materials comparatively easy to prepare and use, but it has little else to recommend it. The more radical and experimental approaches generated by the communicative 'revolution' have produced activities that are interesting, interactive and varied, but my own feeling (Ed.) is that the organisational relationships amongst these activities are often still uncertain, more so in fact than in the days of structural syllabuses. In a coherent curriculum the organising principles on which the programme is based need to be stated and understood. Those principles need to go beyond the traditional concern for structural order and vocabulary control to encompass the full range of communicative functions and language skills. 'Feeding' relationships in this broader context are more complex now than in the days of structuralism and audio-lingualism, but no less essential.

Andrew Littlejohn and Scott Windeatt consider the content of the language programme rather than its organisation, and the unintended as well as the intended effects upon learners which may result from the realisation of syllabus specifications as language teaching materials. They acknowledge the difficulty inherent in establishing any direct link between 'input' to the learner and 'uptake' by the learner (a problem discussed in Part IV), but argue that it is possible at least to identify and evaluate what is 'available to be learnt'. This they do under six headings: general or subject knowledge offered in the materials; views of what knowledge is and how it is acquired; views of what is involved in language learning; role relations within the classroom; opportunities for the development of cognitive abilities; and the values and attitudes presented in the materials.

In their title, Littlejohn and Windeatt see these issues as going *Beyond language learning...*' It seems to me however that, on their own evidence, these issues directly affect both the processes of learning, and the nature of the learners' communicative competence on completion of the programme, and that therefore they constitute essential elements within any discussion of programme implementation.

The further important point emerges that 'mismatch' may exist between the language curriculum and the broader aims of society and education as well as within the curriculum itself. To return to the metaphor of the curriculum as an ecosystem: coherence, like the balance of nature, is necessary but by no means sufficient to ensure an acceptable quality of life for all the participants.

Part IV: Classroom implementation

The fourth set of decisions to be made in the curriculum development process relates to classroom implementation. These decisions determine the nature of the teaching and learning acts that will be performed, with the latter being unarguably the most crucial for the success of the whole of the curricular enterprise. Resourceful, intelligent and determined students achieve their aims in spite of ill-conceived policies, poorly formulated syllabuses, inadequate resources and incompetent teaching. Conversely a well-planned curriculum with appropriate aims effectively realised and implemented achieves little if students are apathetic and unmotivated. This fact in itself explains the inconclusive results of much research and will continue to bedevil curriculum research and evaluation until the role of the learner is acknowledged and, more difficult, taken into account in research design.

The notion of the learner as an empty vessel to be filled by a teacher from a predetermined curriculum has been unacceptable for some time, replaced by the current more positive perception of the active role played by the learner. Nevertheless enthusiasm for various reformulations of syllabuses, and for new styles and methods of materials design and pedagogical presentation has continued largely unconstrained by the growing evidence that learners' aims and the means they adopt to achieve them are not necessarily those of the official curriculum.

In the first paper in this section, David Nunan focuses upon the decisions of the learner, and the evidence from various studies that learners have 'hidden agendas', derived partly from their own aims, partly from their preconceptions about the learning process, and partly from their lack of understanding of the aims of the official curriculum and the means adopted for achieving those aims. Nunan argues that every aspect of curriculum studies needs to be expanded to include these hidden agendas. In this way, curriculum planning, development, implementation, evaluation and research would take account of learners' perceptions of the learning process as well as those of the theorist, of what happens rather than what ought to happen and of what is learned rather than what is taught. Nunan is particularly concerned with the practical implications of the hidden agenda hypothesis in the classroom, and he proposes techniques for achieving a synthesis between the official curriculum and that of the learner.

One problem inherent in this situation is precisely that the learner's agenda is hidden, and may be inaccessible to the outside observer and indeed to the learner himself. What can be observed however is the interaction between the learner and the learning task. It is here that the official and the hidden agendas come into direct contact, the point at which the learner interacts with, and is able to operate on the curriculum. Mike Breen analyses language learning tasks in terms of three 'phases': the task as workplan (what is intended); as process (what is done); and as outcome (what is achieved). The second is seen as being the most important, the least understood, and as having the most to contribute to language curriculum development. The task evaluation cycle proposed by Breen focuses primarily on this aspect of task, and it aims at involving the learner in the analysis of tasks and in the formulation of proposals for their revision. Like Nunan, Breen sees the role of the teacher as mediator between the curriculum and the learner in a two-way process which revises both the 'agenda' of the learner and the curriculum itself to bring the two into line.

In the last paper in this section, David Stern traces the changes in emphasis in language teaching research from 'Method' as an abstraction to 'natural' learning or 'acquisition' outside the classroom, to the realisation emphasised by the two previous writers that we must come to grips with the process of language curriculum implementation inside the classroom. Stern maintains that classroom research so far has proved of limited value, because it has lacked any explicitly stated theoretical base, and consequently, in the accumulation of a potentially infinite quantity of detail, it has proved difficult if not impossible to see what is and is not important. The theoretical framework which Stern proposes to remedy this situation has three interdependent levels: theoretical concepts, policy directives and classroom behaviour, similar as levels of abstraction to those proposed by Anthony, 1963 (*Approach, method, and technique*) and by Richards and Rodgers, 1986 (*Approach, design, and procedure*). Stern maintains that the findings of classroom research can be interpreted only in so far as they can be related systematically to policy specifications, and the theoretical constructs (or approach) on which the curriculum as a whole is based; i.e. it is impossible to evaluate classroom behaviour unless the aim of that behaviour is clear. Similarly, approaches to language teaching and learning cannot be evaluated unless those approaches have been effectively realised in classroom behaviour.

On a personal note, I am very pleased to be able to include this paper by David Stern. I met him in 1987 after many years of admiring his work and was equally impressed by his wisdom and vitality. It was a shock and a great loss to applied linguistics when he died. Very few people have been as successful in '*Seeing the wood AND the trees*', the title of his paper, or have contributed as much to theoretical aspects of language curriculum studies. The Core French project in Canada, which he initiated, is a model of conceptual clarity and attention to detail and seems, at its present stage of development, a near perfect example of coherent language curriculum development.

Part V: Evaluation

In each of the preceding sections, it has been emphasised implicitly if not explicitly that curriculum development and renewal can only proceed effectively if supported by evaluation.

James Brown defines evaluation as the 'systematic collection and analysis of all relevant information necessary to promote the improvement of a curriculum and assess its effectiveness and efficiency as well as the participants' attitudes within the context of the particular institutions involved'. He examines key definitions and distinctions within the literature related to language programme evaluation, and the various approaches developed over the past thirty to forty years, culminating in 'decision facilitation approaches'. Brown argues that these developments have been evolutionary rather than revolutionary, each building on what was learned previously. His discussion of the various 'dimensions' of evaluation: formative and summative, product and process, quantitative and qualitative, leads to a set of procedures and steps for developing and implementing language programme evaluation.

Bachman and Hudson focus upon the problem of what should be measured and the means by which measurement should be carried out. Both are dissatisfied with current approaches based on standardised, norm-referenced tests and largely undefined notions of global proficiency or skills. Their approaches are very different however. Bachman is looking towards the future and the point at which evaluation, or at least testing, can be carried out without direct reference to each particular programme under consideration. Hudson's approach is programme-based and he is concerned with practical measures which can be implemented effectively in the light of current knowledge (and the lack of it).

Lyle Bachman's proposals for establishing a theoretical base for criterion-referenced testing are based on generally accepted models of communicative competence. In line with these models, he seeks first to specify a domain of communicative language ability and second to define scales of proficiency at a level of abstraction which makes them independent of contextual features of language use. Criterion-referenced tests based on this model would provide scores that would be comparable across differing sets of instructional objectives, and would provide a valid basis for comparison across language programmes. As Bachman points out, neither the theory nor the tests exist as yet beyond a rudimentary stage of development, and he argues the need for empirical research (rather than arm-chair model building) which will guide test development and at the same time refine and validate the theoretical framework.

Thom Hudson focuses upon student performance, which he considers to be 'the key in evaluation', in terms of student mastery or non-mastery of language programme objectives. Mastery testing establishes absolute rather than relative standards (cf. tests which are intended to rank-order students). It enables the evaluator to determine whether a particular programme has achieved its intended goals, and if not, the areas in which it is deficient. However, these absolute judgements raise in acute form problems which underlie all testing: epistemological (mastery of what), ethical (how will the results be used), and technical (in this case, the problem of the cut-off point which determines whether mastery has or has not been achieved). In dealing with the first of these, Hudson compares two approaches to test data, as a sign of underlying competence, or as a sample of performance. He discusses the implications of each for the definition and demonstration of mastery, with the solution, i.e. which approach to adopt, depending upon the ends and means of the curriculum being evaluated. On the technical (and ethical) question, Hudson takes up the issues of reliability and validity in criterion-referenced measurement. He proposes statistical solutions to the former, but the latter remains problematical, with validity and therefore the ethics of mastery testing having to be argued, again on the basis of the policy and pragmatic constraints of the programme in question.

Warwick Elley's paper provides a down-to-earth conclusion to the collection. It deals with language curriculum evaluation in the broadest sense and as it is rather than as it ideally ought to be; i.e. in situations where few of the desirable prerequisites have been met. The resourceful evaluator needs often to make judgements, to quote Elley: '... about which hallowed principles are essential, which are desirable, what might be feasible under the circumstances, and what is to be avoided at all costs'. He offers pragmatic advice on how to proceed in relation to the choice of evaluator; assessing the importance of the information to be gained; identifying the aims of a programme; selecting the evaluation design and the sample; selecting/developing the instruments; administration and marking; the importance of process as well as product; and the analysis of results. His approach suggests that there are very few curriculum situations so hopeless that they cannot be enlightened and improved by a sensible and sensitive evaluator.

For the future, it may be assumed that more rigorous accounts of communicative competence and how it develops will inform the processes of planning, implementation and evaluation of the language curriculum. In the meantime, however, the experience, enthusiasm, tradecraft, careful planning, hard work and good will of all those involved seem to be the primary contributing factors to the achievement of a coherent and successful language curriculum. Whatever theoretical advances are made, the importance of these factors seems unlikely to diminish.

PART I
1 CURRICULUM OVERVIEW

1 A decision-making framework for the coherent language curriculum[1]

Robert Keith Johnson

Introduction

In this introductory paper, I have three major aims: first to provide a framework for discussing the language curriculum; second to define the notion of a 'coherent' language curriculum, the theme of this book as well as the title of this paper; and third to show how the other papers in this volume and the particular aspects of development they focus upon relate to the curriculum process as a whole.

The word 'curriculum' is defined here in its broadest sense, to include all the relevant decision making processes of all the participants. The products of these decision making processes generally exist in some concrete form and can be observed and described: for example policy documents, syllabuses, teacher-training programmes, teaching materials and resources, and teaching and learning acts. The processes themselves are usually more difficult to identify and analyse. They involve such questions as: Who is supposed to make the decisions and who actually does? How are these people selected and what qualifications do they have? What are their terms of reference? What resources in time, money, information and expertise are available to them? etc. Other 'process' factors such as prejudice, preconception, ambition or laziness are even harder to examine, but may be no less influential in their effects.

The framework consists of three sets of constraints on curriculum decision making. The first is policy. A curriculum which appears in all other respects to be successful, but which fails to achieve its aims, is hard to justify however much the participants may have benefited from their experience in other ways, for example socially or financially. The second consists of pragmatic considerations such as time and resources, human and material. Any curriculum design must take adequate account of these

1 I would like to acknowledge the valuable comments of David Stern, Patrick Allen and in particular Merrill Swain on the draft version of this paper, and also the assistance of the Modern Language Centre staff at O.I.S.E., where work on the preparation of this collection was completed.

constraints or fail to achieve its aims. The third consists of the participants in the curriculum process and the ways in which they interact. Their task is to reconcile policy and pragmatics and to achieve and maintain, at each stage of development, products of the decision-making process which are mutually consistent and compatible. Such a curriculum is said to be 'coherent'.

Factors which promote coherence or its opposite 'mismatch' are discussed in the sections which follow in relation to each of these three dimensions and 'process' and 'product'. The final section considers the role of evaluation in curriculum decision making. Brief comments along the way show how the topics of other contributors to the book fit into this framework.

Policy decision making

The four stages or decision points in policy implementation are:

1 Curriculum planning
2 Ends/means specification
3 Programme implementation
4 Classroom implementation

These four headings with 'Evaluation' also make up the five section headings of this book. The planning stage consists of all those decisions taken before the development and implementation of the programme begins. Ends specification relates to objectives, and means specification to method; programme implementation involves teacher training and materials/resources development. Decision making at the classroom implementation stage has as its products the acts of the teacher and the learner (Table 1).

The term 'policy' is used to refer to any broad statement of aims whether at the level of a national curriculum (for example Japanese should be taught as a foreign language in secondary schools), or as a 'good idea' a teacher or learner may put forward for the classroom (for example: let's have a debate on Friday afternoons). In this sense the stages of policy determination, specification and implementation are ordered. The policy or idea must exist. It must then be operationally defined. Any necessary resources must be prepared. These must then be presented (a teaching act) so that learning acts may follow.

Curriculum planning

Policy makers are responding to 'needs'; their own, other people's or those of an entire society. They determine the overall aims of the

TABLE 1. STAGES, DECISION-MAKING ROLES AND
PRODUCTS IN CURRICULUM DEVELOPMENT

Developmental stages	Decision-making roles	Products
1. curriculum planning	policy makers	policy document
2. specification: ends	needs analyst	syllabus
means	methodologists	
3. programme implementation	materials writers	teaching materials
	teacher trainers	teacher-training programme
4. classroom implementation	teacher	teaching acts
	learner	learning acts

curriculum and are influenced in varying degrees by special interest groups who are able to bring pressure to bear.

In different educational contexts, different people will play the role of policy maker and the policy will be stated more or less formally. A language learner who hires a tutor is the policy maker. However, the teacher may influence the learner to modify that policy, or may subvert it by implementing an inappropriate curriculum, for example the one that happens to be available, without mentioning the fact to the learner.

A commercial language school makes its own policy and sets this out in a prospectus. Students decide whether the aims stated coincide with their own. Policy in this case may be determined primarily by market forces.

National language policies are determined by socio-political pressures which vary from one culture and socio-political system to another; the primary consideration of most governments being to maintain, and if possible extend their power, influence and acceptability.

Policy statements tend to be utopian. 'Promises are cheap', 'hope springs eternal', and there are no limits on what is desirable. It is not the business of language curriculum specialists to tell governments or the public what they should want, but it is our business to state what is and what is not attainable and the costs of implementation. (Swales in Part II discusses the concept of 'opportunity cost' in this broad 'ecological' rather than economic sense.) There are well-established constraints on what can be achieved, for example in situations where opportunities for learning are brief and intermittent, opportunities for forgetting almost infinite, and where there is no contact with the target language outside the classroom (for example Strevens, 1977: 29). However, governments and language schools which promise only what they can perform are likely to go out of business, and language educators who criticise policies as unrealistic sometimes find their career opportunities have not been enhanced.

There is in fact an inherent danger of mismatch between policy and the learning outcomes which the implemented curriculum is capable of achieving. Rodgers, in the paper which follows this one, maintains that decisions taken at the curriculum planning stage, and what he refers to as 'polity factors' generally, have a far greater impact on the success of curriculum development than decisions relating to the implementation of the curriculum *per se*.

Ends/means specification

Policy statements, however detailed, are directives not specifications. They are not formulated to meet the requirements of curriculum development. Ends/means specification is the process by which policy, and the means by which it is to be implemented, are operationally defined. Ends specification should provide an exact characterisation of the target proficiency. Means specification should prescribe the method by which that target proficiency will be achieved. Those who make decisions about these specifications are referred to here as syllabus writers, and the formal product of their decision making as a syllabus. If the specifications in the syllabus are inadequate, the curriculum becomes potentially less coherent (i.e. divergent decisions may be made inadvertently at subsequent stages in the developmental process) and actually more difficult to evaluate, since criteria would have to be inferred.

In the case of the Friday afternoon debates, to continue with that example, these might be designed in various ways: with advance preparation or without; with the teacher or with a student as chairperson; as a means for selecting the school debating team; to provide opportunities for the best students to extend themselves or to facilitate maximum participation by all students; to provide fluency practice; to promote vocabulary expansion, for general interest or as an opportunity to spot common errors in a 'natural' communicative context. Unless the ends are specified, an evaluator would have to guess what they might be, or impose what the evaluator thinks they ought to be. The debates themselves are in any case unlikely to be concluded successfully unless the teacher and the students have some shared understanding of the ends to be achieved and the means for achieving them.

Where a broader set of aims is concerned (for example Japanese as above), specifications at this stage of curriculum development become even more crucial, since a negotiated approach or trial and error can be successful in the context of a particular course or classroom, but is less likely to succeed where learning outcomes are expected to be comparable and examinable across several institutions or an education system.

ENDS SPECIFICATION

Decision making in this area has tended to follow one of two largely divergent lines of development. In the first, the general concern throughout education for accountability and cost effectiveness has prompted the specification of objectives in behavioural and verifiable forms. This approach, with the growing importance of E.S.P. programmes, has resulted in the development in language education of a technology of needs analysis. Problems of definition and implementation associated with various aspects of this approach are discussed by Berwick and Brindley in Part II of this book. The other approach, more cognitive in orientation, has extended the traditional notion of language learning as mastery of the grammatical system to a broader conception of communicative competence. Model building of the kind initiated by Canale and Swain (1980), supported by research programmes such as the one proposed by Bachman in Part V, may eventually lead to a developed theory of communicative competence which could support and inform decision making in ends specification (and evaluation), but a theoretical paradigm which involves the explanation of so much of human cognition will not be developed easily or rapidly. At this stage, our theories of communicative competence are abstract, speculative and fragmentary, but progress in this area has nevertheless been real. We now know enough about the schemata and processes which guide certain aspects of communication to suspect that lists of target behaviours are inadequate and possibly counter-productive either as ends specifications or as the basis for programme and classroom implementation. What we do not have, unfortunately, is an adequate descriptive account of the constructs of communicative competence that could be used in place of such lists.

MEANS SPECIFICATION

Discussions of language teaching methodology have been influenced by first and second language acquisition theory and a growing body of classroom observation studies. However, no conventional wisdom or consensus has yet emerged, as is demonstrated by the proliferation of methods, claims and counter-claims, since the demise of audio-lingualism. The communicative revolution in language teaching has broadened and enriched the repertoire of techniques available to language teachers and materials writers, but it does not as yet offer a principled basis for selecting amongst them or for elevating a particular set of techniques into a globally applicable method. Even if theoretical purity could be achieved, it would remain less important for effective curriculum implementation than accommodation to the usually impure constraints of a particular educational context. The eclectic approach, a combination of experience, local knowledge, intuition and trial and error, is widely adopted for precisely this reason.

MISMATCH IN ENDS/MEANS SPECIFICATION

The practical value of a theoretical paradigm in any field of activity is that it establishes a consensus about a way to proceed and things to do. To the extent that the paradigm is established, detailed specification becomes less important; to the extent that it is not, the specifications themselves provide the primary means for achieving coherence. The communicative approach to language teaching provides many insights, but no paradigm, and the coherence of curriculums at present lies not in shared assumptions but in operational definitions. It is necessary to demonstrate that the ends specification matches the policy, and that means and ends are compatible. The grammar-translation method notoriously did not promote oral fluency, and an oral/aural approach does not develop writing skills. A Council of Europe style 'ends' specification may look like what a syllabus 'ought' to look like, but this style may be inappropriate for a policy whose aim, for example, is to promote study skills. 'Procedural display' (behaviour which enables participants to appear to be doing a good job when in fact they are not) is not limited to the classroom.

Above all, there must be no mismatch involving 'hidden' syllabuses. In many education systems the key question for students, teachers, parents, school administrators, and even inspectors is not, 'Are students gaining in communicative competence?' but, 'Are they on course for the examination?' In such a situation the examination is the ends specification, the item types constitute the means specification, and the official syllabus depends for its credibility on the extent to which the content of the examination is an adequate sample of that syllabus. Item types in examinations need to be selected and constructed with this 'washback' effect in mind. For example, if cloze is used in testing, doing cloze passages will occupy a considerable portion of teaching and learning time. If oral skills are judged by reading aloud, reading aloud will be practised, conversational fluency will not. A great deal of classroom behaviour which appears inexplicable and even bizarre in terms of the official policy can be readily understood once the 'hidden' syllabus has been identified.

Programme implementation

In the programme implementation stage, all those decisions are made which cannot be deferred until teachers and learners are preparing for or performing classroom acts. These decisions relate to the development of teaching and learning resources, and the preparation of teachers to ensure that the resources are used effectively; i.e. in accordance with the means specifications and with a clear understanding of the objectives to be achieved and the reasons for achieving them. As with earlier stages, these decisions may be made formally or informally, explicitly or implicitly, and the products are consequently more or less amenable to evaluation, revision, and transfer or adaptation to other educational contexts.

PROGRAMME RESOURCES

Teaching and learning materials provide the corpus of the curriculum. They normally exist as physical entities and are open to analysis, evaluation and revision in ways that teaching and learning acts are not; and they have a direct influence upon what happens in classrooms, which policy documents, syllabuses and teacher-training courses do not.

If the ends/means specifications constrain the materials writer too closely, creativity tends to be stifled. If the ends/means specifications are too loose, there is the possibility of mismatch, with the materials writer introducing an alternative curriculum which cannot easily be detected. My feeling is that, ideally, the materials writer should be closely associated with the process of ends/means specification (as a member of the syllabus committee for example) but should have considerable freedom in actual implementation; for example the materials writer need not be required to implement the ends/means specifications in a particular way, but must show, formally, that the specifications have been met. In practice, this idea is rarely achieved. Government curriculum units may be too rigidly constrained, commercial writers too little. The latter are usually excluded from syllabus committees on principle (to avoid charges of favouring particular publishers) and may have little understanding of the particular educational context they are writing for, particularly if they have an international rather than a specific market in mind. Commercially produced materials are generally piloted in schools prior to general release, at least by the more reputable publishers, and materials are often significantly modified as a result. However, this exercise is generally aimed at adjusting the product to the potential market rather than at evaluating the product itself. Financial and practical considerations ensure that the publisher must accommodate to the market and not the market to the publisher, who is rarely in a position to mount extensive teacher-training programmes. Many excellent language teaching programmes have failed, their promoters falling into the hands of receivers or multinationals, because the materials were too alien, too complex, or too expensive for local taste.

These 'facts of life' notwithstanding, it is encouraging to note situations, particularly over the past ten years, where materials have been developed through curriculum projects involving materials writers, publishers, ministries of education and other consumers. On a smaller scale, E.S.P. projects have also sometimes achieved a high level of co-ordination. Collaborative ventures of this kind go a long way towards ensuring that the planning and development of a curriculum is coherent. Also, in case I should appear prejudiced against commercial publishers, I should add that large-scale materials development projects conducted without their support have rarely produced effective results. Lack of expertise, lack of resources, the impossibility of effective materials writing by committee and many other factors seem to contribute to this failure, including the low status of those involved in curriculum development within ministries of education. Talented individuals tend either to move into the commercial field or to be promoted to administrative positions which have little effect on teaching and learning outcomes, but which nevertheless carry more status, better pay and better long-term career prospects.

Even in the most highly developed materials projects, commercial or otherwise, the principles governing the selection, grading, organisation and presentation of contents are rarely stated in explicit and operational terms. A fully argued account of the relationship between the policy which is to be implemented and the constraints affecting the manner of implementation is even more rare. Teachers' guides offer advice at the level of 'procedure', stating often in considerable detail what to do with the materials, but not why the materials exist in the form that they do (F. C. Johnson, 1973, was a notable exception).

In smaller institutions, and in programmes developed by individual teachers, materials are often fragmentary, and poorly organised (for example as unordered piles of stencils in a cupboard) with little or no guidance as to how the materials should be used. This does not mean that the programme is incoherent as taught, though it may be, only that the curriculum exists primarily within the minds of its creators. When staff changes occur, the teaching materials, the only tangible evidence of that curriculum, make little sense to the newcomers. It is often easier and less frustrating to throw out what exists and begin again from scratch. However, where staffing continuity is relatively assured, the need for formalising the curriculum and for rigorous evaluation of course materials may be questionable in such institutions. A less formal, 'in-service' approach is likely to be more practicable and more productive.

Low, in Part III, discusses organising principles in materials design which seem most readily generalisable across educational contexts. Other decisions, such as what is relevant, interesting and appropriate can only be considered within the context of a particular teaching and learning situation. Here too, the role of the materials writer is of critical importance. Littlejohn and Windeatt explore ways in which the materials writer can generate mismatch, not only within the curriculum, but between the curriculum and the broader aims of education and society.

TEACHER TRAINING

If the materials writer provides the body of the curriculum, teacher training should provide the spirit. In a coherent curriculum, teacher training would clarify policy aims as expressed in the syllabus, would show how ends and means relate, how they are embodied in the teaching programme and how particular classroom procedures complement the programme materials and optimise learning opportunities. The teacher trainer forms the bridge between the syllabus committee and the classroom, and is ideally placed to facilitate formative evaluation, to aid syllabus revision and to engage in ongoing curriculum development in collaboration with materials writers.

The reality is often the opposite of the ideal. At one extreme, the theoretical, teacher trainers tend to be specialists in applied linguistics in general, and methodology in particular. Their knowledge of the curriculum they supposedly serve is often limited, their attitude towards it may be dismissive and their efforts directed towards revolutionising rather than implementing it. They are critical of programme materials but have little contact with materials writers, and may urge teachers to create their own resources. They often have little sympathy with official policy and would like it changed, usually in a direction better suited to their favourite 'Method'. Meanwhile they espouse the cause of that method anyway, and when it conflicts, as it inevitably does, with the official examination, teachers are urged to ignore the examination. However justified their criticisms, these teacher trainers gain little credibility and have little influence, least of all with teachers. The problem is that they do not play the role which is pre-eminently theirs, that of promoting coherent implementation and development within the curriculum.

There are very different problems at the more practical end of the teacher-training continuum. These specialists are master craftsmen and they have a great deal of credibility with teachers. They see their task as one of handing down tried and tested techniques for implementing a particular programme in the classroom, and they rarely consider or ask teachers to consider the programme as an integrated whole. Their approach often makes the best of a bad programme, but it does not make the bad programme better.

In the first paper of Part III, Pennington provides a model of staff development as an integrated component within curriculum design, while Breen *et al.* describe the evolution over a number of years of a learner-centred approach to teacher training. As both these papers show, a teacher-training programme is a curriculum within a curriculum, embedded at the point of programme implementation. Its policy and pragmatic constraints are, or should be, determined to a large extent by those of the 'host' curriculum, but its role must be active and developmental as well as passive and implementational.

Classroom implementation

Teachers, learners and programme resources combine and interact to create learning opportunities, in ways discussed by Breen in Part IV. Classroom implementation is the final stage in the curriculum development process and also the most important, because ultimately learning acts determine curriculum outcomes. All other decisions merely, though importantly, constrain the decisions which inform those acts.

When implementing a language programme in the classroom, a major cause of mismatch is a difference between the actual proficiency levels of learners and the level assumed by the materials writer. Writers are bound to accept the ends specification in the syllabus as their target, otherwise their materials will not be used. If these ends are unrealistic, writers must either assume a higher level of proficiency on entry than actually exists, or must push learners forward at a pace more rapid than most of them can sustain.

Given the tendency for policy makers to be over-optimistic about what can be achieved, this form of mismatch is a frequent cause of curriculum failure. It is in my experience the most frequent cause of what is generally called 'poor' teaching, but is in fact 'survival' teaching. Its function is to enable students to continue in a curriculum which is too advanced for them. As an example, teachers may prepare students for a reading or listening task by anticipating problems and supplying answers until the possibility of error, along with challenge and genuine engagement with the text, have been virtually eliminated. However, when completion of the teaching programme in a given time is mandatory, it is unfair to blame teachers for the strategies they adopt to achieve that end. The problems associated with survival teaching are rarely caused and even more rarely solved at the classroom stage of development alone.

TEACHING ACTS

Where the 'official' curriculum differs radically from a teacher's beliefs about the roles of teachers and learners and the kinds of activities which promote language learning, what happens in the classroom is likely to conform to this 'alternative' curriculum. Since the programme was not designed to serve either the ends or means of this alternative curriculum, the outcomes are usually unsatisfactory. Gross mismatch is again easy to detect but hard to remedy. For example, where teachers refuse to use group or pair work in a curriculum designed for it, it is not just a matter of changing attitudes. The teachers are in effect being asked to change their trade, to abandon tried and tested techniques for an unknown world in which they doubt their own and their pupils' competence. Successful teaching depends to a large extent upon confidence and upon responses automatised by experience. As so many papers in this volume suggest, evolution not revolution must be the aim in language curriculum development, particularly at the classroom level. Radical change, whether well-motivated in terms of policy or an ill-motivated attempt to be fashionable, usually results in a loss of coherence which may take many years to remedy.

LEARNING ACTS

The decisions which inform learning acts are as I have said by far the most important in determining learning outcomes. They are also the least likely to be consistent with the official curriculum. Many factors affect language learners' decisions (for example Schumann, 1978) and little has been established about the ways in which these factors interact or the relative weighting they may have for different learners in different educational contexts. Students may, in some situations, choose not to perform their designated role at all, a privilege largely denied to the paid participants.

Assuming that learners are motivated and responsible, their decisions may still render the curriculum incoherent. 'Learner training', comparable to teacher training, rarely exists as an effective component in language curriculum development, and the role of the teacher as learner trainer (teaching students how to be effective learners in a given curriculum) rarely receives the emphasis that it should. Successful students have been shown to follow their own strategies; for example formulating and testing structural hypotheses in a communicative activity, or 'talking to walls' as many Chinese students do when following a grammar-translation programme in order to gain oral fluency. Observations of unskilled learners are equally unenlightening about the effectiveness of the official curriculum. In this case, the learners have no strategies, i.e. no principled basis for making constructive use of learning opportunities, and it seems doubtful whether the acts performed under these circumstances should be regarded as evidence of a 'learning style' any more than the motions of someone drowning should be regarded as evidence of a 'swimming style'. Problems such as these have bedevilled language curriculum research and evaluation and will continue to do so.

The need to discover and to respect the 'hidden agendas' of learners is discussed by Nunan in Part IV. He proposes ways of approaching the problem and of reconciling the approaches of the learners and the official curriculum. The larger question of classroom research and its place in language curriculum studies is taken up by Stern.

Policy determination and implementation: conclusion

The causes of mismatch within a curriculum are numerous. It may result inevitably from decisions made or not made at the curriculum planning stage or from inadequacies in the specification and implementation of the policy at any or each succeeding stage. A great many of the possibilities seem likely to have been instantiated somewhere in the language teaching world at some time or another. The potential forms of coherent language curriculums are equally varied. The only characteristic which they must all share is the absence of mismatch; but this is not so negative a virtue as it may appear. Achieving and maintaining coherence requires the active engagement and co-operation of all participants throughout the life of a curriculum. The process depends upon good will, but it also requires the existence of organisational structures which facilitate its achievement and can then sustain it.

The next section describes the roles played by participants in the decision-making process under different styles of language curriculum management and considers the potential those styles of management have for promoting coherence in different educational contexts.

Participant roles in policy determination and implementation

The left-hand column in Table 2 identifies the participants involved in the curriculum in terms of the primary roles that they play. These roles are associated with specific stages in the curriculum process, and the participants are assumed to have particular expertise in decision making in relation to those stages. The role category does not preclude a participant from playing other roles or from involvement in decision making at other stages. Thus in one interpretation of a learner-centred curriculum, learners determine policy through their perceptions of their needs. A teacher-centred curriculum would maximise the influence of the teacher, while the so-called 'teacher-proof' curriculum seeks to minimise it, decisions relating to teaching acts being taken *a priori* by the teacher trainer and materials writer. Different styles of management determine participation in the decision-making process in different ways and place different values upon the contributions of different participants.

TABLE 2. DECISION MAKING IN 'SPECIALIST' AND
'LEARNER-CENTRED' CURRICULUMS

		Stages in curriculum development						
			Syllabus		*Programme*		*Classroom*	
Participants	*Policy*		ends	means	materials resources	teacher training	teaching acts	learning acts
policy makers								
needs analysts								
methodologists								
materials writers								
teacher trainers								
teachers								
learners								

specialist ⧄   learner-centred ⧅

Table 2 compares two approaches to policy determination and
implementation, the specialist approach and the learner-centred
approach, and the discussion which follows outlines the mirror image
strengths and weaknesses of each. The most effective curriculum
management style might be one which, within the constraints of a
particular educational context, utilised the strengths of both. Neither of
the extremes described here would be found in practice. Consultation
and feedback exist in even the most authoritarian systems (specialist
approach) and learners require the support of teachers and/or suitable
resources if a learner-centred approach is to be implemented effectively.

Participant roles in the specialist approach

STRENGTHS

The 'specialist' curriculum has a simple, military style chain of command.
Responsibility for the various decisions is clearly defined and decisions
are made by people who are 'experts' in their respective fields and know
what resources are required. All the decisions passed down the chain of
command have to be explicitly formulated so that they can be understood
by the experts at the next stage. Consequently the curriculum can be

evaluated. It can also be transferred; i.e. it can be used by teachers and learners other than those involved in initial development. All decision makers can be held accountable for their acts and the preconditions for further development and innovation exist.

WEAKNESSES

The flow of information is in one direction only, and there is no consultation or interaction amongst those assigned to play the various roles. False assumptions cannot be formally challenged and consensus cannot easily be achieved. Commitment to successful implementation will be uncertain, and heresy (adherence to 'false' curriculums, for example an examination) may be hard to detect and eliminate. The one-way flow of information means that policy makers would need a) to be aware of all pragmatic constraints and b) to take them fully into account when establishing and implementing policy. Neither condition is likely to be met.

Participant roles in the learner-centred approach

STRENGTHS

The learner-centred curriculum has a unified view of policy. All participants are involved at every stage of decision making with maximum provision for interaction, consultation and co-operation, and maximum potential for the development of consensus, commitment and motivation. The approach is responsive to changes in perceived needs, to 'good ideas' and to pragmatic constraints as they emerge.

WEAKNESSES

There is no chain of command. No one has specific responsibility for carrying out decisions. There are no 'experts' and limited understanding initially at least of resource implications. The consensus *is* the curriculum, which does not exist in a formalised and explicit sense. It is not therefore easily transferable to new learning situations, it cannot be formally evaluated and it is accountable only to the participants themselves.

Participant roles in an integrated approach to policy determination and implementation

In an integrated curriculum (Table 3) all role-players would be aware in general terms at least of decisions made at all stages in the curriculum process and would contribute to the developmental process through formative evaluation or by other means. The integrated curriculum

TABLE 3. DECISION MAKING IN AN 'INTEGRATED CURRICULUM'

Participants	*Stages in curriculum development*						
	Policy	*Syllabus*		*Programme*		*Classroom*	
		ends	means	materials resources	teacher training	teaching acts	learning acts
policy makers	▨						
needs analysts	⊠	▨					
methodologists	⊠	⊠	▨				
materials writers	⊠	⊠	⊠	▨			
teacher trainers	⊠	⊠	⊠	⊠	▨		
teachers	⊠	⊠	⊠	⊠	⊠	▨	
learners	⊠	⊠	⊠	⊠	⊠	⊠	▨

input to product of decision making ▨

input to process of decision making ⊠

therefore has many of the virtues of the learner-centred approach while, as in the specialist approach, the responsibility for implementing the decisions made at each stage lies ultimately with those considered best qualified.

Pragmatic constraints

So far, this discussion of the decision-making framework has concentrated upon policy decisions, with policy constraints acting from left to right (figure 1) from policy document or 'good idea' to learning acts. Where policy determines what counts as a successful learning outcome, pragmatic constraints determine whether those learning outcomes can be achieved. In figure 1, these constraints operate from right to left, beginning not from the policy makers but from the learners, whose characteristics and expectations influence teaching acts, teacher training, materials content and methodology and ultimately the policy which can be implemented. The characteristics of teachers and other participants also act as constraints upon the curriculum; so does the availability and type of non-human resources. Pragmatic constraints operate from outside as

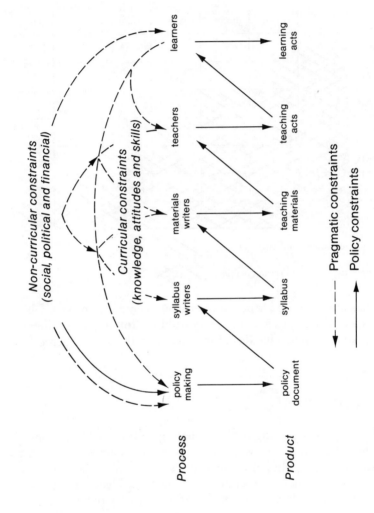

Figure 1 Policy and pragmatic constraints on curriculum decision making

well as inside the curriculum, affecting policy and influencing styles of teaching and learning as well as the content of programmes and the eventual learning outcomes.

Pragmatic constraints from outside the curriculum

Many of the constraints upon what can be achieved in any particular curriculum are beyond the control of any of the participants in the curricular process. The time and money available are prime examples, with little scope for a trade-off between the two; i.e. more money compensates very inadequately for insufficient time, while more time and other measures to improve proficiency gains tend to result in exponential increases in costs, with smaller classes and more highly selected students, a more intensive programme and better qualified teachers, more resources, provision for time to be spent in the target community etc. In a broader sense, the policies of most language curriculums have to be justified to some external agency or group, and the movement towards 'accountability' has meant that influences from outside the curriculum are increasingly effective (for good and ill) in constraining policy and its implementation. The validation criteria set up by the outside agency, or the tests which operationalise them, can and do constitute the new 'hidden' curriculum in many institutions and education systems. Values from outside the curriculum may also impose themselves in other ways: the Friday afternoon debate, for example, may have to be discontinued, regardless of its merits, because the school principal thinks debates are a waste of time, or because the parents' and citizens' association has objected to one of the topics.

Pragmatic constraints from within the curriculum

Pragmatic constraints within the curriculum include the knowledge, skills and attitudes which the participants possess and which constrain their ability to perform their roles. In the case of learners, proficiency level on entry, motivation, previous learning experience, 'cognitive style' and preferred learning strategies might all need to be taken into account by teachers, materials writers, and syllabus writers. Similarly teachers' qualifications, academic and professional, their previous teaching experience and preferred teaching strategies as well as their proficiency in the target language all constrain the options of the materials writers and syllabus writers. Since the number of materials writers and syllabus writers required is small, it is usually possible to obtain the services of experienced and well-qualified specialists, but where teachers or learners attempt to take on these roles themselves or where a larger organisation feels constrained to use available personnel, the quality of the 'products' may be adversely affected. Even where specialists are employed, they still have their preferred styles of operation, which may not match the approach best suited to implementing a particular policy in a particular context. Like learners and teachers, they may do what they have always done rather than what the policy or the context may require.

Matching pragmatic constraints and policy

A coherent language curriculum reconciles what is desirable (policy) with what is acceptable and possible (pragmatics). When the last concession has been squeezed from a reluctant agency or institution, expectations about what can be achieved have to be adjusted downward to what is practicable. Ideally this would be done during planning, but a full assessment of pragmatic constraints is difficult if not impossible to achieve at this stage and coherence can normally only be achieved through the fine-tuning of on-going evaluation and revision. As mismatch is (belatedly) revealed, policies, teacher training, teaching materials, prerequisites for admission, etc. need to be reviewed.

Ultimately, if what is learned is shown to be totally inconsistent with what is required, the curriculum should be discontinued. However, where jobs and career opportunities are at stake, not to mention social consciences (i.e. where the admission of educational failure has unacceptable political/social implications) any curriculum may be considered better than no curriculum. As a result, unwarranted optimism may survive along with the ill-fated curriculum, and rigorous evaluation may be avoided or its findings ignored.

Process and product in each stage of decision making

In this section I would like to sharpen the distinction between decisions relating to process and those relating to product. Process here refers to the ways in which decisions are made and product to the ways in which decisions are presented.

The processes of decision making

Process decisions are about management: Who will be involved? What are their powers and terms of reference? What resources will they have available to them, what constraints will they be under and what procedures will be followed? These management decisions may themselves ensure that policy reflects the wishes of a particular person or pressure group, of the general community, the governing body of an institution or the learners themselves. Decisions about conducting a needs analysis, a literature search or an evaluation are also process decisions and may be made more or less formally by any participant, within the framework of the official curriculum or outside it. As other examples of process decisions, teachers decide what and how and perhaps most important, whether to prepare for lessons. Learners (like syllabus and materials writers) decide whether to work as required or whether to copy from a 'friend'. Where the outcome of the decision-making process is inadequate or inappropriate, the most obvious step is to see how the input could be improved. Would a more explicit statement of ends and means solve the problems of the materials writer? Would a better 'Teachers' Book' or in-service teacher-training programme remove the mismatch between the requirements of the curriculum and what the teacher is actually doing? etc.

Additional input helps to overcome ignorance, but may have little success in overcoming self interest or a well-established alternative curriculum. Policy documents may continue to reflect the prejudices and preconceptions of a powerful pressure group regardless of the rec-ommendations of an evaluator. Teachers may reject the methodology of the 'Teachers' Book' or in-service programme and continue to teach in what they regard as the 'proper' way. However, to repeat this point, if the constraints on decision making are formally stated and explicit, and if the decision-making processes are effectively monitored, the products of the decision-making process are more likely to adhere to the official than to an alternative or hidden curriculum; and mismatch, where it occurs, is easier to identify and, potentially at least, to remedy.

Product: the presentation of decision outcomes

At the end of each decision-making process there is a 'product': a policy document, a syllabus, a set of teaching materials, a teacher-training programme and teaching and learning acts are products in this sense. While any participant, and even non-participants, may contribute to the decision-making process, the right to present these products is usually reserved for designated specialists whose appointment is subject to stringent conditions. Learners have to meet specific entry requirements regarding age and/or proficiency level. To continue as learners they have to meet other requirements about where they go and what they do during specified periods of time. If they fail to observe these requirements or cannot meet them, they cease to be learners in that curriculum. The conditions on who is permitted to perform teaching acts are equally stringent. Most national education systems go to considerable lengths to ensure that teaching acts may only be performed by certificated teachers. The skills of materials and syllabus writers are even more highly specialised, and policy statements, in so far as they are commitments, may have the force of legal documents and need to be framed as such.

A role change, where a specialist product is to be presented by a non-specialist, normally has to be sanctioned. A learner may perform teaching acts, as in peer teaching, but this is sanctioned by the teacher. If a school wishes to set up its own teaching and learning programme, this has to be approved by the designated specialists within the relevant education authority. Acts of parliament, or their equivalent, determine what policies are acceptable and the constraints upon groups which may want to set up independent teaching and learning institutions in which to pursue policies of their own.

Designated specialists are therefore in a particularly strong position to impose an alternative curriculum upon the official one. They are in charge of the product, and each product is the major policy constraint on the next stage in decision making (see figure 1). If formative evaluation could be carried out on the product of each stage before the decision-making process at the next stage began, subsequent formative evaluation could focus primarily upon classroom processes and learner outcomes: i.e. the assumption would be that policy decisions up to that point had been implemented consistently, and that teachers and learners were faced with the task of implementing a coherent language programme rather than surviving one which was not. In practice, a staged approach of this kind would rarely if ever be possible, as the pragmatic constraints revealed through implementation in the classroom would inevitably have implications for the redevelopment of earlier stages. An on-going, interactive and recursive process of decision making seems to be far more likely to succeed.

Evaluation

As Hargreaves points out in the last paper in this section, evaluation is not a stage in itself, it is the result of a further set of decisions built into curriculum planning and implemented at each of the subsequent stages of development. My intention here is to comment briefly on the relationship between curriculum research and evaluation, argue the need to evaluate both process and product if either is to be meaningful, and summarise points already made or implied in this paper on the role of evaluation in a coherent and integrated curriculum.

Curriculum research and evaluation

Curriculum research and evaluation would seem to have complementary aims, but the premisses on which each is based are very different. Planning in curriculum evaluation depends upon the purposes for which its findings will be used, and the usefulness of an evaluation depends upon its appropriacy to a specific educational context, points made particularly strongly by Hargreaves and by Hudson and Elley in Part V. Evaluation findings are not expected to be replicable in or generalisable to other educational contexts, and their validity is determined primarily by the effectiveness of the decisions which flow from them. Pure research, as opposed to applied, is not concerned with the uses to which its findings might or might not be put. Its findings must be generalisable or must lead towards research which could give generalisable results. Its validity depends crucially upon its replicability in other contexts, and its validity is judged in terms of theoretical rather than practical criteria.

The researcher and the evaluator come closer together as a theoretical paradigm (i.e. of language and language learning) is established. I have argued (above) that no developed paradigm currently exists in language curriculum studies, and until it does, the relationship between evaluators and researchers needs to be one of considerable caution.

Brown, in Part V, traces developments in the theory and practice of curriculum evaluation over the past forty years, emphasising the importance for language curriculum development of work in the mainstream of educational curriculum studies. In looking, perhaps over-optimistically, for paradigms of our own, we may too often have ignored those which already exist in related disciplines and which could be applied to the solution of at least some of our problems.

The interdependence of process and product evaluation

The evaluation of process and product in curriculum development cannot usefully be separated. Knowledge of products and in particular global products such as scores on proficiency tests, have limited value for decision making unless evaluators know the learning processes by which the outcomes were achieved. Success may have been achieved in spite of the official curriculum, or failure because it was never implemented (the course books did not arrive; there were no qualified teachers; the students were on strike). A 'product' approach to evaluation can offer an initial insight into the coherence of a curriculum; i.e. it can check the products of the four stages of development for mismatch and it can assess summatively the performance of learners against the original aims. However, once mismatch has been identified, its elimination depends upon an adequate understanding of causes. The knowledge that mismatch exists offers no basis in itself for remedying the situation.

The investigation of processes without consideration of their product (a feature of some approaches to teacher evaluation) is no more helpful. It assumes that the outcomes of certain procedures are so well established that they may be taken for granted. There is no evidence which supports this assumption, and a great deal which shows that it is false. The evaluator may also need to look at inadvertent as well as intended outcomes, social as well as academic, and at the processes which brought them about: for example the students of Japanese may have performed well, but they discontinued their studies; the debates went well, but students conducted an open forum on school policy which led to the expulsion of the ringleaders.

Evaluation and the coherent curriculum

The implication of the argument I have presented here is that all decisions influencing the acts of any participant in the curriculum process should be regarded as potential causes of mismatch. Needless to say, this approach takes the language curriculum as a whole far beyond the scope of any formal evaluation, however thorough and extensive. The only practicable way forward is to increase the professionalism of the decision makers (all the participants) themselves, so that they achieve the knowledge and skills necessary for effective curriculum maintenance and revision. Maintenance requires participants to evaluate their own acts in relation to the curriculum as it is; revision requires them to identify potential areas of mismatch and to propose remedies.

In terms of the 'ideal', integrated curriculum discussed earlier, development and renewal would consist of a process of continuous adjustment and fine-tuning, a 'bio-feedback' mechanism involving all the participants. In the less than ideal circumstances of real life curriculum evaluation, mismatch may be virtually institutionalised within the curriculum, and its removal might require radical changes in the policy, the programme, the participants or the society itself. Nevertheless evaluators can still play a valuable role, as Elley demonstrates in the last paper in this collection, if the means at their disposal are employed sensibly and sensitively, and if participants are involved in the process to the fullest extent that this is possible.

Summary and conclusion

In this paper I have outlined a framework for the decision-making processes which cumulatively result in a language curriculum. I have identified major constraints on the decision makers, the participants in the curriculum, as being of two kinds: those relating to policy and those relating to pragmatics. Policy constraints operate successively on each of the four stages of curriculum development, 1 planning, 2 ends/means specification, 3 implementation as a language programme, through teacher training and the preparation of materials and resources, and 4 implementation in the classroom through teaching and learning acts. At each of these stages, pragmatic constraints (time, money, human and other resources) have to be accommodated.

At each curriculum development stage, there are decisions relating to the processes or management of decision making: (Who should participate? What resources of information and expertise should be available? etc.) and to the products of decision making: (Who is responsible for formalising the outcomes, as syllabus documents, teaching materials, teaching acts etc. and how should it be done?) The aim of the decision-making process as a whole is to achieve coherent curriculum development, maintenance and renewal, where a coherent curriculum is defined as one in which policy has been reconciled with pragmatic constraints, the products of each of the four stages of development are mutually consistent and complementary, and learner achievements correspond to the aims of the curriculum.

I have argued that coherence can only be formally demonstrated and mismatch remedied to the extent that the processes and products of decision making are accessible to investigation. Without this precondition, it is difficult if not impossible to carry out effective evaluation. If this precondition can be met, evaluation should be integrated into each stage and aspect of the decision-making process in ways that have been discussed.

At some time in the future, an adequate theoretical base may be established in applied linguistics to support the 'technology' of language curriculum development. If this were established, consensus amongst decision makers could be achieved and processes could be monitored (to some extent at least) by reference to principles and procedures external to the curriculum. For the present no generally accepted and explicitly formulated theoretical paradigm exists, and the integrity and coherence of each language curriculum has to be established and maintained primarily from within.

2 Syllabus design, curriculum development and polity determination

Theodore S. Rodgers

Introduction

In this brief paper, I want to examine evidence which suggests that program innovation has not worked very well as a strategy for educational renewal. I contend that good programs are central to good education and that failures in program innovation are not as often failures of content as failures of contextual planning.

I want to draw distinctions between three types or levels of educational program planning. I label these levels

1 Syllabus design
2 Curriculum development
3 Polity determination

I propose that in the same sense that curriculum development is a contextually enlarged view of syllabus design so polity determination is a contextually enlarged view of curriculum development. I propose that examination of and planning within the relevant political context is critical to the success of any educational program and that program failures are often attributable to shortcomings in the sort of planning I call polity determination.

Finally, I propose a polity planning framework, which though necessarily limited in scope, has helped planners of three language education programs to become more aware of and be able to accommodate for those factors of a polito-pedagogical nature which often decide the success or failure of educational programs.

Success and failure

'Innovations or revisions in programs have had only about 20 percent success rate in education.' This conclusion from a large-scale study of educational change efforts has been supported by analyses from a wide variety of studies (Parish and Arrends, 1983). I assume the success rate of new language education programs is no higher and, given the thorny nature of language education, possibly lower.

Parish and Arrends conclude that the primary cause of educational program failure is attributable to incongruities which exist between administrative priorities and teacher priorities.

'Administrators control access and adoptions; therefore strategies for adoption and training include interaction with the formal system. Teachers control implementation; strategies must be used that involve and include the informal networks and ways of doing things that exist in each school.' (Parish and Arrends, 1983: 65). Parish and Arrends claim that program implementation strategies rarely satisfy both sets of priorities.

I feel that this analysis is too limited and at best not too helpful, since no program development and implementation group, however well-intentioned and informed, is likely to be able to respond adequately to the 'ways of doing things that exist in each school'. However, the general thrust of the Parish and Arrends argument seems well taken and needs to be thoughtfully and thoroughly considered by language (as well as other) program developers. We need to see successful language education programs as considerably more than a composite of well-chosen linguistic inventories, well-tested procedures and well-designed classroom materials. Perhaps even more than educational programs in other fields, language programs are necessarily political in nature and need to be proposed and planned with political acumen.

Syllabus and curriculum

At the heart of the educational enterprise is the educational program offered. Until fairly recently most educational authorities have considered the *syllabus* to be the educational program. It has been the syllabus which has received the most attention in educational design and implementation. It has been syllabus reform which has been seen as central to educational reform. When new educational goals are sought or old goals are felt to have been inadequately realized, specification of a new syllabus has been the typically favored solution.

Consideration of syllabus change as but one element in a constellation of related elements is a fairly recent phenomenon in discussions of educational renewal. This larger view of educational planning has been often labelled as *curriculum development*. In his study of the implementation of the Malaysian Upper Secondary English Language Communicational Curriculum, Rogers defines the syllabus/curriculum distinction as seen in Malaysia in the mid 1970s. 'The assumption implicit in the formulation of syllabi, as a basis for school programmes, has been that syllabi and curriculum are synonymous. Syllabi, which prescribe the content to be covered by a given course, form only a small part of the total school programme. Curriculum is a far broader concept. Curriculum is all those activities in which children engage under the auspices of the school. This includes *not only what pupils learn, but how they learn it, and how teachers help them learn, using what supporting materials, styles and methods of assessment*, and in what kind of facilities.' (Rogers, 1976)

Conventional and consultational

In the field of second language teaching, then, thinking about design of language education programs in curriculum development rather than syllabus design terms is reasonably recent and still somewhat unformed. I think it fair to say that most second language educators are not familiar with the extensive literature of curriculum design, development and dissemination, nor do they feel thus handicapped in their capacity to design language education programs (Richards, 1984b). This lack of attention to curriculum development and dissemination issues among second language educators stems, I think, from two primary causes. First, there has been a tendency to regard language learning, even formal school-based language learning, as different in kind from learning in all other disciplinary areas. Thus, the professional literature on design and implementation of curricula in algebra or history has seemed highly irrelevant to the concerns of the second language educator. As well, second language teaching has been typically defined as a kind of applied linguistics rather than as a kind of education. There are several reasons for this, not the least of which is the relatively higher academic prestige accruing to linguists than to educators. Since curriculum development and dissemination issues are discussed in the educational rather than the linguistic literature, they have often been ignored or overlooked by applied linguists interested in language teaching.

Language educators thus may not be fully aware of some major discussions current in professional education circles about educational programs and the nature of educational change processes. These discussions have particularly tended to challenge what have become the 'conventional' paradigms for curriculum development, program evaluation and educational decision making. Criticisms of the conventional models in these three areas have arisen somewhat independently. They have been based, however, on similar sorts of critical concerns and have led to similar sorts of proposals for remodelling. The concerns expressed and solutions proposed usefully preface our discussion of polity determination and so will briefly be reviewed next.

The conventional view of curriculum development is one that derived from governmental systems design and has been described by Tyler (1949), Taba (1962), Dick and Carey (1978), etc. The curricular systems design model has been prescriptive and rule-driven. It defines a linear sequence of events comprising formulation of objectives, selection of content, task analysis, design of learning activities, definition of behavioral outcomes and evaluative measures for determining the achievement or non-achievement of these outcomes.

In the hey-day of large-scale curriculum development in the U.S., policy makers required specification of curriculum development plans by program administrators in the format outlined above. Permission to proceed typically turned on receipt of a systems-formated development plan, usually with attached time lines. A typical development proposal was submitted as 'will do' items affixed to linear time-lines such as defined in a program evaluation and review technique (PERT) chart.

The conventional model of program evaluation is based on the hypothetico-deductive paradigm of experimental science and dictates a sequence of procedures to be followed in conducting an evaluation. 'Program goals subject to evaluation are selected, success criteria are stated, measures are selected/constructed, an evaluation design is developed, treatment and comparison groups are formed, data are collected and analyzed, conclusions about the effectiveness of the program are drawn, and a report is written.' (St. Pierre, 1979)

The conventional view of educational decision making holds that there are two major kinds of decision makers with two kinds of decisions. *Policy makers* make decisions which focus on large questions such as whether a particular program's services should be maintained, eliminated, expanded or revised and *program administrators* make decisions that turn on problem identification and solution and types of procedural changes (Cronbach *et al.*, 1980).

These views are conventional not only in the sense that they are discussed at conventions but in the sense that they have tended to be formal and quantitative (rather than informal and qualitative) and in the sense that they have been embedded in customary practice and have often been contractually mandated, most typically in publicly-funded educational development projects.

As I initially observed, the conventional wisdom and practice in the areas of curriculum development, program evaluation, and educational decision making have recently come under increasing attack.

The systems design model for curriculum development has been challenged by contemporary planners who view educational design as a non-linear, multi-directional, organic, context-dependent process (Short, 1983) and as one primarily shaped by intermediate rather than one-time, long-term, decision making (Yinger, 1980).

The use of the experimental science paradigm of hypothetico-deductive methodology for program evaluation has been critically challenged by evaluation specialists who propose more situational (Parlett and Hamilton, 1976), more qualitative (Patton, 1980) and/or more interactive (Guba and Lincoln, 1981) methods of program evaluation.

Finally, educational decision making is seen by many current educational specialists as an on-going and wide-ranging process involving teachers, trainers, tax-payers and students themselves. All of these participants are seen as exercising important educational decision-making roles (Cronbach *et al.*, 1980).

Current critics of the conventional approaches to curriculum development, program evaluation, and educational decision making thus tend to reject linear, quantitative, top-down, participant-restricted models in favor of more multi-dimensional, qualitative, interactive, and participant-extended options. They urge that these processes be more deliberative and less deterministic in operation.

We now turn to consideration of a framework to support such a deliberative approach to educational program planning.

Programs and polity

The language syllabus is typically defined as the selection and organization of linguistic content to be taught. In current syllabi, linguistic content is held to include not only vocabulary and grammar but *notions* that the learner needs to communicate about and *functions* that the learner needs to communicate within. Syllabus design is thus the process by which linguistic content – vocabulary, grammar, notions, functions – is selected and organized.

The language *curriculum* includes specifications for providing inputs to syllabus design and for measuring outcomes of syllabus-based instruction. Language curriculum development processes are typically seen as needs analysis, goal setting, syllabus design, methodology and evaluation (for example Richards, 1984b). Curriculum design derives generally from three design considerations which I have elsewhere called learner considerations, knowledge considerations and instructional considerations (Rodgers, 1980).

The analyses of educational program failure with which this paper began suggest as critical an even larger domain of concerns and attendant planning process than those defined as curriculum developmental processes. These sets of issues are political concerns, in the largest sense; their analysis, political considerations; their resolution, political decisions. The process of arranging, analyzing and responding to political considerations, I call polity determination.

Polity determination is a bit awkward but I think reasonably apt. 'Polity' is dictionary-defined as 'political organization' or a 'specific form of political organization' and also 'the prudent management of public affairs'. I consider the polysemy fortunate in that I want to suggest by polity determination both 1) the analysis of the existing socio-political context into which a new educational program is to fit as well as, 2) the development of strategies to optimize the probable success and effectiveness of the program in such a political context. Polity determination seems to have the right level of ambiguity to suggest both the carrying out of political analyses and the construction of political strategies.

There, perhaps, has been implicit in the discussion thus far an assumption that those in general education have been sensitive to the political context of successful educational program implementation whereas language educators have not. This would be unfair and incorrect to imply.

John Munby (1978), for example, has undertaken to present a system for specifying syllabus content that is relevant to the communication needs of different types or groups of foreign language learners and to place syllabus content thus derived in the context of socio-political, logistic, administrative, psycho-pedagogical and methodological concerns. However, Munby makes no attempt to specify the nature of these contextual concerns. He also holds that he has constructed a system from which syllabus content can be derived a) algorithmically and linearly and b) *a priori* to any consideration of the contextual concerns. As indicated previously, I question both of these views.

Other language educators have dealt more specifically with the nature of contextual constraints than does Munby. Maley (1984) and Hawkey (1983) describe 'constraint-based' syllabus concerns in China and Zimbabwe and Candlin (1984a) describes a German project, central to which is concern with the degree to which the conceptual model deals with 'the real world problem'. These three authors list what some of the constraints and real world problems are. Maley, for example, lists 140 constraints in his constraints check list.

What I think now needs to be focused on is 1) how constraints or problems are to be de-limited and organized for consideration in 'real time', 2) how scarce resources for 'clearing of constraints' (time, energy, money) are to be allocated and 3) how constraint consultation among planner and client groups can best be focused and co-ordinated. I want to focus on these issues in the remainder of my paper.

I propose below a polity planning framework consisting of a set of factor scales organized under the categories of considerations in curriculum design earlier mentioned; *i.e.* learner factors, knowledge factors, and instructional factors. I have also added another category, administrative/management factors.

The polity planning framework is a device to stimulate group discussion, evaluation and problem solving. We know that curriculum development is typically a group planning process. Group planning plays an important part in almost all curriculum development projects which have been analyzed (see for example Schaffarzick and Hampson, 1975 and Walker, 1971). But how can group educational planning be most effective? How should planning groups be constituted and how should they operate? And particularly, to what factors should planning groups direct their attention?

The factors proposed here are ones that have emerged as worthy of early consideration from 20 years of curriculum design experience of our staff at the Curriculum Research and Development Group at the University of Hawaii. The factor inventory has been revised several times and will undoubtedly be revised again. At this point, the factor inventory is intended to be more than suggestive but less than comprehensive.

POLITY PLANNING FRAMEWORK

Knowledge factors		1	2	3	4	
1 Subject area	familiar					unfamiliar
2 Knowledge base	defined					undefined
3 Knowledge structure	simple					complex
4 Relevant materials	available					unavailable
5 Knowledge outcomes	facts					values
Learner factors						
6 Group size	limited					general
7 Homogeneity	homogeneous					heterogeneous
8 Teachability	easy to teach					hard to teach
9 Motivation	aspiring					non-aspiring
10 Attainment expectations	basic					sophisticated
Instructional factors						
11 Curriculum design	simple					complex
12 Educational plan	well-researched					intuitive
13 Instructional media	technically simple					technically complex
14 Teacher retraining possibilities	extensive					none
15 Target schools (system)	coherent					disjoint
16 Target schools (problems)	known/simple					unknown/profound
17 Competing programs	none					many
Management factors						
18 Change effort (breadth)	local					international
19 Change effort (depth)	partial					complete
20 Development time	extensive					limited
21 Development team	experienced					inexperienced
22 Agency reputation	excellent					poor/unknown
23 Agency leverage	great					limited
24 Development resources	large					small

The scales are organized so that low difficulty factors are on the left and high difficulty factors on the right. For example, if a proposed program's *Subject area* (factor 1) is already highly familiar to educators and the community (for example reading) the assessment would suggest 'low difficulty' loading on this factor. If subject matter is highly unfamiliar (for example discourse analysis) assessment would indicate 'high difficulty' loading on this factor.

In use, each member of a planning group is given a framework sheet. The proposed educational program is described by the team leader and substantive questions are entertained. Each of the factor scales is 'read' and briefly discussed to insure a more or less common interpretation of the factor. Each of the participants then privately provides an assessment indicating which of the four scalar points on the scale best represents the current status of that factor and marks the scale accordingly. The exercise leader may want to 'pulse' this so that participants consider each factor equally and complete this phase of the exercise together. Participants then divide into sub-groups of about four or five, each group containing a mix of people with different sorts of educational affiliations. The groups then discuss each factor (or a sub-set of factors) and comment on their individual assessments. A group secretary then records a group assessment on a clean framework sheet. Consensus and disagreement are both important to note. The group then reconvenes as a whole and secretaries report the results of the sub-group discussions.

The group can then make several kinds of polity determinations. For example:

1 How 'difficult' does the project look as a whole? (Do assessments bias to the left/low difficulty or to the right/high difficulty end?)
2 What 'high difficulty' factors are most susceptible to manipulation which could make them less difficult?
3 What factors will be most critical in the likely success or non-success of the project?
4 When considerable disagreement exists as to assessment rating, why is this so? Would more data/more discussion help?
5 Which factors contain the greatest unknowns? Could/should more information be gathered on these factors?
6 Do representatives with the same affiliations assess factors similarly? What are the implications for inter-group/intro-group communication and co-operation?

To help clarify the kinds of polity determination that results from deliberation built around the framework let me provide two brief examples.

Case A: A national communicative curriculum is proposed to replace a grammar/literature upper secondary syllabus in an EFL situation. The planning group notes that communicative approaches are unfamiliar to teachers (factor #1), locally relevant materials are unavailable (factor #4), and time and resources for development and for teacher retraining are highly limited (factors #14, 20, 24). Deliberation suggests that because these and a number of other factors are weighted towards the high difficulty end of the factor scales, a modest subject matter change should be initially attempted. Using the principle of 'least change', (Au and Jordon, 1981), a program built around communicative pair practice of exercise types familiar to and favored by teachers and maintenance of a literature element is proposed.

Case B: A computer-based guided composition program has been devised by a university team and tested for secondary school age students in the university laboratory school. Several enthusiastic school administrators are now proposing to install the program regionally. A budget is proposed for equipment purchases and for teacher in-service training at the university.

Polity factor analysis indicates 'guided composition' to be an unfamiliar educational technique for most teachers (factor #1). Current administrative disagreements regarding computer choice, software design, and equipment security and maintenance also yields a 'high difficulty' rating for factor #13. The university team has high prestige (factor #22) but little leverage (factor #23). After deliberation, a decision is made a) to introduce guided composition techniques through a newsletter with sample reproducible paper and pencil exercises, b) to form a town/gown consortium to test and promote the new guided composition program and c) to hold in-service training sessions in familiar and easy-to-reach local schools rather than at the university.

Obviously, the factor list can be extended almost indefinitely (witness Maley's list of 140 constraints). The factors need to be comprehensive enough to be realistic and yet capable of group deliberation in a reasonable period of time. Exercise planners will find suggestions for alternative factors in the Maley, Hawkey and Candlin pieces cited.

I have seen the framework used with several educational planning groups including three groups considering new language education programs. My sense is that the framework exercise, as described, has several benefits. It helps planners

1 to conceptualize educational planning in a new way;
2 to find out what they don't know that they need to know;

3 to focus on issues of feasibility in education renewal;
4 to become more sensitive to the concerns of other individuals and
   agencies involved in educational change;
5 to identify factors requiring more detailed analysis;
6 to plan allocation of time, energy and resources.

Perhaps, most critically, the exercise of group deliberation built
around the framework helps the planning group to develop cohesiveness
and a deliberative style which facilitates more difficult problem resolution in the tasks that lie ahead.

3 DES-IMPL-EVALU-IGN: an evaluator's checklist

Peter Hargreaves

The place of evaluation in the anatomy of a project

There is no need to belabour the point that evaluation – whatever that involves – is typically the least well articulated and supported limb of a project's anatomy. There are many reasons for this but among the more obvious are the lack of immediacy and urgency in what evaluation is concerned with; it is usually the second volume of the course book or the programme for the next in-service course which are needed by tomorrow, rather than the perhaps inconclusive assessment of the effectiveness of the first volume of the course book or the previous in-service course.

If evaluation is sometimes underrated, it is, perhaps more often, simply overlooked. One of the problems is that the three major aspects of a project – *design, implementation* and *evaluation* – are all too frequently treated as *linear* and *discrete*:

DESIGN ⟶ IMPLEMENTATION ⟶ EVALUATION

I deliberately attach the arrows to →IMPLEMENTATION and →EVALU-ATION because these are invariably perceived as dependent limbs in a project: →IMPLEMENTATION presupposes DESIGN: →EVALUATION presupposes DESIGN and →IMPLEMENTATION. DESIGN, on the other hand, is, at worst, considered separately from both →IMPLEMENTATION and →EVALUATION or, at best, DESIGN →IMPLEMENTATION together are seen as a self-contained entity separate from EVALUATION.

The only way in which *evaluation* will receive the attention I believe it merits is for us to move away from a *linear, discrete* view to a *cyclical, integrated* view of these three aspects of a project:

It is outside the scope of this paper to discuss in detail the relationship between DESIGN, IMPLEMENTATION and EVALUATION represented in the diagram above. Suffice it to say that even this fails to capture fully the inter-dependence of the three aspects, in particular, that IMPLEMEN-TATION and EVALUATION are actually *part* of the DESIGN. It is in fact the complete package or process represented by the second diagram above that constitutes the DESIGN of a project.

One way to get this across might be to use a different word for design-as-aspect/component, for example, CONCEPT (a term which I notice is used nowadays for the mock-up stage of new cars demonstrated at motor shows). Another, admittedly unaesthetic, way would be to coin a portmanteau word such as DES-IMPL-EVALU-IGN. This, if it has no other merit, at least graphically illustrates the fact that DESIGN is not complete without IMPLEMENTATION and EVALUATION. A third way, which I suggest not entirely with tongue in cheek, is to incorporate all three aspects into a kind of logo (somewhat on the lines of the British Standards Institute):

LOGO   =   DESIGN   +   IMPLEMENTATION   +   EVALUATION
                                                        (superimposed)

This might perhaps be awarded to, or stamped on, a project that met the desired criteria; i.e. achieved a *cyclical integration* of all three aspects.

If I have spent some little time emphasising the place of evaluation in the anatomy of a project, it is because, until and unless its place is fully recognised and acknowledged, not much attention is likely to be paid to its detailed physiognomy – which forms the subject matter of the rest of this paper.

Evaluation: a checklist of factors

The checklist used in figures 1 and 2 (below) is made up of broad headings of factors relevant to evaluation whether of time-bound projects or on-going programmes. Each factor (target audience, purpose, focus, criteria, method, means/instruments, agents, resources, time factors, findings, presentation of results and follow-up) covers a number of options which are exemplified and expanded in the columns below the headings. The checklist assumes no particular theoretical model; it has been built up over a number of years as a result of contact with a variety of English language projects and programmes overseas, which include:

curriculum development, syllabus design, materials production, teacher education, test design and administration. Similarly, the way the checklist is drawn up is not meant to imply that there is any *necessary* number or order of factors in project evaluation.

In practice, it is usually convenient to consider the factors from left to right, i.e. starting with *target audience*, but many of the factors are interdependent. Choices from one set of options will naturally determine or affect choices from others and continual revision or modification – both backwards and forwards – is necessary as each factor is considered in turn. Further, as illustrated below, the number of factors that apply to a particular project or programme will vary according to what is appropriate. Some factors will tend to be universally applicable, for example, *purpose, agents, means, follow-up* (action). Other factors, such as *presentation of results*, may only be applicable to the more formalised cases of evaluation.

Like most checklists, this one is not intended to be exhaustive or definitive. No doubt there are other factors which could or should be included in an evaluation checklist and it may well be that some of them will be added to this particular list as and when they come to light through my experience with other projects. (For a somewhat different but overlapping list of factors see Rea, 1983: 89ff.)

I shall now say a little about each of the factors in turn.

Target audience

The evaluation of a project or programme may be undertaken for the benefit of – and therefore directed at – a target who is either a *specialist* or a *non-specialist* or both. The same evaluation might in fact be directed at two or more different targets simultaneously, for example a host government, a funding sponsor and a specialist supervisory body. If so, though some of the other factors in the checklist are likely to be the same for all of the targets, for example *agents, resources, time factors*, others would almost certainly be different, for example *focus, criteria, presentation of results*.

Purpose

Evaluation is either *formative* or *summative* in purpose – or both. Formative evaluation is typically periodic or recurrent, since its function is usually to check the progress of a project or programme and make modifications if/where necessary. Summative evaluation, on the other hand, assesses the effects or impact of a project when it is completed – or perhaps when a particular stage has been reached and it is necessary to take stock before, for example, further investment is made.

An essential feature which formative and summative evaluation have in common is that they both need to be built into a project at the *beginning* of its life in order to ensure adequate planning and provision of such factors as *method, means/instruments, agents* and – above all – *resources* and *time factors*.

Projects, by and large, will involve *both* formative *and* summative evaluation and, if the former has been carried out effectively, the latter is less likely to bring with it too many surprises.

Focus

I find it convenient to subdivide *focus* into *direct* and *indirect*, but one could in some circumstances substitute – or, indeed, add in as a further distinction – overt and covert. A typical example of a *direct* focus for evaluation is the language proficiency of a group or groups for whose benefit a project or programme of language improvement (for example through new textbooks, in-service courses, etc.) was set up. The evaluation would be looking to see what changes – if any – had come about as a direct or immediate result of the project or programme.

I use *indirect* focus to refer to the effects typically brought about or influenced by the *direct* results of a project, which may (or may not) have been specifically intended to achieve these effects. Indirect effects may be ELT-related, for example changes in teacher behaviour as a result of the introduction of new textbooks/materials for the benefit of their pupils. Often, however, the effects in question are of a socio-economic kind, for example changes in work patterns, efficiency, etc. in an industrial context as a result of improved communication with English-speaking advisers.

It is worth noting that the direct/indirect distinction does not correspond to primary/secondary. It may well be that the socio-economic effects of a project – though an indirect focus as defined above – are in fact a primary focus for certain targets (particularly non-specialist) in the evaluation of that project.

An evaluation may be concerned with one or more foci and these may be either direct or indirect. An example where both a direct and an indirect focus are relevant relates to a project in a Third World context, in which an English Language Proficiency Examination is being developed for adult learners, who 'missed out' during their school years. In evaluating this project – or to be precise this *part* of the project – a direct focus will be the design and implementation of the examination itself. Briefly, this will be concerned with such matters as the reliability, validity (relevance to context, etc.) and practicality (matters of administration, continuity, etc.) of the examination. An indirect focus of any evaluation of this project is certain to be the effect of the examination/certificate on the employment prospects and patterns of the candidate group, many of whom require (an appropriate qualification in) English for low and intermediate level jobs in other countries, where English is used as a medium of communication.

Another focus for this project, which is arguably direct or indirect, will be the effect that the new exam has on both other EL exams/tests and teaching, since backwash effect has been a major feature of its design and implementation.

Criteria

The evaluation of a project should in most – if not all – cases proceed on the basis of specified criteria by which the success or effectiveness of the project can be judged. There may be rare occasions when an evaluation has no pre-specified criteria, when it is entirely exploratory – simply seeking to establish what effects have taken place as a result of a project, without reference to any prior expectations. But I would not regard this as an evaluation in the strict sense, since evaluation necessarily entails making judgements about past and/or future action – and this implies the existence of criteria or expectations against which such judgements are made. Even if an 'evaluation' does proceed on the basis of no pre-specified criteria, this should be a conscious decision on the part of targets, agents, etc., not – as is sometimes the case – simply a matter of oversight or omission; for the failure to spell out criteria at the outset can lead to disagreements at a later stage about what constitutes 'success'. Though such disagreements may still arise if criteria *have* been spelt out at the outset, they are much more likely to be capable of resolution, especially if – as should be the norm – the criteria have been previously agreed by the key parties involved (targets, project 'des-impl-evalu-igners', etc.).

There is naturally a close relationship between the *criteria* of evaluation and the original objectives or goals of a project. But it is unlikely that there will be an exact correspondence, if only because the evaluation criteria are related to specific foci, some of which may not feature in the original objectives. One could also add that evaluation criteria are almost certain to be different from the original objectives simply because of the dynamics of a project and changes that need to be made as it develops. However, this *ought* not to lead to significant differences between project objectives and evaluation criteria since it is my view that the former should be periodically revised along with other aspects of a project as it develops.

Looking a little more closely at criteria, I draw a distinction between, on the one hand, *global* criteria and, on the other hand, *relative* criteria. These are not in mutually exclusive opposition but at either end of a continuum reflecting the extent to which the criteria are modified or not by the circumstances (constraints, etc.) of the particular project. At the *global* end of the continuum, criteria of success or effectiveness are such as might be applied generally to similar projects (or foci of projects) and therefore tend to be less shaped or modified by local circumstances. At the *relative* end of the continuum, criteria are tailored to the specific situation and are correspondingly less generalisable outside it.

For many projects the evaluation criteria come somewhere in between the two ends of the continuum. In terms of their formulation, they often start more towards the *global* end but in the process of being agreed by the key parties involved they may well finish up more towards the *relative* end. A recent example comes from a project involving the development of a new set of course books in Europe. In evaluating the course book component of this project, it was felt by some of the key parties that it should be appraised on the basis of (what I describe as) *global* criteria, i.e. the extent to which the course books matched up to current thinking/ developments in the design of materials and related pedagogy – without making major concessions to the constraints of the local situation. It was clear, however, from the wider objectives of the project that, if the course books were to be accessible to the traditionally trained teachers who formed a substantial proportion of the target group, they would only be able to go so far down the 'progressive' road. Just as – if not more – important, trialling of the course book materials in draft at an early stage in the project revealed that a number of modifications were needed to meet 'traditional' expectations and give teachers the confidence to deal with the more 'progressive' aspects. It was, in fact, a typical example in project development of a sensible compromise. *Global* criteria of the kind referred to above simply would not have been relevant or appropriate.

Method

Under the general heading of *method* I draw a basic distinction between *a priori* and *empirical* methods in evaluation. The first typically involve assessment of an aspect, product, etc. of a project by experts in the relevant field in terms of (ideally, previously agreed) *global/relative* criteria. The second typically involve the comparison of a situation 'before' and 'after' in order to gauge the changes brought about by a project. Often both *a priori* and *empirical* methods are involved and it is frequently the case that empirical evidence (of change, etc.) forms part of the data scrutinised by the 'experts', along with project products such as textbooks, supplementary materials, guidance notes, etc.

Means/instruments

The distinction *a priori* and *empirical* follows through from *method* into *means/instruments*. *A priori means* might involve, for example, analysis of project documentation, proposals, reports etc.; scrutiny of procedures for consultation, for revision of objectives, timescales, etc.; comparison with relevant precedents, schemata, etc., i.e. with established or agreed 'expert' opinion of what an effective project of the kind under review – and its products – *should* be like (hence *a priori*). *Empirical means* will vary according to whether the evidence being sought is of a *quantitative* or *qualitative* kind or both. Simplistically, the first is generally concerned with counting heads, seeing, for example, how many of a target group show evidence of changes in their language behaviour resulting from the project; the second is generally concerned with describing the impact of a project in all its ramifications but, for reasons of economy and practicality, using only a small selection of the target group. (On the *qualitative* view of evaluation see for example Parlett and Hamilton, 1972; and for the quantitative versus qualitative approaches to evaluating the same project see Beretta and Davies, 1985, and Carroll, 1980.)

A crucial point about *means/instruments* is that an evaluation which is based on empirical evidence, whether quantitative or qualitative, almost invariably depends on the collection of initial or 'base-line' data against which a subsequent comparison can be made. Without such base-line data it can be difficult, if not impossible, to assess the nature and extent of any changes resulting from a project. This is one of the clearest reasons why evaluation must be built into a project DES-IMPL-EVALU-IGN at the outset.

Agents

By *agents* I mean all those involved in planning, carrying out and following through an evaluation.

I subdivide *agents* into *internal*, i.e. those directly or indirectly involved in some aspect of the project, and *external*, i.e. evaluators brought in from outside, who may not even be familiar with the project.

It is typically the case that whereas *formative* evaluation (see under *purpose*) is carried out by internal agents, *summative* evaluation is 'entrusted' to external agents. One reason for this is that summative evaluation is often undertaken in the interests of accountability, for example in order to justify previous investment or make a case for further funding. In such cases it is no doubt felt that external agents will maintain a measure of independence and detachment from a project which would be difficult or impossible for internal agents. Whatever the truth of this, it is evidently perceived as such by some *target audiences* and for this reason alone it may be necessary to make use of external agents.

There are, however, two points I would wish to stress about the use of external agents. The first is that calling in the external 'expert' does not absolve project teams from the responsibility of evaluating. Evaluation is not something that can be left to someone else to do. Above all it is not the preserve of the 'expert evaluator'; along with design and implementation it is an integral part of the DES-IMPL-EVALU-IGN of a project. The second point is that, even where external agents are used, it is in almost all circumstances bound to be the case that, the closer the collaboration between external and internal agents, the more thorough and effective the evaluation is likely to be. In fact, it makes sense for any external evaluating agents to be in on the DES-IMPL-EVALU-IGN at the outset. For, otherwise, how will it be possible to ensure that appropriate base-line data (see above under *means/instruments*) are collected or that project decisions etc. are properly recorded for subsequent analysis?

If there is one single point that I should like to highlight from this article, it is that there can be little or no justification for what so often happens in the case of summative evaluation viz. the jetting in of external 'evaluation experts' to assess the impact of a project, with which they have had no previous contact; which may have started anything up to ten years earlier; where base-line data do not exist and important project documentation is irretrievable; and – most important of all – after the project team has already dispersed and is no longer accessible.

Resources

Under *resources* I include *agents* – considered from the point of view of their time, how it is allocated, financed, etc. – and *funding* – for staff, assistance with testing, interviewing, data collection and analysis, etc.

Two common problems with resources for evaluation are, firstly, that they are easily underestimated or – perhaps more often – accorded a low priority; secondly, they are inadequately planned for in the DES-IMPL-EVALU-IGN. The first point is in a real sense the 'bottom line' for evaluation. The priority accorded to it can usually be gauged by the amount or proportion of resources planners, sponsors, des-impl-evalu-igners, etc. are willing to commit to it in the face of competing claims – that is, assuming they are, or have been made, aware of what resources are required. For, moving to the second problem, it is all too often the case that evaluation and the resources required for it are overlooked in the planning, as pointed out at the beginning of this paper.

Such planning includes allocating a percentage of staff time to the work of evaluation *and writing it into the job descriptions of staff* so that they know it forms an integral part of their responsibilities. I recently had the occasion to look at some well worked out proposals for evaluating courses in language schools but was surprised to find that there was no provision for the work of evaluation written into the job description of the supervisory staff involved.

Time factors

Time factors are very much bound up with *method, means/instruments*, and *resources*. I give them a separate heading, firstly, because time factors are a crucial part of planning, particularly in the case of the periodic, formative evaluation; secondly, because time can often be the deciding factor in the choice of method, means/instruments, etc. It needs to be stressed, however, that there is only so far one can go in the compression of the time-scale before a meaningful evaluation becomes impossible – whatever the pressure from sponsors, policy makers, etc. In one project in Asia the development phase of part of the project, which was to have led into a final phase after formative evaluation, has – for reasons of time and other constraints – been turned into the final phase itself, without the formative evaluation being completed or acted upon. And there is no doubt that this sort of thing will continue to happen unless and until planners insist on due time and place being given to the evaluation process.

Findings

This heading is in the checklist as a reminder that it should be established or agreed by the key parties (target audience, agents, des-impl-evalu-igners, etc.) at the planning stage what the status of any findings will be. This is particularly important in the case of evaluation at the end of a project phase, where external agents are involved. Will, for example, any recommendations be mandatory and binding? Or will they simply be advisory – to be implemented only subject to agreement, availability of funding, etc? It is also important to establish whether the findings themselves will need to be *agreed* by the key parties rather than simply presented, unilaterally, as a *fait accompli* by the external agents.

While it should be clear from the discussion of other factors above that my own view would incline towards the agreed, negotiated outcome of any evaluation, my main point in including *Findings* as a separate heading is that *whatever* is decided on should be clear to all parties at the outset. It can be just as frustrating to external agents in an evaluation to find their recommendations largely ignored as for the internal agents to find recommendations with which they do not agree being imposed upon them.

Presentation of results

It is no exaggeration to say that an evaluation can stand or fall on the presentation of the results. Given that an evaluation may be directed at a whole host of different specialist and non-specialist target audiences and for a range of different purposes, this is hardly surprising. There is little point in, for example, providing a vast amount of specialist detail in a report directed at sponsors or policy makers, nor, on the other hand, dwelling at length on the need for more resources in a report for colleagues who are powerless to increase the budget.

It may be that, for reasons of economy or time, a variety of purposes and target audiences will need to be served by a single evaluation exercise. In that case, more than one presentation or write-up will be necessary, with different findings selected or highlighted and different supporting evidence, to reflect differences in the purposes and the targets.

Follow-up

Most, if not all, evaluations will lead to (hopefully, agreed) recommendations for action, either for the project which is the subject of the evaluation (typically formative evaluation), or for future projects of a similar kind (typically summative evaluation). Such recommendations should wherever possible specify by whom and by what date (and if relevant with what resources) action is to be carried out. With the best will in the world, however, it is often difficult to ensure that all the recommended action is carried out, even if it has been agreed by the key parties.

One measure which can help in this connection is to build some kind of follow-up into any recommendations for action. This may take the form of an agreement to report back on recommendations after a specified period, indicating where action has or has not been taken and, if not, why not. Alternatively, in some situations the follow-up might itself be part of the process of carrying out the recommended action, for example, through the setting up of an action group or committee to oversee implementation and keep a record of progress.

A useful prompt for follow-up to a formative evaluation is to put an expiry date on any points of action recommended. Such prompts might have a greater impact if they took the form of date stamps such as we commonly find on perishable food such as INTRODUCE BY ... or BEST BEFORE ...

Target audience	Purpose	Focus	Criteria	Method	Means/instruments	Agents	Resources	Time factors	Findings	Presentation of results	Follow-up
Non-specialist	*Formative*	*Direct/indirect*	*Global/ 'absolute'*	*A priori*	*A priori*	*Internal*	*Staffing/ funding*	*Timing and timescales*	*Nature/ status of findings*	*Format*	*Action*
e.g. clients, sponsors, policy makers, resource allocators, etc.	e.g. to revise, modify, monitor, assess progress/ need for adjustments, etc.	e.g. programme relevance; social impact; e.g. teacher behaviour, perceptions, etc.	e.g. adequacy/ success judged without reference to local constraints, etc.	e.g. scrutiny by 'experts', etc.	e.g. analytical procedures, etc.	e.g. by self (i.e. where targets and agents are same); by one set of people involved with a programme/ project for another set of people involved with it, e.g. programme designer for resource allocators	e.g. - agents; people needed for 'means' e.g. testers, data collectors and analysers, etc. (with responsibilities spelt out and time allocated); - adequate funds to cover costs	e.g. timing of formative and summative evaluation; adequate time allowance for collection of data, etc. built into planning	e.g. advisory; mandatory; etc.	e.g. report; recommendations; etc.	e.g. what (in general/ in detail)? by whom? by when? etc.
Specialist	*Summative*	student enrolment, proficiency, exam results, etc. affective factors such as motivation, attitude, etc.	*Relative*	*Empirical*	*Empirical*	*External*					
e.g. designers of programmes, curricula, syllabuses, courses, materials; teachers; students; etc.	e.g. to justify change/ investment, etc. (Accountability)		pre-determined/ agreed criteria according to local/ immediate requirements, needs, etc.	comparison of situation before implementation with situation during and/or after implementation	collection of base-line data and subsequent comparison - quantitative study: measurement via tests, questionnaires, observation, etc. - qualitative study: description via case-study, diary-study, observation, interview, etc.	'independent' evaluators brought in from outside					

Figure 1 An evaluation checklist – example (1) of application: a formal, summative evaluation of a curriculum development project by external evaluators

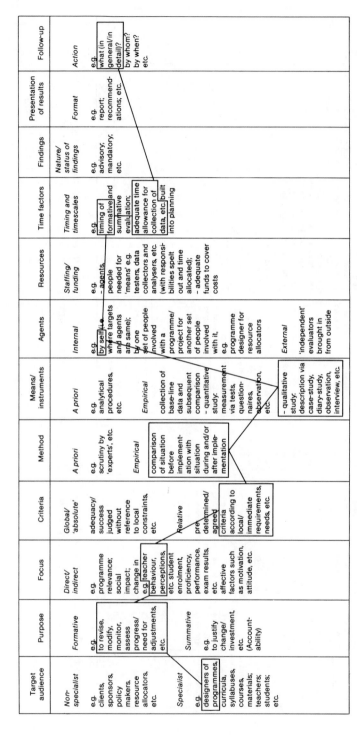

Figure 2   An evaluation checklist – example (2) of application: a small-scale, internal, formative evaluation of a postgraduate TEFL programme

Conclusion

By way of conclusion I would simply like to provide two illustrations of the application of the checklist.

In the introduction to the checklist I pointed out, firstly, that not all of the factors will necessarily apply to every case of project or programme evaluation and, secondly, that choices from one set of options under particular headings will naturally determine or affect choices from others. These two points are illustrated by the two flow charts figures 1 and 2. Figure 1 shows the factors involved in a formal, summative evaluation of a curriculum development project in Asia, undertaken by external evaluators. Figure 2 shows the factors involved in a small-scale, internal, formative evaluation of a postgraduate TEFL programme in the Middle East. The differences in scale and emphasis between the two exemplars of evaluation should be clear from the flow-charts, which also illustrate how the checklist can be used to cover a wide variety of evaluation types.

PART II
ENDS/MEANS SPECIFICATION

4 Needs assessment in language programming: from theory to practice

Richard Berwick

Introduction

This paper is about how teachers and others involved in language programme planning can describe the language needs of prospective learners and about the tools they may employ to fashion their descriptions. It is also about the conceptual baggage planners inevitably bring to the planning situation – often unclarified beliefs and positions about learning and teaching which translate eventually into positions about learners' needs, needs assessment processes and syllabus design.

I want to examine the juncture between theory and practice in language needs assessment first by outlining what I think are some essential concepts in educational planning which do not ordinarily receive the credit they deserve for influencing the ways language programme planners undertake language needs assessment. Next I will try to relate general concepts and methodologies in educational needs assessment to our particular concern with needs assessment in applied linguistics. Finally, in my conclusion, I will try to isolate several key variables in the needs assessment process which planners in institutional situations will want to consider *before* they are overwhelmed by the forces of a large-scale language needs assessment. Throughout the discussion I will stress that language needs assessment is shaped by the local work environment and especially by the commonsense thinking of practising teachers about their work.

Ultimately my goal is to move beyond the aspects of methodology which ordinarily dominate needs assessments and to suggest what factors – largely subjective in nature – influence the interpretation and use of data during the assessment process.

Theory

Orientations to planning and decision-making

Most modern accounts of the origins of planning in educational systems, particularly in public education, begin with a discussion of purposes and sources of curricula. Although Tyler (1949) was not the earliest advocate of systematic curriculum planning he is perhaps the clearest and arguably the most influential. Even though his name has rarely surfaced in the body of professional literature we are ordinarily exposed to, Tyler's four questions outlining the bases of school curricula will strike a responsive chord in anyone who has had to think seriously about programme planning and syllabus design in applied linguistics:

1 What educational purposes should the [teaching establishment] seek to attain?
2 What educational experiences can be provided that are likely to attain these purposes?
3 How can these educational experiences be effectively organised?
4 How can we determine whether these purposes are being attained?

Answers to these questions in the world of educational planning can take a nearly infinite variety of forms. Some of the broad possibilities (see, for example, Eisner, 1985; Elias and Merriam, 1980; Mohan, 1978; Saylor and Alexander, 1974) which have at one time or another found representation in our area of educational practice, applied linguistics, include the following:

Designs based on an organised body of knowledge This has been the predominant design until relatively recently. It emphasises the direct link between an academic discipline (or other established body of knowledge) and content and procedures used during instruction. The focus in this design is generally on the intellectual development of the learner, although, as in the case of structural or functional syllabuses, the primary point is transfer of a systematic body of knowledge – the essential grammar or communicative functions of a language, for example. The main academic sources for designs in language programming include literature and linguistics.

Designs based on specific competencies These emphasise performance objectives and learning of skills for particular purposes, although 'skills' can be taken to mean almost any level of specificity (the 'four skills' – reading, writing, speaking, listening – versus using the target language to confirm an order for a meal in a restaurant). Specification of objectives is a major component of this kind of design, especially in programmes designed to teach language for specific purposes.

Designs based on social activities and problems   This approach to planning has been most influential in second (as opposed to foreign) language teaching, i.e., for immigrants or new residents of a culture in which the target language is viewed as a tool for coping with the social and economic demands of daily life. Heavy emphasis is placed on language as a tool of survival and on exposure to experiences in the community which will assist survival.

Designs based on cognitive or learning processes   This orientation has always been a peripheral rather than mainstream way of approaching instructional design. It stresses the ways learners think (over the content of instruction *per se*) and aims at strengthening the learners' ability to examine and solve problems on their own. Perhaps the best developed application of this approach in applied linguistics can be seen in the organisation of composition courses and materials (for example Lawrence, 1972), although a theoretical basis for process approaches in instructional syllabuses has been developed in Widdowson (1984b). (See also Hansen and Stansfield, 1981, for a discussion of matching learning situations and learning styles.)

Designs based on feelings and attitudes   These approaches represent the humanistic, affective end of the planning spectrum, an appealing region to those who believe that learning must bring people together and that the capacity to learn increases with one's openness to others. Miller (1976) and Rogers (1969) offer exemplary rationales for this design in educational planning. Those who apply humanistic values in language programming would emphasise development of the person *through* language (see, for example, La Forge, 1983; Moskowitz, 1978), and thus would view language more as a tool than an object.

Designs based on needs and interests of the learner   This approach to planning has generally supported rather than supplanted other approaches, although needs-based curricula have been in vogue for the past twenty years, particularly in public education systems. It constitutes a strong justification for the decisions planners make about instruction, for example, to say that their way of organising it will meet learners' needs. The central characteristics of the approach include *systematic* assessment of learners' language needs, along with consultation of learners at appropriate points in the planning and instruction processes. Influential advocates of this orientation in applied linguistics would include Stevick (1971), Munby (1978) (largely in connection with the technology of specific-purpose syllabus design) and, in general, The Council of Europe (see, for example, Richterich, 1983; Richterich and Chancerel, 1980).

These six orientations do not, of course, constitute the final word on the subjective bases and educational values which underlie language programme planning. They do, however, represent the most influential streams of thought in educational curriculum design which have found their way into applied linguistics. The main point I want to make here is that their influence has filtered down to language teaching professionals, whether or not such professionals clearly understand the bases of their systematic planning efforts. Moreover, the importance of needs-and-interests designs in our field closely parallels their popularity in public and adult education generally. I next want to examine the reasons for this popularity along with the theoretical bases for implementing needs-and-interests designs in language planning. At the same time, I will emphasise the persistence of other orientations within needs-based approaches which influence planners' – most often teachers' – perception of learners' needs.

Learner needs in language syllabus design

What are the sources of our fascination with needs? To what extent have approaches to needs assessment been mixed with other approaches to educational planning?

Two major streams have fed the interest in needs-based designs in language programme planning. The first was a legacy of public aid to education in the United States during the mid 1960s – a period of rapid social change which government was prepared to support. Needs assessment activities undertaken by various publicly funded educational and service-providing agencies were largely motivated by federal and state legislation requiring the identification of needs as a condition of receiving financial support (Saylor and Alexander, 1974; Stufflebeam *et al.*, 1985; Warheit *et al.*, 1978). The need for convincing precision in educational needs assessment was also reinforced during this period by the 'behavioral objectives' movement in educational planning, particularly in North America, which insisted on specifying in measurable form all goals of importance within an educational system (Mager, 1962, is an exemplar of the literature in this field). The emphasis on precision and accountability clearly influenced the appearance of needs assessment as a form of educational technology and its diversification into a collection of educational research methodologies (see, for example, Kaufman, 1972; Witkin, 1977).

This positivistic faith in the power of applied science to secure new knowledge and to protect us from the unreliable application of mere 'common' sense has very much made its mark in planning language-for-specific purposes (LSP), the second major source of interest in needs assessment in language programme planning. The direct link between LSP and needs assessment is examined in Mackay and Bosquet (1981), Mackay and Mountford (1978), Munby (1978), Robinson (1980) and Schutz and Derwing (1981). Munby, who represents probably the most technically satisfying approach to needs assessment in LSP, describes the link in these terms:

> The most crucial problem at present facing foreign language syllabus designers, and ultimately materials producers, in the field of language for specific purposes, is how to specify validly the target communicative competence. At the heart of this problem is a reluctance to begin with the learner rather than the text and the lack of a rigorous system for finding out the communicative needs that are prerequisite to the appropriate specification of what is to be taught.
>
> (Munby, 1978: iv)

Here we have the beginnings of a rationale which centres on belief in the power of technical solutions to help people develop specific language competencies. Although Munby's rationale is among the clearest and best-founded in LSP syllabus design, the method for implementing it has been largely lost upon the vast majority of practitioners (Hawkey, 1983, 1984 notwithstanding) because of its complexity. What we do have now is a relatively open-minded attitude among practitioners about undertaking systematic assessment, the ideological and methodological underpinnings having been provided from a wide variety of sources in education.

What is needs assessment, then, how is it accomplished and what are its effects?

Essential principles

Definition   The definition of need is the basis of any needs assessment. Unfortunately, an operational definition must be constructed anew for each assessment because its elements will change according to the values of the assessor or influential constituents of an educational system. In general, however, the skeletal structure of a definition is most often expressed as a gap or measurable discrepancy between a current state of affairs and a desired future state. Thus, as a waiter, my need for being able to confirm an order for salads and sandwiches in a target language (TL) could be based on some of the following: Experience and opinion indicate that confirming an order in the TL is essential to fulfilling it properly; I cannot, at the moment, confirm an order in the TL; therefore,

I need to learn how to confirm orders in the TL, possibly drawing content from lists of words and phrases typically used for the purpose. This all may sound very reasonable and precise, until we learn that my need for learning the subjunctive forms in Spanish, or perhaps how to distinguish subject and object particles in Japanese, could just as well be indicated by the results of a grammar test and the preference of a teacher for a grammatical syllabus. The problem with defining needs, then, lies in the specification of who needs what, as defined by whom (Coffing and Hutchison, 1974; Richterich, 1983) – and a clear understanding by clients or prospective learners that the syllabus will inevitably represent a collection of authoritative, informed opinions about what should be taught (Berwick, 1984b). The subjectivity of needs definitions is thus probably the main conduit by which alternative philosophies of planning are able to find their way into needs-based syllabuses.

Preferences for particular forms of needs assessment   Stufflebeam *et al.* (1985) note a variety of needs assessment types in educational practice, including what I have already described as analysis based on the discrepancy between what people know and what they ought to know (*discrepancy analysis*). Exponents of this form of needs assessment in various areas of applied educational research include Kaufman (1972) in public education curriculum planning, Knowles (1970) in adult education programme planning and, by examination, Munby (1978) in applied linguistics syllabus design. One of the disadvantages of this approach to needs assessment is that areas which are difficult to measure tend not to be included in the assessment. Moreover, discrepancy analysis gives the impression that needs can be discovered with mechanical simplicity once observations have been quantified, leading stakeholders in the assessment process to accept the validity of both the design and the process without close examination.

Although this form of assessment seems most familiar to language professionals who have thought of measurement in terms of tests, or who are accustomed to thinking of lists of structures or functions from which needs can be selected in supermarket fashion, other needs assessment types have emerged in other areas of social science research. Stufflebeam *et al.* (1985: 7) also list *democratic* approaches which emphasise examination of a reference group's views: when a majority of the reference group wish a change in some form of educational practice and make their wishes known, a need is thereby expressed. A democratic approach is going to have great public relations value in situations involving educational constituencies (beyond the prospective learner, of course), although democratic consensus on a large scale would not ordinarily be a useful way of specifying objectives and content for the language syllabus. In practice, the democratic (or, perhaps more accurately, learner-centred) aspects of needs assessment in language syllabus design generally entail consultations or interviews with prospective learners (see, for example, Richterich and Chancerel, 1980) in order to accommodate individuals' goals.

An additional view of needs assessment involves reliance on informed judgement, or expert opinion, and in practice can require elaborate methods to obtain statements of needs. This *analytic* view of needs assessment is reasonably familiar to applied linguists who, after all, comprise the 'experts' most often involved in goal-setting, sentiments about democratic procedures notwithstanding. Because the knowledge base of language courses is likely to emphasise language over content, the technical expertise of linguists will be the predominant source of syllabus specifications. The abstractions drawn from linguistic science may be very difficult to operationalise validly – the emphasis is on applying theory to practice – and the complexity and utility of linguistic descriptions may simply be beyond the interest of practitioners in the field. So far, what I believe is the methodology of choice for this expert-centred approach to needs analysis – the 'delphi study' (Linstone and Turoff, 1975), which helps to systematise consensus building among experts (see *Methodologies*, below) – has not made much of an impact in our field. Moreover, I think we are going to have to re-think the issue of *who* the experts are in needs assessment and the means by which their opinions are to be included in the assessment (Berwick, 1984b).

One final view of needs assessment in educational research, the *diagnostic* approach, comes from the social services (see, also, Bradshaw, 1974, on normative needs) and may have its greatest application in second language learning situations – situations in which 'survival' seems to be the major rationale for course content. Here a need is defined in terms of the harmful consequences of a deficiency. Thus, not knowing how to ask the manager of a supermarket where the cereals are might be considered a deficiency serious enough to require treatment in a syllabus if experts are able to diagnose particular groups or individuals as 'suffering' from the deficiency (Berwick, 1978).

Although compensatory training of this sort operates at the level of fairly basic survival needs, it might be argued that expert perception of such needs is quite subjective and arbitrary, that a person suffering deprivation may have no such perception and may want none of the proffered help.

These views of needs assessment seem to fit particular preferences for curricula (for example, diagnostic designs based on social activities and problems + designs based on specific competencies), and, more important for our purposes, suggest how much approaches to needs assessment are dependent on and mingled with other approaches to curriculum planning. One explanation for 'slippage' between theory and practice in needs assessment, then, may be that models for assessment offered to planners unrealistically assume that planners will buy the whole package and nothing but the package. In fact, as we will see, language programme planners are likelier to 'buy' a number of packages and use them in wonderfully patchwork fashion when they have a syllabus to get out.

Types of need

I have looked at types of needs assessment without much consideration for the ways in which needs themselves have been described in the literature. What are some of these types and how might they apply to language needs assessment?

One of the most enduring distinctions among needs is that between 'felt' needs and 'perceived' needs. This is a useful distinction since it lets us locate the source of need and strike a philosophically satisfying balance between learner-centred and teacher- (viz. authority-) centred inputs to the planning process. Felt needs are those which learners have. The connotation which has developed for the term is one of unsophisticated, egocentric expressions of a desired future state which individuals can be induced to express if planners ask the right questions. Felt needs in this revealed state are sometimes referred to as 'expressed' needs and, depending on the preferences of the people doing the assessment, may be (and often are) devalued by viewing them as 'wants' or 'desires'. The range of responses to 'mere' wants can include ignoring them, interpreting them, and, of course, applying them directly to planning operations – developing a kind of people's syllabus, a smorgasbord of responses to wants – whatever else professional planners may say about their educational value.

I think the usual response is the middle ground where interpretive expertise is applied to what learners say they need. Even Freire's radical methodology for discovering the motivating themes of local groups (Freire, 1970) is fundamentally an interpretive strategy and depends for its success on experts' sensitive understanding of what they think people really need. Thus 'perceived' needs represent the other side of the coin – judgements of certified experts about the educational gaps in other people's experience. Once again, perception of needs can be expressed as a range from sensitive consideration of learners' statements about themselves to largely insensitive prescriptions about learners who may have had the bad luck to fall under the control of an educational despot. This reminds me of the claim one of my teachers made a long time ago – perhaps times have changed – that all students need a good shot of Latin to straighten out their thinking. Such perceptions may be wise, but it is difficult to think of them as being 'true'. After all, we have no absolute basis to dispute anybody's values (particularly if they carry the weight of authority). Along these lines, perceived needs have been described as 'normative' needs (see Bradshaw, 1974; Griffith, 1978; Monette, 1977), and even as 'real' needs (Chambers, 1980) or 'objective' needs (Richterich, 1980) – although we should be wary of prescriptions for language learning which claim to be more than informed perceptions and preferences about learners' futures.

Practice

Methodologies

I don't want to unnecessarily abbreviate this discussion of values and authority in needs assessment – issues which are, after all, at the basis of all educational planning – but I think that, in their theoretical guise, they are essentially intractable and uninteresting for most people involved in the planning process. Thus, I want to take educational values into the field of practice in this section and will begin here by emphasising the very practical point made rather cursorily earlier on – that our perceptions of need develop from what we believe is educationally worthwhile, that needs are not simply 'out there' waiting to be counted and measured with the latest innovations of educational technology (see Monette, 1979a, for a helpful explication of the point).

What educational technology does offer, however, is a highly versatile collection of methodologies to suit various planning situations, ranging from assessments for the individual learner to massive programmes of the sort likely to be found in multi-national corporations. I will list and briefly outline those which I think are among the most innovative and likely to be of greatest utility and then try to round out the discussion by drawing together several key generalisations which I hope will begin to link theory with practice. The reader also is directed to more complete discussions of needs assessment methodologies found in Richterich and Chancerel (1980), Stufflebeam *et al.* (1985) and Witkin (1977).

Inductive (category-dependent) methods

One of the earliest systematic approaches to assessing language needs at the individual level is Stevick's 'Socio-topical matrix' (Stevick, 1971; Buckingham and Pech, 1976). The matrix is drawn so that the kinds of people the learner most urgently needs to interact with are arrayed against the things a learner is most likely to want to talk about. An optional linguistic dimension (this could take the form of language structures or functions) can also be used to broaden the scope of the grid with the intersecting cells producing the content basis of an entire course. Individuals with similar socio-topical profiles can be easily grouped.

Another inductive approach to language needs assessment is Freire's 'dialogue' (Freire, 1970) in which important themes in the lives of prospective learners are gradually clarified through graphic and verbal exercises. The method combines in-depth observation of people in various locations and life situations along with classification of salient themes which keep appearing during extensive discussions with and observations of members of a defined community (a group of farmers or factory workers, for example).

The broad range of what might now be called 'target situation analysis' (see Chambers, 1980; Jupp and Hodlin, 1975) also fits within the tradition of inductively organised applied research, although it is clear that the political and social values which underlie Freierian 'dialogue' do not govern the more technically-oriented analysis of communications in work situations. The emphasis of target situation analysis is on the nature and effect of target language communications in particular situations (in offices, on assembly lines, in meeting rooms, in content-area classrooms, for example). Expert analysis of communication establishes standards against which current performance can be gauged. 'Needs' in this context are perhaps more appropriately described as 'objectives' for learners who will eventually have to demonstrate competence in the situations.

Clearly, within the framework of target situation analysis, reliance on candidates who face instruction to describe their needs (as opposed to merely offering evidence of them during observation) is not going to prove very fruitful, given the strong emphasis on technical analysis of communications which these candidates are unable to handle in the first place. One interesting variation in this approach to language needs assessment is the case study (Schmidt, 1981) which requires intensive study of an individual engaged in language-dependent tasks and then generalisation about the individual's language problems in the defined learning situation. Schmidt finds the greatest values of case studies to be greater understanding of process-oriented needs (needs arising during the learner's attempts to gain knowledge in a field) and establishing a basis for designing a questionnaire or interview battery (see *Deductive methods*, below).

A method which resembles target situation analysis, but which traditionally employs groups in artificial, target-like situations is the 'Critical Incident Technique' (see Flanagan, 1954; Cohen and Smith, 1976). In language needs analysis critical incidents might be breakdowns or difficulties in communication which learners experience when attempting to solve a motivating problem. Competent verbal solutions serve as points of contrast with problematic ones and serve as standards for analysis of the communicative record. The technique requires some faith in the representativeness of the situation under scrutiny and plenty of time to conduct a sensitive analysis, but it does suggest some interesting extensions of needs assessment into such areas as simulation and role play, which ordinarily are only viewed as approaches to instruction (Berwick, 1984a, 1984b).

One final inductive method I want to mention is the 'delphi study', originally developed at the Rand Corporation in the 1960s to assist futures research (see Dalkey, 1969; Linstone and Turoff, 1975; Weatherman and Swenson, 1974; also, Holmes, 1977 on adult ESL programme planning). Use of the technique entails asking stakeholders or experts in a given field (who never meet each other during the delphi process) to rank items which constitute important or desirable future conditions. This ranking continues for several rounds and is influenced by informing the individuals involved about the degree of support each item has received to date. Individuals are asked to reconsider their previous choices in the light of an emerging consensus on particular items.

The technique can be described as inductive when the initial list of items is developed by the raters during the first round, although variations on the delphi study also allow for presenting the raters with a list and then asking them to respond (a deductive approach to t e process). Application of delphi methodology to language needs assessment could, for example, have panels of managers and specialists in a company, who face the task of creating a comprehensive language training programme, propose specific language uses of value to the company; these would eventually find their way into a needs assessment questionnaire in the form of items to be evaluated by prospective learners.

Deductive (category-dependent) methods

Deductive approaches to language needs assessment are the natural complement to the kinds of inductive approaches outlined above. They are also the more typical way into needs analysis, constituting an extension of the tests-and-measurement tradition of educational research into applied linguistics. Unfortunately this collection of deductive methodologies, ranging from simple questionnaires to highly complex sociolinguistic typologies and surveys, generally has no special justification as instrumentation to assist needs assessment. Concepts of need are almost never clearly defined, values are generally left unexplicated, and category-generating methodologies (see *Inductive methods*, above) are typically not invoked to support the selection of categories and items used to generate data.

At the same time, the typologies, surveys and questionnaires which are most frequently used in language needs assessment are valuable resources for the programme planner. I will list some of the best and most accessible deductive approaches here and hope that my cursory treatment will not be taken for disinterest.

Richterich (1983) and Richterich and Chancerel (1980) are two fundamental documents in the Council of Europe's attempt to outline a framework for language needs assessment. What they offer to the planner is a comprehensive list of topics under which data may be collected by a variety of methods of interest and use in local planning situations.

Trim (1980) has noted the extraordinary number of possible combinations of information-gathering categories and sub-categories in Richterich's early model (see Richterich, 1980, originally, 1973): basic demographic features, agents, roles, times, places, environments, functions or purposes of communication, references to affective status, attitudes, means of communication and so on – many of which have found their way into the work of Richterich and Chancerel. This latter guide for practitioners of needs assessment organises data collection into three basic information categories: identification by the learner of his needs, identification of the learner's needs by the teaching establishment, and identification of the learner's needs by the user-institution (i.e., the 'social unit making use of one or more foreign languages to enable it to operate properly', Richterich and Chancerel, 1980: 43). Again, the number of categories in the framework a planner will have to deal with (and may choose to ignore) is stunningly large, although I think the level of organisation to be found in the framework will be a boon to people who have yet to undertake a full-scale assessment of language needs.

Actual data collection methods of potential use are listed, although not explained, and range from surveys and questionnaires to language tests and attitude scales. A companion text (Richterich, 1983) provides case studies which greatly assist the planner to think about data collection and analysis in a wide variety of typical adult learning situations.

Munby's (1978) 'Communicative needs processor' is, perhaps, the most highly developed model-mechanism for the interpretation of specific language learning needs. I want to emphasise that it offers a rationale for its inclusion of categories (to be filled with data on the basis of interviews with candidate learners) and that it has found application in a number of planning situations (see, for example, Hawkey, 1980, 1983). However, as in the case of the Council of Europe framework, the whole of the model is likely to be unwieldy in most planning situations. Perhaps a more fundamental point is that we are going to have a great deal of faith in what appears to be a comprehensive categorisation of 'micro-functions' in the second stage of the processor: Do we believe that learners 'need' language functions, or at least those functions offered for choice in the typology? I have the impression that the system's precision unrealistically limits our view of alternative interpretations of need and that, at the same time, it leaves largely unexamined the problem of interpreting data. Interpretation is probably the most practical problem any needs assessment manager is going to encounter (raw data rarely 'speak' very eloquently), with artful construction and description of needs at the subjective heart of the whole process (Schutz and Derwing, 1981, make a similar point in a description of their needs assessment in Taiwan). In other words, the Communicative Needs Processor gives us exemplary mechanisation when perhaps more art would do.

This observation is just as applicable to the closed-ended questionnaire or other survey instruments, although a fair perspective on category-dependent methodologies would have to allow for their relative ease of use. I want to briefly mention several kinds of questionnaires which have been published and are of potential value in bringing the needs assessor to the actual point of interpretation.

A number of questionnaires apply a useful distinction between needs felt by the learner and needs ascribed to them by administrators of the programme in which they study or will study (recall the felt needs/perceived needs distinction discussed above). Examples of felt/ascribed questionnaire content include Holmes's (1977) study of community survival topics for ESL courses in Los Angeles and Mackay's (1978) study of English for specific purposes at Mexico's National Autonomous University. Although no clear definition of need is offered in either study, need is apparently indicated by high frequency, overlapping responses to choices available on the questionnaire. This is a fairly straightforward approach to locating areas for emphasis in programming and tends to satisfy the constituents of a needs assessment that their interests will be represented in the eventual educational product.

Harlow *et al.* (1980), on the other hand, focus exclusively in their survey on *student-perceived* communication needs in French. According to the authors, the questionnaire employed for the survey can be completed in less than 15 minutes. It contains opportunities for students to evaluate the probability of using French in various future situations (for example, study, travel, etc.) and asks respondents to evaluate the importance of 65 functional descriptors under six general categories of language use (getting things done, socialising, showing emotion, and so on). The categories of language use and descriptors were based on authoritative lists, produced by the Council of Europe and notional-functional specialists, and on introspection. Items likely to be incorporated into a syllabus resulting from the needs assessment would be those which received high rankings in one or more categories of use.

Finally, Carrier (1983) offers a sophisticated method for eliciting respondents' evaluations of 'language subskills' (analogous to Harlow *et al.* 'descriptors' of language use but at a more specific level). Respondents are asked to evaluate a list of subskills of possible importance in an office or factory, for example, from four different work-related perspectives: necessity, priority, problems (caused by ineffective use of the subskill), and importance. A simple check-mark on the questionnaire accomplishes the respondent's evaluation of an item, a process repeated until all items have been evaluated.

Although it is unclear from Carrier's description whether current or future language use is being evaluated (this must be sorted out in any application of the questionnaire format), once the data are gathered and stored in a computer they can be used quite flexibly. For example, it might be useful to combine several of the use categories and then obtain a printout of the names and section addresses of employees who indicated high priority and problems for use of such combined subskills as organising, writing and revising research reports in English. This kind of flexibility – common to all computerised data bases – does not obviate the necessity of interpreting the data in whatever form requested. Nor does it eliminate the burden of deciding how to request data in the first place. There will always be some concept of need, some vision of a syllabus, some preference for method and content underlying the collection and display of information about language needs.

What happens when theory and practice collide?

A clear direction I think it is a fundamental of needs assessment that at some point in the process the assessment will be given a clear direction, or it will fail. By 'clear direction' I mean something like an action plan that satisfies sources of authority in the system and furthers their goals. It is at this breakthrough point that clients and planners may come to blows, since a planner's educational values may conflict with those of a client willing to assert the client's values. The planner's preferences and expertise may find little recognition in the outcomes of the needs assessment – a risk professional planners who are likely to possess clear educational preferences – will have to take. But I really want to note the more typical pattern at the other end of the scale, the case of non-professional planners, generally teachers in an institutional programme, who may lose themselves in the masses of detail which inevitably accumulate as the needs assessment progresses from concept to analysis of a data base to applications within the programme.

Managers in a company language programme, for example, may suddenly awaken to the fact that information is going to be gathered about people in their sections, and may start to register some subtle and not-so-subtle objections to violation of the status quo. Although there are numerous consequences for failing to assuage sources of influence in the institutional system, one of the more likely consequences is that the needs assessment will be forced to simmer on the back burner until consensus has been reached on the basic goals and methods of the assessment. The process may wait for years to restart; it may never be revived. Teacher-planners who may possess only a thin, eclectic collection of ideas about the goals and methods of language learning are going to be at a serious disadvantage when they discover the machine beginning to stall. The point I want to make is that educational and institutional values ought to be insinuated into the needs assessment at the outset, when control over the direction the assessment is going to take is most firmly in the hands of educational planners.

In practice, this will mean that a consensus on goals and strategies for interpreting data should be developed fairly early between those who have responsibility for planning and those who are stakeholders in the products of the needs assessment. Very likely, planners will want to begin with what I have called 'category-generating' methodologies in order to expand their own perspectives on possible content for instruction (or for such other purposes as testing and evaluation) and to lay the groundwork for later methods of data collection which build on themes of actual importance to the institution.

A view of the future   The attempt at data collection itself is meaningless, of course, unless the planners know reasonably well in advance what kinds of analyses will be made of the data – what questions, for example, will be 'asked' of piles of computer printout as they accumulate on some unfortunate person's desk. Leaving space on a questionnaire for the respondent's telephone number may seem an obvious thing to do when designing a form, yet it was just this lack which almost killed the usefulness of a recent, massive English language needs assessment at a major Japanese steel company involving nearly 10,000 respondents – one of the largest formal needs assessments ever undertaken at a single institution in Japan.

Under normal circumstances (and here I mean circumstances in which the planner is relatively inexperienced, has lots of other responsibilities and is never very sure about reliable co-operation from the rest of the teaching unit) foresight of the type described here may be hard to come by. However, finding a 'clear direction' obviously also means knowing pretty well how the assessment is going to end up – knowing, for example, whether it will be used to help design short courses or workshops, and whether the content for such courses will be expressed as language functions or structures or topics or something else. This sort of commitment to a defensible strategy for use of data (one which must, by the way, be communicated frequently and simply to non-planners) is very much what Monette (1979b: 548) had in mind when he argued that 'objectives are required to define needs'. Thus I think the crystal ball isn't nearly as useful in language needs assessment as a planner's vision of the language programme in six months' time.

5 The role of needs analysis in adult ESL programme design[1]

Geoffrey Brindley

Introduction

One of the fundamental principles underlying learner-centred systems of language learning is that teaching/learning programmes should be responsive to learners' needs. It is now widely accepted as a principle of programme design that needs analysis is a vital prerequisite to the specification of language learning objectives.

Over recent years, however, there has been a good deal of disagreement in ELT circles over the meaning of 'needs' and what 'needs analysis' should entail. This disagreement has resulted in the emergence of two orientations to needs analysis. The first of these is based on what could be termed the 'narrow' or 'product-oriented' interpretation of needs whereby the learners' needs are seen solely in terms of the language they will have to use in a particular communication situation. Needs analysis therefore becomes a process of finding out as much as possible before learning begins about the learners' current and future language use. On the other hand, proponents of the second interpretation of needs, which I will call the 'broad' or 'process-oriented' interpretation, see needs primarily in terms of the needs of the learner as an individual in the learning situation. If this view of needs is adopted, then needs analysis means much more than the definition of target language behaviour: it means trying to identify and take into account a multiplicity of affective and cognitive variables which affect learning, such as learners' attitudes, motivation, awareness, personality, wants, expectations and learning styles.

The necessity of finding a balance between these two approaches to needs analysis and by extension, to curriculum design, has been pointed out by numerous authors (Holec, 1980; Bowers, 1980; Coste, 1983). In the words of Richterich (1983: 4):

> It is clear that we must find a happy mean between the technocracy of needs, which claims to be able to define and foresee everything

1 Revised version of a paper presented at the 18th Annual TESOL Convention, Houston, Texas, March 6–11, 1984. I would like to thank David Nunan and Chris Candlin for their helpful comments on the original paper.

and by which everything is imposed, and the infinite diversity and mobility which makes all action absurd and futile.

In this paper, I want to suggest directions which might be taken in order to find the happy mean to which Richterich refers. In order to do this, I shall first examine the two orientations to needs mentioned above, after which I shall attempt to clarify the notion of 'need' as it applies to the teaching of English to adult immigrants. I shall then propose a type of learner-centred system of adult ESL which allows for differing perspectives on needs to be taken into account, drawing on the results of a research project into needs analysis and objectives in the Australian Adult Migrant Education Program. It will be argued that such a system can only acquire the flexibility it needs to operate effectively if regular and ongoing consultation and negotiation between teachers and learners takes place. However, since the feasibility of fruitful consultation and negotiation is a subject which provokes a good deal of controversy amongst teachers, I shall also examine some crucial issues relating to learner/teacher roles in a learner-centred system.

Objective needs as a starting point

It is now generally accepted that the analysis of what Richterich (1972) calls 'objective' needs will not produce a teaching syllabus. It is nevertheless difficult to see how one could dispense with it as a starting point in programme design. Learners cannot learn the entire language in any given course of instruction, so choices have to be made. If instruction is to be centred on the learners and relevant to their purposes, then information about their current and desired interaction patterns and their perceived difficulties is clearly helpful in establishing programme goals which in turn can be translated into learning objectives.

At the same time, the teaching institution needs information on learners' ability to use English, as well as a certain amount of biographical data such as their educational and occupational background, their lifestyle and interests, in order to make decisions on matters such as class placement and learning mode.

Yet as Richterich (1983) notes, this initial phase of objective needs analysis is only a first step. It will establish broad parameters for programme design but once learning begins, it is likely that, first, these language-related needs will change and that second, particular *learning* needs will come to light which were not identified pre-course. It thus appears that two types of needs analysis are necessary, one aimed at collecting factual information for the purposes of setting broad goals related to language content, the other aimed at gathering information about learners which can be used to guide the learning process once it is under way. These two types of analysis could, in Richterich's (1980) terminology, be referred to as *objective* and *subjective* needs analysis. To clarify this distinction, however, it is necessary to examine the notion of 'need' more carefully.

Definitions of needs

It is difficult to find a usable definition of 'needs' in the context of second language learning. As Richterich (1983: 2) comments:

> The very concept of language needs has never been clearly defined and remains at best ambiguous.

It is therefore useful to borrow some insights from the field of adult education, in which needs are conventionally defined as being something like 'the gap between what is and what should be'. What is important to note here is that someone has to decide what should be. In other words, needs statements are open to contextual interpretation and contain value judgements. They do not have of themselves an objective reality. In the words of Lawson (1979: 37):

> 'Needs' are for the educator to define against a background of normative concepts of almost infinite range and variety. His task is to select those normative areas in which there appear to be deficiencies and to match them up with what the educator *qua* educator can supply or provide. Where a deficiency can be remedied by the help of some educational process, an 'educational need' is established.

However, Lawson notes, one cannot be sure in all cases, that the educator's diagnosis and prescription are accurate. The diagnosis made will be based on the practical experience of symptoms of those who diagnose the need, and therefore:

> what is finally established as a 'need' is a matter for agreement and judgement not discovery.
>
> (Lawson, 1979: 37)

Teachers' views of needs

If we apply Lawson's statement to adult second language learning, it follows that teachers' approaches to 'needs' will be heavily influenced by their practical experience as well as by their personal philosophy and conception of their role. It is therefore not surprising that teachers often end up talking at cross purposes when discussing the role of needs analysis in programme design. In order to illustrate this, I shall refer to a survey of over 100 adult ESL teachers conducted as part of a research project to investigate the feasibility of implementing a learner-centred system in the Australian Adult Migrant Education Program (Brindley, 1984).

When asked the question, 'what do you understand by the term "student needs"?', teachers gave a variety of answers which can be roughly categorised under three headings: the 'language proficiency' view of needs, the 'psychological-humanistic' view and the 'specific purposes' view (Table 1, after Trimby, 1979).

Proponents of the first view interpreted 'needs' as the gap between current and desired 'general' proficiency level, and hence tended to stress the importance of language proficiency as a criterion for grouping learners. Despite the demise of the Unitary Competence Hypothesis (cf. Oller, 1983) these teachers spoke as if the notion of 'general proficiency' was universally accepted as fact. It was assumed that learners of a similar level, as evidenced by a rating on a general proficiency rating scale such as the Australian Second Language Proficiency Rating Scale (Ingram, 1984) would have similar needs – in other words, that there was a 'common core' of language which could serve as a basis for specifying course content and objectives. Needs analysis, seen from this perspective, would thus consist mainly of using samples of learners' language performance in the productive and receptive skills to make placement decisions and set course goals.

Frequent reference was also made to the recurring difficulties of certain types of learners in particular language skills. Many teachers felt that these could be predicted, even in the absence of the learners, for example, pronunciation and listening comprehension problems of Indo-Chinese learners.

The responses of those teachers who adopted the 'psychological-humanistic' perspective emphasised learners' affective and psychological needs which they saw as a gap between a current and a desired psychological state – usually one of a higher level of confidence, motivation or awareness. While not denying the importance of language-related needs, these teachers regarded the building of confidence and positive attitudes to learning as a vital prerequisite to the acquisition of language learning skills. They also highlighted the necessity of assisting learners to develop and use independent learning strategies.

The responses of the third group of teachers tended to highlight the 'instrumental' needs of learners which were seen to arise principally from their stated purposes for learning. This view of needs was similar to the 'goal-oriented' definition proposed by Widdowson (1981b: 2), i.e., 'what the learner needs to do with the language once he has learned it'. Thus their responses often focused on the necessity to align course content with the learners' occupational or academic goals.

TABLE 1 COMPARISON OF APPROACHES TO NEEDS ANALYSIS

	'Language proficiency' orientation	'Psychological/humanistic' orientation	'Specific purposes' orientation
View of the learner	Learner as a language learner	Learner as a 'sentient human being' in society with the capacity to become self-directing	Learner as a language user
View of needs	Objective needs stressed. Needs seen as gap between present and desired general language proficiency	Subjective needs stressed. Needs seen as gap between current state of awareness and state of awareness necessary for learner to become self-directing	Objective needs stressed. Needs seen as gap between present language performance in a specific area and language performance required in a particular communication situation
Emphasises	Ease of administration Where the learner is at in terms of language proficiency in one or more skills Relevance of language content to learners' proficiency level	Sensitivity to adults' subjective needs Where learner is at in terms of awareness Relevance of learning content and methods to individual learning styles	Collection of detailed data on objective needs Where the learner is going in terms of language performance Relevance of language content to learners' personal goals and social roles
Educational rationale	Language learners learn more effectively in a group containing learners of a similar proficiency level. Language learners learn more effectively if programme content is geared to their proficiency level	Adults learn more effectively if they are involved in the learning process through consultation and negotiation Their past experience and present capacities should be valued and taken into account	Language users learn more effectively if programme content is relevant to their specific area of need or interest General language proficiency is not as important as the ability to operate effectively in specific areas relevant to the learners' needs and interests

⋙→

	'Language proficiency' orientation	'Psychological/humanistic' orientation	'Specific purposes' orientation
Type of information	Biographical information Information on learners' language proficiency Information on learners' language difficulties	Biographical information Information on learners' attitudes, motivation and awareness Information on learners' personality and learning style Information on learners' desires and expectations about learning English	Biographical information Information on native speakers' use of language in learners' target communication situation Information, where relevant, on the needs of other parties in the relevant communication situation e.g. factory foremen
Method of information collection	Standardised forms* Language proficiency tests* Observation	Standardised forms* Observation Counselling/interviews* Oral surveys* Group discussions* Written questionnaires followed by discussion*	Standardised forms* Intensive language analysis in target communication situation Language proficiency tests* Surveys of learners' patterns of language use* Surveys of needs of particular bodies or individuals outside A.M.E.S.
Time of information collection	Mainly pre-course Some in-course diagnostic assessment and feedback, depending on teacher	Pre-course Constant in-course consultation and feedback	Mainly pre-course Some ongoing in-course consultation and feedback depending on teacher

	'Language proficiency' orientation	'Psychological/humanistic' orientation	'Specific purposes' orientation
How analysis of information is used	Decisions made concerning learners' current ability to use English. Decisions made concerning language learning priorities in light of present proficiency and diagnosed difficulties	Decisions provisionally made about types of learning environment, methods, and content which might be appropriate for learners' subjective needs, taking into account their attitudes, motivation and awareness. Decisions constantly revised and objectives modified in the light of ongoing negotiation	Decisions made on appropriate language content to meet communication needs of learners. Reconciliation of language needs of learners with those of other parties (e.g. management)
Purposes for collecting information	So that learners can be placed in groups of homogeneous language proficiency. So that teachers can plan language content relevant to learners' proficiency level	So that adults' individual characteristics as learners can be given due consideration in providing learning opportunities. So that adults can be helped to become self-directing by being involved in decision-making about their own learning	So that learners will be presented with language data relevant to their own personal goals and social roles. So that motivation will be enhanced by the relevance of this language content and learning will thus be facilitated

* All of these procedures for information collection may require bi-lingual assistance of some kind.

Objective and subjective needs

These views reflect a tension between two types of needs and by extension, between two types of analysis, i.e. between *objective* and *subjective* needs (Brindley, 1984; Quinn, 1985). The first of these terms, as we have seen, refers to needs which are derivable from different kinds of factual information about learners, their use of language in real-life communication situations as well as their current language proficiency and language difficulties. The second term refers to the cognitive and affective needs of the learner in the learning situation, derivable from information about affective and cognitive factors such as personality, confidence, attitudes, learners' wants and expectations with regard to the learning of English and their individual cognitive style and learning strategies (see Table 2).

Although in theory it would be possible for teachers to subscribe to all three of the approaches to needs analysis outlined above, their responses showed a tendency for some kinds of needs to be emphasised at the expense of others. In general, it appeared that while most teachers were attempting to diagnose learners' objective needs through collecting some combination of personal data, information about their language proficiency and interaction patterns, they had much more difficulty in systematically identifying and catering for subjective needs. This, of course, is not surprising, given the elusive nature of the variables in question, the current rather messy state-of-the-art of affective measurement (see for example, Oller, Prapphal and Byler, 1982) and the relative dearth of information on learning style differences in ESL (see Willing, 1985a).

Communicative language teaching and needs analysis

The different perspectives on needs analysis I have outlined reflect the shift which has taken place in language teaching from language-centred to learner-centred approaches, as Hawkey (1984) demonstrates.

During the early stages of the communicative movement in language teaching in Europe, objective needs were the focus of needs analysis, since language learning was seen as a means to an end: effective communication in the learners' current or future domain of language use. As theories of adult learning indicated that adults learn better when programme content is geared to their immediate concerns, language teaching tended to concentrate on the end *product*: the actual language which learners had to use.

Subjective needs were thought at the time to be unpredictable, therefore indefinable (Richterich, 1980). Since analysis of language needs was carried out and content specified once and for all at the beginning of a

TABLE 2. TYPES OF INFORMATION REQUIRED BY TEACHERS IN A
LEARNER-CENTRED SYSTEM OF ADULT SECOND LANGUAGE LEARNING

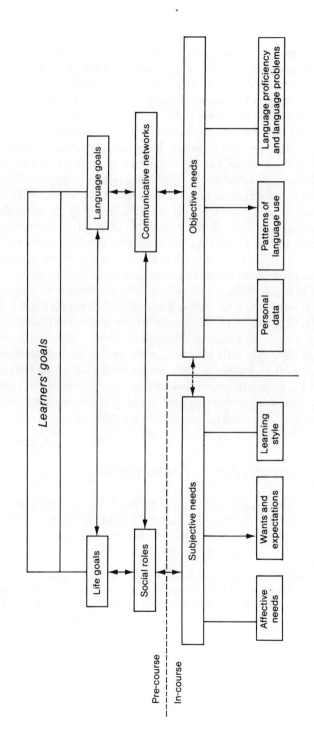

course, teachers were able to avoid the extremely difficult business of taking these unpredictable affective and cognitive variables into account: the *learning content* of the course was identified with the *language content* derived from the teacher's diagnosis of objective communication needs, as Widdowson (1981a) points out. Consequently, the importance of methodology in communicative courses tended to be downplayed in relation to the content (Johnson, 1979; Brumfit, 1979).

However, with the spread of 'humanistic' approaches to language teaching (exemplified by Community Language Learning, Silent Way, Suggestopaedia, etc.), there has been a renewed interest in the role of cognitive and affective variables in adult language learning. At the same time, a lot more information is becoming available to teachers about self-access, individualisation and self-directed learning. As a result, the focus on language content which characterised much 'communicative' teaching in the 1970s is shifting back to the learning process itself: assisting learners to 'learn how to learn' is now for many teachers as much a goal as promoting effective communication (Rubin and Thompson, 1982; Willing, 1985b) and a whole new movement of classroom-based research is under way (Allwright, 1983). However, the balance between subjective and objective needs which Richterich (1983) talks about has not always been easy to find and for this reason, the debate on communicative teaching still abounds with similar dichotomies which remain to be resolved: *communicative* versus *pychological/humanistic* (J. Roberts, 1982), *linguistic/analytical* versus *psychological/pedagogical* (Stern, 1981), *new-style behaviourism* versus *spontaneous self-direction* (Coste, 1983), *syllabus-centred* versus *learner-centred* and so on.

The role of consultation and negotiation

Corder (1977) in speaking of the need to break down a similar sort of division – that which the English language arbitrarily makes between *teaching* and *learning* – draws attention to the fact that the language learning process is a co-operative enterprise:

> In the end successful language 'teach-learning' is going to be dependent upon the willing co-operation of the participants in the interaction and an agreement between them as to the goals of their interaction. Co-operation cannot be imposed but must be negotiated.
>
> (Corder, 1977: 13)

If subjective psychological needs felt by the learner are to be taken into account as well as objective communication needs, then some kinds of mechanisms have to be built into the learning process which allow for systematic consultation and negotiation between the two parties. Information has to be exchanged about roles and expectations, both teachers' and learners' awareness of each other's needs and resources has to be raised, and compromises have to be reached between what learners expect and want and what the teacher feels he/she can and ought to provide. This process of 'validating' a need through consensus is the crux of needs analysis in a learner-centred system (Holec, 1980; Richterich, 1983).

However, the necessity for consultation and negotiation between teachers and learners is not something that all teachers agree on. When surveyed during the research project mentioned previously, many teachers expressed scepticism about the feasibility of designing a language programme in consultation with learners. The view was frequently expressed that learners cannot generally state what they want or need to learn. The point was also made that it is almost impossible to get learners from certain backgrounds to participate in decision making, owing to the rigidly defined social roles of the teacher and learner in some societies.

We were subsequently able to test out these propositions by interviewing 115 learners from a variety of language backgrounds. From the responses of learners, some *prima facie* evidence emerged to support teachers' claims. When asked (literally) what they wanted to learn, the majority of learners gave vague answers expressed either in terms of language skills ('I need speaking') or less commonly, situations they commonly encountered ('I need English for going to doctor'). The main exceptions to this rule were a number of well-educated learners with high levels of language proficiency who had been in Australia for more than a year.

Some of the comments made by learners about the learning process also confirmed the teachers' observations on preconceptions about learning:

– Without the grammar you can't learn the language.
– I don't want to clap and sing. I want to learn English.
– I want something I can take home and study.
– I just want a programme so I know what I have to learn. They're the teachers. They know their job.

Views of language learning

It appeared that many learners held rather fixed ideas about what it was to be a learner and to learn a language. These ideas, not always at a conscious level, ran roughly thus:

– Learning consists of acquiring a body of knowledge.

- The teacher has this knowledge and the learner has not.
- The knowledge is available for revision and practice in a textbook or some other written form.
- It is the role of the teacher to impart this knowledge to the learner through such activities as explanation, writing and example. The learner will be given a programme in advance.
- Learning a language consists of learning the structural rules of the language and the vocabulary through such activities as memorisation, reading and writing.

The corresponding set of assumptions for many teachers who hold a 'learner-centred' view of language teaching would probably be something like the following:

- Learning consists of acquiring organising principles through encountering experience.
- The teacher is a resource person who provides language input for the learner to work on.
- Language data are to be found everywhere – in the community and in the media as well as in textbooks.
- It is the role of the teacher to assist learners to become self-directing by providing access to language data through such activities as active listening, role play and interaction with native speakers.
- For learners, learning a language consists of forming hypotheses about the language input to which they will be exposed, these hypotheses being constantly modified in the direction of the target model.

This potential conflict of ideas strengthens the case for consultation and negotiation as a basis for classroom management. If learners and teachers do not share their perceptions of each other's expectations about the learning process, learners may become demoralised, threatened, or in some cases, hostile, when their expectations are not met (Bassano, 1986). If, for example, they cannot transfer their learning strategies to the new situation, or the course content or methodology does not conform to their expectations, dissatisfaction may result. For example, Nunan (1986a) illustrates the dramatic mismatches which may exist between teachers' and learners' perceptions of the utility of certain common classroom learning activities.

Accommodation and compromise

Where there are areas of potential conflict, reconciling teacher-diagnosed objective needs with learner-perceived subjective needs is of crucial importance in a learner-centred system. It would, however, be naive to suggest that this is easy or that cultural perception of learner-teacher roles would not make compromise difficult or even impossible, at times (see Maley, 1985). Nonetheless, in many cases, sharing of information regarding each other's expectations is a first step which can help to avoid such conflicts, as Bassano (1986) demonstrates. Subsequently, allowing learners a choice of learning activities corresponding to their preferred learning modes and styles has been shown to be an effective way of involving them in the management of their own learning while at the same time reducing the risk of conflicting expectations (Littlejohn, 1985).

A particularly notable example of a mismatch in expectations which is probably amenable to negotiation is the issue of 'grammar'. In surveys carried out as part of the study referred to previously, teachers and learners expressed quite different views on the role of grammar in second language programmes: learners lamented the lack of it, while teachers complained that learners continually asked for it (Brindley, 1984: 105).

After more detailed questioning of learners, it became apparent that 'grammar' was in fact being used by many of them as a blanket term behind which lay a variety of meanings, some of which were more related to *preferred ways of learning* rather than to programme content. These included, *inter alia*:

– a 'systematic' approach
– formal explanation of grammatical rules
– more class time spent on doing written exercises
– a formal presentation of the English verb tense system

Although some learners appear to be saying 'This is *what* I want to learn', in some cases they may, in fact, be saying 'This is *how* I want to learn.' This potential confusion can lead to serious misunderstandings between teachers and learners. Since teachers usually believe (with some justification) that they know more about language and how it is learned than learners, they may not be prepared to negotiate about learners' preference in regard to course content in cases where they feel that this content is inappropriate (for example formal grammar). However, if this preference is seen as an expression of a 'subjective' need (in this case, the desire to learn in a particular way) rather than an attempt to compete with the teacher in diagnosing an 'objective' need related to course content, then there is room for negotiation and compromise.

If, therefore, as a beginning in the negotiation process, learners and teachers were able to arrive at an agreed definition of 'grammar', it would help both to work towards common objectives.

It is also worth noting in this context that the time is ripe for a serious re-examination of a lot of the assumptions that are made by teachers and material writers about learners' cognitive styles and learning strategies. Teaching approaches, methods and textbooks often have a particular cognitive style bias which may be to the disadvantage of learners who have a different style. Are we being reasonable to expect adults to employ 'discovery learning' strategies if they have learned deductively all their lives? Are we correct in assuming that strategies such as rote learning and memorisation are ineffective and therefore to be discouraged in the classroom? As Widdowson (1981b), and Rivers and Melvin (1981) have pointed out, if learning is to come about, then learning tasks need to be attuned to the cognitive style of the learner. Meeting needs arising from individual differences in cognitive style would therefore involve on the one hand exploiting the strategies learners already have, and on the other, assisting them to acquire new strategies. Examples of ways in which teachers can assist learners to do this are outlined in detail by Willing (1985b).

Needs analysis in a learner-centred system

Since teachers and learners are likely to have differing expectations about what should be learnt and how, we have seen how misunderstandings may arise unless information is shared by both parties about their expectations. This information can form the basis on which compromises can be arrived at between what learners want and what teachers think they need.

However, information sharing is only a beginning – negotiation is a complex and subtle process which takes time. It may also involve, in the case of language learning, a change in the power structure in the classroom, which as Stevick (1976) and Richterich (1983) have pointed out, is extremely threatening to some teachers as well as to learners who wish to play the role of 'pupil-acquirer of knowledge'. Ongoing negotiation therefore has to be seen as part of a continuing cycle of needs analysis as outlined in Figure 1.

This dynamic view of needs analysis is similar to the approach taken by the Council of Europe Modern Languages Project group: the learning process, by being responsive to learners' expressed needs, becomes a source of its own change (Richterich 1975). If feedback and consultation are built into the learning cycle, a learning activity can in itself become a kind of needs analysis which allows the teacher to perceive and provide for needs as they arise.

It is important, however, to stress that in a learner-centred system, needs analysis and setting of learning objectives is not something which happens only once at the beginning of the course. It is quite unrealistic to expect learners to be able to participate fully in such an enterprise at this stage for the simple reason that people can't make a valid choice until they have experienced whatever options are being offered. In other words, if learners are asked about their preferred methods of learning,

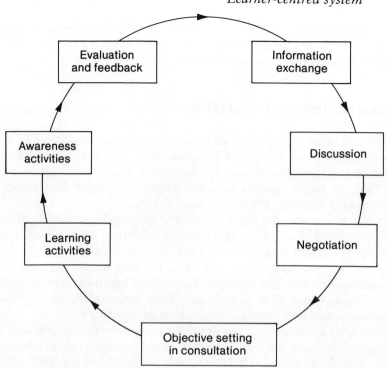

Figure 1   Elements of a learner-centred system

learning materials, and language content at the beginning of a course before they have tried them out, they will most likely give vague or even meaningless answers which are useless to the teacher trying to plan appropriate learning activities.

At this point, what the teacher can do is to use the pre-course information she or he has about the learners' objective needs, such as their goals, social roles, interaction patterns and language proficiency, to plan preliminary learning activities. After learning has begun, methods such as surveys (Richterich and Chancerel, 1980), group discussion, counselling/interviews (NCILT, 1980; Harding and Tealby, 1981; Hoadley-Maidment, 1983), communication awareness activities (NCILT, 1980; Haycraft, 1983) and learning contracts (Tough, 1971) can then be used to assess needs as they arise and are expressed. Objectives can thus be modified in the light of feedback from learners. By suggesting the use of such methods however, I do not mean that we should return to the cumbersome pseudo-scientific instruments used in the early 1970s. Rather, what Richterich (1975: 6) calls 'light rapid techniques' can be used. These could include such tools as Shaw's *ad hoc* needs analysis procedure (Shaw, 1982), Allwright's learning strategies profile (Allwright, 1982) or Marti Viano and Orquin's learning preferences survey (Marti Viano and Orquin, 1982).

Needs analysis and the real world

In the context of a large-scale educational operation such as the Australian Adult Migrant Education Program (AMEP) which caters for over 150,000 ESL learners annually, the implementation of curricula based on the type of needs analysis outlined above is fraught with difficulty (Nunan and Brindley, 1986).

In the first place, the administrative implications of moving from a subject-centred to a learner-centred curriculum are far-reaching. Using information about learners as a basis for course design and involving them in the management of their own learning necessitates adequate counselling services and bilingual support. In addition, a great deal of organisational flexibility is required, since catering for diverse needs entails different timetabling and grouping arrangements.

Secondly, a learner-centred system makes for greater demands on teachers. Not only do they need classroom management and teaching skills, but ideally they also have to be able to identify all the various kinds of needs we have mentioned, to counsel learners, to negotiate the curriculum, to assess learning processes and outcomes and to prepare their own materials if those available are inappropriate. It is thus not surprising that Butler and Bartlett (1986), in a recent survey of AMEP teachers conducted as part of a major review of the programme, found that teachers, although they were in favour of a learner-centred curriculum model, were experiencing severe difficulties in putting such a model into practice. Clearly, if they are to become curriculum developers in their own right, teachers need the time and support resources to do so.

In the light of these difficulties, a number of initiatives are underway in Australia to investigate and document the practical ramifications of implementing a learner-centred system and to pilot systematic means of evaluating the curriculum (Dowsett and Shaw, 1986; Nunan, 1986b).

In addition, a number of experiments are being carried out into alternative ways of grouping learners according to needs other than those determined by their language proficiency level (Brink, Mullins, Pedler and Reade 1985). A substantial body of evidence is thus being accumulated on both the administrative and pedagogical consequences of curriculum change. As more evaluative data become available, it should be possible to gauge better the extent to which the range of needs we have identified previously can be met in a large-scale adult ESL programme such as the AMEP.

6 Service English programme design and opportunity cost

John Swales

Observations on programme design papers

This paper reflects upon the creation and maintenance of adequate service English provision in tertiary institutions where English is wholly or in part the medium of instruction and study. It thus discusses the classic English for Academic Purposes operation that has variously arisen in many parts of the world following the precipitate advance of English as the world's leading language of research, scholarship and advanced training, and following the changing patterns of non-native speaker enrolment in English-medium universities. However, if the subject matter of this paper is clear, an appropriate treatment of that subject matter remains somewhat obscure. As the ethnomethodologists would put it, there is some doubt as to what 'counts as' a paper on programme design. Even more difficult is the question of how we are to judge the *value* or *usefulness* of such a paper. Should we be after sense, sensibility or schematics? Should we be searching for Yeats's 'paradigm that plays upon the spume of things' or expecting reports from the 'Hard Knocks' school of life? Or somehow both?

One important reason why such questions are perplexing is that they expose to us the divided nature of the ESL world. The answers will very likely differ according to whether the respondents see themselves as working within an American or British ESL tradition. For instance, if we take *TESOL Quarterly* as the flagship of U.S. ESL thinking, then we will find therein a concentration of papers dealing with second language acquisition, classroom-centred research, the validation of tests and so on. Thus, from the viewpoint of the range of variables that potentially affect the efficacy of ESL teaching, this important journal tends to publish 'micro' investigations rather than 'macro' studies. There are of course exceptions, and a recent one that bears indirectly on this paragraph is Richards's *The secret life of methods* (Richards, 1984a) in which he touches on 'national styles of thought and practice' and valuably differentiates the support networks for American and British activities. Obviously enough, it is not the case that Americans – and the many others they have trained and influenced – are somehow unconcerned with field experiences, with ESL policy at home and abroad, with ESL lessons from history or geography, or with the uncertain status of the profession. Rather, it is that such issues are seen as *secondary*, at least in the sense that they are adjudged as non-contributive to ESL development at the highest level. It therefore comes as no surprise to find that they have little place in the flagship, but are relegated to the fleet auxiliary of *TESOL Newsletter*, with its miniscule print and magazine style ('continued on page 7'), or appear in lesser periodicals.

There is no close European equivalent to *TQ*. *ELTJ* is conspicuously teacher-oriented and is only comparable to the *Forum* section of *TQ*. The British publication that comes closest to *TQ* is probably *ELT Documents*, which carries longish referenced articles, often written by the more senior members of the profession. Here, in vivid contrast, we find a fully-fledged tradition of non-experimental case reporting, of descriptions of programme design embedded in curricular principle and offering operational generalisations. Indeed, since *ELT Documents* is thematically constructed, some issues like *Language Projects for the Third World* are expressly designed to be an anthology of field experience. Comparable publications also emanate from the Regional English Language Centre in Singapore, a recent volume being *Trends in Syllabus Design* (1984). It is my firm impression that publications such as these are little known and little read in the United States, whilst *TESOL Quarterly* passes surprisingly unnoticed in British libraries and British Council libraries overseas.

Inevitably enough both traditions have their internal critics. Horowitz (1986a), from within the pages of *TESOL Quarterly*, has recently attacked certain orthodoxies of contemporary U.S. ESL composition research. The British tradition of wide-ranging description also has its own detractors:

> It is undoubtedly true that not only editors but also readers of journals can find it exercising and on occasion fruitless to wade through a series of anecdotes about English teaching through different approaches with different resources in unrelated and possibly esoteric contexts: war stories and romances, tales of experience and the unexpected, echoes in the background of 'I did it *my* way'.
>
> (Bowers, 1980b: 71)

In fact, Bowers goes on to argue that field reports can be both a necessary and a valuable part of the ESL professional literature, but only in so far as certain criteria are adhered to. These criteria are that the reports must 'be comparable within the field of language teaching as a whole, relatable to the particular learning contexts which are the concern of the individual reader, and capable of being evaluated as accurate and comprehensive statements of pedagogic activities and the pedagogic results of those activities' (1980b: 71–2). In this way, Bowers argues, we can make useful comparisons between one project and another and assess the extent to which particular projects achieved their agreed objectives. Ultimately, Bowers claims that reported observational studies which meet the criteria of comparability, relevance and validity/reliability provide their readers with a platform of learned experience which can then offer 'general prescriptions for the next wave of innovation and experiment by means of which the profession will progress'.

Bowers' 1980b paper can therefore be seen as outlining a way of evaluating project-type programme design papers. It expresses cautious approval for the right kind of authentic educational studies 'in which the heterogeneity of the natural learning context has been reported'. Indeed, Bowers goes on to argue that such studies will be of greater value than experimental work 'where the variables have been controlled but reliability and focus attained at the cost of immediate relevance to authentic contexts'. Even if we temporarily side-step the issue of experimental investigation, there remains, I believe, something unfinished about Bowers' characterisation of a valuable paper on programme design. In today's world of a large and increasing ESL literature, there is lighter justification for reports, however explicit, of what was done and how it was done, especially as the *what* and the *how* are more accessible to experimental study and formal evaluation. Rather, I would argue, the situated rather than speculative programme design paper achieves greater utility when it concentrates on *why* certain key decisions were made. It is this kind of deeper descent into cases that requires us to relate strategic, theoretical and technical considerations in ways that would seem at present to be totally beyond any experimental testing of variables.

If Bowers' reconsideration of war stories and romances can be taken as representative of a British view of course design papers, then Long's 1984 *TESOL Quarterly* paper might represent the American. In this paper Long argues persuasively for a process evaluation of ESL programmes as a valuable addition to the better-established product evaluation (i.e. to what extent is it true – if at all – that the experimental programme can produce better results than the standard programme. Process evaluation is defined in decidedly 'micro' terms as 'the systematic observation of classroom behavior with reference to a theory of (second) language development which underlies the program being evaluated' (1984: 415). He then illustrates the procedures by taking the case of an English Language Institute of an established structural orientation setting up an experimental Natural Approach programme in two classes following the recent 'conversion' of the director and a group of her teachers 'to a radically different set of beliefs about how adults learn a second language'. (The procedures themselves involve recording, transcribing and coding sample lessons in order to establish relative frequencies of salient features associated with one or the other of the approaches, such as teacher correction and referential questions.) Long is surely correct when he observes that a process evaluation of this type has much in common with recent work in classroom-centred research and can consequently borrow methodologies and operational definitions from this field.

It seems clear that process evaluation could in principle be incorporated into a rigorous observational account of the type advocated by Bowers and, only a little less certainly, ought to be so incorporated. However, it seems equally clear that not all the variables in an innovative programme are as open to process evaluation as those that are centrally concerned with methodology. Innovation, after all, is rarely a simple matter of modifying classroom behaviour, but is more likely to be accompanied by concomitant shifts in class size, the degree of homogeneity among the learners, the number of contact hours, the socialising or intellectualising of the course content and so forth. A way must therefore be found to identify aspects of the innovation that are both thought to be significant and yet open to process evaluation.

One possible way of structuring the decision-making process is to utilise the simple but powerful economic concept of *opportunity cost.* (Opportunity costs are real or full costs because they take account of the deficits created by the forced abandonment of other alternatives. Thus, the opportunity cost of going to graduate school for a Ph.D. in ESL is not only the tuition, books and living expenses etc., but also the cost of giving up a regular position to do so – with deleterious effects on income and on the independent work experience section of the vita.) Long estimates that the minimal opportunity cost – although he does not put it like that – of carrying out the process evaluation in his illustrative case would be 75 hours of staff time (and this without any allocation for producing a document for presentation or publication). The issue for the programme design team can now be seen as weighing up the gains and losses associated with particular courses of action. It may turn out, of course, that undertaking the process evaluation will produce a useful contribution to classroom centred research (and that possibility can be factored in), but research advance cannot of itself be the primary purpose, which must reside in the gathering of information for the purposes of decision making.

If the revealed rationale for decision making is recognised as a valuable feature of programme design papers, then it follows that programme design requires a wider perspective than methodology. In Long's illustration, for example, there is a case for discussion of both subsequent and prior decisions. We may assume, on the one hand, that the evaluation produces encouraging results. What happens next? Is there a hold-out group of committed and skilled structuralists, and what's to be done about that? We may assume, on the other, that the findings from the evaluation are discouraging. In such a case, it is hardly likely that there will be a tame return to the previous *status quo*; indeed, what kinds of experience and evidence might persuade the 'converted' group to apostatise? And in that context, it would be useful to have some disclosure of the reasons for the *conversion* in the first place. These reasons may after all be complex: a sense of boredom, intellectual persuasion, external pressures, a wish to be 'state of the art', a managerial belief in creative disequilibrium, or some rich compendium of all of these.

In this opening section I have tried to make a case for locating the value and usefulness of a programme design case study in its capacity to illuminate the decision-making process. Further, I have borrowed the concept of opportunity cost as a means of evaluating that process. As it happens this broad characterisation has interesting points of contact with the perceived roles of case studies in other professions. Medical case studies typically discuss the decision-making process in anomalous cases, law uses case reports to help the apprentice lawyer identify features that crucially distinguish one legal decision from another (Bhatia, 1986), whilst the widespread use of case studies in advanced business training follows from the belief that in the real world 'wisdom can't be told' (Charles, 1984).

Methodologies of programme design: analysis and opportunity cost

Within the EAP context, those that write about – and perhaps teach – approaches to programme design occupy a range of positions with regard to two key but inter-related issues: the permeability of principles to local conditions, and the extent to which the programme design process can be systematised. As is well known, the *opus classicus* of impermeability and systematisation is Munby's *Communicative syllabus design* (1978). This work has given rise to considerable debate (Swales, 1986) but the controversy over *Communicative syllabus design* is now jejune given that Munby has recently modified his position:

> Some constraints (type A) e.g. political factors affecting the target language and homogeneity of the learner group, should be applied at the needs analysis stage. Others (type B) e.g. time available for the course, state of resources, styles and traditions of learning, should be applied at the content specification stage. I previously advocated leaving all constraints until after the specification of content, but in practice we found some constraints cannot wait. However, if the designer starts at the outset with all the

constraints, he will not know what is needed. Deference to type B constraints should not be made independently of objectively obtainable information on the learner's communication needs.

(Munby, 1984: 64)

In some ways, this extract would appear to offer a *modus vivendi* for the programme designer. Immutable type A factors can be taken on board at the outset, whilst potentially negotiable type B constraints are held in reserve until investigations into the learner's communication needs are carried out. Indeed, opportunity cost analysis may show that there are at least a couple of circumstances that can justify the undertaking of a needs analysis exercise even when there is no realistic expectation that the results could be fully utilised in any pedagogical sense. First, there is the *realpolitik* situation, well established in administrative and institutional settings, in which managers have to argue for twice as much resourcing as the situation demands in order to obtain half of what they need. A needs analysis capable of specifying fully the extent of the gap between the target ESL learners' present position and where they need to be can be a valuable card to play. (However, as we all know, if it is played recklessly it can be trumped by higher authorities with the resounding crash of yet another set of ambitious ESL proposals. As Markee (1986b) observes, there may be a transparent need for our ESL product, but this does not necessarily mean that there is a *market* for it.)

The second circumstance in which we may wish to push the needs analysis forward is when there exists considerable uncertainty about the target situation for which the students might be being prepared (Chambers, 1980). After all, there are few who are likely to dissent from Christison and Krahnke's conclusion:

> We believe that sound curriculum design in ESL programs for academic preparation would be based on empirical data that reflect what is really useful to students and not only on the intuitions and the expertise of the teaching personnel.
>
> (1986: 78)

In fact getting at those data can be extremely difficult. Nevertheless, it may be important to persevere, if only because a number of studies have shown how deceptive can be appearances and how distanced from prior expectation can be reality. Herrington (1985) analysed the contexts for writing in two Senior classes in the same Chemical Engineering department and was able to show that 'these two courses represented distinct communities where different ideas were addressed, different lines of reasoning used, different writer and audience roles assumed, and different social purposes served by writing' (1985: 331). This kind of finding casts doubt on any straightforward vision of a monolithic disciplinary culture. Horowitz (1986b) analysed the writing tasks required of undergraduates at Western Illinois University and found them to be highly structured with clear specifications as to what should be attempted in each section of the response. He then raises the issue of whether ESL writing instructors are behaving appropriately in devoting so much time to the structuring and organisation of their students' writing when these are apparently predetermined by the subject instructors. Candlin *et al.* (1976), in their well-known study of doctor–patient interaction in casualty, were able to show that utterances ostensibly designed to inform and reassure the patient such as 'I think we'd better give you a little jab' were contemporaneously designed to be overheard by nurses as instructions – in this case to prepare an anti-tetanus injection. Thus, the unexpected multifunctionality of speech in this context both underlines the great demands here being made on the non-native speaker and also calls into question the monofunctionalism of speech act theory and its derivative, the notional functional syllabus. Wickrama (1982) was able to show that understanding the set textbook for his Sri Lankan law students partly depended on their recognising that the chapters were organised very differently according to whether the subject matter fell within a Common Law tradition. Here then is a counter-example to the belief that a textbook is an internally consistent entity. Finally, Swales (1980), at a loss to explain the failure of a new course in writing field reports for Sudanese students of geology, eventually discovered that over the years the department had surreptitiously dropped its official grading procedure of giving equal weight to the report and the map and had 'let it be understood' that only the map counted.

Therefore, *realpolitik* arguments for a fuller delineation of the skills and abilities that students may need can, on occasion, be strengthened by opportunity – cost arguments in favour of a target situation analysis. And these in turn may be bolstered by gains in the reputation and visibility of the Service English unit and by gains (via presentation and publication) in our understanding of the complexity and variability of communication within professional and academic settings. As I have argued elsewhere (Swales, 1985), this type of enquiry can both draw upon and make a contribution to the *Great Game* of the sociology and cultural anthropology of knowledge. Clifford Geertz, one of the outstanding players of the game, observes:

> We are all natives now, and anybody else not immediately one of us is an exotic. What looked once to be a matter of finding out whether savages could distinguish fact from fancy now looks to be a matter of finding out how others, across the sea or down the corridor, organize their significative world.

(1983: 151)

English for Academic Purposes has on occasion ventured down the corridor.

Methodologies of programme design: trials and tribulations

One of the most interesting aspects of the descriptive programme design literature is the discussion of 'problems'. It is interesting because a number of problems seem to recur. Seven of these I list below:

1 Difficulties with the processes of higher-level decision making, problems arising from pre-project decisions, and difficulties in changing institutional perceptions and attitudes. (Crocker, 1984; Frankel, 1983; Lilley, 1984; Maley, 1984; Markee, 1986a)
2 Uncertainties about the 'home base' of Service English, its status and role and those of its staff. (Bowers, 1983; Drury, 1983; Johns, 1981, Lilley, 1984; Swales, 1984)
3 Problems arising from mis-match of expectations among the relevant parties. (Drury, 1983; Dudley-Evans and Swales, 1980; Maley, 1984; Markee, 1986a; Rea, 1983)
4 Problems with staff development, motivation and retention. (Crocker, 1984; Frankel, 1983; Maley, 1984; Rea, 1983; Swales, 1984; Wingard, 1983)
5 Problems with time-tabling, contact-time, room-allocation and material resources. (Barmada, 1983; Candlin 1984; Drury, 1983; Hawkey, 1984; Hiragama-Grant and Sedgwick, 1978; Johns, 1981; Maley, 1984)
6 Difficulties in keeping to project schedules. (Bowers, 1983; Frankel, 1983; Rea, 1983)
7 Uncertainties about participants. (Drobnic, 1978; Maley, 1984)

One striking feature of this compilation is that the most commonly identified problems are those that are structural or managerial. Apart from 2 and 5, they could have occurred in any kind of innovative project: urban renewal, agricultural reform, comprehensive schooling, or whatever.

A little more substantially, I have extracted from this literature four concluding remarks. These have been selected because they emphasise, in their different ways, the importance of pragmatic elements in course design:

1 Again the efficiency of the programme was seriously impaired by largely non-linguistic factors which no amount of syllabus design would have avoided. (Maley, 1984: 103)

2 There is no direct, diversion-free, syllabus design route from 'needs to materials via constraints'. (Hawkey, 1984: 131)
3 ... in the real world of ELT, there has to be creative synthesis of theoretical principles and practical constraints, and ... where these conflict, as they sometimes do, the latter must take precedence. (Frankel, 1983: 130)
4 Our syllabus design seemed to conform to a logic when viewed in retrospect; however in reality *ad hoc* decision making, intuitive, and educated guesses provided much of our momentum and direction. Because of their strong influence, these factors merit more attention in the literature of ESP, even if they cannot be included in models of the design process. They should be neither disguised nor concealed. (Hiragama-Grant and Sedgwick 1978: 331)

The Maley quotation implies that there may be situations where the wiser course would be not to embark on a new programme (unless opportunity-cost arguments suggest that the programme will need to fail first time around if it is to have a chance of ultimate success). The comment by Hawkey would seem to suggest that Munby's attempt to salvage the systematic approach by incorporating certain constraints into the operating cycle may not work after all. Certainly, many local features can be constraining by virtue of the fact that they are unpredictable, such as mislaid mail, strikes and other sundry acts of God. Frankel makes full allowance for local contingencies, whilst Hiragama-Grant and Sedgwick believe in letting the truth be known about the unsystematic nature of the course design process, even if – in 1978 – they do not see a way of incorporating such entropy into models of the design process.

I do not wish to imply in any way that those many colleagues who write on programme design are generally insensitive to the interactions between theoretical principle and pragmatic reality. Even a simple model like that of Allen and Spada (1983) shows the interactive process between administrative guidelines and syllabus. Rea's model (1983) schematises this relationship by having the core ELT project processes surrounded by layers of increasingly broad educational and administrative factors. Bowers (1983) places the curriculum development project at the centre of a 'spider's web' of other variables that include personnel, facilities, funding and management. An elaborated three-dimensional model like that by Johnson (Introduction to this volume) allows alternatives to a top-down decision-making process: 'less institutionalised teaching and learning situations *may* allow materials writers, teachers, and learners to determine, or at least influence, aims and pedagogical strategies to be adopted, through a process of "negotiation"' (my emphasis). However, I have argued in this paper that it is these issues of how and why aims are determined and how and why strategy is formulated, that are of fundamental importance, and thus provide a *raison d'être* for descriptive case studies. I further suspect that a recognition of the importance of the decision-making process, plus a realisation that attempts to preserve the ideal may be counter-productive, have given rise to a new approach to programme design that has been variously labelled 'ecological' or 'means analysis' (Holliday and Cooke, 1982; Holliday, 1984), 'learning environment analysis' (Crocker, 1984) or 'Appropriate Technology' (Markee, 1986b).

The 1982 Holliday and Cooke paper tackles the issue of 'how to make ESP take root, grow, bear fruit and propagate in the local soil (1982: 124). They follow Breen and Candlin (1980) in seeing programme design as a dynamic and recurrent interplay of negotiations involving purpose, syllabus, method and evaluation within a milieu of attitudes and expectations of all the parties involved (cf. Bowers' 'Spider's web'). However, they break fresh ground when they perceive this milieu as an *ecosystem* in which all the competing but interdependent elements need to survive if the ecosystem is not to suffer damage. The study of an educational ecosystem principally involves understanding the prevailing classroom culture, the management processes and the functioning of the infrastructure. In traditional terms, some of the emerging features could be seen as constraints. However, Holliday and Cooke reject this attitude because 'to view them as such would merely mean that our preconceived notions about how the job should be done would be unacceptable to the ecosystem' (1982: 33). The approach now becomes one of trying to make best use of local features, both promising and unpromising, so that the long-term viability of the project can be assured. (Crocker, 1984, and Markee, 1986b, voice similar concerns although in different metaphorical language.) For example, an apparent 'constraint' might be that ESL classes will have to remain very large. However, Holliday (1984) argues that this unpalatable circumstance in fact makes a stronger case for introducing group-work in the eyes of the various elements in the ecosystem than would have been likely if class size had been 15. The ecological approach is thus one of cautious gradualism, much influenced by anthropological considerations, and yet marked by the optimism of an alchemist.

The ecological approach would seem to suggest that room for initiative on the part of a programme designer or project director may be more straitened than aid agencies or specialists in curriculum development would like to believe. On the other hand, the importance that the approach gives to understanding how the system works, and hence understanding where and how the system will resist change, creates a sense of working within the system rather than against it – which may provide chances for development likely to be denied in a more adversarial context. However, the ecological approach does not itself provide an easy way of determining priorities in strategic decision making. For that we will need to incorporate the concept of opportunity cost.

The factors that to me seem of decisive relevance to the EAP programme designer are summarised in the following diagram:

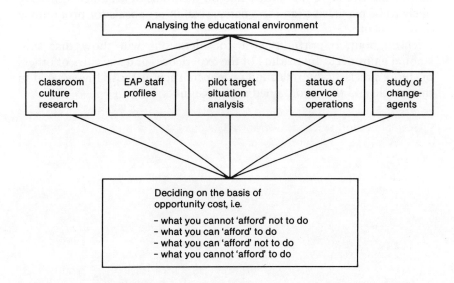

Figure 1   Setting programme objectives in EAP contexts

Some of the elements in the analysis have already been discussed. Classroom culture research will follow the direction established by means analysis. The second element will provide information about the ELT staff's strengths and weaknesses and their hopes and fears. Target situation analysis has already been sufficiently discussed. In contrast, the perceived role of service teaching has received very little consideration in the programme design literature. Drury (1983) is one of the very few to have given it serious attention:

> Service course directors sometimes do not fully appreciate the suspicion a service course can generate in a rarefied academic environment. It has already been discussed, but it cannot be overstressed, that the innovative and remedial nature of most service courses lend themselves to suspicion ... In addition, they usually do not have the examination orientation which often provides a necessary study impetus, even though they are in part tools for easing the burden of these very examinations.

(Drury, 1983: 127)

Drury was writing about an African university, but in any context time spent on understanding how the host institution views service roles is likely to be a useful investment. The final element in the preliminary considerations focuses attention on the mechanisms by which curricular innovation can be set in motion and on the kinds of arguments that are likely to be persuasive (and less persuasive) in proposals for programme development.

Throughout, opportunity-cost considerations will show that substantial gains occur by reading of the experiences and activities of others or, more precisely, by reflecting on papers such as those I have cited in this article and those contained in this volume.

PART III
PROGRAMME IMPLEMENTATION

---

7 Faculty development for language programs

Martha C. Pennington

Introduction

The heart of every educational enterprise, the force driving the whole enterprise towards its educational aims, is the teaching faculty. Hence, the nature of the faculty, in both its overall composition and the characteristics of its individual members, to a large extent determines the unique character of any language program. As stated by Eskey (1982), in a brief article on the faculty of intensive ESL programs: 'The single most important feature of any program ... is the teaching faculty. ... [G]ood teachers make good programs ...' (p. 39).

In what follows, the nature and development of language program faculties is explored in detail. The concept of faculty development is taken to embrace three areas:

The Education and Training of Language Teachers
The Organization of a Language Program Faculty
The Evolution and Growth of a Language Program Faculty

Figure 1   Aspects of faculty development

Each of these aspects of faculty development is taken up in turn. The first of these topics addresses both pre-service and in-service teacher preparation and training. In this section, a number of different approaches to teacher training are outlined, and a general model for conceptualizing the teaching act is proposed. The second section includes discussion of faculty structure in the larger organizational context of a language program. Under the third heading are included matters of faculty evaluation, supervision, continuing education and professional growth. In this section, a comprehensive model of the teaching cycle from the perspective of long-term faculty development is proposed. Practical concerns relating to faculty development are addressed in each section, and suggestions relevant to both autonomously functioning language programs and those housed within larger academic units are offered. In addition, the discussion is set in a theoretical framework based on literature in teacher education, ESL/EFL and other aspects of language teaching.

The education and training of language teachers

Comparison of training approaches

Just as in any other field of specialization in which certificate or degree programs are offered, language teaching requires education and training:

> A major problem world-wide in the field of language teaching is the popular belief that anyone who can speak a language can teach it. The fact is, however, that language teaching requires a special combination of knowledge and skills that is always hard to find, and finding teachers who have it should be the first concern of any good administration.
>
> (Eskey, 1982: 39)

Language teacher training includes pre-service (usually graduate) degree work in addition to in-service training programs and workshops offered on site or through continuing education or university extension courses. There is general agreement that preparation for language teaching requires certain types of knowledge, skills and attitudes. The following figure is a sampling of approaches to language teacher preparation taken from ESL/EFL.

(1) Strevens 1974; Britten, 1985	(2) Hancock 1977	(3) Lee 1977
Skills training	*Command of target language*	*Experience learning a language*
Didactic (pre-active) Pedagogic (interactive, reactive)	*Language analysis*	*Language analysis*
	Culture	*Methodology*
Information	*Teaching-learning process*	*Practical teaching skills*
Education Syllabus and materials Language	*Professional components*	
Theory Psychology Linguistics		

Figure 2   Approaches to language teacher preparation

Those who educate language teachers differ in their views about the appropriate orientation for pre-service preparation. Some, for example Fanselow (1977), advocate a competency-based approach for preparing teachers. This approach is described by Smith (1969) as having the following characteristics:

1 The job of teaching is analyzed into tasks that must be performed.
2 The abilities required for these tasks must be specified.
3 The skills or techniques through which the abilities are expressed must be clearly described.
4 Training situations and exercises for the development of each skill must be worked out in detail.

(p. 77)

Others, such as Larson-Freeman (1983), believe that what is needed is a holistic approach to teacher education which goes beyond training to prepare 'an individual to function in any situation, rather than training for a specific situation ... preparing people to make choices' (Larson-Freeman, 1983: 265). These two general approaches can be compared in Figure 3 below, which shows the differing emphases of each.

Holistic	*vs.*	*Competency-based*
Personal development		Component skills
Creativity		Modularized components
Judgment		Individualization
Adaptability		Criterion-referencing

Figure 3   Differing emphases in two approaches to teacher training (based on Britten, 1985)

The emphasis of holistic approaches to teacher preparation is on the development of the individual in personal dimensions which are relevant to professional dimensions. These include increasing creative potential for syllabus and materials preparation, refining the sense of judgment for purposes of assessment in the planning and conduct of lessons, and learning to adapt teaching approach to meet the needs of individual students, classes and teaching situations. In the competency-based approach to teacher education (CBTE):

the certification of teachers through observation of their teaching rather than on the basis of completed courses is not meant to ignore the evaluation of the knowledge required of second language teachers. But in addition to knowing that teachers have learned certain information and theories, CBTE is interested in the ability to apply the knowledge in teaching.

(Fanselow, 1977: 138)

Competency-based teacher education is directed towards criterion-referenced evaluation of teaching performance in individual areas (component skills) of teaching competence. It therefore allows for individualization of the training program through division of the course into independent training modules.

In-service or continuing education for language teachers might include training modules focused on the use of new techniques, methods, materials or equipment, or on the upgrading of individual classroom skills or areas of knowledge. In some cases, in-service workshops might be intended not only to upgrade and expand teaching capabilities but also to reorient teachers to cope with changing conditions in the field or in the society at large which affect the priorities and objectives of the school or which require changes in the language program.

For both pre-service and in-service teacher education, modalities requiring practice and active participation refine skills and prepare the teacher for the active role of classroom teaching. In addition to supervised classroom teaching, individual and group experiences involving case studies, problem solving, video viewing and analysis, direct observation, roleplay and simulated teaching experiences (micro-teaching) help trainees to develop classroom skills while also directing their perceptual and cognitive experience as students. Such participatory experiences can therefore focus the trainee's attention on fundamental issues and concepts in language teaching, while sharpening observational skills and the ability to analyze and evaluate classroom events. Structuring experiences – for example, through various uses of video in teacher training (cf. Pennington, 1985b) – helps the trainee to form attitudes about effective instruction, and to formulate a personal theory or philosophy of instruction.

For trainees as well as teachers already in service, work on attitudes may be as essential as work on methods, and may in fact be a prerequisite to any successful program to improve teaching methodology. Unless teachers from the outset of training have the proper attitudes or frame of reference within which to receive new ideas, work on methodology will have little effect on their actual teaching behavior. Regardless of the kind of training teachers receive, their classroom behavior will reflect their underlying attitudes towards the students, towards themselves and towards the entire educational enterprise. 'For while skills execute, it is attitudes that command' (Britten, 1985: 122).

Recognizing the fact that no amount of purely methodological training can neutralize attitudes imprinted from previous experience, Pennington (1986) advocates a training program for ESL/EFL or multicultural education in which methodology is introduced after several phases aimed at 'attitude adjustment':

Stage one: Educational awareness

Stage two: Self awareness

Stage three: Student awareness

Stage four: Methods and materials

Figure 4   Stages in ESL/EFL/multicultural training (Pennington 1986)

In Stage one, the aim is to provide a basic introduction to the interface of language, culture and education, while leading the trainee to realize the need for specialized training to work in ESL/EFL or multicultural environments. In Stage two, trainees examine themselves as cultural and social beings, looking at how they appear to others and how they can improve their classroom image. In this phase, the concepts of ethnocentricity and stereotyping are introduced as relevant to both teacher and student. In the third stage, trainees consider the classroom from the student's perspective, examining cultural differences that affect classroom interaction and student achievement, language standards and speech varieties, and the special needs of second language speakers. Not until the last stage does the program move to a methods focus for developing language skills through interactive and content-oriented activities.

The goal of such a pre-service or in-service course is to shape or reshape the attitudes that govern student treatment and other aspects of classroom performance. In a multicultural educational system, the difference in attitudes can be represented as follows:

≫→

	Pessimistic perspective: non-empathic, monocultural	Optimistic perspective: empathic, multicultural
a) Student needs and desires	All of the students have differing needs and desires. This makes it very difficult to plan any kind of lesson and puts an added burden on the teacher to individualize instruction.	As is inevitable in any group situation, the students represent a multiplicity of needs and desires. This is the normal circumstance in the classroom and points up the importance of individualizing instruction.
b) Linguistic proficiency	Students are not fully proficient in the language of the classroom. This creates a major barrier to communication and will cause them to make all kinds of mistakes in their work.	Students are fluent in one or more languages. Hence, they are ready to learn academic skills and content as they acquire a good command of English and learn about the other languages represented in the class.
c) Cultural experience	Students do not share a common core of cultural experience. Thus, it will be hard for all of them to fully participate in the lessons and activities of the class.	Students bring to the classroom a variety of cultural experiences to share. This variety should add interest to classroom activities and expand the horizons of teacher and students alike.
d) Values	Because of dissimilar cultural experience, students do not share a common set of values. This will make it difficult to bring the students under the teacher's control.	We can learn to understand and respect the different values represented in the class. This will encourage the teacher and the students to open themselves to new ways of looking at things and of doing things in the classroom.

Figure 5   Contrast in attitudes towards the multicultural classroom (Pennington, 1986)

Thus, a primary goal of the multicultural or ESL training program must be to move teachers or prospective teachers from the relatively narrow, monocultural attitudes reflected in the left hand column to the broader, multicultural perspective reflected on the right.

Conceptions of the teaching act

Teacher preparation programs and systems for faculty evaluation and development reflect differing views of what teaching is. The teaching act has been described in many different ways, and there is much disagreement about what constitutes a good performance. As a basis for an effective pre-service and in-service faculty development program, however, it is important for program designers and administrators to clarify their view of what (good) teaching is. Towards this goal, different ways of conceptualizing the teaching act can be compared and contrasted. This has been done in Figure 6, where different conceptions of teaching are represented as lying along a continuum from context-dependent to context-free acts.

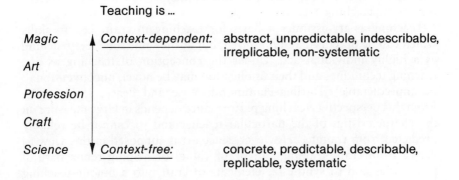

Figure 6   Differing conceptions of the teaching act

The analogy of teaching to magic is meant to emphasize the importance of individual variables in describing and evaluating acts of teaching. Teaching from this perspective is highly context-dependent, in that it is impossible to predict or to fully describe what happens in actual instances of teaching. In the conception of teaching-as-magic, therefore, no insight is possible into what is going on in a classroom and how a teacher succeeds in teaching. Under this radical conception of teaching, in which no analysis of the teaching act is possible, there is no rationale for teacher training or evaluation of any kind. From this perspective, teachers are born, spontaneously as it were, when they stand in front of a class and begin to teach. Hence, the only relevant experience for prospective teachers is actual teaching.

In sharp contrast, teaching-as-science conceives of pedagogy as susceptible to comprehensive analysis and full description. From this perspective, teaching behavior can be broken into component skills which have high observability and which can be learned and evaluated based on specific behavioral objectives. The view of teaching-as-craft likewise regards pedagogy as comprised of component skills but differs from the 'scientific' view of teaching in the degree to which such skills are expected to be describable and in the presumed difficulty of mastery of those skills or specialized techniques (cf. Darling-Hammond, Wise and Pease, 1983: 291). A 'craft-based' approach to teacher training assumes that an extended period of classroom practice is necessary for learning how to apply teaching skills in actual teaching situations, whereas a 'science-based' approach assumes that the major part of training can be accomplished under idealized conditions outside of any actual teaching experience. The perspective of teaching-as-science is in this sense 'context-free'. The work of Stevick (1980) exemplifies a more context-dependent, mystical view of language teaching, while that of Long (Long and Crookes, 1986) represents a more context-free, empiricist conception of the teaching act.

Teaching-as-art assumes a basis for teaching in craft, i.e., in skills which can be practiced and mastered, but at the same time sees teaching as a highly individual act. 'Under the conception of teaching as art, teaching techniques and their application may be novel, unconventional, or unpredictable' (Darling-Hammond, Wise and Pease, 1983: 291). From this perspective, teaching performance depends in large measure on the characteristics of the particular teacher and so cannot be reliably predicted from training. However, since art is supposed in this view to derive from craft, training can be of value for helping refine natural proclivities and to synthesize elements of craft into a unique teaching style. At the same time, training is viewed as of limited value for many individuals who lack natural talent, 'personality' or instincts for teaching.

Teaching-as-profession, in contrast to the view of teaching-as-art, assumes that the majority of those who receive adequate preparation, through a combination of skills training and holistic education, can be successful as teaching professionals.

> Under the conception of teaching as *profession*, teaching is seen as not only requiring a repertoire of specialized techniques but also as requiring the exercise of judgment about when those techniques should be applied (Shavelson, 1976; Shavelson and Stern, 1981). To exercise sound professional judgment, the teacher is expected to master a body of theoretical knowledge as well as a range of techniques. Broudy (1956) makes the distinction between craft and profession in this way: 'We ask the professional to diagnose difficulties, appraise solutions, and to choose among them. We ask him to take total responsibility for both strategy and tactics ... From the craftsman, by contrast, we expect a standard diagnosis, correct performance of procedures, and nothing else' (p. 182)

Standards for evaluating professionals are developed by peers, and evaluation focuses on the degree to which teachers are competent at professional problem-solving. ... This view of teaching work assumes that standards of professional knowledge and practice can be developed and assessed, and that their enforcement will ensure competent teaching.

(Darling-Hammond, Wise and Pease, 1983: 291)

The view of the teacher-as-professional therefore respects individual differences while providing competency standards for the field, viewed as a coherent profession. Within this framework, teacher preparation aims at the attainment of a certain level of competency for all individuals, and professional growth is a continuing goal throughout the teaching career.

Organizing a language program faculty

Faculty development in the first sense is essential for guaranteeing that there will be a competent pool of teachers to draw on when setting up a language program and hiring instructors. Faculty development in the second sense is a critical determinant of the ultimate success of a program. Here, faculty development means bringing good teachers into a program and structuring the faculty as a whole to achieve the best possible fit with program objectives and structure. This type of development begins with a conception of the program as a whole and how the faculty structure will fit into the network of interlocking program components as the language program is being designed. All aspects of the structure of an educational program are interrelated, so that any decision made about the design or development of the program in one area will affect and be affected by the choices which can be made in other areas. For example, the type and number of classroom spaces, class size, faculty composition, size of enrollment and the number of proficiency levels in a program are all interrelated factors (cf. Taylor, 1982). Theory and experience, in addition to program-internal and externally imposed guidelines and operating constraints, will guide the decision-making process involved in setting up or running a program.

To take a concrete example of the interlocking nature of programmatic decisions: The number of students in an educational program, especially in the case of a self-supporting unit, affects and is affected by the programmatic structure in several other areas, as illustrated in Figure 7.

Increasing enrollment projects to an increasing *number of classrooms*. On the other hand, a limited amount of space may limit the possibilities for increasing enrollment. (Housing availability is also related to projected growth in a program.) The *number of proficiency levels* possible in

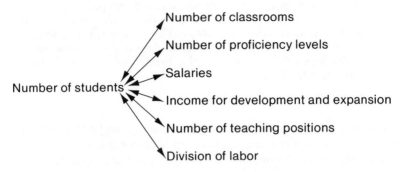

Figure 7   Relationship of enrollment to other program features

a program is directly related to the size of enrollment. For example, if an average class size of fifteen is desired, then a regular average enrollment of ninety students is required to support six proficiency levels on a continuing basis. Larger enrollments support larger financial outlays for *salaries* and provide *income for* program *development* (for example, for provision of reference and supplementary classroom materials or equipment) to improve the quality of the program and for *expansion* to a wider student audience. These larger expenditures are expected to result in large enrollments but there is a sort of 'vicious cycle' here, as the larger expenditures must continue to be supported by large enrollments if the program is to remain financially sound.

The *number of teaching positions* is closely tied to the *number of students* projected to be or actually enrolled. At the same time, if the faculty is large, then enrollment needs to be maintained or increased to avoid position cuts. Regarding the *division of labor*, as a program grows – i.e., as there is an increasing number of students and teachers – there is the possibility and also the need for more non-teaching staff. New positions intermediate between the program director and the instructors (for example, a faculty supervisor), between the director and the other administrative staff (for example, an assistant director) or between the director and the students (for example, a student services coordinator) may be created. If a program shrinks, the division of labor will shift: certain staff members may suddenly need to spend a great deal of time on recruitment and promotion or lobbying with a higher authority to justify the continued existence of the program. Under these conditions, the program staff will eventually have to shrink back to a smaller number of job categories and fewer actual positions.

The first part of the personnel process in structuring a faculty is the determination of staffing needs, both immediate and long-range. This determination takes place before any faculty members are hired and again every time a new position opens up. In many language programs, staffing needs change over time, depending on the number and the character of the students enrolled. Staffing needs also vary according to the interests and strengths of those who have already been hired. Faculty positions may therefore change in nature or in number as a response to fluctuating characteristics of the student body and of the faculty as a whole.

The structuring of the faculty is related to choices in the area of curriculum design. At the extreme, a language curriculum based on a certain method or set of materials requires for its implementation teachers specifically trained in use of that method or those materials. In the less extreme and more usual (and desirable) situation which exists in most language programs, the structure of the curriculum does not so rigidly determine the type of background which a teacher must have in order to work in a particular institution. Nevertheless, faculty structure and curricular structure or course design are interrelated decision areas. For example, a curriculum divided into several different specialized areas dictates hiring of teaching specialists, i.e., those trained to teach in specialized areas such as technical writing, scientific or business language. On the other hand, a generalized course in which there are few curricular divisions – as, for example, when a language course is organized according to functions rather than in terms of individual skills such as reading, writing, speaking and listening – requires a faculty accustomed to teaching language in a more integrated way. A language curriculum which includes both specialized areas and work on general language skills can make good use of both generalists and specialists on the faculty.

In making faculty hiring decisions (or in providing continuing education for faculty members – cf. the discussion of continuing education and professional growth below), it is important to try to match faculty orientation not only to the philosophy and curricular structure of the program, but also to the interests and needs of the students. For example, if the students come from a heavily grammar-based tradition, then it is desirable for instructors to have a strong foundation in the grammar of the language, even if the teaching approach is not grammatically based. If the students are academically oriented, then instructors must be hired who understand this type of orientation and how it differs from a more conversational orientation to learning and teaching a language. In an intensive language program, where the expectations for rapid progress are high, students expect a relatively high level of challenge and a relatively rapid pace. Teachers accustomed to working or trained to work in less intensive educational settings might have difficulty in achieving the right level of challenge and pacing for students in an intensive course.

At the same time as faculty hiring decisions must be consistent with the language program curriculum and student characteristics, there should be some complementarity here, such that the structure of a program can accommodate the differing approaches and interests of individual teachers. Indeed, the faculty should be consciously structured, both at the outset when a program is first designed and later in the life of a program when new positions are added or faculty members replaced, to incorporate a measure of diversity in teacher characteristics. A degree of heterogeneity in faculty characteristics ensures programmatic flexibility to meet the generally unpredictable and fluctuating needs of the student body. Planned diversity within the teaching faculty provides the program with a wide array of internally generated resources for the growth and development of the program as a whole as well as for the individuals who work together on the faculty and who serve as resources for each other.

Diversity can be achieved by structuring the faculty to include a balance of types of positions. Inclusion of some part-time or teaching assistant positions allows for administrative flexibility in scheduling and class organization. At the same time, a core of experienced full-time professionals is desirable in most situations, since these teachers provide for program continuity, stability and progressive development and improvement of the curriculum and operations. A balance of experienced and new teachers ensures continuing input of fresh ideas and maintenance of faculty enthusiasm.

Once the necessary faculty positions have been established, qualifications and expectations for each should be written out in concrete terms and in some detail to guide selection and recruiting. Before the job is advertised, the process of application and the methods to be used in screening applicants need to be determined. In interviewing top candidates, interviewers should attempt to probe the applicants' qualifications in particular areas related to the advertised position, as well as personal characteristics which will help to determine what positive features the individual might bring to the organization.

Throughout the faculty selection process – from determination of needs to screening of applications, interviewing and hiring decisions – it is desirable to have involvement by persons other than the program administrator, for example, a hiring committee composed of faculty members and other administrators. Hiring decisions made on the basis of input from several different sources and through a process of discussion and negotiation are on a firmer foundation than those made by one individual based on that person's necessarily limited perspective.

When a new faculty member is hired, there begins a formal or informal probationary period of orientation and adjustment, generally lasting six months to a year. During this period, the new teacher is expected to become familiar with the curriculum of the program, as well as with its administrative policie and procedures, adapting prior experience and training to meet the needs of the particular program and its students. The administrator and other faculty members can help in this adjustment period, in which the new faculty member benefits greatly from guidance and feedback (see below on faculty supervision). In most cases, new teachers will succeed in adjusting to a new position within a year and will achieve a regular and acceptable level of performance by the end of that time period. However, when the adjustment is not made within the limits of the probationary period and performance has not achieved an acceptable level, it may be necessary to terminate employment. When this is necessary, it is highly desirable to terminate within the first six months to one year, that is, before the period of regular employment beyond the probationary period begins. For this reason, a formal probationary period which includes several observations of teaching and other assessments of teaching capability may be desirable.

The evolution and growth of a language program faculty

The third aspect of faculty development begins after the faculty members have been hired and are performing their jobs. Development in this third sense relates to the professional growth and changes which both organizations and individuals experience in their career history. It thus includes an ongoing process of evolution of the faculty as a functional unit within the larger organization of the program as well as the realization of potentialities and goals of individual faculty members. The three major aspects of this process are: evaluation, supervision and continuing education.

Faculty evaluation

As stated above, the ultimate success (or failure) of a language program hinges on the initial decisions related to the hiring of instructors and the structuring of the faculty as a whole. Once the faculty has been organized, the continuing success of a program is dependent on development in the other sense, that of providing an orientation for the program and its individual faculty members towards continual improvement and change, i.e., a focus on the future. From the administrative perspective, development means innovation and growth, and a continual evolution of the organization in a certain direction. From the faculty perspective, development means growing and evolving as a professional in the field. In the ideal case, personal goals develop in parallel to the goals of the program. Hence, the system and methods of faculty evaluation and supervision in a language program should be tied to a professional development plan which encourages individuals to further the goals of the organization through their own professional expansion or improvement. In such a system, motivation derives quite naturally from explicit opportunities for professional growth.

A formal performance evaluation system is a set of written documents and specifications for conducting periodic performance reviews. The performance evaluation system comprises a number of components, as shown in Figure 8.

Standards – What

Evaluators – Who

Procedures – How

Purpose – Why

Results – How much

Figure 8   Components of a performance evaluation system

The *standards* component specifies the expected performance in areas related to teaching and other aspects of the faculty member's job. A detailed faculty job description or a written statement of standards of performance can be provided for those just hired as part of their orientation to a new teaching assignment and as a reference item providing the framework for faculty performance review. Job-related areas which might be addressed in these written standards include: general conduct of classes, homework and outside assignments, curricular emphasis and standards, assessment and grading, relationships within the program (with students, administration and other faculty members), performance of non-teaching duties, and adherence to policies and procedures of the program.

The *evaluators* component of the system specifies whose input will be solicited in the evaluation of faculty members and who will make the final interpretation of that input. Input from students, the supervisor, and from faculty members themselves may be formally or informally solicited as part of the evaluation *procedures*. This component describes the evaluation process in detail, including the types of input which will be solicited (for example classroom observations by faculty supervisor, review of lesson plans or course outlines by faculty supervisor, teaching evaluations performed by students, peer reviews or self-evaluation of teaching performance), and the phases of the process and their timing (how often and in what sequence observations, meetings and formal evaluations are to take place). For formal input, special forms must be devised or located.

Two important aspects of faculty evaluation systems which are often overlooked or not explicitly addressed are the *purpose* and the guidelines for interpretation of evaluation *results*. The evaluation purpose should in large measure determine the other components of the system. In the area of *results*, criteria must be defined for interpretation of the data gained in the evaluation process with reference to the *standards* specified at the outset. Moreover, criteria for advancement or other employment action, including explicit grounds for termination of employment, should be determined and made known to the faculty before any aspect of the evaluation system is implemented.

In the design and implementation of a faculty evaluation system, it is important to realize that every organization functions both as an autonomous unit and as part of a larger context, including the institution within which the organization is housed and the larger field of which the organization is a representative. The functioning of the organization in this larger context may put different demands on the organization than what is required for internal day-to-day functioning. In general, 'external demands for accountability are at odds with internal organizational needs for stability and trust' (Darling-Hammond, Wise and Pease, 1983: 286). Thus, while it may be desirable from the perspective of the faculty members in a program to have a formative focus for teacher evaluation, referenced to program-internal norms and conditions, an outside authority or program administrator may impose instead a summative focus for evaluation of teaching performance. A program-external or summative focus in faculty evaluation may function as part of a larger programmatic evaluation or as the basis for decisions about future employment of individual faculty members. However, such a focus may run counter to the formative goals of continued growth and improvement in the faculty and the program as a whole:

> It is one thing to define and measure teacher competence in a
> standardized fashion; it is quite another to change teacher
> performance. Research on individual and organizational behavior
> suggests ... that successful approaches involve processes that may
> be inconsistent with those used to derive summative evaluation
> judgements. That is, the context-free generalization necessary for
> implementing a uniform evaluation system may counteract the
> context-specific processes needed to effect change in individual or
> organizational behaviors.

(Darling-Hammond, Wise and Pease, 1983: 288)

The development within the faculty of an evaluation system which meets criteria specific to a particular program is more likely to result in a successful program, both in terms of teaching behavior and in terms of other equally important motivational and organizational factors:

> The process of developing evaluation systems is an occasion for
> many things in an organization such as the interaction of
> constituencies, celebration of important values, and the joint
> recognition of problems. Whether or not performance objectives
> are met by a specified proportion ... of teachers, the *indirect*
> results of such efforts may have considerable impact on staff
> enthusiasm, beliefs, or behavior, with ultimate benefits for
> students.
>
> (Knapp, 1982: 18)

The success of a system of evaluation which is intended to produce
positive change and improvement hinges partially on the degree of
involvement in the evaluation process by the teachers themselves.
'Research on individual and organizational change indicates that the
degree of control and autonomy characterizing participants' roles in the
implementation process is critical to success of a planned change effort'
(Darling-Hammond, Wise and Pease, 1983: 313). Thus, if faculty
evaluation is intended to effect change, it should have a strong 'bottom-
up' impetus (Johnson, 1980), in which design, implementation and
interpretation phases involve participation by individual faculty
members or a representative faculty committee. In the Redfern (1980)
Management by Objectives model and other teacher evaluation models
described by Lewis (1982), the evaluation process begins with the setting
of individual objectives, the development of a plan of action and the
determination of measurable indicators of progress by the individual
faculty member in consultation with the supervisor.

Through such a cooperative evaluation process, the character and
standards of the program will become more and more representative of
the particular faculty members who comprise it, and personal standards
and organizational standards will co-evolve. The evaluation process then
becomes a vehicle for effecting change in the organization: 'Effective
change requires a process of mutual adaptation in which [participants] at
all levels can shape policies to meet their needs – one in which both the
participants and the policy are transformed by the convergence of
internal and external reference points' (Darling-Hammond, Wise and
Pease, 1983: 317). Change occurs realistically and gradually, through
'transformation' rather than (involuntary) 'conversion' (Fenstermacher,
1978).

Faculty supervision and continuing education

In many contexts, faculty supervision and coordination of the academic
aspects of the language program will be provided by a person specifically
designated as 'faculty supervisor' or 'academic coordinator'. Whether
department chair, director or faculty supervisor, whoever is coordinating

the faculty should be experienced and highly skilled in the techniques and procedures of the language teaching field as well as in human interaction. As emphasized in Pennington (1985a): 'In educational administration, perhaps more than in any other type of administration, human skill is essential' (p. 306). Faculty members expect to negotiate and interact with the program administrator in a climate of participative decision-making.

Faculty evaluation and supervision should be processes through which faculty motivation is enhanced, rather than diminished or destroyed. Faculty morale-building is an important function of the program administrator because:

> self-perceptions of efficacy both affect performance and are affected by others' perceptions of a person's efficaciousness. Research on this topic indicates that perceived self-efficacy better predicts subsequent behavior than does actual performance attainment.... More important, substantial research also suggests that an individual's sense of efficacy can be influenced by interactions with others as well as by organizational factors....

> (Darling-Hammond, Wise and Pease, 1983: 315)

Freeman (1982) and Gebhard (1984) describe a variety of supervisory approaches for working with language teachers, from directive to non-directive 'Rogerian' approaches. In my view, the type of supervisory and professional development approach should vary depending on the career stage of the faculty member. A general model of these stages is presented in Figure 9.

Curricular assignment		Professional orientation	Supervisory approach	Sources of input
Advanced stages	*Initial stages*			
(5) supervising teaching	(1) supervised teaching	training	directive (providing direction)	Su, St Fa
(6) developing curriculum	(2) teaching across the curriculum	exploring the curriculum	supervisory (suggesting alternatives)	Su, St Fa, Se
(7) developing materials	(3) teaching in favorite areas	specializing	facilitative (providing resources	Su Fa, Se
(8) developing new areas	(4) teaching in new areas	expanding competencies	collegial (sharing resources)	Fa, Se

(Su=supervisor, St=students, Fa=faculty members, Se=self)

Figure 9   Stages in faculty development: the teaching cycle

In the model above, it can be seen that a different type of curricular assignment and supervisory approach is appropriate during each of these career stages, which can be expected to last from one to three years. Stage (1) represents the initial training phase of faculty development in which trainees work under the close direction of experienced teachers. In this phase, directive supervision is needed to build the teaching repertoire and a sense of security and confidence. Input from supervisor, students and other faculty members is needed to help refine observational and critical skills so that continuing improvement can result in a consistent teaching style. Stage (2) is the period in which the new teacher is trying the approaches learned in Stage (1), exploring the curriculum by teaching in a variety of areas. At this point, the teacher begins to be able to make productive use of self-evaluation of teaching performance, along with continuing input from a wide range of other sources, as in Stage (1). In Stage (2), the supervisor can be most helpful in providing alternatives and suggestions for approaching the teaching task from a variety of perspectives. In Stage (3), the instructor has stabilized teaching performance and prefers to work in certain areas of the curriculum, based on personal tastes, interests and teaching strengths. At this point in a teacher's career, student feedback on performance becomes predictable and so may be dispensed with, while feedback from peers and input from the supervisor in the form of provision of new resources is helpful.

After some period of time in Stage (3), the faculty member generally begins to tire of the routine teaching assignment and is ready to go off in a new direction, Stage (4). By this time, the faculty member has gained in maturity and self-reliance and no longer needs the guidance of formal supervision. Thus, the program administrator can encourage the potential of the faculty member who has passed through Stage (3) by allowing that individual to move beyond a primary emphasis on classroom teaching to the higher level activities shown in Stages (5) through (8). In this way, the faculty member moves to a higher level of professional development, and of development and participation in the program, as shown by the loop connecting the initial stages with the advanced stages.

The faculty supervisor ought to be aware of faculty career phases such as those outlined above and to try to match curricular assignment and supervisory approach to the needs of individual faculty members following their developmental profiles. Also, at each of these stages, a different type of continuing education will be most valuable and effective, based on the interests and needs that are present at that time. Some teachers may move naturally through the career cycle shown above, while others may need some help in identifying a new pathway at certain stages in their career. Thus, a faculty supervisor should be on the lookout for signs that a certain job assignment may have outlived its usefulness for a certain instructor. If a faculty member seems to be dissatisfied or to be stagnating or performing below standard in an assignment, it may be advisable to try to move that teacher out of one curricular assignment and into a more advanced stage in the teaching life-cycle.

As a response to performance review and as part of the ongoing professional development of faculty competence, in-service and continuing education opportunities of many different types can be made available to instructors. The administrator should encourage any kind of professional activity, whether engaged in by the faculty as individuals or as a group, by offering release time or other types of allowances and incentives, including raises and promotions. For as faculty members increase their status and mature professionally, so does the program in which they work. Moreover, faculty members who are benefitting professionally from association with a program gain in loyalty and job satisfaction and are likely to maintain a high level of productivity throughout their careers. In contrast, those who do not grow and change in their jobs become bored, frustrated and dissatisfied, often remarking that they suffer from 'burnout'.

Professional development opportunities may involve teachers in outside activities such as conference attendance or continuing education courses, or may draw on the resources of the program and its internal needs. For example, after-class workshop activities can be instituted based on case studies, role-play or problem-solving activities built around typical classroom situations which faculty members are encountering and which are the source of stress or are of particular interest to them. It is also advantageous for the administrator to involve faculty members in projects aimed at external promotion or improvement of non-teaching aspects of the program. For example, a faculty committee might oversee design and implementation of a conversation partners program; an individual faculty member might serve on a school-wide committee which advises on student services in all units; another faculty member might help in disseminating information about the program to potential students. In this way, faculty members, while experimenting with new job tasks, come to have a personal interest in the welfare of the program and a stake in its continued existence.

Conclusion

As has been argued above, teachers are the driving force in every educational enterprise, so that the success or failure of any particular program rests largely on faculty development. In self-supporting language programs, the nature and quality of the teaching faculty can literally 'make or break' the operation. In state-subsidized institutions, too, the character of the faculty is largely responsible for many overt indicators of success or failure, such as reputation, size and income from grants. To ensure its continued health and existence, it is in the best interests of a language program for the administrator to commit considerable resources of time, personnel and money to faculty development.

In the larger context outside of individual programs, it is of benefit to the society as a whole to offer high-quality, specialized training for language teachers and to promote the best interests of those teachers. For it is through the profession of language teaching, more than any other type of work, that the languages and cultures of the world are preserved and spread to new domains. Hence, we can agree with Eskey (1982) that language program administrators must cultivate their teaching faculties and help to gain acceptance of the idea that teaching is among the most important and admirable of human pursuits:

> Despite the relatively low estate which teachers seem to have fallen into lately, teaching arguably remains the quintessential human activity. Since culture is learned, not inherited, every culture's first concern must be perpetuating itself. In this respect, teaching, the passing on of culture to each new generation of students, has a special importance and merits greater respect than most people now feel for a profession regarded as a home for 'those who can't' as opposed to 'those who can' and do. The trouble with the can/can't argument, however, is that those who can soon become those who could. George Bernard Shaw, who penned the original aphorism, has been dead for some time, and it is mainly thanks to teachers that a few cultured people still read his plays – and thanks to language teachers in particular that there are so many people in so many places who can understand the language that he wrote them in. . . .

(p. 44)

8 The evolution of a teacher training programme

Michael Breen, Chris Candlin, Leni Dam and
Gerd Gabrielsen

Introduction

This paper provides an account of an in-service programme for teachers of English as a foreign language in secondary schools in a European country. The programme was initiated in 1978 and is still in operation. The authors have been the training team throughout the programme, although they have been supported from time to time by certain specialists.[1] During the eight-year period between 1978 and 1985 well over a hundred experienced teachers have participated, and they have had a significant influence upon the nature of the evolution described in this paper.

The paper has three purposes: i) to provide a description of the main characteristics of the in-service programme; ii) to offer an account of the ways in which the programme has developed, particularly with regard to changes in the priorities, roles, and activities of trainers and trainees; and iii) to deduce a number of principles for in-service training from our experience of the programme which may be of interest and value to others engaged in in-service work.

We believe the programme may be unusual in its coincidence of eight specific characteristics:

1 It is a long-term experience and therefore facilitates a cyclic process from training input, through trainee implementation in the classroom, to subsequent feedback and later training input in response to classroom experiences.

2 A main source of continuity in the programme has been the presence of

1 Claus Faerch of the University of Copenhagen and Handelshjskolen of Aarhus made a valuable contribution to one of our training workshops. His untimely death has deprived us of a good friend and wise colleague. We dedicate this paper to him. Our thanks are due to Sarah Mann of the Centre for the Study of Management Learning, University of Lancaster, and to Scott Windeatt of the Institute for English Language Education, University of Lancaster, who made valuable contributions to some of the training workshops. We wish also to record our gratitude to the Education Authority of Greve Kommune, Danmarks Laererhojskole and the British Council in Denmark and London for financing this programme over the extended period of time.

111

the same four trainers throughout. About a fifth of the teachers have also maintained contact with the programme over several years, although the training policy has been to invite a greater proportion of completely new participants every year so that what is offered may be more widely and locally shared.

3 Teacher participation is purely voluntary and the teachers apply to attend the training workshops.

4 Many of the teachers who have participated come from schools in the same or in neighbouring areas of the country so that continued contact can be maintained if they so wish.

5 As is the case in many European countries, the participating teachers do not see themselves as language specialists alone. They are generalists with some training as language teachers and are qualified to teach in more than one or two subjects. Accordingly, they relate any in-service training in language teaching to their work in education in general and perceive language teaching as part of broader school policies.

6 The programme emerged in response to local demand and interest. When we started, we never anticipated such a long-term involvement and we had no longer-term strategy of training. The continued demand and interest was significantly maintained by the in-country local trainers who sought continual contact with participating teachers. In this way, the programme itself has been more emergent or reactive than planned and proactive.

7 The actual training workshops organised by the visiting trainers (from Britain), although serving as the pivotal events around which the overall programme has taken shape, are undertaken over only *two and a half days* in every year. Therefore, the longevity of the programme has to be balanced by each annual training workshop bringing together a group of not more than twenty participants for about fifteen hours in the year.

8 While the training workshops aim to provide the impetus for new directions in training, two one-day follow-up meetings during the year allow the local trainers to meet the teachers attending the training workshop. The primary function of such local meetings has been to continue and develop the work initiated in the annual workshop.

Given the nature of this in-service provision, this paper will focus primarily on the training workshops themselves. However, we will also try to show how these workshops have been followed through and how they have been shaped by the local trainers' contacts with the teachers in the local meetings. Our account will therefore be of an evolution in training growing out of the interaction between the annual training workshops, the locally-organised follow-up meetings, and the teachers' own classroom experiences during their contact with the programme. (From 1978 to 1983, a teacher wishing to attend the programme could work with a group of 10 to 20 fellow teachers and the trainers on three occasions in the year: the training workshop in the autumn and two follow-up meetings organised by the local trainers. Since 1984 we have established a definite two-year cycle of contact which most teachers follow through.)

We shall begin by briefly describing the context within which the programme was initiated. The main body of the paper details the evolution of the programme in terms of its three phases. We believe this reveals a gradual transition from i) training as *transmission*, to ii) training as *problem solving*, to iii) training as *classroom decision making and investigation*. We offer an account of each of these phases in turn. The paper ends with a number of discoveries of possible general relevance for in-service training.

The start of the programme

In 1978, the two Danish authors of this paper (Dam and Gabrielsen), familiar with the work of the Lancaster trainers (Breen and Candlin) in communicative language teaching, invited them to Denmark to offer a short intensive in-service course for a group of teachers of English in local secondary schools. At that time, the four people involved in this initial venture had no idea that the proposed course might blossom into the kind of continuing programme which is the subject of this paper. It was the wish of the Danish trainers to introduce the teachers to new developments in communicative language teaching and, in particular, to the adaptation and design of English teaching materials incorporating communicative principles.

The local teachers at that time expressed a particular concern with their current teaching materials. The textbooks which they used in their schools were felt by the teachers to be rather 'old-fashioned' and constraining in terms of the kind of language teaching activities they felt they ought to engage their learners in. Such perceptions of published materials are not, of course, unique to Denmark. Danish teachers, however, remain sceptical of the published materials they use despite the fact that they freely choose these themselves. Materials are not imposed by Ministry or school but merely require approval of the parents' representatives on the School Board. The teacher's choice is primarily constrained by cost. Published materials provide a focal point for teachers through which they, directly or indirectly, express more general and often deeply felt concerns with language pedagogy and the motivation to improve it in whatever ways may be feasible. Although we did not fully appreciate it at the time, this initial focus on teaching materials provided a doorway into wider and more important pedagogic issues.

The purposes of the initial in-service workshop were, therefore, twofold. The trainers' priority, on the one hand, was to introduce the teachers to certain characteristics of communicative language teaching; we assumed our task was to update the teachers' thinking and to generate innovation through teachers' views of the possibilities of language teaching materials. The teachers' shared interest, on the other hand, was to hear of ways in which published textbooks might be best used in addition to those approaches they had developed through their own experience. These two slightly different sets of assumptions had an important shaping influence upon what followed.

Given this context, the Lancaster trainers approached the initial course as a short intensive introduction to communicative language teaching, likely – in their common experience – to be a 'one-shot' contact with a group of unknown teachers. Aware of the obvious limitations of such 'flying-visit' in-service provision, their intention was to offer a spring-board for possible local innovations which the in-country trainers might then build upon. They saw themselves as offering principles and ideas, rather than prescriptions for classroom techniques, in the hope that these could be reinterpreted locally through classroom practice. Perhaps somewhat inevitably, the Lancaster trainers saw themselves in the role of catalysts from outside who could deliver a sufficiently stimulating message so that the local trainers could take things further. Assuming this role, the Lancaster trainers adopted a particular approach to the first training workshop. It was one which, although clearly shaped by circumstances, is prevalent in many situations while not being perhaps the most appropriate model for in-service training. In this first phase of the programme we launched into training as *transmission*.

The first phase: training as *transmission*

In describing this initial training approach, exemplified in the first two annual workshops, we refer to five related matters:

1 trainer and trainee roles
2 the purposes of the workshops
3 the general content and method of the workshops
4 the outcomes for the trainees' classroom practice
5 the weaknesses we deduced in our training approach which we felt we needed to reduce or eliminate.

So that the reader may compare the three phases of the programme and observe thereby its gradual evolution, we refer to these five major features in each phase we describe.

Trainer and trainee roles

The role the visiting trainers adopted, and a role the local trainers for a variety of reasons expected of us to some extent, was that of missionaries. We were 'bringers of good news'; the assumed sources of expertise, greater knowledge and innovative ideas from the outside. The trainees, on the other hand, were placed in a state of assumed deficiency. They were willing and no doubt interested recipients but to some extent simultaneously obliged to 'have faith'. At the same time they were a little defensive of their own assumptions and practical experience in the face of visitors proposing at least implicitly that they should change or improve upon what they currently did. This obvious asymmetry of roles and expectations, however justified they might or might not be, was not merely imposed in some way by the trainers but was mutually sustained by the trainees. Such a conspiracy we believe to be far more common in the teacher-training process than many trainers would wish. We do not feel that we have described it in too stereotypical a fashion but we now believe that this characteristic asymmetry of roles and expectations has to be confronted and worked on as part of the training itself.

The purposes of the training workshops

Each training workshop lasted usually fifteen hours and consisted of intensive work sessions over two and a half days. The teachers obtained release from their schools for much of the time although they were also obliged to give up some of their own time in an evening or at the weekend. Initially our purposes were twofold: first, to convince the trainees of the 'rightness' of communicative language teaching, and second, to involve the trainees in a critical evaluation of their current textbooks including the classroom exercises and activities they contained, with a view to adaptation along more communicative lines and use in more communicative ways. In essence, our purposes were to introduce what we took to be genuine innovation and to achieve this through focusing on an aspect of the teachers' classroom resources which might then metamorphose these innovative ideas into classroom practice.

The content and method of the workshops

We launched the workshops in a way which typifies training as transmission. The visiting trainers devoted the first third of the time to providing lengthy presentations, in this case on the nature of language as communication and the nature of language learning. Such presentations represented the trainers' syntheses of current theory and research, providing – for them – the rationale for the innovations they believed the teachers needed to be aware of. Such syntheses were well motivated and of interest and value to the trainees. The convincing rationale, however, provided the basis for everything that followed. From what they had presented, the trainers deduced key criteria for 'good' materials.

The second step in the workshops was to involve the trainees in a critical evaluation of their current textbooks. The trainees were required to uncover positive, negative and lacking characteristics of the materials, and closely evaluate the nature of the published exercises in terms of their requirements on learners. Having analysed their materials in these ways, the trainers moved to the adaptation and redesign of materials. On the basis of what the teachers felt the textbooks lacked, and, crucially, given the criteria we had provided for 'good' materials, the trainees undertook to design their own classroom activities which would supplement what was lacking in the textbook and which would be more communicative in nature.

We saw this redesign or new design of classroom materials as the pivotal workshop activity. Subsequent sharing of newly designed materials enabled the trainees to evaluate each other's designs, and to consider the extent to which they had compensated for what the textbook exercises had lacked, and had incorporated the criteria we had given them as a blueprint for their designs.

The outcome for classroom practice

Less than a quarter of the teachers attending these initial workshops took their newly designed materials into their classes and tried them with their learners. A further group claimed in subsequent local meetings that they had discovered alternative approaches to using published materials in the classroom. Thus, less than half of the original number of participants followed up the ideas offered in the workshop or wished to continue to explore the ideas and develop their own practice through contact with the local trainers and by attending a further workshop. Where there was a strong willingness to take newly-designed materials into the classroom, it derived not least from the investment of creative energy devoted by the teachers themselves to their new designs. As we subsequently discovered, the perceived value of the workshop for the trainees was related to two factors: the extent of their personal dissatisfaction with the textbooks, and the degree of conviction they had reached – and the extent of new approaches subsequently tried – in relation to the ideas proposed by the trainers. From our viewpoint as trainers, however, the new materials designed during the workshop varied on a continuum from those capturing *some* of the criteria we had insisted on to those differing hardly at all from the original activities and exercises in the much maligned textbook.

These outcomes provided the visiting trainers with food for thought. In that they assumed that these first workshops were the end of the affair as far as they were concerned, it was not that the visiting trainers themselves believed that they could do much about the fate of their initiatives. They had done their bit, and the rest was to be left to the teachers themselves and the local trainers to explore further if they wished. (At the time, the visiting trainers were in a position of assuming that they would not be asked to return to face the actual consequences of their well-meaning efforts to introduce innovation.)

The weaknesses of training as transmission

With hindsight we deduce the following major weaknesses in our initial transmission approach. Such weaknesses were revealed partly by the actual outcomes from the initial workshops but were also uncovered precisely because the continuation of the programme gave us the opportunity to learn from our mistakes.

1 We, the trainers, decided what was important for the teachers to know, and what they should try to do both during the workshop and subsequently in the classroom. There is a tendency, however unintentional, to attach less attention and less value to what teachers already know and experience in their own classrooms. The assumed source of change and development is the expertise of the trainer. This expertise derives primarily though not exclusively from theory and research, sources other than classroom practice. However acceptable and *welcome* these ideas are to the teachers, their immediate practical concerns become overlaid in 'top-down' fashion by academic expertise. Such a process has two major consequences.

a) First, the partly justifiable passive reaction from some teachers. This reaction is expressed by them in terms of theory and research being too 'ideal'. This does *not* mean that teachers reject theory and research. Our experience throughout the programme suggests quite the opposite. Passive reaction arises from two aspects, the relationship between theory/research and the daily classroom experience of the teacher. First, theory and research are often perceived by teachers as characteristically narrow and selective in their focus, while day-to-day classroom life is perceived as rich, complex and unpredictable. Second, although teachers find proposals from theory and research as both informative and relevant to their own thinking, they are primarily concerned with action; with what they can *do* in the classroom. The translation of theory and research into action is something hard to achieve if trainers adopt a transmission approach. This is so because such training precisely tends not to meet the teachers and their classroom experiences at least halfway.

b) Secondly, a consequence relating to those teachers who accept the ideas offered and try to put them into practice. In our particular case, two matters transpired which we should have anticipated. In the first case, teachers' own efforts to introduce innovative materials created new pressures, notably their pupils' new-found enthusiasm for the teachers' own materials and *their* growing disillusion with their textbook. The pressure would be on the teachers to produce continually new materials when they simply had no time. Alternatively, teachers' innovations emphasised and on occasion revealed deeper and more general pedagogic problems. How to teach the grammar of the language through materials emphasising communication? How to cope with mixed-ability groups of pupils whose very differentiation was at present hidden? How to maintain pupil interest and motivation regardless of the materials with which they were being asked to work? What we can say is that those teachers who were enthusiastic proponents of the innovation became more sensitive to these deeper issues and problems, only some of which we list here, and which any partial innovation can only partly address.

2 Training as transmission not providing any direct follow-up of classroom implementation through further work with trainers (as was initially the case here) can be damaging. Where teachers try implementing the innovation and something fails, those teachers may reject the innovation and, in addition its origins and rationale. Or, after the initial 'failure', teachers need adequate support to continue trying for fear that they attribute responsibility for the failure to themselves. We might conclude that training as transmission might only benefit those with considerable self confidence who have robust personalities from the start.

3 The tendency to unidirectionality in training as transmission emphasises the gap between the cocoon of the training workshop and classroom realities rather than reducing that gap. By its nature, innovation entails teachers in processes of personal readjustment and gradual accommodation in thinking and practice. *The teacher needs time to make the ideas and practical suggestions his or her own; to interpret them and adapt them to particular classes and pupils.* It is equally important for teachers to have time and means to *evaluate* any changes they bring to their classrooms from training. More significantly, teachers need to be able to evaluate the *whole* classroom

process in the light of the innovation. Even small changes in ways of working can reverberate throughout classroom procedures. This re-evaluation should in turn shape and inform the training itself. By its nature, training as transmission is insensitive to teachers' own individual problems in accommodating what is being proposed. It tends to be closed to any thorough evaluation of its own effects, including those that are unexpected and which go beyond the specific innovation being introduced. If evaluation ensued from such training, then as in our experience, the training would have to cease being transmissive.

More positively, perhaps, this initial phase did provide openings and growth points for ourselves and the teachers. We were struck forcibly by our own inconsistency. Our way of working with the trainees did not exemplify the principles of communicative language teaching we were endeavouring to convey. At least, we needed to reexamine the relative roles of trainer and trainee if we were to claim the primacy of learner experience and assert the changes in teacher and learner roles implied by communicative language teaching. The *way* in which we worked with the trainees needed to reflect the nature of the innovation we were advocating. Secondly, we had been fortunate in our decision to focus upon principles and ideas that could be explored by teachers in their own ways, rather than trying to prescribe particular classroom techniques for immediate transfer to the classroom. This obliged us to listen to teachers' reinterpretations of the principles and ideas offered through their subsequent activity in the workshop. In essence we had begun a dialogue about how principles and ideas might *variously* be turned into practice.

The second phase: training as *problem solving*

Fortunately for many of the teachers who participated in our initial workshops, the local trainers set up small working groups of teachers who wished to follow through the new ideas that had been offered. These working groups met to share their own progress and problems in trying to develop the practical application of the ideas and their own materials design. One major outcome from these meetings was the request to the visiting trainers that they return to face the music, so to speak, and to clarify those aspects of their tasks and suggestions which had either proved indigestible on first hearing, or unfeasible in practice. With this, the programme entered a new phase which was to continue for some four of the following annual training workshops. This phase was characterised by a primary concern with those more general pedagogic problems experienced by the teachers in their day-to-day classroom work. Some of these we had helped to bring to the surface by our own initial workshops and most were articulated by the teachers in local follow-up and planning meetings.

Trainer and trainee roles

As trainers we placed ourselves in a consultancy role in relation to the teachers. Perhaps we should say that the teachers *rendered* us consultants because they wished us to address those problems they brought from their classrooms. These included the wish to become more communicative in how they undertook work with their learners. This central issue was pursued in part because many new workshop participants had been made curious concerning what had been done by the earlier groups, through informal contacts they had with former participants in their own schools or at local meetings. The teachers' chief role was to identify and prioritise particular problems they had themselves experienced in classroom practice, problems which they felt they had to sort out in order to be clearer and more confident in what they were doing, and, thereby, to solve classroom management problems. They were involved in sharing pedagogic problems with each other and with the trainers, itself a difficult and sometimes threatening experience, but one which the teachers felt unanimously to be of personal and professional benefit. This phase represented an important shift in the relationship between the teachers and the workshops. The teachers were now using these for their own purposes rather than being obliged to accommodate to the priorities of some pre-planned workshop topic or content.

The purposes of the training workshops

In this second phase our purpose as trainers became both the introduction to and the support of innovation. We now *knew* from the local trainers' follow-up meetings that the teachers were interested in trying to implement communicative language teaching. We had taken this matter somewhat for granted in the initial phase. Rather than exploit materials as the direct target and means of innovation, however, our purpose was to explore with teachers two routes along which innovation might usefully travel. First, to consider ways in which the innovation of more communicative approaches to teaching and learning language might *help solve* those problems identified by the teachers from their own classroom work. Second, intentionally complementary, to build on the teachers' own knowledge and awareness of *their own learners* so that the rationale and essential principles of communicative language teaching could be closely related to the teachers' views of their learners and the language learning process they undergo. Thus, as in the initial phase, the training workshops still had the overriding purpose of introducing innovation.

They had two related aims, however, that of exploring the possibilities of the innovation through a search for solutions to teacher problems, and that of encouraging teachers' own reflections on the nature of the language learning process. Both these stood in contrast to the assertion of innovatory ideas and the subsequent channelling of these into materials and design.

The content and method of the workshops

The workshops were built on two main inputs. The first, that of teachers' problems with their classroom practice, required an introductory step of problem identification. Through particular activities, teachers individually highlighted those matters they saw as problems in their language classes. They were asked to state such problems in as precise a form as they could in terms of particular questions, and these were subsequently shared in the workshop. The second input was provided by the visiting trainers at the request of the participating teachers and the local trainers. This involved the Lancaster trainers in providing a rationale for communicative language teaching *through* a consideration of the language learning process and its implications for the ways in which learners might work in classrooms.

The next step involved ways of working on these two issues: teacher problems and learner process. In one approach, teachers were asked to form working groups to choose and focus on one of these problems identified earlier. The principles of communicative language teaching were presented by the trainers in the form of a check-sheet of the characteristics of communicative activities. Groups were then asked to design a lesson (or an activity for a lesson) exploiting the particular communicative principles which seemed to them to offer a possible solution to their original problem.

In another approach, the participants were asked to analyse a number of language learning exercises from their own current textbook to deduce as precisely as possible what the exercises required their learners to do: what learning operations, or processes or strategies the exercises required of learners if they were to complete them successfully. It had been our original wish as trainers to encourage the teachers to reflect closely on the actual requirements made by the language-learning process on their own learners, but such a focus was further validated by the teachers themselves in discovering that a good proportion of their own stated classroom problems referred to difficulties experienced by their *learners* during classroom work.

From their deductions of the learning process requirements of typical language exercises and the relationship of these requirements to the range of difficulties the teachers perceived their learners to have, teachers were then asked to design new exercises or classroom activities. These should both encourage the learner to work in particular ways, enabling him or her to overcome learning problems through alternative ways of working or alternative strategies, and incorporate those characteristics of a communicative activity which the teachers believed would most help learners in this regard.

From these approaches the participants shared and evaluated lesson plans, classroom activities or new exercises which the various working groups had developed.

The outcome for classroom practice

In this phase a greater proportion of the participants took the plans for classroom action from their working groups into their own classes. Evaluation of implementation was followed up by many of the teachers when they met again with the local trainers in post-workshop meetings, and this evaluation was fed back to the Lancaster trainers and *used as a basis for subsequent workshops*. In this way, a new cycle became established whereby the search for solutions related to teacher problems and learner work served as a basis for initial workshops. Through practical application and subsequent sharing of experience from implementation, more precise problems and issues could be identified for later workshops. At the same time, and feeding into these workshops, small working groups of teachers were being formed through meetings held by the local trainers. Here participants from earlier workshops could pursue their particular problems or practical matters of interest.

A new development emerged where a small proportion of the teachers began to initiate and co-operate in action research in their own classrooms and share their discoveries with their colleagues. In local meetings later in this phase, participants carried out plans for the documentation and later analysis of classroom work. Such documents included observation schedules, teacher diaries, collections of samples of pupils' work and *pupil* evaluation of both their own work and of several aspects of the classroom process. A small number of the participants and one of the local trainers began to videotape their own lessons. These videotapes were later used as a basis for discussion and as a stimulus for sharing and trying out new ideas. These unforeseen developments have had a strong effect on the way of working in the third and most recent phase in our programme.

The weaknesses of training as problem solving

Once again, because of our long period of co-operation (despite the relative brevity of the annual training workshops) and because of the continued evaluation of the outcomes from workshops by participants, we have come to learn that training as problem solving also has its limitations. These are perhaps less serious than the constraints coming from training as transmission, and there are indeed certain positive features of this particular approach. (See the final section of this chapter.) A major discovery was the high value placed by virtually all participants on the discussion and sharing of practical classroom problems. Although we had felt that such problem raising might be approached cautiously by many teachers, requiring as it does self confidence and trust, none the less it was continually identified by teachers as one of the most positive features of each workshop. This helped us to realise that teachers very rarely have the opportunity of sharing classroom experiences with colleagues, and that the process of identifying and sharing problems itself has a positive effect on many teachers' later views of their own work. A second discovery for both trainers and teachers was the true nature of the rocky road of innovation. It became clear that the demands of the process of introducing change were far more subtle and numerous than any of us had initially anticipated.

The following weaknesses of the *problem-solving* approach adopted during this phase emerged:

1 Although welcomed as consultants in the search for possible solutions, the visiting trainers were still placed in an 'expert' role. This was so even when they were in far less of a position to judge the relative significance of a problem or contribute to its solution than the teacher who identified it. The local trainers, however, had the advantage of being seen as people closer to the real problems and actual working processes experienced by the teachers. Indeed, one of the local trainers shared her own efforts and experience of innovation from her own classroom. That one of the trainers could reveal that she was practising what she preached has been one of the influential aspects of the whole programme (Dam, 1982).

2 Perhaps not surprisingly, every workshop group identified far more problems than even small sub-groupings could address and try to seek solutions for in the time available. The more careful focus on specific problems, significant or not, is always only a partial endeavour. The problems themselves were symptoms of a larger, underlying issue, that of the day-to-day management of the language classroom in the context of the school and its responsibility to the local community. While certain problems could be solved, and certain lessons, activities or exercises proved helpful to both teachers and taught, the phenomenon of the teachers' greater sensitivity to emergent and wider problems remained. (For an account of 'complexes' of teacher problems see Gabrielsen, 1985.) What was still needed was to address

classroom management in ways in which teachers could confront practical problems, independently of the workshops in the continuing life of their classes. We had no doubt that the teachers *did do* this. They would have had to do so to deal with the realities of classroom work as they experienced them. What we might be able to offer was a systematic framework and starting point for the clear location of problems, and a suggestion for alternative ways of working for teachers to adopt as part of their own classroom management. Merely sharing problems and searching for solutions did help, but the inevitable selectivity and partiality of the solutions collectively generated proved to be insufficient.

3 A major difficulty with the problem-solving approach lies in the teachers' own views of their problems. Teachers may feel frustrated in a workshop that requires them to articulate their work problems when trainers do not provide a point of reference, from theory, research or current practice. Teachers may need to *relate* their problems to a framework provided by an overriding issue or debate. Or, some teachers may find it difficult to articulate their experiences in terms of problems. They have the concrete experience, but not perhaps the words to capture that experience, or the familiarity with problem raising in the company of fellow teachers. Problem raising has to be a slow, delicate process involving a deeper reassessment of the role of the teacher and the learner and of the functions of the classroom itself. Problem solving often uncovers much more than specific difficulties. Positively, this can be a means towards a broader re-evaluation of teaching and learning. Negatively, it may highlight what is difficult to achieve rather than what has been achieved.

4 The risks of teacher 'failure' were again possible, as was the case with transmission (already discussed under 'The first phase'). In some ways, such risks were intensified because the workshops focused on issues identified by the teachers as important to *them*. The responsibility for continued innovation and the greater sensitivity to learner problems were clearly of mixed benefit for many teachers. Paradoxically, the closer the teachers analysed the ways in which learners might work on particular activities or exercises, the more complex their own job appeared of helping their learners.

As trainers, we therefore had to consider ways in which the workshops might achieve the purpose of introducing innovation while also encouraging participants to pursue innovation *independently* in their own classrooms. We had to think of ways to facilitate innovation while making the supportive comfort of our workshops redundant. We needed to establish a way of working which would encourage teachers to interact with each other and with trainers as equal participants with equally innovative ideas in the search for solutions to immediate problems. A further motivation for this new way of working emerged, one which might forge links between the training workshop and the teachers' classrooms. We considered we might work with the teachers in the ways they might themselves work with their own learners in the classroom.

The third phase: training as *classroom decision making and investigation*

The *raison d'être* of our training programme has been to introduce innovation. At the outset, in adopting a transmission approach, we assumed that the trainers were the catalysts for innovation. Later we recognised that the teacher could be the main agent for change if the innovation was itself motivated by and related to problems defined in the classroom context, and if the innovation was perceived as helping the learning of *both* teachers and pupils. Continuing evaluation of workshop outcomes through local meetings revealed that participants interpreted the innovation in their own terms, and that many perceived change and development in classroom work. A good proportion however had been rejecting or doubting the value of what we intended.

Any innovation offered for classroom practice from outside is obviously vulnerable to rejection. Every innovation will inevitably be reinterpreted by teachers in order to be made manageable for them in practice. It is, however, also changed in the process, so that the teacher's version of the innovation may only loosely resemble the original intent. Over the years a fair number of the teachers have expressed their rejection of the innovation for several reasons. Their views can be summarised as follows:

1 The innovation came from trainers who were outside the teacher's own classroom experience, and were not ideas or proposals drawn directly from this experience. Put simply, it was someone else's innovation from another context.
2 The apparent demands on the teacher were too burdensome. This was primarily because the innovation itself implied a change in the teacher's role which was found unacceptable.
3 The innovation involved too many risks of failure, and this was expressed in terms of likely learner rejection.
4 It was too ideal in terms of being a world away from the reality of the teacher's own classroom and his or her wider responsibilities to the school and to parents. What theory and research might propose seemed unfeasible in practice or insensitive to the *social* world of the teacher and the constraints of that reality.

5 It was irrelevant as an innovation because the teacher had already put into practice alternative innovations or had gone further than what was being proposed.

Teachers' varied expressions of these five reasons for rejection of the ideas offered by the workshops seemed both understandable and valid as perceptions from the teachers' viewpoint, however difficult for us to confront. Although supported by those who pursued the ideas we worked on together, we were sure that at least a third of the participants did not gain from our offerings. Perhaps we were either unrealistically optimistic to expect a large measure of success in our introduction of innovation, or else blinded by our own faith in the innovation itself.

The latest phase of the programme, characterising our workshops since 1984, tries to anticipate these problems which any innovation is likely to meet. It also reflects several discoveries we have made over the preceding six years' contact with participating teachers. First, the actual implementation of innovation certainly does not depend on the trainers alone, nor does it depend on trainers and teachers together. Second, training workshops, though a luxury for many teachers, can perpetuate themselves as a necessity for some who see themselves as trainer-dependent. This is partly because they perceive training as questioning what they already do as classroom teachers, and, in consequence, weakening the currency of their own skills and experience. Third, there is a significant gap between what teachers think and do together in workshops, and what an individual teacher thinks and does in the classroom; a gap between thought and action giving workshops at best therapeutic value, and making them only an indirect means for action within the classroom. Finally, although the trainer may be informed about the innovation, and through evaluation procedures advised of the nature of its possible implementation, he or she often remains least informed about the happenings in the trainee's own classroom. Paradoxically, the assumed 'expert' is less aware of matters than the trainee and, more important, further away from the innovation in practice than the trainee's own learners.

The discovery process we have been able to undertake during the programme has led us to perceive trainers as *participating in the learning* with the teachers. The training workshops have become exploratory activities with the teachers as our informants. Genuine dialogue can be established between ourselves, the participating teachers and their own learners. We have come to believe that the trainees' classrooms and their learners are the *key training resources*. The classroom as a working group and the learners as members of that group are not only the obvious location for any innovation or development, but they are also the primary means to them. Our training workshops have begun to reflect that realisation by focusing on classroom decision making and the kinds of action research teachers may themselves initiate in their classrooms. Training should avoid the limitations of trainer-centredness and teacher-centredness and become classroom-centred in the sense that the workshop itself becomes a window on classroom work. In this way training can facilitate ways of exploring what classrooms can offer as a contrast to the belief that training is *for* the classroom and to be taken unidirectionally from workshop to the classroom.

Trainer and trainee roles

Training as classroom decision making and investigation puts the trainer in a team both with participating teachers and the teachers' own learners. Trainers are *facilitators* within the team, assisting a dialogue between themselves, teachers and their learners. Trainers act as ignorant outsiders in the sense of wanting to find out with the teachers how classroom management decisions about learning are made, and how learners undertake their own language learning. Trainers consider with teachers the range and the means of classroom decision making, offer proposals, and seek teachers' proposals as to how the decision-making process might more directly engage learners themselves, in order for it to become more sensitive to learning needs and experiences. As a complement to this focus on decision making and as a way of informing it, trainers plan with teachers varied ways of undertaking small-scale investigations in the classroom.

During the workshop, teachers identify and discuss decisions to be made in the work and procedures of their classroom. They plan, with the added suggestions of the trainers, alternative ways in which decisions can be shared with learners. They also identify aspects of the language-learning process they wish to discover more about, and then explore how they might investigate one or other aspect using their learners as informants and co-investigators. Participants, both trainers and trainees, plan together alternatives in classroom decision making and classroom-based investigations.

The purposes of the training workshops

As trainers we now have two related aims emerging from our original wish to help innovation. This wish and the continuation of the programme, informed continually through feedback, itself gave rise to a change in how our major objective might be realised. A current purpose is to discover whether or not particular innovations are *needed*, and if they are, how they can evolve with direct learner participation through more explicit sharing of decision making with teachers. A second purpose relates to our original intention to inform teachers about current language learning theory and research, as the bases for motivating innovation. Instead of telling teachers what other researchers may have discovered about language learning in the past – research rarely based on classroom investigation – we now want the teachers to become their own researchers, so that what they discover from and with their learners can provide the basis for the development of classroom work. The location of theory and research in our work has shifted. Instead of presenting current theory and research to teachers for possible reflection and application, we now build on teachers' own investigations and evaluations of actual classroom occurrences, and then relate these to relevant theory and research. There is now a more balanced dialectic between *teacher* ideas and discoveries and those offered in the research literature.

In trying to introduce innovation, and in participating in a training programme which included implementation and subsequent evaluation, our more immediate major objective has been turned on its head. Instead of infusing innovation into the classroom from our training, we now see ourselves as exploring with the teachers the *possibilities of the classroom* in terms of its members' own initiatives in change and development. Ironically, perhaps, but certainly fortuitously, trainees have introduced innovation into the training.

The content and method of the workshops

The actual work undertaken during the most recent phase of the programme can be best described with reference to four areas of development:

1 The time and the timing of contacts between teachers and trainers.
2 The introduction of an additional workshop organised one month prior to the usual annual workshop by the local trainers.
3 The current nature of the annual training workshop involving visiting trainers.
4 The organisation of the two follow-up meetings locally on two separate days between the workshops.

TIME AND TIMING OF TRAINER AND TEACHER CONTACTS

Until this third phase, the programme involved local teachers in a one- or two-year pattern of contact, each year offering participation in the training workshop plus follow-up and planning in two separate one-day meetings with the local trainers. When teachers currently apply to participate they know that they are entering a two-year cycle of contact with the trainers in a group of about 15 to 20 fellow teachers. The group will meet on four occasions in each of the two years: for two and a half days at the start of the school year (*local trainers' workshop*); for two and a half days about one month later (*the annual training workshop*); and for two separate days with the local trainers during the period before the next year's cycle. In quantitative terms, the 15 hours devoted to the visiting trainers' workshop is now complemented by a 15-hour local workshop and 12 hours (over two days) of local follow-up and planning meetings.

If a teacher continues working with his or her group for a second year (and the majority do so), such in-service work offers 84 hours of contact with colleagues and trainers. This most recent pattern has emerged in response to the recommendations of previous participants, balanced by the obvious constraints of release time from schools. This cycle of contact is, however, also based on two underlying motives, seen to be crucial by both trainers and participating teachers. First, it provides for a basis of professional *support* to the teacher who wishes to become more explicitly engaged in the management of innovation in the classroom. As we deduced earlier in the programme ('The weaknesses of training as *transmission*') the interpretation and gradual implementation of innovation requires time and confidence. Both of these benefit from contact with colleagues who are also undertaking a similar process. Secondly, the extended period of contact offers scope for systematic implementation and evaluation. In this way what may be planned for classroom-based work in the initial training workshop can be monitored and analysed in subsequent meetings. In turn, what is discovered provides the basis for plans for classroom action once the teacher completes the two-year cycle and works independently of the group.

THE LOCAL TRAINERS' WORKSHOP

The introduction of this additional locally organised workshop was motivated by the kinds of problems we had discovered concerning innovation, particularly the implicit re-evaluation of teaching and learning which even partial innovation requires of the teacher. This workshop is attended by the teachers at the very start of their involvement in the programme and again midway through the cycle. It has three related purposes:

1 to draw out from the teachers *their* ideas and proposals for change in classroom practice;
2 to share plans for change and to evaluate changes implemented by the teachers;
3 to identify areas of knowledge and skill participants feel they need to achieve their plans, so that these areas will be addressed and worked on in the annual training workshop organised by the visiting trainers.

In the first introductory workshop, the focus is on raising possibilities for change in classroom work. Open discussion of such possibilities is initiated by the teachers' evaluation of video recordings of classroom work made by teachers from earlier workshops. Subsequent discussion is aimed at identifying particular aspects of classroom work which might be developed. Participants then plan together ways in which the developments or changes may be implemented. The second major theme of the programme is then introduced, that of the nature of language learning and learner difficulty. Participants identify particular aspects of learning in which they are interested, and initial ideas are explored as to how these aspects might be investigated in class. The two themes are brought together through considering ways in which changes might be evaluated and reported on in subsequent meetings, and how classroom learning data might be collected. In this way the rationale for and basic methods of action research can be introduced to the group as a means for monitoring planned change and investigating learning.

The local trainers perceive the introductory workshop as an awareness-raising process; as a means for participants to propose innovations and to pursue them in practice. The trainers seek to enable the teachers to be less concerned with classroom techniques and more involved in considering principles and criteria for classroom management and innovation. The assumption is that exploring possibilities at the level of more general ways of working, say that of greater learner involvement or of systematic evaluation of what happens in classrooms, allows participants greater flexibility and adaptability in the longer term once they complete their programme.

When participants attend the second local workshop, they present and evaluate what they have tried out on the basis of their previous year's planning. Various types of documented classroom work are shared and discussed so that links can be made between an individual's experience of innovation or investigation and generalisable conclusions and principles. Here we address explicit issues of innovation management and action research. In the most recent workshops, the first has been discussed through the theme of teacher responsibility for the assessment of pupil learning, securing of parental understanding and co-operation in relation to particular changes the teacher wishes to introduce, and ways of sharing changes with colleagues. In the context of pursuing innovation in their own classrooms, teachers need to consider how any change will affect the totality of the pupil's school experience. Therefore the workshop addresses innovation management in relation to the broader school context.

By this point in the cycle, classroom investigation becomes a matter for refinement and more detailed planning. Aspects of research methodology are more closely considered on the basis of initial and sometimes tentative investigations. Areas of need are identified for the subsequent training workshop and new plans drawn up for future investigation in the classroom.

THE ANNUAL TRAINING WORKSHOP

The training workshop has now become more directly a *response* to participants' identification of areas of knowledge and practice which can serve their own management of change in the classroom and their investigation of classroom learning. Teachers now specify at the local trainers' workshop one month in advance those matters which the training workshop should address and explore. The visiting trainers plan the annual workshop on the basis of the teachers' own priorities. The content and method of these workshops therefore follow directions the teachers want to pursue.

In the most recent training workshops we have followed two main routes for exploring the potential of the classroom. Workshop groups have proposed one or other of these alternatives. One route begins from *teacher decision making*, itself a major element of classroom management and one closely linked to the range of problems participants had identified in earlier workshops during the second phase of the programme or in the new local workshop. Using teacher decisions and related problems as input, smaller working groups of teachers could identify and discuss possible ways in which their *learners* could provide alternative solutions to both teacher management problems and their own learning problems. This focus has led to the planning of specific activities in which learners are engaged in seeking among themselves and proposing alternative solutions or decisions concerning ways of working in the class, including the role they wish the teacher to play. More broadly, other sub-groups of participants are now engaged in developing a 'process syllabus' with their learners where major classroom decisions are negotiated and jointly agreed between teachers and pupils (Breen, 1984; Candlin, 1984b).

A second route is more overtly that of *action research*. It begins from the teachers' earlier identification of aspects of the individual learning process (for example learning strategies, learning progress, learning difficulty etc.). Here, working groups of teachers identify and consider various ways in which a particular aspect could be investigated with the direct co-operation of learners during classroom work. From this, small-scale research plans evolve which include classroom activities involving learners in the collection and analysis of data from themselves and by themselves, the teacher acting as a research co-ordinator.

THE LOCAL FOLLOW-UP MEETINGS

The two one-day follow-up meetings now have two major functions: first to maintain the momentum of planned innovations and investigations initiated by the local and training workshops, and, second, to provide that important support during the year between the workshops so that teachers can share progress and difficulties with colleagues in their group.

In this way a sense of loneliness in a period of important changes can be reduced.

The first year of meetings serves as a sharing of initial experiences through the first body of data brought from classrooms. In the second year, this focus is maintained but by then the teachers are about to complete the cycle and leave the programme. Given that the teachers have undertaken 'pilot' investigations in the first year and have refined their plans for action research in the second year workshops, the follow-up meetings are for teachers to present what they have discovered from their more developed methods of investigation. Here the related theme of innovation management in the classroom can also be addressed. In these later meetings, however, new directions are proposed from what has been tried out and discovered by the teachers since joining the programme. Plans for following through these new directions are also drawn up. These final meetings are therefore intended as a springboard for the teachers' personal work of completing the programme. In this way the impetus generated through work with the trainers and fellow teachers can be more directly maintained in the new ways of working the teacher has by now introduced into his or her own classroom groups.

The outcomes for classroom practice

We cannot yet be clear whether individual teachers from the workshop groups have gone some way on the routes set out so that they are now enabled to evaluate the implementation of shared decision making or their own action research. This is a new phase in our work and we have made only tentative beginnings. None the less, so far feedback from participating groups seems promising. Most participants have given reports of changes in their patterns of classroom work, especially in terms of greater learner involvement. Three quarters of the teachers have wanted to complete the full two-year cycle, and this represents a 200 per cent increase in continued participation compared with our initial phase in the programme.

Although teachers' action research, now informed by learners' views, was intended as the basis for new directions in classroom work, the involvement of learners in exploring the language learning experience is as vulnerable as any innovation in the language class. We feel as trainers we have come closer to the teachers' classroom experience through our present ways of working with them. Teachers are bringing more to the workshops so that training is more reciprocal and complements classroom action. None the less we still await learners' reactions and retrospective accounts from the teachers of their process syllabuses and the findings from their investigations. In a real sense, our programme is now in an even more experimental phase than when it first began.

The weaknesses of training as classroom decision making and investigation

We suspect our current approach to training within the programme will reveal its own special weaknesses. One immediate problem is *our* new dependency on the teachers to provide us with what they have discovered and upon the reactions and contributions of the learners. It is they, after all, for whom the in-service training is ultimately intended. The workshops themselves now directly mirror the uncertainties and gradualness of innovation experienced by teachers in classrooms when they try to innovate. We see this, however, as a strength. Trainers, teachers and learners are placed in an *interdependent* role relationship. In a way it is the *learners* who now act as the source of training, and the workshops are a forum for teachers and trainers to plan cautiously and thereafter to share and evaluate what has been achieved and uncovered by learners.

The workshops are thus located in a cycle from classroom management or learning problems, through planning for decisions or investigation, through implementation to evaluation of what has been discovered. This phase of training requires teachers to allow and encourage their learners to do much more in the classroom and in more overt ways. Trainers and teachers are involved in discovering the learners' perspective so that planning and practice may be better informed. Classroom-centred training as a means for introducing innovation must begin from the shared discovery of what actually happens in participants' classrooms for any innovation to be related to that reality. In asserting this it seems we may have reverted to a stage in our wish to innovate which was logically prior to the introduction of the innovation.

Introducing innovation: some deductions for training

In this paper we have described three phases through which one particular in-service training programme has passed. Initially, our training approach could, as transmissive, only indirectly influence what went on in the classroom, and that only through the confidence and determination of certain teachers. Later, by adopting a problem-solving approach we managed to get closer to the experience of participating teachers but still failed to establish a direct link to classroom implementation. Most recently we have tried to make the training workshops windows into the classroom, reactive to what the classroom and its learners revealed to us, so as to serve as a planning forum for enabling decisions to be shared by teachers and pupils. We might summarise the evolution of our programme as a gradual movement of training based on the trainers' views of teaching and learning to one based on the classroom world as seen by language learners.

From our own experience to the more general issue of in-service training, we conclude this paper with a number of deductions drawn from our joint work with teachers and their learners and revealed during this evolutionary process. We hope that in so far as they are not already well known, they will be of value to those engaged in in-service training.

1 An in-service training course or programme is likely to be most useful if it grows directly out of the experiences, assumptions and perceived problems of the trainees. This implies that trainers need to be prepared to devote the initial part of any training to a variety of modes of bringing such experiences, assumptions and problems out into the open. Trainers will also need to consider *how* the process of reflecting on these matters will be undertaken by the trainees. (See 'The weaknesses of training as *problem solving*'.)

2 It seems teachers attempt too much in their classrooms. Trainers may be most helpful to them by joint exploration of teachers' responsibilities in classroom work and by examining which of these might be taken on by their learners (by shared decision making, identification of learning achievements and problems etc.).

3 The trainee's own classroom and the learners within it are a major source of information on the nature of the language-learning process. The training course or programme could offer teachers ways of investigating that process. In that way theory and research may benefit and, more important perhaps, teachers can explore the potential of classroom language learning in order subsequently to relate those findings to outside theoretical and research developments.

4 In-service training should focus on what is *done* in the daily life of the language class, the decisions, activities, tasks and learning experience. This requires time for the collection and sharing of classroom data. It also requires the trainers' respect for the ways trainees articulate their perceptions of the classroom process. For the trainer, the teachers' interpretations of what is done in classrooms are as important as the data from the classroom itself.

5 Any innovation premissed on training is most usefully introduced by building on what teachers currently know and do and what occurs in class. Rather than maintaining that these matters must be changed or replaced, training might best entail reflection and development rather than assume 'deficiency' on the part of trainees. More often than not, assuming the latter leads to blocks towards willingness to change.

6 Any training will be converted to action to the extent that it is seen as valuable and necessary to teachers and, as important, to learners. They will, however, reinterpret it in their own terms. Trainers need to be open therefore to issues raised by trainees as relevant to *them* despite such issues perhaps initially seeming to be peripheral in the

trainers' experience. Training acquires direct relevance if trainees' own learners and their classrooms can be offered as key resources in the training process and the primary focus for an exploration of the possibility for change and its implementation.

7 Training should encourage a three-way interaction and interdependence between trainers, teachers and learners.

8 The training course or programme must include evaluation of its outcomes and effects. This will be most informative for trainers if it occurs during the process of training and if there is subsequent evaluation by the teachers in terms of what happens in their classrooms. Ideally such evaluation should form the starting point for future in-service provision.

9 Training might be best seen as an investigative process where the trainer explores possibilities with trainees by drawing on their contributions from classroom experience and from their learners. Trainers are outsiders, but the advantage of this position is the ability to act as a neutral participant wishing to find out more from teachers and classrooms, in order that their potential is realised, related to and built on through the trainers' own knowledge and experience.

10 In terms of the three phases of our programme, we believe now that training could begin ideally from *classroom decision making and investigation*. If this is impracticable for trainers, then training as *problem-solving* is a feasible first step which will reveal other possibilities to both trainers and teachers.

11 Our programme has developed from a focus on materials, through a focus on learning to a focus on classroom-derived information, and from there to aspects of classroom management involving learners. We continue to be concerned with the introduction and implementation of innovation in language teaching. Other starting points and other teaching contexts may open the exploration of other routes and a different evolutionary process than ours. We are confident of two matters, however: first, whatever the specific initial focus of the in-service training, once a dialogue is established between trainer and trainee the focus of concern will expand from the particular to more general and underlying aspects of the management of classroom language learning. Second, the trainer needs to be open to the likelihood that the programme may lead in unexpected directions. Training as *transmission* forecloses both these possibilities. The convenience of its less unpredictable and less exploratory nature has to be balanced against the limited influence of transmission training for change in actual classroom practice.

9 Appropriate design: the internal organisation of course units[1]

Graham Low

Introduction

It is hardly controversial to note that teaching materials are one of the major determinants of what gets taught in language teaching programmes. Indeed, it has been suggested (Hawkes, 1983: 99) that recent communicative programmes assume an even greater role for materials than has traditionally been given to them. It is therefore of considerable importance that appropriate techniques of materials evaluation are developed. Although almost everyone connected with a teaching-learning enterprise will have some interest in examining the materials, they will not all be asking the same questions. There is thus no single all-purpose approach to evaluation. If evaluation is not to be time-wasting and possibly self-defeating, the evaluator must not only ask relevant questions, but have access to an adequate amount of the sort of information that can help to answer them. As a brief illustration, a teacher planning a course is likely to want to know whether Book X suits the needs and interests of the students concerned. An inspector, on the other hand, might be more interested in the extent to which a course matches an official syllabus and in the ultimate level of language proficiency which learners demonstrate, irrespective of details of how this came about. Both of these viewpoints have generated a number of appropriate evaluation techniques (Low, 1987).

The present paper focuses on the position of the materials designer, who is in a rather different position from the teacher or inspector, being concerned to know how materials appropriate to a range of teaching-learning situations might be designed in the first place, and secondly, how small details could best be modified in the light of people's experiences with them. The types of evaluation developed to help teachers select course books, or researchers to assess ultimate proficiency, can only provide data of limited usefulness.

1 My thanks to Susan Fearn, Gregory James, Ken Methold, Celia Roberts and Mary Underwood for reading and making helpful comments on the earlier draft of this paper, which was presented at the Seminar on the Assessment of Language Teaching Materials, University of Exeter, August 29–31 1985.

136

In crude terms, the designer wants to know two things:

1 What sort of activities are likely to promote (or conversely to hinder) effective performance and learning?
2 How might such activities be constrained or elaborated, and organised in terms of a publishable course?

There have recently been several serious attempts to explore the effects of certain types of language-teaching task, much of this under the label of 'task-based' approaches to second language acquisition research. As an illustration, three of the more interesting findings, which have obvious implications for materials design, may be cited. These are i) that inter-actions between learners can prove as good as, or superior to, inter-actions between learners and native speakers, when it comes to preserving certain important features of native speaker conversations (Gass and Varonis, 1985); ii) that 'jigsaw' or 'two-way' oral tasks, where each participant does not have access to all the information, produce different types of conversation from tasks where all the information is pooled (Long, 1983; Long and Porter, 1985; Duff, 1985); and iii) that since we now have some idea how the ability to summarise accurately develops and roughly how long it takes (Brown and Day, 1983), it has become clear that summarising is an activity which should be handled with great care in courses (and tests) aimed at younger children.

On the question of how tasks and activities might profitably be controlled and structured, the designer can make use of a reasonably large body of work on syllabus design, most of which approaches the problem from a 'global' viewpoint. Much less help, however, is available when it comes to detailed decisions about how to construct, or modify, individual course units. This paper is an initial attempt to develop a design-oriented approach to the evaluation of the internal organisation of course units. It tackles the area at the level of 'Method' (Anthony, 1963), or 'Design' (Richards and Rodgers, 1982), because that is the level at which designers generally work. It also assumes a particular, and no doubt simplistic, model of the design process whereby designers i) begin with an idea of what they want to teach, ii) envisage the construction of a unit embodying the 'content', as a design problem to be solved, iii) consider various ways of solving it, iv) adopt the solution that seems preferable in the circumstances and v) edit the resulting unit. Ideally, this editing would involve at least three things: a) exploring the possibilities offered by the design solution chosen, b) removing tasks or language which might hinder learners and c) maximising the adaptability of the unit to different teaching-learning situations.

Course unit, learning unit and lesson

I shall try to use these terms in a consistent way. A 'learning unit' is defined by Gibbons (1980: 44) as the set of tasks felt by the designer to be necessary for the teaching of an item on a syllabus. A 'course unit', on the other hand, which is the focus of this paper, is an arbitrary structural unit which simply denotes a major division of a course. In practice, designers often tend to make course units equivalent to learning units, but there is no theoretical limitation; one course unit may contain several learning units, and one learning unit may be spread over several different course units. Both concepts are clearly distinguishable from a 'lesson', which denotes actual teaching and learning, and thus exists at the level of 'technique', or 'implementation', rather than method.

Design-oriented evaluation questions

The model of the materials-writing process outlined above suggests that design decisions may well be interrelated. A designer may at times envisage an entire unit as having a certain type of structure, or alternatively, she or he may find that the decision to do one particular activity in a certain way constrains the form and sequence of some, or even all, of the others in that unit. Either way, decisions about Exercise A are related to decisions about Exercise B. This conclusion suggests the formulation of a number of detailed design-oriented evaluation questions, such as:

1 What sort of shape does this unit have?
2 What is the rationale and justification for this shape?
3 Why do these exercises take the form that they do?
4 Why do they come at precisely this point and in this sequence?
5 Might other possible design solutions be preferable?

The rest of the paper consists of an attempt to find a way of answering these questions. It takes the form of an examination of six or seven possible approaches to structuring all or part of a course unit. An attempt is made to consider the implications of each, in terms of advantages and possible (or probable) pitfalls. Some attempt is also made to consider interactions between solutions.

Two sources of evidence are used to derive the comments which follow. First is my own experience of writing, teaching and evaluating language courses, plus discussions with other materials writers. Second is a detailed analysis of thirty-two language course books from about 1970 up to 1987. The database has been used in two ways: i) as a check on the validity and generalisability of several of the comments made; and ii) as a source of occasional frequency counts. It should perhaps be emphasised that the object of this paper is not to provide either a state-of-the-art summary of recent trends in course design (which would look very different), or an evaluation of specific texts (which should ideally be done in conjunction with classroom trials, as in Mitchell *et al.*, 1981). Its purpose is rather to help formulate a framework for text description and evaluation which emphasises the relatedness of the individual parts of a course unit.

Traditional unit structure

From the late 1960s or so, a large number of major courses have adopted a sort of four-phase structure. In this design, the course unit is considered identical to a learning unit. Although individual designers have made minor modifications and invented their own labels, Table 1 appears to be a reasonable summary of the general design.

TABLE I. TRADITIONAL UNIT STRUCTURE

---

1 Presentation a) of language to be learned.
             b) of language description.
2 Controlled exploitation.
3 Free exploitation (generalising to areas other than those in the presentation).
4 Synthesis (pulling disparate strands together and sometimes creating an 'end-product').

It is sometimes argued that there should be a revision phase at the start of each unit (for example Gibbons, 1980). The reason it is omitted from Table 1 is simply that only one of the courses examined had an explicit revision phase built into the students' book. Several texts had specific revision units, but that is more of an inter-, rather than intra-unit problem.[2]

Courses which adopt this 'traditional' design in an unmodified form tend to start with a reading or listening passage (frequently in the form of

2 As the system developed by C.R.E.D.I.F. has proved so influential in the design of language courses, it may be wondered whether it is compatible with that set out in Table 1. I would be inclined to put their *Présentation*, *Explication* and *Répétition* under my *Presentation* and their *Transposition*, *Restitution du commentaire*, *Exercises sur le film du sketch* and *Exercises en images* under my *Controlled Exploitation*. The function of role play is discussed further under 'The learner-as-observer syndrome'. This classification would seem to accommodate the modifications suggested by Gross and Mason (C.R.E.D.I.F., 1967: 8–10) for the teaching of young children, namely the abolition of repetition as a discrete phase. Many audio-visual practitioners have privately suggested the need for a revision phase before the *Présentation*, but there is no mention of one in C.R.E.D.I.F., 1967, 1970 or 1972 at least.

an invented dialogue) which leads directly to a set of comprehension questions and/or repetitions of the text, plus short grammatical drills. There is often an attempt to use the language in assorted situations and the unit may well end with a writing passage designed to bring back the main points of the unit and commonly set for homework (for example C.R.E.D.I.F.: *Voix et images de France*, 1962). Whether or not the designer makes suggestions to the teacher about how actual class periods should be structured, the fact that the phases are rigidly sequenced across the whole course unit makes it in practice very hard to have much structural (in the design-related, not grammatical, sense) variety in the course of a single lesson. This problem, which seems to be inherent in the design, has proved to be quite a serious one for audio-visual courses in particular. Unmodified traditional structure would seem to require fairly short units and thus to be more appropriate perhaps to add-in material than to complete courses.

The single presentation solution

Teaching material intended to last an academic year is frequently divided into about ten to twenty units (50 per cent of the general course books analysed had fewer than twenty units and 63 per cent fewer than twenty-five), a procedure which results in an easily readable contents page for potential buyers and/or users. More important perhaps, such a division also implies, that, unless it is intended as add-in material, each unit will have to contain a reasonable amount of new language. If a single presentation solution is adopted, then all of this 'reasonable amount' must be input at the same point in the unit. From a design point of view, it follows that the presentation passage or dialogue is going to have to be long, if the distribution of new information is not to be too dense. The likely classroom implication of a single long dialogue is that a disproportionate amount of class time is going to have to be devoted, without a break, to getting the students simply to comprehend it. This of course further implies that, if all ten to twenty units are to be covered within the year, little time will be left for the other phases, and that student concentration and motivation may suffer accordingly. The problem has arisen in particular in the case of class-based audio-lingual and audio-visual courses, but is not restricted to these and can occur, with the same degree of seriousness, in self-study materials. It can be reduced either by increasing the number of course units, or failing this, by otherwise decreasing the information density of the individual units.

A second, more general problem with the single presentation design is the fact that it can encourage the designer to restrict the focus of the unit to one set of people solving one single problem via one single text. A single presentation can make it difficult to have language (or problems) transferred across text types and formality levels, and thus it is unlikely to be highly suited to attempts to help learners understand how things are *not* used and to establish the limits of appropriateness. It is, of course, theoretically possible for a single presentation to show a relationship developing and changing as time passes and as new problems, social or otherwise, are resolved, and it is obviously possible to have new characters entering a text as the theme develops, but it is hard to see how the learner could be made aware of the concept of a speaker, deviously perhaps, deciding between various possible tactics and strategies in a range of related situations, without the text becoming impossibly long and complex.

It is fairly common to find courses which adopt a single presentation solution putting the presentation text (whether it involves listening or reading) at the start of the unit. Despite the possible advantage of the learner associating a fresh unit with fresh texts and ideas, there are two serious disadvantages to positioning a single presentation text at the very start of a unit. The first relates to the fact that the text concerned has to be such that the students cannot fully understand it, since the whole point is to introduce and contextualise all the new language for the unit. Unless special precautions are taken, one of two results (both equally undesirable) can easily follow. The first is that the students, far from being trained in the language and in 'text attack' strategies, are simply tested on how far they already understand the passage and on whether they can use a dictionary. This can be, and frequently is, partly remedied by 'pre-teaching' exercises, which introduce the new language, or sensitise students to new skills and topic areas. It is perhaps more important for the designer to develop explicit pre-teaching exercises for self-study courses than for class-based ones, since it is probably reasonable to assume that a trained teacher would create them, if there were none in the published book. The other possible result is that the teacher goes through the text in minute detail with the class. If a single presentation solution has also been adopted, then the initial comprehension phase can take up virtually the whole time available for the unit.

The second problem with the single-text-first solution is that there is a strong tendency for the text, particularly where it is an 'authentic' one, written by someone other than the course designer, to dictate the content, and frequently the structure, of the rest of the unit. For example, the comprehension questions and drills which follow the text tend to depend to a great extent on what happens to turn up in it. If it is also felt that the text, or dialogue, should be exploited in a representative way, in the sense that every two or three lines should have an associated drill or comprehension question, the exploitation material is almost bound to be constructed in a very piecemeal fashion. That is to say, individual questions and drills are likely to be unrelated to each other ('structurally discrete'), and have no clear social or discoursal purpose.

If the designer is justifying the material explicitly on the grounds that it relates to what people do and think when they use language, as is commonly the case with 'communicative' courses, then there is likely to be an attempt to make the unit task-based in some way. The problem of the discreteness and lack of pragmatic motivation associated with a single initial text can make it very difficult to design a structurally coherent task-based unit. For example, how many activities begin with an unprepared, possibly purposeless, reading of, or listening to, a text? A few, like reading an unexpected letter which has just been delivered, do, but not many. Even headlines, or in this case, postmarks and the handwriting, create expectations about the writer, the content and the sort of treatment likely to be given to it. If the questions and drills are based on the presentation text and not on tasks, they tend, as has just been noted, to be arbitrary, and teaching can easily be forced into a pattern of being text-specific rather than generalisable, bitty rather than coherent, and random rather than purposeful. If teaching the use of language is envisaged, in large measure at any rate, as teaching learners how to control language, then the text-first solution, particularly when combined with the single presentation idea, is really only likely to be appropriate for teaching such things as low-level syntactic rules, certain types of clause structure, or terms marking the internal structure of arguments; that is to say, things which do not require reference to speakers and listeners, interactions, other texts, or events in the outside world.

This is not, of course, to suggest that a text at the start of the unit can never serve a useful function. For example, C. Roberts (personal communication) has suggested that adult learners on vocationally-oriented courses often prefer to get a general overview of an event before working with the details. This seems eminently sensible where the unit will ask learners to initiate situational role plays and the initial text serves to orient the learners and allow them to indicate where they cannot cope. It should be noted that this is not a presentation text, as the term is usually understood, as what is being 'presented' is a skeletal frame of known language into which new language can be progressively inserted, and which can itself be systematically modified over the course of the unit, to cope with new strategies or alternative solutions to problems raised. Designs like this are better seen as involving multiple presentation, and are discussed in the next section.

Before doing so, however, it is worth pointing out that, where a single presentation text is felt to be an appropriate design, putting it, not at the start, but at the end of the unit can have several advantages. The designer can then take the disparate strands of the text and build, in various ways, towards longer and longer chunks of reading or listening, culminating in the text itself, which the learner should finally be able to read with considerable understanding. One problem which does tend to arise with putting the presentation text last is that it can sometimes prove hard to think of enough different techniques to use, and the temptation can become strong to adopt what we may call 'crossword' rather than 'natural language' processing. The designer begins to jumble letters, words and even sentences and asks the learner to solve the anagrams thus created. The problem lies in the fact that many people seem to have great difficulty thinking in this way, and, possibly as a result, it does not appear to form part of many real-life language or communication tasks. Personal experience suggests that the introduction of this mode of thinking can cause a serious slowing of pace and loss of motivation when the material is actually used in the classroom, even with postgraduate university students. As so few real-life tasks involve crossword processing, the course writer also faces a structural problem, in that adopting it makes the creation of meaningfully linked exploitation material very difficult indeed. Even so, despite the practical difficulties, the presentation-last design can prove preferable to presentation-first particularly in the case of self-study courses, where long presentation sections are often used, but no help from a teacher is available.

The multiple presentation solution

One way round the difficulties associated with single presentation formats is to opt for short amounts of presentation material spread throughout the unit. The main advantages of doing this are first, that information density can be controlled with great precision, and second, that the content, style and length of each chunk of text can be matched to expected characteristics (such as the concentration span) of the target learners. An additional bonus for the designer is the fact that it is comparatively much easier to edit short passages (after test trials, for example) than long ones, which are likely to involve far more complex patterns of cohesion and coherence. Moreover, the possibility, and indeed the desirability, of controlling the relations between the individual presentations is also highlighted and pushed to the fore in a way that is not always true where one is dealing with the component parts of a single presentation. It becomes important to decide which will come first, which second, and why. The sequencing will depend on the nature and strength of the desired relationship. Storylines and tasks can be used which provide real-life (or at any rate extralinguistic) justifications for locating things at specific points, and multi-text complexes can be devised such that texts reinforce each other, contrast with each other, involve jumps of formality or style, contradict each other, build patterns of things some-times hinted at, sometimes asserted and so on. Multiple presentation thus provides an escape from the dichotomy that at least some designers feel exists between an 'initial model text' and a 'freely negotiated interaction' which uses 'self-selected data' (Hawkes, 1983: 100). What is more, it does so in a way that provides maximum flexibility and maximum control.

The advantages of the multiple presentation solution can be reduced and even virtually negated under certain circumstances, however. An approach occasionally adopted (for example C.R.E.D.I.F. 1970, *Voix et images de France, Leçons de transition*) is to provide a long presentation dialogue and to divide it into sections. Each section is considered as a separate learning unit and all relevant phases are applied sequentially to it. The problem arises when the course fails to provide adequately for the later phases, especially free exploitation and synthesis. There is super-ficially multiple presentation, but a) the absence of the later phases creates an undue quantity of highly controlled language work and b) the absence of links between the presentations, other than the fact that the extracts happen to come from the same text, remove most of the discourse- and task-related advantages of the multiple presentation. A related problem is where the unit contains nothing else but the presen-tation text, plus perhaps a few drills. This form of 'presentation-dominated design' can and does occur in both class-based and self-study courses, but is likely to be appropriate only where the material is intended primarily as add-in textual enrichment. It is perhaps worth pointing out that many of the 'listening first' approaches to language teaching such as Total Physical Response (Asher, 1972, Asher *et al.* 1974) in fact require large amounts of exploitation and, surprisingly perhaps, would not work well with 'presentation-dominated' designs.[3]

Feeding and bleeding solutions

One important dimension of structuring either a course unit or a learning unit is the nature of the relationships between presentation material and

---

3 Chaudron (1983: 722), in the context of adult special-purpose courses, makes an interesting suggestion about the inverse situation, namely the effects of an over-emphasis on controlled exploitation. He hypothesises that where the learners are working with the (non-linguistic) content of the materials outside the language classes, and are thus fairly familiar with them, the expected effect would be for even semi-controlled exercises to be performed more mechanically than the designer originally intended. However, he also argues, surprisingly perhaps, that this may in fact be highly appropriate for many special purpose situations, as automatic recognition of the force of certain types of utterance by the learners could well be one of the major objectives of the course.

any accompanying exercises, and between the exercises themselves. The terms 'feeding' and 'bleeding' were introduced by Kiparsky in 1968 to denote the implications of two ways of sequencing phonological rules in a traditional generative system. With a bit of poetic licence, the two terms, particularly the idea of 'feeding', can be quite helpful when describing the sequencing of parts of a unit. A loose definition would be to say that an exercise 'feeds (into)' another if it provides something that is needed for the second one. A stricter, and possibly more useful, requirement would be that the second exercise could not be done (by all or most learners) unless the first had already been completed. An example using the looser requirement would be an exercise introducing the difference between 'Yours faithfully' and 'Yours sincerely' which could be said to feed into a subsequent exercise asking for a particular type of letter to be written. If the relationship were to be feeding according to the stricter requirement, the first exercise might need to contain the relevant information about the addressee required for the letter in the second exercise. If a unit is described as 'task-based' by the designer, then one would, it seems to me at any rate, expect to find most or all of the exercises feeding each other in either or both of the ways being suggested.

Once the decision has been taken to make use of feeding relations, a whole range of new possibilities opens up. The simplest is a straight-forward linear series, where each exercise feeds directly into the one following. If a multiple presentation solution is adopted, then presen-tation passages are simply slotted into the line, with the addition of appropriate continuity material, such as 'At this point your aunt enters the room and the three of you argue violently'. A variation on the linear sequence is the multi-text task which perhaps starts with one text, but where at each subsequent stage another, or perhaps even two more, are fed in. At various points the learner must integrate, or otherwise make use of, several texts concurrently. This can mean asking the learner to change direction, or possibly re-edit previously introduced text(s) to cope either with new arguments and different perspectives, or else with the necessity of modifying specific aspects of language (e.g. formality level). In this way, the learner is asked to cope with greater and greater subtlety, but the density of new information is controlled. A brief outline of the structure of a simple possible multi-text sequence is given in Figure 1.

Although feeding would seem to be eminently suited to courses labelled 'communicative', there can be problems. These are considered together with storylines and other lines of development in 'The storyline solution'.

It is less clear what a 'bleeding' relationship between two or more exercises/texts might usefully be understood to mean. It is obviously not just the absence of any observable link, but ought, if the spirit of the

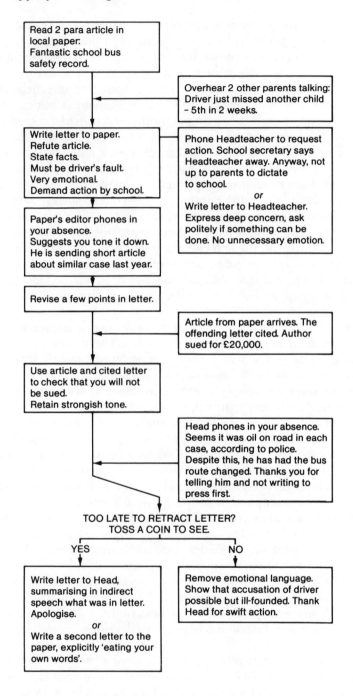

Figure 1   Outline of a possible multi-text sequence

term is to be retained, to be a relationship such that the first exercise takes away the value of the second and renders it, if not impossible, at least worthless. For example, the solution to a problem might be given before the problem itself, a definition introduced far too late to be of use, or a hint given about the ultimate outcome of a task or interaction, thereby removing all motivation on the part of the learners to try to persuade or convince the person(s) involved. Few designers would aim at this intentionally, but it is certainly something for which materials should be checked.

In practice, of course, the distinction between a feeding and a bleeding relationship is unlikely to be as clear-cut, when used for the purposes of course evaluation, as it is in phonology. If an exercise is used to provide guidance for the one following, this would be described as feeding. However, it is quite possible that the addition of one extra, inappropriate, word would give too great an indication of the answer to the following exercise. A serious element of bleeding would thus be introduced. Whether the result is described by the evaluator as primarily feeding or bleeding, however, would ultimately be a matter of personal judgement.

The writing-last solution

This is a fairly popular option in both general language courses and add-in materials. The unit ends with a writing task, such as an essay or a letter, which pulls together the grammatical points covered in the rest of the unit. Several problems frequently arise, though as the device concerns the end of the unit only, the unwanted effects do not cause major structural problems with the unit as a whole, and tend to be, as it were, masked. If one of the aims of the course is, in fact, to teach writing (beyond the level of teaching control over the script), then a) written language needs to be consistently and purposefully compared and contrasted with speech and b) the learner needs to be helped to cope with texts of differing types and of varying degrees of complexity. This means that model texts are needed, and a reasonable number of them. It also implies that learners are frequently going to need to move back and forth between the various model and presentation texts and texts of their own construction. Even this is unlikely to prove adequate for any but the most minimal purposes, and learners will need guidance about how certain types of reader might react in given circumstances to what has been written. The exploitation of the multiple presentation solution to provide multi-text tasks, as suggested in the previous section, would seem ideally suited to teaching control over written language in particular. It then becomes a relatively simple matter to devise preliminary activities concerned with the content, style, purpose, and strategies to be adopted.

Various devices have been adopted at times to mitigate the effects of the writing-last solution in its crudest form. For example, the problem of minimal feedback by the designer on the texts that the learners produce is sometimes lessened by either making the writing itself partially guided (via such devices as a skeleton, or framework, into which relevant expressions are slotted and perhaps modified), or by introducing a guided exercise in front of the final writing task. Though both solutions are fairly common, neither gives the learner much idea of the ways in which written language differs from spoken language, particularly in situations where the two interact. More important, neither solution allows learners to explore the implications of what they have written with respect to the material contained in the rest of the unit, or allows them to see how else they might have approached the task. In essence then, unless precautions are taken, the unit-final writing task can easily end up as a summarising exercise, which functions more as a test than a teaching device, and which is structurally poorly integrated into the unit.

It is perhaps worth digressing slightly at this point to consider how improvements might be made in one of the problem areas mentioned above. The question of whether or not to differentiate between spoken and written language in a particular course is beyond the scope of this paper, but if one does want to do so, the design solutions discussed above suggest a possibility which could be used even at beginner, or near-beginner, level. Instead of asking for a final written summary of a presentation dialogue, the unit could involve a series of multi-text activities which involved the production, not necessarily of coherent texts, but of short, purposeful notes. These might derive from a variety of linked presentation texts such as telephone calls, announcements, short letters, or fragments of conversation. Clearly, each set of notes could be used to interpret further texts, aid the progress of further tasks, or lead to various types of understanding, erroneous planning or communication breakdowns. Learners could also be asked to help repair interactions by checking whether their notes were accurate, in order to determine who was at fault. Thus, exercises and presentation texts could be related without too much difficulty in quite complex feeding relationships. By exploiting processes of comparison and contrast, and by varying the type of notes requested, longer and longer texts could be built as the course progressed, each set having a specified purpose, being geared to a specific readership and relying on appropriate text-summarising conventions. This solution has the additional merit that it allows the designer (or the class teacher) to decide how far writing need be taught, especially in the early stages, via full sentences, with all the extra problems that this brings (see Low and Lau, 1983 for further discussion of this point). Integrating writing tasks with a multiple presentation design has three advantages over the writing-last solution, in that it offers considerable design flexibility, a high degree of 'fine control', and also allows learners to explore the implications of what they write.

The storyline solution

There are so many ways in which coherent lines of development can be put through teaching material that the following section is no more than a brief outline of a number of basic approaches and the expectations they create.[4]

One fairly commonly adopted device, used primarily to provide an obvious link between the units of a course, is to have a story text which runs the length of the materials, with one episode per unit (for example O'Neill *et al.*, 1971, *Kernel Lessons Intermediate*). In such a case, it is important for each episode to be sufficiently self-contained to be readable on its own. This is crucial when designing adult courses likely to be used in evening classes, for example, where few individuals will in all probability attend every class, or for courses which happen to have long units. The content of the story is equally important. As most learners below advanced level will not have enough language to make it possible to have a story with much depth or subtlety as regards emotion and characterisation, it could well prove preferable to have something other than a downgraded novel running through the units. If that something else could be integrated with both the aims and content of the course, and not just the lexis and syntax of the unit(s) concerned, then it is likely to prove more acceptable. An interesting sidelight on episodic story texts is the unfavourable reaction sometimes accorded by adult second language learners to the use of complicated detective-style plots. The negative reactions that I have experienced seem to stem from a) the fact that it is very hard to remember intricate details when the reading of two episodes can be separated by several weeks, b) an unwillingness to spend valuable time revising something which is felt to be a not very relevant or integrated adjunct to the course and c) a general inability to identify with the characters, due to their often inevitable psychological shallowness and resulting lack of credibility.

An alternative to having a story in addition to presentation material is to make the presentation text itself into a story. The problem here is that the very fact that the presentation material is completely self-contained makes the task of designing a structurally integrated unit, where the presentation is but a part, very difficult indeed. That is to say, giving presentation material the form of a coherent story can make it hard to devise purposeful and/or motivating exploitation material. So, while a

4 Some further aspects of storyline structuring, though in the context of language proficiency test designs, rather than language teaching materials, can be found in Low (1986).

story presentation may be perfectly appropriate as a one-off solution, or for certain types of add-in material, it may well not prove very suitable as the basic pattern for a whole series of units.

The combination of the two solutions, resulting in an inter-unit storyline occurring as the presentation text in each unit, can have quite complex effects. On the negative side, the problems of memorising the plot, avoiding boredom due to lack of characterisation, or just overexposure to the same storyline, remain, and the difficulty of creating an effective climax is exacerbated. Moreover, it is not at all clear that resolving the question of overexposure (for example by restricting the story to alternate units) will not make it correspondingly harder to remember details of the plot. On the positive side, however, the extended storyline makes it rather easier for later sections of a unit to introduce extra information on the characters and/or extra texts which resolve mysteries created in the main presentation. An example of this is *Track* 1, Unit 22 (Palmer and Byrne, 1982), where a letter resolves a mystery built up in Units 18, 20 and the story/dialogue presentation of Unit 22. Moreover, quite complex feeding relations could easily be built such that extra texts actually made the learner revise or reinterpret the main presentation.

It was pointed out earlier that there is a version of the multiple presentation solution, where a single, coherent presentation text is divided into a series of shorter segments, and the phases of comprehension and controlled exploitation are applied to each segment in turn, giving the effect of a continuous recycling. In this case, one might wonder what would happen if the designer chose to structure the whole text as a story. If the recycling period was short, then the narrative structure would stand some chance of emerging, but if the cycle of explaining, questioning, repeating and drilling took a long time, then this, plus the continual focusing on linguistic form rather than on meaning or rhetorical effect, would tend to negate any motivational advantages which might be gained in other situations by using a story. The aspect of the story which one might expect to cause the most problems would be the ending, as it would be extremely hard to create a climax which, after all the controlled exploitation, would have any effect at all on the learners. One way round the problem might be to let learners create their own endings, or select from a set of possible endings, as is sometimes done in first-language storybooks, though even here, it is hard to see how, without some help and some idea of purpose, inventing one's own ending would avoid many of the problems already discussed in connection with the writing-last solution.

It has generally been assumed up to this point that the presentation and exploitation material can usually be linked together to simulate a (controlled) progression through a task or story, and that this, if done well, can be a very useful device, especially where one wishes to base the teaching on context effects and/or on the idea of individuals trying out and modifying strategies in the course of such activities as holding conversations or writing documents. In these cases, the design involves putting one or more lines of development through an entire course unit, and not just through part of a unit or an individual text. However, the fully integrated storyline solution is not necessarily the optimal one in all situations, despite the (generally desirable) emphasis it places on true multiple presentation, the use of feeding relations between exercises, controlled text build-ups and monitored, purposeful feedback to the learner. The major problem involves the interaction of the course unit with the actual lessons taught. A large number of special purpose courses, and almost all courses used for evening classes, need to be reasonably modular, since attendance is erratic and the learners generally spend the time between lessons concentrating on things other than the structure of the course units! In this sort of situation, it is frequently very difficult to maintain a storyline successfully across two or more lessons, and a unit structure composed of several short lines of development can often prove far more successful. A second reason why total integration via a line of development may require modification is the simple fact that from time to time people, being human, like doing something different, just for variety. Therefore, a unit with odd bits and pieces which provide short interludes of light relief can sometimes be more successful than one which may appear to a detached reviewer to be structurally and pedagogically perfect.

While this last point is unlikely to arouse much in the way of violent argument, it does have a less obvious and considerably more controversial corollary, at inter-unit rather than intra-unit level. It is frequently felt that all units of a course should be structured in an identical way, thus divorcing the structure of the unit totally from its content and its purpose. Where a justification for uniform structuring is given, it tends to be based on either, or both, of two claims. The first is that an ideal teaching method has been discovered and is simply being applied to all areas of the course; the second is that, if all units are similar, then the learners do not have to devote valuable lesson time adapting to the methodology and to working out what sort of response is required of them. But, if courses should be structured to allow for variation, and if methodological detail is to be justified with reference to what people do with language outside classrooms, then the arguments in favour of uniform structuring would seem to be far less convincing. One arrives at a similar conclusion if the criterion of 'pluralism' (proposed by Stevick, 1971 and Young, 1980, which holds that learners get bored if everything in a course is continually done in the same way) is adopted and applied to the concept of unit structure. The preferable conclusion would appear to be that structuring should be appropriate to the unit in question, unless a positive overriding reason in favour of uniform structuring can be found.

The learner-as-observer syndrome

If a text or task is introduced into a unit, then the designer needs to think about how the learner is going to be asked to relate to it. This is fairly obvious in the case of a task, such as writing a letter, since training the student to cope with the various demands of letter writing is likely to be one of the major objectives of the unit. A format commonly adopted in this sort of case is that of partial simulation; the learners are given a guided tour through the task, having things commented on and perhaps explained at some points, and being asked at others to make decisions which take into account what has been covered thus far, both situationally and linguistically. Although they are at times observers of what is happening, at each decision point they are themselves actively involved in creating pathways through interactions and tasks. How keen individual learners are on the decisions they must take, depends upon the choice of task and the way it is handled, but the possibility exists of limiting the degree to which learners are simply observers describing what happens in the texts in a detached way. Where each learner is being him or herself, there may well be no serious problems, but many people do appear to dislike (sometimes quite violently) playing the role of someone of a different age, sex, or personality from themselves and attempts to involve older students in particular, by asking them to change personality, can go badly wrong. Hawkes (1983: 95) argues that such exercises should be flexible enough to be 'turned around' or adapted to the personality of individual learners, but an easier (for the designer) and more controllable solution might simply be to provide alternative pathways at the particular points in the unit where personality change exercises occur.

Turning from the relationship between learners and tasks to that between learners and presentation texts and drills, the same design logic can be applied. If, for example, the presentation text consists of a discussion between three people about the details of a space flight and the learner is asked first to comprehend, perhaps by answering questions put by the teacher, then to repeat and finally to substitute bits of the language, or perhaps to write a description of what was said, then the learner is acting as an observer and is quite uninvolved in creating the texts and resolving the situations. The same is true of reading a story, especially if one does not identify strongly with the characters. If this is a consistent pattern through the course, the advantages which may be gained by the use of partial simulation are simply not obtained and the learners are likely to become increasingly bored and frustrated. While it is probably true that the learner-as-observer position is necessary for part of the course (see Low, in press, for a discussion about certain metaphors, like 'hit the roof', which appear to be restricted to reports of action, rather than performances) it would seem to make sense, even in the most 'observer-centred' of Special Purpose courses, to alternate between this and a position where the learner is personally involved; indeed the jumps from one position to the other offer considerable scope for creative exploitation.

Not infrequently, an attempt is made to reduce the effects of the learner-as-observer position by adding in role-playing exercises, arguing that these necessarily involve the learners actively. It has already been noted that many learners seem to take exception to role plays involving personality changes. Another problem is that if the role play is given no justification (there being no real reason why the learner should act out such a situation at the point in the unit at which it occurs), then she or he may well have difficulty performing. A third problem, especially in a 'communicative course', is with instructions like 'Imagine you are walking along the pavement, see a fight and try and break it up. What do you say?' (taken from a public examination paper). Contextual information is crucial here, yet all necessary clues are missing. The result is hard for many people to act out even in their first language.

Conclusion

The assessment of language teaching materials, even when supplemented, as it should be, by empirical studies, remains, like the evaluation of hi-fi equipment, something of a 'black art'. Designing appropriate materials is not a science; it is a strange mixture of imagination, insight and analytic reasoning, and this fact must be recognised when the materials are assessed. The purpose of the present paper has therefore been to suggest, for one specific area of course evaluation, a method of working which is compatible with the design process as I understand it. The method is based on envisaging structural possibilities in the design of a course unit and on the likely implications of specific choices that are made. It also requires the evaluator to spot ways in which a designer has recognised the existence of a problem and tried to avoid it, or has modified a common design solution, in order to tailor a course to a specific learning situation. The design solutions discussed in the paper do not permit an exhaustive description of the structure of a unit, or the prediction of every single possible problem. But they do make meaningful cross-course comparisons feasible, allowing the evaluator to note, for example, how far new ideas about language teaching are in fact reflected in the structure of the teaching materials.

At several points in the paper, the argument has had to take inter-unit matters into consideration, but without the possibility of relating them to a coherent body of research concerning inter-unit design possibilities. As inter-unit and intra-unit designs are demonstrably interrelated, future research might fruitfully extend current work on ways in which certain syllabus types might be implemented to include general structural possibilities and their related problems.

10 Beyond language learning: perspectives on materials design

Andrew Littlejohn and Scott Windeatt

In this paper we want to set out a number of perspectives on materials design which focus on learning outcomes other than those relating to the acquisition of the second/foreign language. The idea of looking beyond the immediate, stated objectives of educational materials is not a new one. Dewey, for example, remarked in 1938:

> Perhaps the greatest of all pedagogical fallacies is the notion that a person learns only the particular thing he is studying at the time.
>
> (1938: 48)

More recently, however, Jackson (1968) has introduced the idea of a 'hidden curriculum' within teaching, referring to learning outcomes apart from those intended in the 'manifest curriculum'. Similar ideas have been expressed by a number of other writers, who see a 'sub-surface' (and frequently pernicious) element to teaching or teaching materials. Freire (1972), for example, is in no doubt as to the 'philosophy of man' projected by conventional approaches to adult literacy:

> We begin with the fact, inherent in the idea and use of the primer, that it is the teacher who chooses the words and proposes them to the learner. Insofar as the primer is the mediating object between the teacher and the students, and the students are to be 'filled' with the words the teachers have chosen, one can easily detect a first important dimension of the image of man which here begins to emerge. It is the profile of a man whose consciousness is 'spatialized', and must be 'filled' or 'fed' in order to know.
>
> (1972: 23)

This point has been developed by a number of educational sociologists and psychologists who see important implications of a hidden or 'latent' curriculum. Writers such as Bourdieu and Passeron (1977), Apple (1979, 1981) and Giroux (1983) (discussed in Auerbach and Burgess, 1985) argue, like Freire, that a curriculum is not neutral but reflects a particular view of social order, implicitly or explicitly. According to Bloom (1972: 343), this hidden curriculum is far more effective than the manifest, planned curriculum because 'it is so pervasive and consistent over the many years in which our students attend schools'.

One of the main problems in making claims for the impact of a hidden curriculum is the determination of a direct link between *any* teaching and learning outcomes. Within the field of language education, the existence of a gap between 'teacher's input' and 'learner's intake' is already well acknowledged (see Corder, 1981) and various theories have been developed to account for this mismatch (for example Krashen's notion of an 'affective filter', 1982). If such problems beset an analysis of the impact of the manifest curriculum then one needs to approach with even greater caution the suggestion that it is possible to discover other 'non-language-learning' learning outcomes within materials.

The key variable in arguing for additional learning outcomes is the unpredictable nature of each student's interpretation of a set of materials and their own personal reaction to it. In attempting to account for why aspects of the hidden curriculum are seemingly not 'intaken' by learners, writers such as Apple (1981, quoted in Gordon 1984) have introduced the idea of student 'resistance' to any aspect of teaching or teaching materials:

> Schools are not 'merely' institutions of reproduction, institutions where the overt and covert knowledge that is taught molds students into passive beings ... Student reinterpretation, at best only partial acceptance and often outright rejection of the planned and unplanned meanings of schools are more likely.
>
> (Apple, 1981: 30)

It seems clear, however, that although one cannot specify with any degree of confidence what may actually be learnt from a specific set of materials, it should be possible to argue for a particular view of what may be *available* to be learnt, suggesting a broader basis of 'input' from which 'intake' may result. As has been indicated above, this broader basis will relate to a number of areas, to which we now turn.

Areas available for learning

Exactly what may be available for learning will, of course, vary from materials to materials, learner to learner, classroom group to classroom group. In examining materials, however, we have found it useful to focus on six main areas. These are: 1 'general' or 'subject' knowledge offered in the materials; 2 views of what 'knowledge' is and how it is acquired; 3 views of what is involved in language learning; 4 role relations within the classroom; 5 opportunities for the development of cognitive abilities; and 6 values and attitudes presented in the materials.

'General' or 'subject' knowledge offered in the materials

One of the most obvious ways in which materials may offer opportunities for additional learning is in the 'carrier content' that is used as a basis for language work. Most frequently, this carrier content is fictional in nature, involving imaginary characters in imaginary situations. Materials may, however, serve as a vehicle for several different types of content, such that they address wider 'educational' goals. A common way of doing this is through the inclusion of texts which offer information about some aspect of the natural or social world or about famous people, as the preponderance of passages about volcanoes, wild animals and Elvis Presley in ELT materials shows. Cook (1983), however, outlines wider possibilities for 'real content' in materials, including i) another academic subject; ii) student-contributed content; iii) language itself; iv) literature; v) culture; and vi) 'interesting facts'. To Cook's list there would seem to be at least two other potential categories which we may add. The first is 'learning itself' and the second is 'specialist content'.

Little has yet been made of 'learning' as content for FLT materials but it seems likely that in the wake of the currently popular notion of 'learner training' we will see an increasing number of texts and tasks in course materials which deal with aspects of the learning process. An example of such a task is from one recent course book, where an attempt is made to integrate 'learning to learn' into 'learning English'.

Learn to study

Everybody loves to hate homework, but it's important when you're learning a language. It gives time to think and to experiment. There are basically three types of homework: learning for a test, reading or listening to prepare for the next lesson, writing of some kind to practise writing letters etc. in English, or to revise words and grammar.

1 Look at the suggestions below. They are about homework. Tick (√) those items in each box that you do, and cross (×) those that you don't do.

1 Learning

a ☐ Check you understand what you're learning.

b ☐ Learn a little often; don't learn everything at once.

c ☐ Find ways of learning that suit you. (Not everybody learns in the same way.)

d ☐ Learn with the help of clear notes.

e ☐ Don't learn when you're tired.

f ☐ Work with a friend, ask each other questions.

In the case of 'specialist content', however, there exists a wide selection of 'specific purposes' materials which include texts and tasks concerned with 'professional topics'. The principal problem with much of these, however, is that they are 'frequently of such a conventional or simple-minded nature as to fail to interest the learner' (Hutchinson and Waters, 1984: 112). In other words, they generally present learners with aspects of their profession with which they are already familiar and therefore offer no opportunities for additional, non-language, learning. To remedy this, Hutchinson and Waters argue for the use of content about which the learners have 'a reasonable background knowledge, but with a new or unusual slant to it' (ibid.). Just how 'new or unusual' the material is will, of course, depend very much on each individual's own experience, but greater opportunities for additional learning outcomes may be provided through the design of materials which involve the learner in working with both the language and the content.

An example of an attempt to offer additional 'special purpose' learning is a recent course book for developing abilities in business correspondence through simulations. During the simulations, learners, working in groups representing companies, are required to make business decisions and then write letters to the appropriate 'company'. The following is an example of a role card from one simulation which the learners receive after their company (a soft drinks manufacturer) has decided to scrap their existing bottling machinery due to maintenance costs and order a new disposable bottle system.

Tasks like these aim to not only improve the learners' ability to communicate in the foreign language but to also increase their understanding of the complexities of the target language situation, dispelling

———— *9* ————

You have just seen this article in the newspaper.

> ## NEW LAW AGAINST DISPOSABLE BOTTLES
> The government has passed a new law forbidding the use of disposable bottles for soft drinks from the end of next year. The new law aims to reduce the amount of pollution caused by bottles thrown away with...

Decide what you are going to do now and then:
- send telexes to make sure you have a working bottling system;
- send any necessary letters to cancel an order you have made.

the myth of an unproblematic, clear-cut world which FL materials often seem to inhabit.

Views of what 'knowledge' is and how it is acquired

Stubbs (1976: 94, drawing on Young, 1971) points out that the selection, classification and relative weighting given to subjects in the school timetable may define for the pupil what counts as legitimate educational knowledge and what boundaries are held to exist between subjects. In this respect, one may view the publication of FLT materials in discrete, self-contained textbooks as both a consequence and reinforcement of established subject divisions since, generally speaking, FLT must not be seen to cross into the domains of other school subjects. This fact alone explains why much FLT material appears bland and contentless.

It is not, however, only in respect of boundaries between school subjects that the nature of FLT materials may be significant for a definition of knowledge. In connection with the study of teacher-pupil dialogue, Stubbs (cited above) argues that we can see how knowledge is divided up into topics and presented to the pupils as discrete 'facts' or as more open-ended suggestions or hypotheses. In that teaching materials may be held to frame what goes on in the classroom, therefore, the organisation of the materials themselves, as well as the kinds of activities and tasks found within them, will contribute towards forming the pupils' perception of the nature of school knowledge and how this knowledge is arrived at.

Nowhere is this moɪ ᵓ evident than in the teaching of grammar. Despite the fact that grammarians typically feel unhappy about making definitive statements about what constitutes a 'correct' grammatical explanation, the image certainly held by most learners and probably most teachers is that it is indeed possible to make clear, unequivocal statements of grammatical rules. This image almost certainly derives from the tone and organisation of most grammar books, which, in the main, admit no suggestion that the 'rules' given are but mere hypotheses. The following extract, taken from a popular grammar book, illustrates this:

Conditional sentences

Conditional sentences have two parts: the if-clause and the main clause. In the sentence *If it rains I shall stay at home* 'If it rains' is the if-clause, and 'I shall stay at home' is the main clause.

There are three kinds of conditional sentences. Each kind contains a different pair of tenses. With each type certain variations are possible but students who are studying the conditional for the first time should ignore these and concentrate on the basic forms.

This contrasts quite markedly with another grammar reference book, which seems untypical in its lack of confidence and its admission that no system of categorisation is watertight.

A common simplification is to say that there are three types of conditional sentences, based on three ways of combining tenses in the *if*-clause and main clause — namely: **1** 'future': <If I see Tom, I will tell him.> **2** improbable/unreal: <If I saw him, I would tell him.> **3** 'unfulfilled past': <If I had seen him, I would have told him.> But this arbitrarily suggests that all other tense combinations are exceptions, which they are not.

Another way of looking at conditionals is to consider them in terms of:
Open (or real) condition (6.22) — open because the events described are a real possibility, already or in the future.
Hypothetical (or 'rejected') condition (6.24) where the condition is 'rejected' as unreal *now* — although in some cases they could happen later (see below).

'Factual' views of knowledge, as in the first grammar extract above, are found quite extensively throughout a number of contemporary course books organised according to a functional syllabus. Here the suggestion given is that it is possible to make definitive statements about the meaning and value a particular sequence of words will have. This extract is taken from a widely used book for advanced students.

> Here are some useful ways of requesting. They are marked with stars, according to how polite they are.

> ★   *Hey, I need some change for the phone.*
> *Oh, dear, I haven't got any change for the phone.*
> *I don't seem to have any change on me.*

> ★★   *You haven't got 10p, have you?*
> *Have you got 10p, by any chance?*

> ★★★   *You couldn't lend me 50p, could you?*
> *Do you think you could lend me 50p?*
> *I wonder if you could lend me 50p?*

> ★★★★   *Would you mind lending me £1?*
> *If you could lend me £1, I'd be very grateful.*

> ★★★★★   *Could you possibly lend me your typewriter?*
> *Do you think you could possibly lend me your typewriter?*
> *I wonder if you could possibly lend me your typewriter?*

> ★★★★★★   *I hope you don't mind my asking, but I wonder if it might be at all possible for you to lend me your car?*

Surveying the organisation and content of most language teaching materials one is reminded of Freire's comment (quoted above), which suggests that, in literacy materials at least, man is seen as something which needs to be 'filled'. Certainly the view of knowledge presented in most language teaching materials, with their emphasis on rules, patterns and definite statements of meaning, seems to rest on what Popper (1972: 61–2) has called 'a bucket theory':

> Our mind is a bucket which is originally empty, or more or less so, and into this bucket material enters through our senses ... and accumulates and becomes digested ... The important thesis of the bucket theory is that ... Knowledge is conceived of as information consisting of things, or thing-like entities in our bucket ...
> Knowledge is, first of all, *in* us: it consists of information which is in us and which we have managed to absorb.

If 'knowledge' in language learning is seen largely as consisting of 'thing-like entities' it is not surprising that the most frequently occurring exercise types in FLT materials focus on the accumulation and manipulation of items. Gap-filling exercises, pattern practice drills and grammatical transformations would all seem to relate in this respect to the same underlying view of knowledge as built up through conscious absorption and manipulation. Indeed, this view of how knowledge is acquired would seem to be so strong that any methodology which emphasises a non-analytic route to a foreign language may be deemed unacceptable. Referring to Krashen's (1982) distinction between 'acquisition' (characterised by exposure to and use of the language) and 'learning' (characterised by the study of grammatical rules), Ager (1985: 14) says:

> ... if we 'acquire' language we do not exercise the intellect; only when we 'learn' is the intellect engaged. And if we equate 'learning' with 'education', then language acquisition, as opposed to language learning, would have no place in the schools.

The important point to make here is that it is not the efficiency or otherwise of 'acquisition-based' or 'natural' approaches to foreign language teaching which is in question. It is simply that, within the context of the established view of knowledge and how that knowledge is to be attained, such approaches are literally 'uneducational'.

Views of the nature of language learning

The discussion above of how materials relate to a view of knowledge has already outlined some ways in which language learning may be similar in nature to other subjects in the school curriculum. Depending on the materials concerned, an image may be projected of, for example, language learning as largely a matter of item accumulation (lexis, idioms, etc.) and the manipulation of rules of structure and/or use. It is likely, however, that the actual procedures of classroom work and the topics involved will be instrumental in defining for the learner what 'learning English' involves. In that most FLT materials are normally organised into 'units' or 'lessons' with a repetitive pattern of sub-sections labelled according to the content or type of activity involved, learners may see learning a foreign language as involving the development of abilities in the specified content areas or activity types. Their perception of what is easy or difficult, enjoyable or unenjoyable, boring or interesting about learning a language may thus be expressed in terms of what they are required to do in each sub-section.

One useful way to get a picture of what view of language learning a set of materials may project is to read through the sub-section headings in each unit and to look closely at the kind of things which learners are required to do. As an example, below are the section headings and rubrics from one ELT course book, together with brief notes of description in italics.

Reading 1
  episode of a continuing story
Comprehension Questions
  A Choose the correct answer. *multiple-choice*
  B Complete each of these sentences with a word from the
     passage. *gap-filling*
Drill Exercises
  A *model 'prompt and response' on a grammar area*
     Now answer in the same way.
     further prompts given
  B *model 'prompt and response' on another grammar area*
     Now answer in the same way.
     further prompts given
Reading 2
  passage related to the theme of Reading 1
  Now answer these questions.
Writing Exercises
  A *model sentence*
     Now write sentences similar to the model sentence using the
     key words given below.
  B Make 5 sentences from this table.
     substitution table

Punctuation
punctuation rule given
Put the (apostrophe/comma/full stops etc.) in the following
sentences.

Assuming that classroom work is restricted to use of the material in the above book in the manner intended, one can hypothesise as to what the likely effect will be for a learner's definition of what learning English involves. At its simplest level, the picture that may be presented by the above sequence of sections is that learning English involves reading texts in detail, attending to items of vocabulary, rules of grammar and punctuation, and writing isolated sentences. At a deeper level, however, it can be seen that each time the learners are required to do something, the activity involves closely following a model or referring back to a text. One can say, therefore, that an underlying message being transmitted to the learners is that to learn English one must complete a series of short, controlled exercises that require reproduction of already presented linguistic facts with little in the way of personal creativity, expression or interpretation.

A slightly different view of what learning English involves is presented by another course book. In this book, there is no consistent sequence of sub-sections in each chapter. Below are the headings from a sample chapter, together, once again, with brief notes of description in italics.

Dialogue
a girl offers a sweet to a boy and a girl
1 Offer and accept.
model 4 line substitution dialogue between 'You' and 'Friend'
followed by labelled pictures of sweets
2 Offer and refuse.
as 1 but this time 'Friend' refuses
3 Offer and accept or refuse.
as 1 and 2, but this time 'Friend' can accept or refuse
4 Thank you for the ice cream, the crisps and the chewing gum.
as 1–3, but 'You' thanks 'Friend' for the items in the picture
5 Write and thank a friend for the following:
Referring to the pictures of sweets, learners complete the
sentence: 'Thank you very much for the...'

In contrast with the first course book headings and rubrics, the above chapter headings suggest no element of 'grammar' in language learning, nor any overt concern with vocabulary and punctuation. The suggestion in this course book is that learning English essentially involves learning fixed phrases into which one can slot different items. For the learner in the classroom, the material may distinguish itself from the first course book by its emphasis on pairwork throughout, but underlying the series of exercises we have a similar view of language learning as largely involving reproduction of the material presented in the book, working within the strict guidelines of each exercise type. Popper's 'bucket' image and Freire's 'spatialised man' would seem to be relevant here.

A quite different picture emerges from looking at a third course book, this time aimed at a somewhat higher language level. Once again, the units have no consistent pattern, but here the sub-section headings do not relate to any overt language syllabus and are merely instructions and/or topic information. Here are the rubrics, with a description in italics, from part of a unit.

> 1 Read this newspaper article carefully. Then complete the map on the next page.
> *newspaper article, giving details of how a kidnapping took place, followed by a map*
>
> 2 Listen to the news report on the tape and then, from the following photos, choose the one that fits the description of the man and woman. When you have finished compare your ideas with your partner.
> *4 photos of a man and 4 of a woman supplied*
>
> 3 The following is the interview between the police and a witness. ... Work with a partner and complete the policeman's questions.
> *text with answers to policeman's questions*
>
> 4 On Tuesday ... Lady Blything received a recorded message. Listen to it carefully and make notes of all the things Lady Blything must do to satisfy the kidnappers.
> *tape to be played*
>
> 5 On Tuesday morning, a note addressed to Lady Blything was found blowing along County Street ... The message was in code, but the police quickly understood it. Can you?
> *text in code*

As the authors themselves point out, this course book aims at providing 'language exposure' so that learning will take place 'naturally'. The view of language learning that is projected is thus quite different from the first two course books since it would appear that in order to learn one simply has to do things with the language, i.e. to resolve a series of problems or tasks. This view is notable for its absence of specified language areas with which learners must consciously get to grips – grammar, punctuation, vocabulary and so on.

Depending on the prior experience of the individual learner, the view of language learning projected by material can be of central importance since it may shape learners' perceptions of their own abilities and of the steps they need to take to progress further. Learners using course books 1 and 2, for example, may see their problems lying at the 'item' level of lexis or set phrases, whilst learners using course book 3 may rather be concerned with the extent to which they can accomplish 'whole tasks'. Each of these views may affect the kind of strategies learners use to learn. Vocabulary lists, punctuation and grammar rules, and exact translations would seem to be suggested by the first two course books. Extensive reading or writing and the need to find 'real' opportunities to use the language might be suggested by course book 3.

Role relations within the classroom

In our consideration of the above three areas, we have already stressed that learner interpretation is the key variable in determining actual, rather than possible, learning outcomes. In turning to an examination of how materials may relate to classroom role relations, however, one needs to consider a further level of complexity; this is the extent to which materials may account for the ways in which teachers and learners interact with each other. It requires no great insight to acknowledge that there are numerous factors which influence how teachers and learners perceive each other, and most of these are well beyond the nature of a particular set of materials. The crucial factor is thus not only how learners interpret what is provided in the materials, but also what actually happens in a particular classroom. Nevertheless, since the construction of teaching materials is a deliberate attempt to bring about certain kinds of interaction in the classroom, we believe it is important to consider materials in terms of what they may suggest for the learning of classroom roles.

One useful concept with which to examine role relations suggested by materials is Bernstein's (1971) notion of a 'frame', which refers to the actual relationship between teachers and pupils and the range of choices which they have over what is done between them. Thus a strong frame will 'reduce the power of the pupil over what, when and how he receives his knowledge'. Whilst Bernstein himself does not consider either classroom interaction or teaching materials, Stubbs (1976: 97–9) relates the concept of a frame to Sinclair and Coulthard's (1974) identification of a teacher initiates/pupil responds/teacher feedback (IRF) discourse structure in many teaching situations. Stubbs argues that, in the IRF structure

> ... the pupil's role is passive: he must respond. It is the teacher who initiates and then evaluates, before asking another closed question. ... the assumption is that it is the teacher who has control over who talks when; and that education consists of listening to an adult talking and answering his or her questions.

In terms of language teaching materials it is not difficult to find numerous instances in which this kind of discourse structure is suggested for classroom work. One device widespread in materials is the drill, which would seem to exemplify the kind of passive learner role which Stubbs depicts. This example, taken from a recent 'communicative' course book is not untypical:

DRILL

1

1 Yes, it (be) very good.
Did you see the film on
television yesterday?
Yes, it was very good.

2 No, he (be) British.
Was the spy Russian?
No, he was British.

3 No, the Professor (shoot)
James Bond.
4 No, Selina (find) the
formula.
5 No, Melissa (jump) from
the helicopter.
6 No, Melissa (help) Bond!
7 No, Rocky (search) for
Selina!
8 No, Melissa (lose) the
formula!
9 I don't know, I (not see) the
end!

Stevick (1976) provides another analysis of drills suggesting an additional source of learning: classroom roles as a parent-child relationship. Drawing on Berne's (1964) theory of Transactional Analysis in which adult relations are seen in terms of ego states labelled Parent, Child, and Adult, Stevick (1976: 78) says:

> In a drill, ... (the learner) is in the sheltered position of a child, or even unborn fetus. It is therefore only natural that his ego state ... should be that of the Child.

Stevick's most important point, however, is not in respect of roles in the classroom, but in terms of what may get learnt: 'ego states are stored along with the basic sentences and structural automaticities' such that 'subsequent attempts to speak the language will inexorably revive this ego state along with the words and phrases' (ibid.). For Stevick, this explains the common feeling amongst many FL learners of an unwillingness to speak for fear of making mistakes and a consequent attempt to avoid FL situations.

A similar passive role for the learner is found in another procedure widely advocated in accompanying teacher's books, choral repetition. The following example is taken from the teacher's notes for a course for eight- to twelve-year-olds, published in 1984.

Stage 2 – Teaching the language in focus

Pictures, words or visual aids from Stage 1 become *prompts* for this stage.

(1) Say the model sentence clearly for Ss two or three times.
(2) The whole class repeats the sentence three times, groups repeat it once each and finally three or four individual Ss repeat it.
(3) Using a *prompt* from Stage 1, try to get the first substitution on the model sentence. A good S should be able to give this new example.
 If a S cannot make the substitution, give it exactly as with the model sentence above.
(4) The whole class repeats the substitution sentence three times, groups repeat it once per group, and three or four individual Ss repeat it.
(5) Using the other prompts, Ss make further substitutions on the original model sentence.
(6) Ss practise these new substitutions as (2) and (4) above.

Following the above procedure, pupils will hear the 'model sentence' and each substitution somewhere between 15 to 20 times, depending on the way the class is grouped. It is difficult to resist the idea that it is not simply the foreign language that is being taught here. For the pupils, the experience of simply repeating sentences after the teacher's prompts would appear to demonstrate clearly that their role in the classroom is largely a powerless one in which they mechanically follow instructions. The fact that this is done *in chorus* adds the sense of anonymity and being 'one of the mass' upon which much social control – inside and outside the classroom – seems to rest.

Perhaps mindful of the implications of chorus repetition and drills, recent materials include a considerable amount of pair or group work. Whilst much of this would appear to be essentially the same in terms of Stevick's analysis of Parent–Child roles (see for example the rubrics for the second course book analysed above), some materials offer opportunities for learners to work more freely. This often implies that the teacher's authority over the class is weakened, and certainly, the more the learners are encouraged to work things out for themselves and to practise without the constant supervision of the teacher, the more the balance of power within the classroom changes. The following extract from a course book illustrates the extent to which the role of the teacher can be altered from that of 'Parent' to that of 'Adult', with much of the decision making of classroom procedures handed over to the learners themselves.

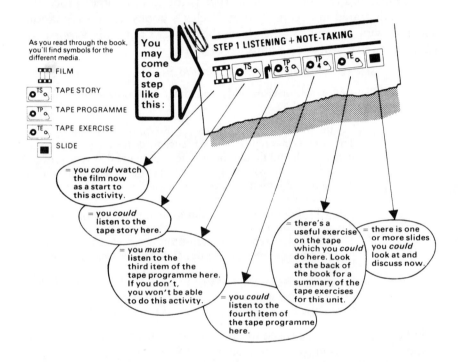

One important point to remember, however, when discussing role relations, is that even the most adventurous materials writer is limited in devising materials which imply a redistribution of power and control in the classroom. Materials must comply with the orthodox view of the nature of classrooms, or they will simply fail to sell – the fate of the material extracted above. That the language teaching profession as a whole is unsure about giving up the role of teacher as 'possessor of knowledge' is evidenced by the fact that publishers frequently produce two versions of a student's book: one with an answer key and one without. As has already been suggested, to a great extent, language teaching materials reflect wider notions of what education is and how it should be carried out. We should thus expect changes in the classroom roles which language teaching materials project to follow developments in other areas of education.

Opportunities for the development of problem-solving abilities

The discussion above has shown how language teaching materials are frequently based on a 'bucket theory' of knowledge (Popper, 1972) and a view of teaching as 'filling' (Freire, 1972) through the emphasis on feeding items of linguistic knowledge to learners for them to absorb and accumulate. At the task level of materials, we can find evidence of this in the preponderance of exercises such as repetition, drills, gap filling, and comprehension questions. The significance of this is that, in the main, materials tend to develop the reproductive and mechanical abilities of learners, neglecting the wider possibilities – and perhaps desirable aims – of language teaching.

We have already seen how language teaching may be used as a vehicle for 'general' or 'subject' knowledge since it is not specifically tied to any content area. In a similar manner, language teaching materials may offer the opportunity for developing 'problem-solving' abilities, by avoiding an emphasis on closed, item-level exercises and instead providing 'whole tasks' which require learners to consider a number of factors at the same time. In recent years, this opportunity has been taken up by a number of authors, although the total proportion of materials which aim to include a genuine problem-solving element is still extremely small. One example of this is the material already cited in our discussion of 'subject' knowledge which provides business simulations as a context for developing writing skills. The following example, this time taken from a book for schoolchildren in the Middle East, is particularly interesting because it attempts to link focused work on an area of grammar with the resolution of a mathematical problem. The aim, then, is not only to improve the learner's abilities in the foreign language but also to develop generalisable skills in problem solving.

≫→

3   Two jugs

Ayoub needs one litre of water. He has only
two jugs. Jug A can hold 3 litres, and jug B can
hold 5 litres. Both jugs are empty now. Ayoub
can fill a jug from the tap. He can also pour
water from one jug into another.

3.1   **If Ayoub fills jug A, how much water will he have? How can
he measure exactly one litre? Look at the pictures and
complete the sentences to find out.**

1   If he ..... *fills* .... jug A with some

    water from the tap, he ....

    ..*3*.... litres in jug A, and jug B ....

    ...*empty*... .

Picture 1

2   If he .... the water from jug A

    into jug B, jug A ....

    .... and he ....

    .... litres in jug B.

Picture 2

3   If he .... jug A again,

    he .... litres in jug A,

    and .... litres in jug B.

Picture 3

4   If he .... jug B with

    some water from jug A,

    he .... litres in jug B,

    and .... in jug A.

Picture 4

On one level, then, the insistence on reproductive and mechanical tasks
in language teaching materials can be viewed simply as a lost opportunity
to capitalise on the unique position of language teaching. On another

level, however, the frequent use of such closed tasks can be seen as having a constraining influence on the abilities of learners. In our earlier discussion of views of the nature of language learning, we suggested that the organisation of materials may influence the kind of learning strategies which learners adopt. Bruner (1960), however, suggests another aspect to this. This is that particular classroom procedures may actually inhibit other ways of working:

> we emphasise algorithmic (rational) thinking at the expense of holistic (creative) thinking [and in doing so] may thus handicap the development of problem solving abilities.

Recent developments in language theory view language use as involving the negotiation and interpretation of meaning, seeing communication as problematic (see Breen, 1987). This view challenges many of the basic assumptions of conventional approaches to language teaching materials, which, in the main, emphasise control of the surface element of language. In the past, materials design has generally responded to innovation in language theory by simply supplementing the existing stock of exercise types and syllabus approaches (for example, the absorption of functionalism). It seems likely, however, that if a negotiation/interpretation view of language use becomes more widely accepted, we will see a basic change in materials away from 'language learning as reproduction' and more towards 'language learning as problem solving'.

Values and attitudes presented in materials

One way to view claims about what may be learnt from a particular set of materials is to consider whether the learning would be brought about *experientially* (i.e. through what learners are required to *do*) or *referentially* (i.e. through the content of the material itself). Contemporary views on education suggest that one may make stronger claims for a learning outcome that is arrived at experientially than for one arrived at referentially (see for example Holt, 1976; Postman and Weingartner 1969; Freire, 1970; Stenhouse, 1975). In this respect, the first area we discussed, general or 'subject' knowledge offered in materials, distinguishes itself from areas two to five in that the first area is principally concerned with referential learning whilst the remaining areas involve experiential learning. The sixth area of possible learning outcomes is, however, similar to the first area, since it concerns how far learners may integrate values presented in materials into their own value system simply through contact with the text.

The doubt over arguing for the transmission of values presented in texts makes all the more interesting recent studies which claim a direct relationship between the values and attitudes learners express and those found in the texts with which they work. Porreca (1984) reviews a number of studies concerned with sexism in teaching materials. In one study (Jenkins, cited in Nilsen, 1977) found a direct correlation between the length of time spent using the *Alpha One Reading Program* (which apparently portrayed girls as 'stupid, dependent, whining and fearful' and boys as 'active and aggressive') and the degree to which pupils' attitudes matched those in the materials. Another study by Bem and Bem (1973) found that when jobs were described using the female generic pronoun women were significantly more likely to aspire to those jobs than when the male generic pronoun was used.

Porreca's own study details fairly thoroughly the extent of sexism in American ESL materials and suggests implications similar to those in the studies described above. Sexism in language teaching materials is, however, just one of an infinite number of areas which one may look for. Others might be ageism, racism, elitism, heterosexism, pro- or anti-smoking, pro- or anti-alcohol and so on, and it is not difficult to identify instances of each of these in LT materials. This example for instance, from a unit on the superlative form, would seem to present a particular view of Arabs:

Similarly, a recent course book, containing hundreds of colour photographs of people in various roles, shows only two black people and both of these fit the stereotype image: one is a muscular athlete and the other is a manual worker. Another very popular course book contains over thirty references to smoking or drinking in the first 25 pages, thereby, some would argue, legitimising and sanctioning such behaviour. The rights and wrongs in international politics are not neglected either, as this example shows.

In order to begin to argue that such features of materials may bring about particular kinds of learning outcomes, however, one needs to show that specific values or attitudes are *pervasive* throughout the text (Gordon, 1984), in the way that Porreca has been able to show with regard to sexist bias in ESL materials. Without this evidence, one may simply object to the inclusion of certain items on the grounds that they offend our own moral sensibilities.

Conclusion

In this paper, we have surveyed some alternative perspectives on materials design which look beyond the goals of language learning itself. We have been able to identify the various ways in which materials may contribute to learners' perceptions (of knowledge, language learning, and roles), to their affective and cognitive development, and to their general stock of information about the world. At various points in our survey we have suggested aspects of materials which, as a profession, we may consider undesirable. Certainly, in citing specific examples from course books we have probably suggested learning outcomes which the individual authors in question would consider unintentional. But materials hold such a significant place in language teaching that it would seem important for us to 'get it right'.

In examining a specific set of materials – either already published or under development – there would seem to be a number of basic questions which we can use to focus our attempt to look beyond language learning. Each of these questions relates to the areas discussed in this paper, and we offer them here by way of a summary of the issues we have touched on. They are:

1 Do the materials extend the learner's 'general' or 'specialist' knowledge?
2 What view of knowledge do the materials present? What implications might this have for how learners attempt to learn?
3 Do the materials develop the learners' understanding of what is involved in language learning and how they may help themselves?
4 How do the materials structure the teacher-learner relationship? What 'frame', if any, is placed on classroom interaction?
5 Do the materials develop the learners' general cognitive abilities? Is language learning presented as reproduction or as problem solving?
6 What social values and attitudes do the materials present?

It is, of course, up to each individual to determine what he or she sees as appropriate and desirable 'non-language-learning' learning outcomes from classroom work, but the process of looking at materials from a number of different perspectives should sharpen our understanding of their complex nature. At the design stage, it is a salutary experience for authors, publishers, advisers and curriculum developers to look at materials under development and consider what overall impression they create. This will almost certainly identify aspects of the materials which need rethinking, supplementing or abandoning. It would, after all, seem unlikely that those features of materials which are unintentional will match the conscious, expressed philosophies of their designers.

For those involved at the implementation stage of materials (teachers, course designers, learners) 'raising to consciousness' the underlying nature of the materials they are using will probably necessitate similar courses of action. A frequent step taken by teachers when they find materials lacking in some way is to supplement them with other materials, either their own or published. This would seem one possible course of action in respect of the issues discussed in this paper, but there are at least two further possibilities.

One possibility is the obvious one of rejecting or abandoning the materials, in favour of using other materials or no materials at all. The other possibility is less obvious and involves retaining the materials but, as it were, 'turning them on their head', making the materials themselves the object of critical focus in the classroom. Of the examples we have given, the view of Arabs projected by illustration is one clear case where the materials themselves could be challenged. Much the same action could, however, be taken in respect of all the areas discussed in this paper by encouraging learners and teachers to reflect on how materials influence what they do in the classroom. We have cited Freire a number of times in this paper and his work would also seem relevant here. One of the key features to Freire's approach to education is that it should be 'problem-posing', aiming to question and analyse the reality in which we live. For language classrooms, such an approach would free teachers and learners from the values, views and ways of working imposed on them, however unintentionally, by the materials they use.

11 Hidden agendas: the role of the learner in programme implementation

David Nunan

Introduction

In this paper, it is suggested that the effectiveness of any language programme will be dictated as much by the attitudes and expectations of the learners as by the specifications of the official curriculum. The assumption that there is a one-to-one relationship between teaching and learning is questioned, and it is hypothesised that learners have their own agendas in the language lessons they attend. These agendas, as much as the teacher's objectives, determine what learners take from any given lesson or teaching/learning encounter.

In order to explore the 'hidden agenda' hypothesis, studies into learner perceptions of learning processes are reviewed and compared with teacher perceptions. These studies provide a basis for the interpretation of classroom interactions which reveal the 'hidden agendas' of the learners in action.

The final section of the paper discusses some of the practical implications of the hidden agenda hypothesis, and suggests some practical techniques for achieving a synthesis between the official and the hidden curriculum.

The scope of the language curriculum

Recently there has been a call for a more systematic approach to language curriculum development. Thus, Richards (1984b) suggests that, in contrast with general educational practice where curriculum development is a 'major educational industry':

> what is understood by curriculum development in language
> teaching has often been rather narrowly conceived. The focus has

been primarily on language syllabuses rather than on the broader processes of curriculum development.

(Richards, 1984b: 1)

Nunan (1985) advocates the development of systematic and integrated procedures for designing courses in which key elements include needs analysis, goal and objective setting, the selection and grading of input, methodology (including the selection of resources and learning activities), learning mode and environment, and evaluation.

In one of the most comprehensive of all contemporary conceptualisations of language teaching, Stern sets language teaching theory solidly within an educational context by suggesting that it needs to be concerned, not only with the nature of language, but also with the nature of language learning, the nature of language teaching, the educational setting and the language teaching background (Stern, 1983: 49–9).

These calls have occurred within the general framework of a learner-centred philosophy which advocates the development of differentiated curricula to provide for different learner needs. In actual fact, however, learner needs have tended to be narrowly conceived, being restricted to considerations of language content, and ignoring the active role of the learner in actual learning processes. Brindley records that:

> In the earliest stages of the 'communicative' movement in language teaching, 'objective' needs received a great deal of emphasis, since language was seen primarily as a means to an end: effective communication in the learner's current or future domain of language use. ... 'Subjective' needs, on the other hand, as we have noted, were thought to be unpredictable, therefore indefinable. Language teachers were thus able, in deciding on content and methodology, to wash their hands of the extremely difficult business of taking affective variables into account: it was the language content derived from a diagnosis of the language-related 'objective' needs which was identified with the learning content of the course. The importance of methodology in 'communicative' courses therefore tended to be downplayed in relation to content.

(Brindley, 1984: 31–2)

In fact, it could be argued that no curriculum can claim to be truly learner-centred unless the learner's subjective needs and perceptions relating to the processes of learning are taken into account. There is anecdotal evidence to suggest that learners are more immediately concerned with the appropriacy of learning processes than with learning content, and it would seem that it is in relation to processes that most teacher/learner conflict occurs (Nunan, 1986b).

Within general education, there has been a great deal of talk about the 'covert curriculum' of the classroom, and the 'hidden agenda' of the teacher. It has been suggested that alongside the 'official' curriculum, as it is enshrined in various documents and statements, there is an 'unofficial' or 'hidden' curriculum (Apple, 1979). It has been further suggested that this hidden curriculum is at least as important as the overt curriculum in determining outcomes. These outcomes will include what gets learned and who will pass.

The hidden curriculum is transmitted to learners through disparities between what is said and what is done. Teachers themselves are often unaware of the covert messages they transmit, verbally and non-verbally. These messages usually reveal teachers' attitudes to many different aspects of the teaching-learning process. The hidden curriculum of language teaching materials has also been documented (Auerbach and Burgess, 1985).

Direct observation and analysis of classroom interactions reveals a great deal about classroom realities, realities of which the teacher is often unaware. There is, in fact, evidence of a disparity between what teachers believe they do and what they actually do in the classroom (Nunan, 1986a).

Learner perceptions of classroom processes

In 1985, two comprehensive studies were conducted into the perceptions of adult ESL learners in relation to classroom processes and activities. The first of these, by Alcorso and Kalantsis, asked learners to nominate what they felt were the most useful parts of their language lessons. The results of their survey are presented in Table 1.

TABLE I. MOST USEFUL PARTS OF LESSON ACCORDING TO STUDENTS

Activity	%
Grammar exercises	40
Structured class discussion, conversation	35
Copying written material, memorising, drill and repetition work	25
Listening activities using cassettes	20
Reading books and newspapers	15
Writing stories, poems, descriptions	12
Drama, role play, songs, language games	12
Using audio visuals, TV, video	11
Communication tasks, problem solving	10
Excursions with the class	7

(Alcorso and Kalantsis, 1985)

The data indicate that learners favour what might be termed 'traditional' learning activities over more 'communicative' activity types. This finding was supported in follow-up interviews with learners in which Kalantsis and Alcorso discovered that:

> There seemed to be a common view about the importance of grammar across respondents with different levels of English and from diverse educational backgrounds ... In explaining their preferences, the learners said they saw grammar-specific exercises as the most basic and essential part of learning a language.

(1985: 43)

In relation to games, singing and dance, it was discovered that:

> These activities were among the most contentious since most students had firm views about their usefulness or uselessness. Again, the divergence of opinion seemed to relate to people's educational background and socio-economic position. The most common comment from high-school or tertiary educated migrants was that, in general, dance, singing and games were a waste of time.

(1985: 48)

Willing (1985a) investigated the learning preferences of over five hundred learners. While his survey instrument and statistical analysis were more sophisticated than those of Alcorso and Kalantsis, he came up with a similar finding in relation to 'traditional' and 'communicative' activities. Despite variations among different learner types, there were certain activities which seemed to be almost universally popular. These included pronunciation practice, explanations to the class, conversation practice, error correction and vocabulary development. Unpopular activities included listening to and using cassettes, student self-discovery of error, using pictures, films and video, pair work and language games.

In a follow-up study, Nunan (1986b) used an adaptation of Willing's instrument to probe the perceptions of teachers. He found clear mismatches between learners' and teachers' views of what was important in the learning process. This can be clearly seen in Figure 1. There are mismatches in all but one activity, and quite dramatic mismatches in half of the activities. (A detailed description of this study, along with a discussion of the implications can be found in Nunan, 1986b.)

While one would not want to draw too many inferences from the data presented here, it is fairly evident that, in general, there are mismatches between teachers' and learners' expectations; that while teachers seem to accept the value of communicatively oriented activities, the learners surveyed place greater value on 'traditional' learning activities. It is reasonable to suggest that the classroom orientation of the learner will

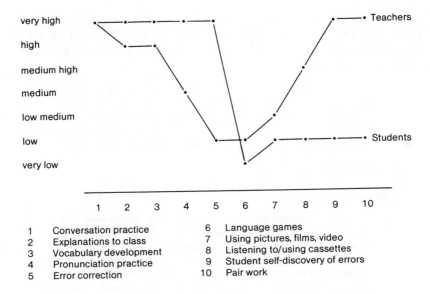

Figure 1   Teacher and learner ratings of selected learning activities: a comparison (Willing, 1985a; Nunan, 1986b)

have a marked influence on his/her classroom behaviour, particularly in terms of the value placed on different learning activities, the attention given and the learning effort made. In short, the orientations of the learner will constitute a hidden agenda and will largely dictate what is learned. In the next section we shall look at a number of classrooms to see what evidence there is in the dynamics of classroom interaction for the notion that learners have their own agendas.

Classrooms in action: another look

If transcripts of language lessons are examined, it is possible to find evidence that while teachers are teaching one thing, learners are often attending to something rather different. One way of gaining insights into learners' focus of concern is to study those points at which they initiate interactions. Such interactions seem to be relatively infrequent in most of the available transcripts of language classes. Even in 'communicative' classrooms, where one might expect a more equitable distribution of power, it is the teacher who determines who will speak, when they will speak, and what they will talk about.

In order to illustrate this point, I should like to refer to a piece of classroom-based research which investigated the degree to which principles of communicative language teaching had taken effect in second language classrooms. In a study of five classrooms in which the teachers were ostensibly teaching 'communicatively', it was discovered that, in fact, there was little genuine communicative language use in evidence. In these classes the teachers decided who would say what to whom when. Teachers nominated almost all of the conversational topics, and also decided who would speak. The only topic nominations which came from students were concerned with lesson procedure, grammar or vocabulary. (A detailed description of the study is to be found in Nunan, 1986a.) The following sample extracts from the study give some insights into the preoccupations of the students as the teachers, ostensibly, set up communicative language activities.

In the first extract, the teacher is trying to set up an information gap activity. The focus of concern for the students however, is whether or not they are going to have a 'quiz' or examination. The rather abrupt topic nomination takes the teacher by surprise, and it takes him some time to work out what the students are trying to convey.

S: Quiss?
T: Pardon?
S: It will be quiss?
It will be quiss?
Quiss?
Ss: Quiz, quiz.
T: Ahmm, sorry?
Try again.
S: I ask you ...
T: Yes.
S: ... you give us another quiss?
T: Oh, quiz, oh. No, no, not today, it's not going to be a quiz today. Sorry.

In the next example, the student initiation is concerned with a point of grammar, rather than with the information gap activity which is the ostensible point of the lesson.

S: Why three bed, er, three bedroom?
Why we don't say three bedrooms?

The teacher's reply is hardly encouraging:

T: Ahhm, oh, I don't know.
S: Is not right.

T: We don't say it. We don't say it. There's no explanation.
But we often do that in English. Three bedroom house.

Another student interrupts to suggest that it is out of order to ask the teacher questions to which he may not have the answer:

S: Don't ask for it.
S: Yes.
T: Well, do ask why, ask why and 99 per cent of the time I know the answer. One per cent of the time nobody knows the answer. If I don't know it, nobody knows. (laughter) Ah, no, I don't know the answer.

The most frequent type of student initiation in the data seems to be on questions of vocabulary. Here is an example from a very low level class:

T: And here is the bottom.
S: Bottom.
T: Bottom of the table, yeah.
S: (pointing under the table)
   An call here?
T: Oh, underneath.
S: Underneath.
T: Yeah.

One of the lessons has a very revealing exchange which demonstrates the learner's attitude towards the locus of control. The teacher has been trying to stimulate learners to 'give opinions' on whether a woman who has been interviewed is an unusual type of person or not.

T: So that's normal or not normal?
   Not very usual?
S: Not usual
T: Yeah, I think ...
   (to student who has been non-verbally indicating disagreement)
   you agree?
S: I have to.

These extracts, which are by no means atypical, seem to support the contention that not all learners will necessarily be focusing on the point of the lesson in hand. In the examples cited, while the teachers are trying to develop communicative activities, with a focus on meaning, the learners are more interested in the formal aspects of the language. Thus the classroom data would seem to support the studies on learner preferences reported in the preceding section. (Similar results are reported in Brock, 1986; Dinsmore, 1985; and Long and Sato, 1983.)

Given mismatches between learner/teacher expectations, hidden agendas and the complexities of the language classroom where there is no obvious one-to-one relationship between the planned curriculum and the implemented curriculum, the obvious questions arise: what is it that has created this state of affairs, and what is to be done? These questions are addressed in the next section.

Dealing with hidden agendas

It has been suggested that one reason for the mismatches which occur at the level of programme implementation is that programme planners and teachers have one set of expectations while learners have others. This seems to be confirmed by studies into learner expectations and preferences as well as by classroom research of the type cited in the preceding section of this paper.

One possible explanation for this apparent conflict between the intentions of the teachers and of the learners is that learners are simply not let into the picture. In other words, it might be the case that learners come to class with their own objectives because they are not informed in any meaningful way of the objectives of the 'official' curriculum, either at the macro programme level, or at the micro level of the individual lesson. In support of this notion, Allwright (1986) presents evidence that learners are confused about the learning objectives of classes which they have just attended. In a study which asked learners immediately at the completion of a class what the lesson had been about, a variety of opinions were expressed, many of which were at variance with the teacher's 'official' agenda.

Allwright also claims that learners have problems in trying to comprehend the facts of the language as explained to them by teachers. He cites a teacher/learner exchange in which the learners are led to believe that the words 'look' and 'see' are synonymous and goes on to suggest that:

> Such little bits of evidence, taken together, and interpreted in the light of years of experience of inspecting classroom data, add up to the notion that instruction may well, much of the time, not make sense from the learners' perspective, because it is fundamentally incomprehensible!

(Allwright, 1986: 2)

Further evidence that much instruction may not make sense comes from quite a different perspective. Based on an analysis of a large corpus of second language data, Johnston concludes that there are strict speech processing constraints on what is learnable at any given stage in the learning process. Regardless of the quality of teaching, learners will not be able to assimilate structures which are beyond their current stage of development as dictated by speech processing constraints.

> ... developmental features are governed by an individual's evolving speech processing capacities in the second language ... as a result of this there is a very strict order for the learning of developmental features. There now exists very strong evidence that there is in fact no way to 'beat' this natural ordering. That is, a learner will only acquire developmental features when 'ready' to do so, 'readiness' being definable here as being well established at the developmental stage prior to the one to which the structures to be learned belong.

(Johnston, 1985: 37)

Johnston has been able to demonstrate that the ordering of structures in most commercial course books is at odds with the 'natural syllabus' of the learners. The implication of his research is that if the linguistic content of the 'official' curriculum is at variance with what learners are capable of assimilating, then the gap between the planned and the implemented curriculum will be exacerbated. Until research and development on the classroom applications of Johnston's work is concluded, it would be best for teachers not to try and force production of language structures which learners seem patently incapable of assimilating.

One response to the data presented in the preceding section, in which the learners under investigation appeared to prefer 'traditional', 'non-communicative' approaches to instruction, is to ignore it altogether and hope that it will not really make any difference to the learning process. At the opposite extreme, the temptation might be to give in to the perceived needs of the learners, and to abandon any attempt at making the classroom more communicative. However, a more positive approach is for teachers to take learners into their confidence and to increase their meta-awareness of the nature of communicative language learning. This can be facilitated by consulting and negotiating with learners on content and methodology, by encouraging learners to formulate their own communicative language objectives, by training learners in self-assessment and course evaluation, and by including 'learning-how-to-learn' components in all language programmes.

There is, in fact, some evidence that sensitisation programmes can be effective. Allwright describes the establishment of a set of procedures for the more flexible use of classroom time, including the incorporation into the timetable of private consultations. He states that:

> I was particularly interested to note that learners began coming to private consultations with purely linguistic queries, but soon changed to talk instead about ways of learning. This change of perspective was further confirmed when, to my surprise, my early morning mini-lectures on language learning ... were greeted with

great enthusiasm. Learning, it seemed, had become a matter of genuine and considerable interest.

(Allwright, 1986: 9)

Classroom-based research is also developing promising strategies for aligning the agendas of teachers and learners. Thus, Long and Crookes (1986) found that increasing the number of referential over display questions and developing what they call 'two-way tasks' led to an increase in the amount of genuine communicative language used in the classroom, and also to higher scores on tests of content. The most likely explanation for this is that the referential questions provided learners with greater motivation to invoke their schematic knowledge representations of the subject in hand, which, in turn, led to greater depth of processing and also greater interest in lesson content on the part of learners (Nunan, 1985).

Allwright suggests that we need to redefine our notions of classroom instruction. He states that:

> Surely all the classroom data ... show quite strikingly that what learners actually get (both in syllabus and method terms, incidentally) is potentially very different from any intended syllabus. My own preferred conception is that what learners actually get is best seen as a set of 'learning opportunities', only indirectly related to the 'official' syllabus. These 'learning opportunities' are themselves the product of classroom interaction, which is a necessary feature of classroom instruction. [...] Classroom instruction proceeds by a necessary joint process of interaction management, and this interaction management makes a difference to what is available to be learned from.

(1986: 5)

Conclusion

Much curriculum development seems to proceed on the rather simplistic assumption that there is a direct equation between planning, teaching and learning. In other words, it is assumed that what is planned will be taught and that what is taught will be learned. Recent studies of what actually goes on at the stage of programme implementation, however, demonstrate that the equation is much more complex. Teachers do not always teach what has been planned, and learners very often learn things other than what has been taught.

This paper produces evidence from a variety of sources to suggest why there might be mismatches between teaching and learning. In the first place, learners may simply be unaware of the 'official' curriculum.

Secondly, they may have different priorities from those of the teacher. Finally, some of the content of a course may simply be unlearnable given speech processing constraints and a given learner's current stage of development.

A number of suggestions are made about ways of bridging the gaps between planning, teaching and learning. In the first place, teachers should be as explicit as possible about the goals and objectives of their courses. They should determine the learners' preconceptions about content and methodology, and, if there are mismatches between the expectations of the learners and the official curriculum, these should be resolved through consultation and negotiation. Finally, it is vitally important that the planned curriculum be seen, not as a prescriptive statement to be slavishly followed, but as a general guide which is capable of modification in the light of on-going monitoring and evaluation.

This last point prompts the conclusion that there is a need to redefine 'curriculum' (or, at the very least, to enlarge its scope). The present tendency is to view curricula 'prospectively', that is, as a set of prescriptions for 'what should be'. However, the studies reviewed here would seem to indicate that the scope of curriculum studies should be broadened to encompass the 'interactive' curriculum. Until this happens there seems little hope of resolving the inherent tension between 'what should be' and 'what is', and consequently little hope for developing a more rational articulation between programme planning, implementation and evaluation.

12 The evaluation cycle for language learning tasks

Michael Breen

Introduction

This paper is concerned with a central issue in language teaching and learning: the efficacy of workplans which are designed to enable the development of an individual's knowledge and capabilities in a new language. Its purpose is to examine both the criteria and the means for the evaluation of language learning tasks. In the paper, I wish to offer particular answers to two major questions. First, what decisions have to be made in evaluating learning tasks and what problems do we have to take account of in the decisions we make? The first part of the paper therefore considers alternatives in the timing, focus, and criteria of task evaluation and the problems which confront us within each of these matters. The second relates to how we might undertake evaluation: what practical procedure might best cope with the problems inherent in the evaluation of learning tasks while also being the most valid means for evaluation currently available to us. My priority throughout the paper is to try to deduce practical proposals, therefore – in addressing this latter question – the second half of the paper suggests ways of implementing a task evaluation cycle.

A language learning task can be regarded as a springboard for learning work. In a broad sense, it is a structured plan for the provision of opportunities for the refinement of knowledge and capabilities entailed in a new language and its use during communication. Such a workplan will have its own particular objective, appropriate content which is to be worked upon, and a working procedure. In using the concept *task* in this sense throughout the paper I therefore intend it to cover a wide range of workplans which are designed to facilitate language learning particularly in classrooms. A simple and brief practice exercise is a task, and so also are more complex and comprehensive workplans which require spontaneous communication of meaning or the solving of problems in learning and communicating. Any language test can be included within this spectrum of tasks. All materials designed for language teaching – through their particular organisation of content and the working procedures they assume or propose for the learning of the content – can be seen as compendia of tasks.

The history of a task: when to evaluate?

If we wish to be more certain of the validity of our tasks, and if we seek to develop new tasks which will be more sensitive to learners and situation, then the timing of the evaluation of any task is a crucial matter. When a task is used during teaching and learning, it immediately acquires a temporal reality of three phases, each phase having its own characteristics, each of which may be a distinct focus of evaluation. These phases are: the task as workplan, the task in process and the task outcomes.

Our pre-designed task is a proposal for language learning work and – however carefully designed – it can be no more than a plan which may or may not be followed according to the 'frame' which it offers to its users. Our *task-as-workplan* is predictive in that it delineates particular learning opportunities through our own selection of objectives, content, and procedure, and our subsequent organisation of these into a learning task. The particular selection and organisation is likely to derive from our knowledge and experience of past plans which seemed to have worked well. Therefore we may prejudge the workplan through our evaluations of previous plans and, significantly, in relation to what happened to these plans when they were used by learners. Tasks-as-workplans are therefore created on the basis of retrospective evaluation, even if such judgements are rooted in the subjective – though experientially informed – best guesses of the designer.

When teachers and learners work upon our task, it is metamorphosed into a *task-in-process* during which teacher and learners redraw the plan in terms of their own 'frames' and their own knowledge and experience of past workplans. If we wish to evaluate our task in terms of the life breathed into it by teacher and learner redefinition, we are necessarily obliged to evaluate within the teaching-learning process itself. The third phase at which we might direct evaluative effort is subsequent to the completion of our task by the learning group. Here we can assess the relative achievements which our task generated in terms of *task outcomes* – choosing, therefore, to analyse what has been learned rather than explore how it is undertaken during the task-in-process.

One way of perceiving the relationship between the three phases of a language learning task is illustrated in the diagram (Figure 1).

This analysis (see also Allwright, 1983; Breen, 1987) suggests that learning outcomes from any task have to be seen as a function of the *interaction* between features of our workplan, variables in learner contributions to the task, aspects of the actual situation in which the task is undertaken, *and* variation in learners' perceptions of each of these three things. Given this complex interaction during the task-in-process of the original task, learner work, situation and learner perceptions, we would be naive to believe that our task could directly 'cause' the

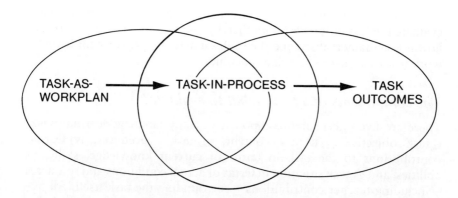

Figure 1   *Three phases of a task*

outcomes it is intended to facilitate. Any task-in-process may generate a range of diverse changes in knowledge and capability, and evaluation of outcomes related only to the criteria of workplan objectives can actually hide more than it will reveal. Even those 'successful' outcomes predicted by workplan objectives could be achieved as a result of variables quite independent of the plan itself. If we assume that our task somehow caused the successful outcomes we sought, we may be led to the deception that any 'failures' which also emerged can be primarily attributed to learners or situational conditions. Unfortunately – and cruelly for our faith in the task – an alternative argument could prove justifiable: that the task caused the 'failures' whilst 'success' was achieved despite it and because of learner ingenuity or situational compensations! Workplans can only provide opportunities for change in knowledge and capability and for successful and unsuccessful outcomes in relatively unpredictable and broad measure. The task-in-process and the teaching and learning activity it engages will *intervene* between the pre-designed task and actual learning outcomes. Perhaps, therefore, evaluative effort would gain greater reward if it was directed upon the task-in-process?

In deciding when to evaluate a task, therefore, we have three alternatives. Evaluation of a task as workplan can explore its validity in terms of anticipated appropriateness of objectives, content and procedure, and potential appropriateness to learners and situation. But such evaluation can be seen to be dependent upon our judgements concerning previous task outcomes or close evaluation of previous tasks-in-process – or a combination of these. An alternative focus upon learning outcomes alone can provide a check on validity and offer information which may be formative in terms of subsequent refinement of the task or the development of new tasks. But the inevitable diversity of actual task outcomes and the opacity of the true origins of these outcomes will render our evaluation partial and possibly misleading. The third alternative is to evaluate the task-in-process and, thereby, explore its validity in terms of how it is actually realised and the routes it actually provides for learning work towards various learning outcomes.

The components of a task: what to evaluate?

There are five interrelated components of any language learning task: i) task objective(s), ii) task content, iii) task procedures, iv) learner contributions to the task in terms of current knowledge, skills, or abilities, and v) task situation in terms of actual conditions and resources – including teacher contributions – surrounding the task itself. All five components exist in continual interaction while any task is being undertaken.

Any language learning task incorporates these components and it will be valid to the extent that it can facilitate a harmonious interaction among all five of them when it is actually worked upon by teacher and learners. Unfortunately for the designer, however, no workplan can inherently guarantee such harmony. Our task-as-workplan is an idealisation; it has to *presuppose* appropriate relationships between objectives, content, procedure, learner and situation, whilst actual relationships are made real in the thought and action of the users of the plan.

The learners' reinterpretations of our task create the actual task-in-process, and through these reinterpretations the five components of a task are very likely to be transformed in the following ways (these are discussed in detail in Breen, 1985b and 1987):

1 The learners' own purposes will be superimposed upon planned objectives.
2 The learners' background knowledge will enable the learners to identify particular aspects of task content which are familiar and, conversely, what is unfamiliar thereby becomes the problematic content. The data and information in our task are therefore transformed from *potential* content for learning into islands of familiar and problematic subject matter. Any potential meanings or communication and any data and information about the language and its use which make up the content of a task will be *redefined* by the current state of learners' communicative and metacommunicative knowledge.
3 Learners will approach task procedure through their own selective and preferred ways of working, and such preferences will *overrule* any explicitly stated task instructions or procedure. Some learners may work closely to a planned procedure only to the extent that it harmonises with their own approach to learning, while many learners – if they are to complete the task at all – will work in ways distinct

from a recommended procedure. Even common learning outcomes will be achieved through alternative ways of working, whilst the usual diversity of outcomes tends to confirm different procedural routes of different learners.

4 Learners will contextualise a task within their own learning process in relation to the immediate language learning experience and in relation to their conceptualisation of the nature of language learning – including the roles and responsibilities this conceptualisation gives them. This *psychological contextualisation* determines what a learner believes he or she should contribute to the task on the basis of their overall approach to learning the language which, in turn, derives from their underlying concept of language learning.

5 Learners will contextualise a task within the actual teaching-learning situation – such as a classroom – within which they work. They will grant a task social significance within the encircling culture of their particular classroom group. This *social contextualisation* locates any task not as an isolated moment of work, but as a social event within specific interpersonal experience, and as subject to both the benefits and constraints which that experience provides.

Some of these learner contributions may be explicit and observable in terms of particular use of skills and abilities during interaction which manifest certain learning strategies and which reveal aspects of the learner's overall approach. But many features of a learner's version of the task can only be indirectly inferred from observable learner work while other important learner contributions during any task will not be observable.

In deciding what aspects of a task we should evaluate, therefore, the first alternative is to evaluate a workplan in terms of its own inherent appropriacy of objectives, content and procedure, their appropriateness to each other, and their anticipated appropriateness to learners and situation. A second alternative is to evaluate the task-in-process with particular reference to the observables of individual and group work upon the task. The third alternative is an exploratory investigation of learner versions of the task. This would involve us in discovering less overt but more comprehensive and highly significant learner contributions to the task. Of course, an evaluative procedure might exploit all three alternatives, although the last alternative enables us to use any task as a window upon important contributions of learners which are very likely to shape a whole range of tasks in particular ways. In other words, the discovery of learner versions of a task can lead us to explanations of how and why learners work upon tasks in the ways they choose and, thereby, provide us with information of a more generalisable kind. It seems, therefore, that we gain most from learner definition and recreation of tasks but this alternative may be more costly in terms of evaluative effort.

The quality of a task: what evaluative criteria?

Every task is, in essence, a means for learning. Its purpose is to provide an opportunity for language learners to move from their present state of knowing and capability towards a new aspect of knowledge and specific use of skills and abilities. To assess a task in terms of its value as a genuine means for learning seems to require us to address criteria within communicative knowledge and abilities which can be *both* prospective and retrospective. Such *means criteria* will refer to those features of a task which directly address learning by explicitly relating the current state of learner knowledge and capacities for learning work to the demands of target language competence. There are three important means criteria against which we can evaluate a task: i) the extent to which it addresses *learner* definitions of progress; ii) the extent to which it is *developmental* towards the demands of the target language and its use; and iii) the extent to which it is open to *diversity and change* in learner knowledge and capability.

Sensitivity to learner definitions of progress, the first criterion, implies that a task should directly address immediate learning needs as perceived by the learners. Second, a task will be developmental if it engages knowledge about language and its use and skills and abilities for communication which the learner already has and which *also underlie* the knowledge, skills and abilities required by the target language. Finally, the third criterion acknowledges that a task cannot predict what a learner will actually contribute to it or learn from it, and that one of its main functions is to positively support the diversity and change which typify a learning process. To serve as a means for learning, therefore, our task needs to anticipate that different learners will bring different knowledge and capabilities to it. It needs to overtly call upon and engage these differences in what learners know and can do as the bases for real change, and it has to positively allow for different learners to learn different things, in different ways, at different moments even in the pursuit of some common overall objective. In a sense, a 'good' task is one which *aims for* such differentiation in order to encourage the inevitably wide range of changes in learning which a task has the potential to facilitate. If a task does not account for differences in learner contributions or positively allow for variation in learner outcomes – so that these may be revealed and shared in a learning group subsequent to the task – then it implicitly subordinates the unpredictable and personal experience of change in learning. It may inhibit more than it could potentially enable. These three means criteria all relate to one another and characterise a task as a bridge between particular ends of language learning and the current state of the learner.

Task design and evaluation therefore seem to require us to respect not one, but three sources of criteria governing the validity of a task. Criteria related to ends, criteria within initial learner needs which derive from their present knowledge and capabilities, and criteria related to the facilitative means which any task must provide. Means criteria entail the other two, but they also suggest the need for an on-going 'dialogue' between the designer and the users if current and future tasks are to harmonise with the actual needs and learning processes of the particular group of learners for whom the tasks are designed. It seems that designing and subsequent evaluating should be undertaken locationally and temporally in close proximity to actual learner work upon the task.

The evaluation cycle in practice: a suggested procedure

A characteristic which is common to all of the conclusions reached so far is that our evaluation of a task would focus mainly upon its implementation during teaching and learning; upon how the learners who use our task actually work upon it, how they perceive it, and *why* they act and think in relation to our task in the ways they do. Evaluation of a task-in-process through learner versions of that task against means criteria seems to be the most informative *modus operandi* both for the validation of our task and towards the refinement and development of later tasks. The task evaluation cycle here proposed will need to occur *within* the actual teaching-learning process itself. The deductions suggest that task evaluation should be part of teaching and learning work *in* the language class, not merely for the sake of developing more sensitive tasks but as a reflexive means for revealing individual learning processes and, thereby, facilitating them through more informed intervention. Therefore the task evaluation cycle can be seen as a positive and highly relevant language learning activity in itself.

In the context of many teaching situations where pre-designed tasks and prescribed materials are the norm and where designers are unavoidably distant from the learners, such proposals may seem inappropriate and unworkable. However, though seemingly radical and fraught with practical problems, the more overt and thorough demands of a task evaluation cycle in the classroom *already* have their roots in what occurs in every language class. Every teaching-learning process involves at least a *covert* task evaluation cycle. As teachers, we have to select appropriate tasks, and we often engage learners in their task selection during classroom work and for individual work so that particular learning problems may be remedied. All our learners also have to locate any task in relation to their own learning process, and this requires them to make judgements about a task in order to render it sensible to them and manageable for them. Even though this selection and judgement of tasks may be part of the less public work of a class, these are nevertheless crucial everyday moments in teaching and learning.

There are, of course, a range of objections which may be raised concerning the implementation of a task evaluation cycle during teaching and learning. Surely the primary subject matter of a language class is the new language, so why allocate precious time to evaluating the means for learning? Questioning the tasks might, perhaps, be seen to challenge the greater experience and good sense of the teacher? And what is the teacher's role in task evaluation? Should we really expect learners to participate in task evaluation, given their inevitably limited knowledge and capabilities in relation to the new things they are supposed to be grappling with? I would like to consider these major objections in the concluding part of this paper, but first wish to suggest a number of practical ways in which tasks-in-process, learner versions of tasks, and means criteria for tasks may be explored in the classroom. In what follows, I hope that these and other objections and problems may be at least partially addressed.

Task evaluation as a diagnostic and formative phase in teaching and learning

Learners are certainly as concerned about task outcomes as are teachers and task designers. In fact, learners invest a degree of affective involvement in the products of their work that is sometimes surprising to us. The assessment phase of learning outcomes is a highly significant matter. Very commonly, however, their perceptions of relative success or failure relate less to criteria which are implicit in the original workplan than to their own reinterpretations of the task. Assessment of their achievement is – crucially – an assessment of their versions of the task. From this we can conclude that helpful formative evaluation of their own progress in learning would involve learners in more directly relating successes and failures *back* to the roots from which these outcomes emerged.

The assessment of outcomes from any task is a crucial diagnostic phase for both learner and teacher. It needs to be imbued with positive value if merely to compensate for the challenge to learner self-esteem which disappointing task outcomes can present. If as many outcomes as possible could be identified, and especially those difficulties and problems which the task generated, learners can come to perceive tasks as valuable starting points for a *more precise* deduction of genuine learning needs. Approaching task difficulty and problematicity as a productive basis for later work is one way of investing 'failure' with positive worth. However, if diverse outcomes can be *related back* to the task itself – and to how learners perceived it and worked upon it – then learners could not only participate in the selection and development of more sensitive tasks, but also become more willing to critically assess the efficiency of their own approaches to language learning.

Working through task evaluation in the classroom

In the sections which follow, I offer a range of proposals for the practical implementation of a task evaluation cycle in the language class. The proposals are offered in a temporal cycle, starting with the evaluation of previously designed tasks, moving on to the choice of most appropriate tasks, and then dealing with the refinement and development of new tasks. However, any one of the proposals within any one of these three phases can serve as a *starting point* for a particular classroom group (see Allen, Howard, and Ullmann 1984; Allen, Barker, and Canale, 1985, and Bennett *et al.* 1984 for other approaches to classroom-based task evaluation).

PHASE ONE: EVALUATING PREVIOUSLY DESIGNED TASKS

Involving learners in collecting and sharing their judgements of currently used or previously experienced tasks can be an obvious first step in an evaluation cycle. A general way into such an investigation is to require learners to identify their favourite tasks or types of tasks. Learners could be asked to base their deductions on language tasks they have worked on in the past and perhaps make deductions with reference to *all kinds* of learning tasks other than those used for language work. This broad search for criteria for favoured task types may be further widened to engage learners in reflecting upon the many things that they will have learned at earlier points in their lives, and thereby deducing the kinds of activity they undertook for such learning which seemed to help them. More narrowly, perhaps, learners might select and specify favourite tasks or task types from immediately available sets of tasks or materials.

An alternative to this identification of favoured tasks – and one which may involve the learners in more precise judgements – is to ask learners to select a currently used task and require them to report (after individual and small-group consideration) on those aspects of the chosen task which they see as 'good', those seen as 'bad', and what features they regard as missing from the task but which they see as desirable in helping their learning. If different groups work on the same task, a diverse range of judgements will emerge. Alternatively, allowing sub-groups to choose any task they wish to evaluate in this way will mean that a range of tasks will be analysed by the class, and a sub-group's *reasons* for the choice they have made can reveal further assumptions and criteria. Perhaps the main advantage in working upon immediately available tasks, whichever of these two approaches is adopted, is that learners' assessment of the aspects and features of a task can be directly related to the actual task in question. That the task is also open to everyone else's inspection further leads to comparing points of view and deducing those judgements which seem most precise, those which are shared across the whole group, and those which represent very different assumptions by different learners.

Although these initial investigations seem based upon simple and seemingly obvious questions, three important requirements upon the group's investigation need to be emphasised. First, individuals and small groups must try to specify *particular characteristics* of the task and organise and categorise these characteristics in clear ways. Second, *reasons and justifications* for favoured tasks and/or *reasons* why characteristics are 'good' or 'bad', and why missing features are desirable need to be sought and shared. Such justification can itself enable learners to attain precision in their evaluations whilst it mirrors for them a range of perceptions and assumptions concerning the things which aid learning. Third, the investigation itself must have a longer-term purpose which provides *a practical benefit* in the eyes of the learners. Initially learners could be asked what they believe might be gained from this analysis of the tasks they have worked on in previous language learning work. Such gains could be listed as the objectives of the investigation.

The teacher knows, however, that the major advantage of this kind of evaluation is that it necessarily draws upon *learner* perceptions of objectives, content, and procedures of tasks. The evaluation cycle will uncover the learners' own learning purposes, their definitions of appropriate content, and their beliefs about preferred ways of working. A significant benefit will accrue in the individual's reflection upon his or her perceptions of the components of a learning task, and from the opportunity to know about fellow-learners' views on these things. A major practical outcome from even this initial evaluation will be the identification by the learners of 'good task' criteria. Preferred design features or 'task blueprints' can subsequently be drawn up. These can then be applied by learners – individually or in small groups – in the later selection of tasks for their own work, or applied to pre-designed tasks so that learners can adapt and refine them along preferred lines. Having carefully deduced a range of 'good task' criteria, learners have the basis for designing and developing new tasks for themselves and for each other with a view to meeting identified and various learning needs. Learner-designed tasks, wherein the knowledge and capabilities already mastered by certain members of the group can serve as a resource to other learners, represent an important outcome from the evaluation cycle, and can also serve as the focus of a new cycle of direct learner involvement in task development. Therefore, even this initial reflection on pre-designed tasks readily available in the classroom has the potential to generate formative criteria for the users' selection and design of new tasks.

PHASE TWO: CHOOSING THE 'BEST' TASKS

The major objective at this phase in the cycle is to discover those task *features* which capture learners' current definitions of most appropriate tasks. Evaluation would draw upon learner perspectives and preferences in relation to *the five components of a task* – its objectives, content, procedure, their contributions to the task, and the role of the classroom situation in relation to the task. Specific investigation could focus singly or in turn upon each of the five components. We can therefore consider starting points with reference to each component.

Deciding on objectives In discovering what learners themselves regard as the most valuable purposes for a task or tasks, the classroom group is necessarily involved in the specification of their needs in learning. A general approach would require the learners to identify as clearly as possible individual and group goals for language learning – the various reasons why they may personally wish to know the new language, and what it may gain for them. It is such longer-term views which provide the learner with personal criteria for 'progress'. Learner goals may be initially vague and certainly change over time and become more refined and realistic. Such change suggests the importance of recurrent, occasional reviews of why learners believe they are working upon the new language.

If we accept that a learner's own purposes will derive mainly from what they believe they have *already* achieved or tried to achieve, then a shared deduction of the most appropriate objectives for future tasks can also start from this particular perspective. Two important advantages are provided by the identification and sharing of i) those things which members of the group already know of and about the new language and ii) what they can already do with and through the language. First, it is an obviously positive approach which values prior achievement as the basis from which any new learning must evolve. Second, the identification and collation of those things which have been achieved in the group can locate sources of knowledge and capability already available in the classroom in addition to the teacher and the tasks. Individual learners who know and can do things which are new can serve as resources for peer work, and as members of 'design teams' whose role would be to seek out or prepare new tasks for fellow learners who are less familiar with the relevant aspects of knowledge or capability.

Subsequently, and on the basis of what learners believe they already know and can do, the group can seek individual and sub-group priorities in relation to those aspects of the language and its use which have proven to be difficult, but which are regarded as important. In this way, immediate learning needs can be defined by learners and worthwhile objectives for future task selection, and motivated learning work would emerge. Involving learners directly in specifying what they believe they do not yet know and cannot yet do in relation to the new language, not only requires them to prioritise objectives which they perceive as worthy of effort, but it also enables the sharing and consideration of those things which different learners regard as important aspects in the learning of a language. Therefore an initial investigation of different needs draws upon and reveals the various conceptualisations of language learning which exist within any classroom group.

Selecting content   Choosing the 'best' tasks, from a learner's point of view, is very likely to relate to the content of tasks. Interest, relevance, or helpfulness of content seem to be very important to learners in making the learning process meaningful and manageable. The content of language learning tasks is, however, ambiguous for the learner. In any pre-designed task, its content will be potentially communicative (concerned with meanings and messages) *and* potentially metacommunicative (providing data and information about the code and its use). Unfortunately, the task designer cannot predict that those aspects of content intended as distinctively 'message-focused' or distinctively 'code-focused' will be similarly interpreted or acted upon as such by a learner. Learners will *redefine* content in their own terms and in relation to the learning purposes which they superimpose upon the content. They will also locate any content in relation to the current state of their own knowledge, skills and abilities – potential content will be translated by the learner into what is familiar and what is problematic. This relatively unpredictable reinterpretation of content provides further motivation for the evaluation of tasks by learners as a means to discovering *their* criteria for 'good' content and those aspects of content which they perceive as useful or problematic.

Three alternative ways of initiating the discovery of learner criteria for appropriate content can be suggested. First, learners can be asked to find examples of target language data – of any type and in any medium – which they regard as 'easy', 'manageable' or 'familiar' etc. Using such data, they could be required to identify as precisely as possible those aspects of the data about which they were *less* sure and which seemed more difficult. Given that a range of data may be chosen and that aspects of these data will be 'easy' and 'familiar' for some learners but 'difficult' and 'problematic' for others, this initial selection of target language data has potential for the identification of both the known and the unknown. The former can serve as input for later work, whilst the latter can reveal new directions for work.

A second alternative to this 'problem-raising' approach to content is to ask learners to locate – and even bring into the classroom from elsewhere – any target language data which personally interest them for whatever reasons. Individuals or small groups could then select from this bank of data on the basis of interest and curiosity and follow a similar 'problem-raising' procedure; carefully identifying what they already know about the data and thence locating and sharing those aspects which cause them problems. The third alternative would involve the teacher in confronting the group with an example or examples of target language data of any kind, with the requirement that individuals and groups discover and state all those aspects of such data which seem familiar to them. In this way, familiar content can be exploited as the starting point for tackling the unfamiliar. It is often surprising to a group of learners how much they already know and how much they can infer from what is, at first sight or hearing, an unfamiliar or 'difficult' example of target language data. The subsequent specification and collation of genuine problems identified within the learning group can then lead in two directions: first, the prioritising of particular problems for later work and, second, the shared solution of chosen problems in groups which contain at least one learner who believes that he or she can help other learners to solve the problem.

The underlying motive for these alternative suggestions regarding potential content for language learning is that the *problematicity* of content as defined by the learner will be the real catalyst for actual learning work. It is the *learner's* view of what is both problematic and worth solving in task content which renders particular aspects of the content as genuine means for learning. However, problematicity has to be seen by any learner through the window of what is already familiar – the former is both identified and made solvable only through the latter. We deceive ourselves as task designers if we assume we can predict with any certainty for any group of learners – however homogeneous – those aspects of content which will prove to be familiar or difficult. We are similarly at the mercy of the learner's imposition of communicative *or* metacommunicative purposes upon any content regardless of any distinctions we might *intend* between data for communication and data and information about communication (Breen 1985a, 1987). Evaluation of appropriate task content would seem to depend upon the discovery of learners' own definitions of content in relation to their own learning priorities and their ways of working upon it.

Choosing procedures Given deduced learning needs as criteria for progress, and given selected content and prioritised problems related to that content, learners can become involved in decisions about the most appropriate ways of working through such content towards agreed purposes. Here we are concerned with learner views of the best ways of learning what they do not yet know – the best ways of applying and developing skills and abilities in learning and using the language. These two issues – increasing knowledge and refining capabilities – can be initially addressed by asking learners to consider *the ways in which they have approached the learning of anything*, and those ways which enabled them to be successful in learning. This sharing of individual approaches to learning in general, and the preferred ways of working which are revealed, can enable learners to be more self-reflective on their own use of skills and abilities and upon the strategies they seem to prefer to adopt during learning. The consideration of others' approaches and preferences can further reveal alternatives in ways of working and, thereby, encourage a toleration of flexibility on the part of individuals who may subsequently tune more finely their way of working to their purposes and to the demands of content. A wider repertoire of working procedures can be revealed by the learning group to the benefit of the individual learner, *and* as a basis both for the evaluation of task procedures and the uncovering of various learner-sensitive procedures even within a single task.

An alternative to a more general investigation of approaches to learning and preferred ways of working upon a new language would be to involve learners directly in *deciding* what shall be done on what content for what period of time and by which procedural routes. Although many learners are often initially teacher dependent, conservative, and relatively imprecise in their proposals for a working procedure through a task, primarily because they have rarely been required to overtly consider these things in the past, the challenge of deciding upon ways of learning offers them the chance to re-evaluate their assumed preferences and to compare alternatives. A subsequent appraisal of the outcomes from an agreed procedure also acquires a new significance for them.

This outcome evaluation phase can be anticipated by involving individual learners within groups in observing and keeping an account of how the group actually worked upon the task and the main characteristics of their approach. Individual learners can also be asked to keep a diary in which they record how they went about certain tasks – when working alone or in a sub-group or within the class. These kinds of important data can be subsequently *related back* to the procedure – or procedures – which were chosen at the outset in order to discover the extent to which procedures were followed, deviated from, found helpful or otherwise, and the reasons for these things. Involving learners in judging their chosen procedures and preferred ways of undertaking tasks can lead them to an accepting awareness of alternatives which can help them to be more adaptable when confronting future learning purposes and different content.

Making the classroom work   The relating of any task to the wider teaching-learning process of the group is an important matter. Learners will contextualise a task in different ways. As part of an investigation of the group's current definitions of most appropriate tasks, we can involve learners in considering and discussing the best uses to which the classroom – and its human and material resources – can be put during a task or tasks. From this, deductions regarding the functions and responsibilities of all members of the group – including the teacher – can be reached. Learners would also be involved in assessing the inevitable constraints of a classroom situation and how these constraints may be overcome in various ways. Therefore, decisions to be made about working procedures can be expanded to cover decisions about the social and material resources in the work situation. Should the task be undertaken individually, in pairs or small groups, or as a whole class? What is the teacher being asked to do as a participant in the task? Also, at what points in the task might participation vary, and in what ways? What additional resources will be needed beyond the chosen data and information? And who is to be responsible for looking for the data and providing them for the group? All such decisions require learners to reconsider their own prior assumptions about their rights and duties in classroom learning, the potential contributions of the other people in a classroom, and the actual benefits of the classroom situation for learning.

The crucial – though often taken-for-granted – role of the classroom situation can also be approached more generally through the learners' identification of the characteristics of a 'good' lesson, of the most helpful things a teacher can provide, and of the most important things other learners can do to make the teaching-learning process of mutual benefit. In addition, the identification of classroom constraints can lead to a consideration of how a 'good' task may compensate for the limits of the situation and available material resources. These issues are particularly relevant in a foreign language learning context where both teacher and learners invest the classroom with a more central role than those groups who can exploit the social situations beyond the classroom in additional ways. (A matter for further decision making within such groups.) The decisions to be reached regarding the contributory functions of the classroom are not trivial background matters in relation to tasks. Learners can be directly involved in contextualising tasks in a more explicit way through decisions concerning: i) types of participation (Who shall work with whom? Who shall do what? How shall things be done?); ii) resources to be used, iii) the timing of the task; and iv) the locating of the task *within* the unfolding curriculum of the group and its particular significance within their own teaching-learning process. This public decision making wherein a task is related to the specific contributions of the classroom can reveal the ways in which learners incorporate any task within the social world of a classroom and transform it into a *social event* with a particular learning purpose. Even a task which does not require overt interpersonal activity is perceived by learners through their definition of a language class and their social role within that class. The evaluation cycle therefore needs to draw out from learners the social significance which they give to a task, and thereby reveal how future tasks may build upon learner contextualisation in positive ways.

PHASE THREE: REFINING AND CREATING TASKS

A major theme of this paper has been that the evaluation which follows the completion of any task is *the* most important and potentially productive moment of classroom work. For learners to be able to relate a task to their original purposes and to perceive progress, they must be engaged in careful appraisal of those things which have been achieved and those which proved difficult or resulted in failure to achieve. It has been suggested that this diagnostic and formative phase can be imbued with a non-threatening and positive value if all outcomes can be *directly* related back to the features of the task – to agreed objectives, selected content, and chosen procedures. Initially, the *full range* of outcomes will need to be identified and shared so that variations in achievement and learning problems can be revealed as a basis for the evaluation of the completed task and 'stored' as the starting points for future tasks. Subsequently, teacher and learners could jointly investigate individual and sub-group answers to the following kinds of questions (their answers being supported or qualified by the reports of task observers and/or by the views expressed in individual learner diaries or work records):

1 To what extent was the task appropriate/inappropriate to our agreed learning objective(s)? And why?
2 To what extent was the selected content helpful/problematic? In what ways?
3 To what extent did the chosen procedure(s) prove to be appropriate/inappropriate? In what ways?
4 What knowledge and ways of working did we actually contribute to the task? What was actually familiar/unfamiliar? What did we actually do in working upon the task? What have we discovered from the task about learning the new language?
5 What have we discovered from the task about each other's contributions during it? What have we discovered about the classroom and the material resources we have used?

These are, of course, example questions referring to each of the five main components of a task. Further questions could certainly emerge from each of these and, prior to the evaluation phase itself, the group could agree on the range of questions to be applied to any one task. When this kind of questioning is pursued by the group in relation to tasks they have selected or planned themselves, the actual role of evaluation itself can be seen by them as highly relevant to their *learning* rather than something which merely focuses upon the products of learning. Decisions about task investigation and how it could be done make the actual process of learning a significant source of subject matter for a language class, whilst the tasks to be worked on are brought closer to the realities of language learning in a classroom group and, thereby, made more sensitive to the benefits and constraints of classroom work *in relation to* the individual learner. The answers derived from evaluation subsequent to the completion of a task crucially provide individual and group criteria for the final phase in the cycle: the group's refinement of existing tasks and their development of new ones. And such refinement and development will be well informed because they emerge from the achievements and problems experienced during previous tasks which have been carefully traced and identified, and they will be characterised by the implementation of the group's own preferred design features.

I offer these *starting points* for a task evaluation cycle within the language classroom on the assumption that the validity of any task has to be discovered during its use. The proposals related to evaluating pre-designed tasks, choosing 'best' tasks, and refining and creating tasks therefore imply that task evaluation can become a central undertaking within the teaching and learning of language. More strongly, perhaps, they suggest that the evaluation and development of tasks can be used as a pivotal language learning activity in itself.

What about the language?

Surely allocating time and energy to the evaluation and refinement of learning tasks is something of a luxury when our priority is the teaching and learning of *the language*? The patient implementation of any one of the proposals I have offered will, of course, take time. But task evaluation will be seen as a 'waste of precious time' only if it is viewed as *something separate* from learning the language. The proposals do not imply that learners will have *less* access to target language or opportunities for using it and discovering how it works. On the contrary. The direct learner involvement in choices and decisions concerning their purposes and needs in the language, about the content to be worked on, and about working procedures in tasks *require learners to make judgements about the new language and relate it – as they see it – to their own learning*. The new language and its use are things about which decisions have to be made as an essential part of the evaluation cycle itself. The language therefore becomes something which has to be planned for and directly related to learning rather than something merely received. The evaluation cycle can serve as a *direct* means for the purposive exploitation of the new language – an authentic language using activity – for the undertaking of a highly relevant decision-making process in a classroom. Task evaluation is therefore both a means towards language development and an immediate and practical use of the new language.

Because task evaluation involves careful reflection and decision making, such work can be *initiated* in a monolingual class through the shared language of the learning group. Later, it can be proposed that the more public sharing of deductions and suggestions should be undertaken through the target language. Gradually the target language can be used as the 'metalanguage' through which a task can be described and categorised, in which observations and records are made, and in which criteria or design features for future task selection and refinement may be expressed. The target language thereby becomes the 'research idiom' of the group. Within the multilingual class, on the other hand, the very need for a common *working* language entails the need for a metalanguage about the target language and about the teaching-learning process directed towards it. Although initiating a task evaluation cycle in a multilingual group may be a slower process than with a monolingual class, the inherent value of learners endeavouring to express and negotiate their views and judgements concerning both the language and the learning of it suggests that task evaluation can be one of the most appropriate and relevant 'situational' uses of the new language in which a class can participate.

Language learning actually *requires* the direct mobilisation of learners' criteria for progress, their exploitation of background knowledge and most productive learning strategies and approaches, and their optimal use of the classroom and the resources within it. Task evaluation directly and overtly engages these things. It is not an activity distinct from actual learning work, but an important means towards language development itself and towards the generation of task types which can better serve this development.

The central role of the teacher

As teachers we have central roles during an evaluation cycle which include at least the following:

1 Sharing with learners the decisions to be made concerning the best ways in which precise information can be gathered and provided by individuals and the group in relation to each phase of the cycle.
2 Provision of a range of pre-designed tasks for evaluation by the group.
3 Co-ordinating the identification and sharing of diverse task outcomes – both achievements and problems.

4 Providing a range of target language data – in any medium – and a range of sources which offer information about the language and its use, all of which can serve as content for new tasks.
5 Co-ordinating the genuine investigatory – or research – process of the group which the evaluation cycle entails.
6 Collecting and sharing key proposals from the group concerning their views of most appropriate tasks – their task design criteria.
7 Being ready, at any moment during the evaluation cycle, to offer our own suggestions and ideas based upon our greater knowledge of the language and wider experience of the language learning process and of the possibilities of classroom work. And being ready to offer these in sympathetic relation to what the learners themselves offer.

In general, however, perhaps the most obvious way in which we can communicate to learners our own need that they willingly identify learning problems and, thereby, confront them more responsibly, is to withdraw from making many decisions *on their behalf* which they should make and which they are potentially capable of making.

Evaluating learners with tasks in mind

Having tried to explain in a brief way in the previous two sections that my particular emphasis upon task evaluation in this paper does not imply a distraction from a working focus upon the language or a reduced role for the greater knowledge and experience of the teacher, I wish to conclude by considering the actual capacity of learners for undertaking task evaluation. Despite the likelihood that some learners may have vague longer term goals in their language learning, assume unrealistic criteria for genuine progress, hold strange views on what may be appropriate content for language work, and seem to be remarkably inefficient in their approaches to such work, *all learners already critically evaluate the tasks they undertake.* They superimpose particular significance on any task and in relation to their view of the wider teaching-learning process in the classroom. They have to contextualise any task within this process and within their individual curriculum for learning the language. They have to make judgements about a task in order to make it amenable and manageable. All learners do such things in mostly covert and personally relevant ways.

In this paper, I have argued that tasks need to be evaluated to determine their validity and with a view to the design of more sensitive tasks. I have also suggested that the covert judgement of tasks which learners already undertake when they reinterpret them in order to make them manageable could become an overt and shared evaluation activity in a language classroom. It is likely that such an investigatory endeavour may initially be a slow process characterised by learners' disbelief that their views and decisions are being genuinely sought. In such circumstances, the full evaluation cycle would not, of course, be immediately embarked upon. However, any one of the proposals offered in this paper can serve as a useful starting point and could well lead towards regular – though appropriately timed – and thorough shared evaluation of tasks. (Alternative task evaluation instruments for classroom use are provided by Potts, 1984 and Breen and Candlin, forthcoming.)

The proposals for an evaluation cycle which I have offered are motivated by the view that task validity and refinement both depend upon *learners'* active participation in judging the tasks they undertake. This participation may be best realised through a task evaluation cycle in the classroom which focuses upon the task-in-process, upon the discovery of learner versions of a task, and which seeks to identify criteria for task design which are closely related to the means for learning in addition to the desired outcomes from learning. This evaluation cycle, though seemingly directed towards the improvement of tasks, also invests tasks with an even greater potential in language teaching than we sometimes grant them. We may use tasks – and the evaluation of them – as a springboard for the more active contributions of a learning group towards the sharing of those decisions and responsibilities which classroom language learning actually demands.

13 Seeing the wood AND the trees: some thoughts on language teaching analysis[1]

H. H. Stern

Introduction

In the development of research on language teaching there has for some years been a tendency to examine more closely 'what goes on in the classroom' and to study classroom discourse (turn taking, error correction, and the like; see, for example, Larsen-Freeman, 1980). This interest in the classroom has a very positive side and must therefore be welcomed, because it is close to the reality of language teaching practice. But there is also a negative side which classroom researchers soon recognise: an over-concern with *minutiae* of teaching and learning, the collection of infinite and unmanageable details, quickly leads to the inability to see the wood for the trees. The contention of this paper is that in order to make sense of classroom discourse and classroom observations they must be placed into a broader context which one might call *language teaching analysis*. In my remarks I would like to outline the main features of such an analysis.[2]

Before doing so we should consider briefly, by way of introduction, why there has been this tendency to become bogged down in the details of classroom observations and classroom discourse. The interest in the classroom as an empirical database has resulted from developments in pedagogy and linguistics.

In *pedagogy*, the disappointment with research on global 'methods', such as comparisons between audiolingualism and cognitivism, had led to a shift of interest from research on *teaching* to research on *learning*. It was recognised around 1970 that different methods are not well-defined entities which can be clearly distinguished from each other and compared by research methods. It is not surprising that, as a reaction, language learning, particularly naturalistic learning *outside* the classroom, received most widespread attention. Eventually, however, it had to be

---

1 I acknowledge with gratitude the Killam Research Fellowship under the terms of which the present paper was prepared.
2 For earlier attempts of systematic language teaching analyses, see, for example, Mackey (1965), Halliday, McIntosh and Strevens (1964) and the feature analyses by Bosco and Di Pietro (1970) and Krashen and Seliger (1975).

recognised that one has also to come to grips with language teaching and learning *inside* the classroom. The nettle had to be seized: to investigate the events of the language classroom itself and to try to understand how and why language learning goes on there as well as how and why it often fails to occur.

On the basis of these reflections classroom observation was attempted in language learning research. Observation schemes, developed elsewhere in education, were adapted to language teaching. New observation schemes have also been developed. The state of the art around 1980 was helpfully analysed in an article by Michael Long (1980) who has examined some twenty odd observation schemes that have been used in language teaching research. But in spite of its comprehensive coverage, Long has, to my mind, not sufficiently emphasised the principal weakness of classroom observation in language learning research: the lack of an explicitly stated theoretical framework in language pedagogy which must necessarily guide any kind of observations in the foreign language classroom.[3]

The other interest in the classroom has been *linguistic*. School classes have been used as a useful database for research on discourse analysis. Here one thinks immediately of the studies in Britain by Sinclair and Coulthard (1975) on classroom discourse. It is important to remember that this research was primarily linguistic, not pedagogic. It was an attempt to develop categories of discourse analysis. Why did Sinclair and Coulthard study *classroom* discourse? Not because it is pedagogically relevant, but because it has advantages for linguistic analysis that other speech settings do not offer: i) in the classroom one can make recordings of what people say without being accused of eavesdropping; and ii) the classroom offers a more clearly defined situation of language use than other situations which are usually more fluid and difficult to capture linguistically; therefore, the classroom lends itself much better to first steps in discourse analysis and to the development of categories of discourse.

For the study of language teaching, this sudden concentration on the classroom from two different points of view has in many ways been confusing and misleading. It has been confusing because the two interests, the pedagogic one and the linguistic one, have not been sufficiently distinguished, and in the literature there is a constant shift from talking in linguistic terms to talking about pedagogy and vice versa. From the point of view of language teaching analysis it has been misleading because the

---

3 Long is of course fully aware of the implicit theoretical bases of such observation schemes: 'Observational instruments are, in fact, no more (or less) than theoretical claims about second language learning and teaching. Their authors hypothesize that the behaviors recorded by their categories are variables affecting the success of classroom language learning. Very little has been done to test those hypotheses' (Long, 1980: 12).

visible events in the classroom and the verbal utterances alone do not necessarily reveal the essentials of a teaching situation.

This article, then, puts forward the claim that what is needed in the study of teaching is a scheme for the analysis of *teaching* rather than a scheme that is designed merely to focus on an individual class out of context and on verbal exchanges occurring in this setting. Within a broad scheme of teaching analysis, however, a more specific scheme of classroom observation that captures the relevant events of a lesson and identifies specific discourse elements can of course be very useful.

In the following remarks I would like to outline the basic categories for a scheme of language teaching analysis which is not focused on an individual classroom in isolation but is conceived more in terms of a case study of a language teaching situation. The categories for such a scheme must of course be sufficiently broad to be applicable to a wide range of situations. At the same time, they must be sufficiently precise to identify and characterise the uniqueness of a given situation.

Such a scheme would serve several purposes:

1 In the first instance it should be designed so as to enable teachers to use it as *a framework for their own decision making*. It is intended therefore to be helpful in a more deliberate and conscious analysis of instructional options.

2 For this reason it should also be useful for *teacher training*. This is of course one of the principal ways in which existing observation schemes have most frequently been used. But in my view they have focused the student teacher's attention too narrowly on the individual lesson and quite arbitrarily on certain behavioural features of the classroom rather than seeing the particular lesson in the total curriculum context and in relation to an underlying philosophy. As a result the observation schemes have tended to make unclear or unstated assumptions which, instead of clarifying, have obscured issues.

3 A broader scheme should have its uses also in *supervision and counselling* where it is often a worry for the practitioner whether the supervisor or adviser sees the lesson under observation in the wider curriculum context, leading to the typical complaint of teachers: 'You've only seen me teach once.'

4 It should have its uses in any form of *programme evaluation* where classroom observation can well provide concrete empirical data which, however, need to be looked at against a broader background.

5 Lastly, such a scheme should be of value to *research on classroom teaching* where, once again, safeguards have to be taken against an overconcern with a mass of behavioural data in isolation. In saying this, I am not siding with scholars who, on principle, oppose empirical enquiries in language teaching (and probably in education generally). I

believe we do not have enough empirical studies in language pedagogy. But without a more comprehensive framework or theory the
study of detailed events can easily be too fragmented. Classroom talk,
for example, is an important aspect of teaching which it is quite
legitimate to focus on. But it is more productive if we have the
instruments to place this particular feature of teaching into a wider
framework.

The framework and broad categories I propose suggest that a teaching
analysis is best viewed as a three-level operation (Figure 1).

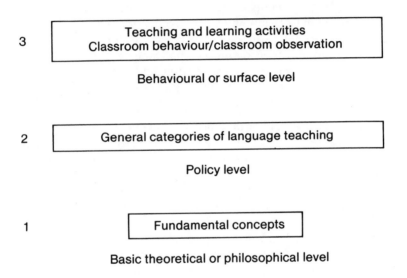

Figure 1   *From 'deep' to 'surface' level in language pedagogy*

At the basic level we visualise the *fundamental assumptions* of a theory of
language teaching, entertained by the teacher, the evaluator, the administrator, the researcher, or even the learner himself. At a second level,
above it, I would place a number of general categories which give
language teaching its particular shape and direction. Let us call this the
policy level of language teaching. It is at this level that the professional
planning and decision making occur. It is only at *the third level*, above
that, that we recognise as surface phenomena the behavioural acts of
teaching and learning, the classroom manifestations which would form
the teaching acts in which the teacher is involved and which are the
subject of classroom observation for a researcher, evaluator or administrator.

My contention is that in many classroom observation schemes there has been a tendency to jump in at the third level and thus to focus on surface phenomena which in themselves are difficult to interpret unless one views them as manifestations of the two deeper levels. Ideally, there would be consistency among the three levels. What happens in the classroom at level 3 should be a true reflection of level 2 (policy) and both levels 2 and 3 should, in turn, be congruent with the fundamental beliefs at level 1. Each of the three levels will now be briefly characterised.

The basic level

At the basic theoretical or philosophical level we visualise a few funda-mental concepts whch are the essential building blocks of a theory of language teaching, concepts of

1 language,
2 society,
3 learning, and
4 teaching.

They are implicit in the language curriculum, in acts of teaching, in policy decisions, even in the learner's conduct. They are also implicit in the observation categories of classroom observation schemes, although they tend to be somewhat lost in the mass of detail that these schemes are apt to gather. It has been a perennial weakness in the past debates on teaching methods that these fundamental assumptions were not clearly enough identified. In other words, differences in basic beliefs, implicit in the method debates, were insufficiently brought into focus.

As a first criterion for assessing language teaching or research I propose the following guiding principle: the more clearly the underlying assump-tions on the nature of language, social context, language learning, and teaching can be called to consciousness, the more sophisticated, the more professional, and the more effective is the operation in question, whether it is language teaching itself, research on language teaching, a language curriculum, a textbook, the evaluation of a programme, and, of course, also an observation scheme.

The policy level

The second level we turn to next is the level of principal instructional options. It is also the locus of pedagogical control and controversies. We can identify four broad categories which are implicit in our teaching but have to some extent been made explicit, partly through earlier decades of

debate about teaching methods, and partly through more recent discussions on curriculum design:

1 categories of content,
2 categories of objectives,
3 categories of treatment or procedures, and
4 categories of evaluation.

As a criterion for the analysis of teaching one can advance the proposition that a sound analytical scheme must somehow concern itself with *all
four* categories. A weakness of the method controversies of the past was
that methods focused too exclusively on procedural treatment factors and
did not concern themselves adequately with the other three. This has led to
the lopsidedness and the constant shifts of perspective in the evolution of
language pedagogy. In the early seventies, the Council of Europe's
Modern Languages Project tried to correct the tendency to be over-
concerned with teaching method by an emphasis on content and objectives. In doing so, the project, in its turn, neglected treatment factors. This
was a deliberate choice at the time in order to focus on linguistic content
and learners' objectives and needs. However, ten years later, the new
project which was started in 1982 was broader and was designed to range
in a more balanced way over a whole gamut of factors, not unlike those
suggested by our analysis of teaching. (Council of Europe 1981, 1983.)

Content and objectives

Let us now briefly look at the first two of the four categories at this level,
content and objectives, which are best represented by a cross-tabulation
(Figure 2). As can be seen from Figure 2, four content categories and four
sets of objectives have been identified. The claim is not made that
language teaching must always pursue all these objectives and content
areas simultaneously and to the same extent. The criterion statement one
might suggest is that a language teaching policy is better to the extent that
it identifies as clearly as possible both its objectives and the content of
teaching, and justifies its priorities on rational grounds, that is, why it
emphasises one or the other content area or this or that objective to a
greater or lesser extent.

Four content categories or 'syllabuses' have been distinguished:

language
culture
communicative activities
general language education

Without dwelling on them here at length, the main point that is being
made is that language cannot be taught in isolation. Language must be

Content	Objectives				Main strategies
	Proficiency	Knowledge	Affect	Transfer	
Language syllabus (L2)	▨	░	░	░	Analytical: study and practice
Culture syllabus (C2)	░	▨	░	░	Analytical: study (knowledge about C2)
Communicative activity syllabus (L2/C2)	▨	░	░	░	Communicative activities (experiential)
General language education syllabus	░	░	░	▨	Comparative (crosslingual/ crosscultural)

Key   Suggested major emphasis
        Suggested minor emphasis   ▓

Figure 2   Example of the interaction between content, objectives and main teaching strategies in a foreign language curriculum.

complemented by other substantive areas which we have called 'culture', 'communicative activities', and 'general language education'. *Culture* as a necessary component of a language programme is in principle well recognised, and need not be elaborated. *Communicative activities* are topics or activities, other than the target language or target culture, which can be regarded as worthwhile in their own right either for their educational value or their interest or concern to the language learner. One such topic area may be the target literature; in many instances of adult language learning it is likely to be topics chosen from the professional interests and activities which may have prompted the learner in the first place to embark on the study of the language in question. In the case of school learners, hobbies, sports and other personal interests fall into this category. Through communicative activities the learner becomes personally involved in communication in the target language. It is the avenue through which personal contact is made with the target language community. *General language education* refers to generalising about language, culture, and language learning, and involves the student in self-reflection as a learner. This is usually a neglected area of language curriculum development, however, see Hawkins (1981 and 1984) and Downes (1984).

Each of these content areas can, in principle, claim equal attention for serious curriculum development. Together the four areas represent a multidimensional approach to the target language curriculum (Stern, 1980, 1982a, 1982b, 1983a, and Ullman, 1982). Whether the emphasis is spread equally over all four areas or restricted mainly to one or two should be a decision deliberately made and justified by the curriculum developer; it should not be a decision based merely on past convention. By and large, it can be said that language curricula have tended to be too narrowly focused on linguistic content in isolation, leading to a working hypothesis that a language programme is likely to be more successful if the language component is not isolated from the other three syllabuses. In other words, the contention is that the curriculum content should normally be multidimensional (particularly so in language programmes at school or university), unless there are specific circumstances where this is inappropriate.

As a generalisation, it can be said that language curricula tend to be too narrowly focused on second language proficiency *in isolation*. The embeddedness of language in culture and society and in the individual's life is not sufficiently reflected in language programmes. A multidimensional curriculum would serve to counteract this tendency.

Turning now to the *objectives* in Figure 2, these, too, have been broadly conceived. They are derived from (and are therefore similar to) the well-known Bloom taxonomies of educational objectives and their application to language teaching worked out by Rebecca Valette over a number of years. Here again, the expression of objectives is multidimensional, not simply proficiency, but besides proficiency, 'knowledge', 'affect', and 'transfer'.

For *proficiency*, which has received most of the attention, there are theoretical definitions available in terms of linguistic or communicative competence (for example, Canale and Swain, 1980), rating scales, usually divided into listening, speaking, reading, and writing, or descriptive inventories, such as the Council of Europe Threshold Level publications, (for example, van Ek, 1975, Coste *et al.*, 1976, Baldegger *et al.*, 1980). A simple criterion proposition might be that proficiency objectives should be defined as clearly as possible in relation to the expected performance levels of the students for whom the curriculum is intended.

As for *knowledge* as an objective, this refers to conceptual knowledge and information about the target language and culture considered worth transmitting to the students within the programme in question. There is also what might be described as 'knowledge of the world' that is expressed in the target language, is specific to the target country, and is likely to have arisen under the 'communicative activities' content area mentioned above. Lastly, there is knowledge about language, culture, and learning in general which is generalised from the work with the target language and culture. Here, once more, our criterion is simply the more clearly the knowledge component has been recognised, the better is the curriculum in question.

Under *affective objectives* we pay attention to the value judgements and to the development of positive and negative attitude and of an emotional set towards the activities in the target language and culture, towards language learning, and towards the self as that of a learner of the particular target language.

Transfer is the construct which represents the idea of learning a language not only for its own sake but as a means to generalise beyond the particular language and culture. Therefore aiming at learning about languages and cultures in general, generalising techniques of language learning, and aiming at developing a positive affect about languages, cultures, and oneself as a language learner fall into this category. This objective is obviously not equally applicable to all language learning situations, but it may be regarded as particularly relevant for school and university language learning where the ultimate uses of a given foreign language are somewhat remote, and language forms part of a general educational curriculum.

This brief outline of objectives suggests that greater diversity of objectives in language teaching is possible and should be envisaged. It should be understood that in this scheme the different *teaching strategies*, indicated in Figure 2, are not just an eclectic potpourri, but they are relevant to the different content areas and the main objectives identified, as will be explained.

Options in curriculum design

With the scheme of content and objectives we have described we have a sufficiently broad, yet precise set of categories to interpret the curriculum policy in a great variety of language teaching situations.

We can summarise the options for curriculum design as being somewhere on a continuum ranging from being narrow and unidimensional to an extreme in multidimensionality:

```
UNIDIMENSIONAL                                    MULTIDIMENSIONAL
  CURRICULUM  <──────────────────────────────>   CURRICULUM
```

Plausible arguments can be advanced for a shift in either direction. For this article the case has been made for a move towards the multidimensional end of the continuum. The possibility of a wider choice of options in curriculum design has been discussed during the past fifteen years. The deliberations by the Council of Europe Modern Languages Project on different principles of designing a syllabus have opened a useful debate on curriculum content and emphasis (Breen and Candlin, 1980; Yalden, 1983; Allen, 1983; Stern, 1983a; and Brumfit, 1984). Of an even more fundamental nature has been the related question to what degree a curriculum should be linguistically controlled, sequenced and carefully structured. This option can be described as follows:

PLANNED		UNPLANNED
	FLEXIBLE	
ORGANISED←		→OPEN
STRUCTURED		UNSTRUCTURED

Little has so far been done to experiment systematically with different options and to study the advantages and disadvantages of differing emphases in curriculum design. A language teaching analysis scheme should certainly attempt to assess the degree of flexibility and complexity of the curriculum design.

The treatment variables

Turning now to the most controversial part of language pedagogy, the treatment variables, some of us have been surprised by a new spate of 'methods' in an era which can be regarded as one of breaking with the method concept in language pedagogy. The new methods (for example Oller and Richard-Amato, 1983) can certainly give focus to specific issues, and they can stimulate experimentation. In spite of these merits of the new methods and the great interest they have aroused, we need categories for the analysis of language teaching methodology which, as Bosco and Di Pietro (1970) and Krashen and Seliger (1975) recognised several years ago, are more fundamental and less rigid than those which have been so prominent in language pedagogy.

The main instructional options can be classified into three broad categories. I refer to them as 'strategies' because they are pervasive features at the policy level of language teaching which at the surface level of teaching manifest themselves in a large number of different techniques and activities:

1 Teaching strategies
2 Timing strategies
3 Social or interpersonal strategies

TEACHING STRATEGIES

The teaching strategies can be said to be derived from the method controversies that have been debated at different times during the last 100 years. For example, *the intralingual strategy* reflects a characteristic of the direct method, the exclusion of the native language, while *the crosslingual strategy* identifies a characteristic of the traditional or grammar-translation method, namely to learn the new language through the medium of the language of origin. *The implicit–explicit option* reflects characteristics of the conflict between audiolingualism and the cognitive theory. The current debate between more structural or more communicative approaches is reflected in the second dimension where we find on one side a more *analytical* and *objective strategy* and a more *experiential, non-analytical* approach to language learning on the other. The *audiolingual–graphic* and *receptive–productive options* represent the experience of over half a century to isolate for teaching purposes the different 'skills' and to combine them in various ways.

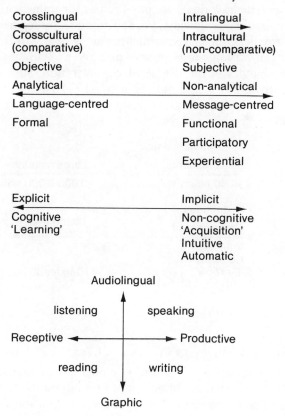

Figure 3   Teaching strategies

Elsewhere it has been shown that these strategy options and the method conflicts which preceded them originate in deep-seated issues of the second language learning process (Stern and Cummins, 1981; Stern, 1983a). These conflicts cannot be resolved by representing them as adversaries. They are best viewed as continua. There is no implicit positive or negative quality judgement on one or the other side of a pair of strategies. Rather they are complementary options which find concrete expression in the more or less of classroom techniques and activities.

TIMING STRATEGIES

While the teaching strategies are largely policy options that, in many teaching situations, the practitioner can select for himself, timing strategies are only partially under the control of the class teacher. They are generally more the responsibility of the administrator or curriculum designer. Nevertheless, there are possibilities for influencing the timing within the individual language class, for example, by segmenting lessons in larger or smaller chunks. Experiments since World War II have opened the possiblity of varying the amount of time given to language instruction and also to changes in the degree of concentration. Some writers, for example, Carroll (1975) and Burstall *et al.* (1974), and some systems of education have attributed a great deal of importance to the time aspect (Stern, 1985).

A. Total amount of time:

Small Amounts	Large amounts
◄───────────────────	
30-60 hours	3,000-5,000 hours

B. Distribution of time:

Concentrated	Distributed
◄─────────────────────────►	
Intensive	
Compact	
'Full flow'	'Drip feed'

Figure 4   Timing strategies

SOCIAL OR INTERPERSONAL STRATEGIES

These partly refer to the size and composition of language learning groups, and as such they are often options for administrators rather than for the individual practitioner. The other social dimension is one in which

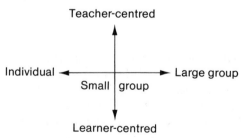

Figure 5   Social strategies

the individual teacher can exercise much more his personal philosophy and policy. There has been an increasing awareness, during the last fifteen years, of the contribution of interpersonal relations to the success of language learning. Teachers have been urged to develop definite strategies of balancing teacher-directedness with more learner participation and learner-initiated approaches. It is certainly an aspect of a language teaching policy to which observation schemes should pay attention.

While none of the teaching strategies can by itself be regarded as either 'right' or 'wrong', their application in a given teaching situation is not a matter of personal whim or fancy. They may be modified in relation to different objectives, to the stage of language learning (beginners, intermediate, and advanced), to the age, maturity, and previous experience of the students, and to the sociolinguistic context of language learning, i.e., whether a language is learnt with or without environmental support. These considerations constitute variables which the practitioner has to bear in mind in deciding on the balance of the strategies to employ. These adjustments of the teaching policy to given circumstances are likely to be made intuitively by the teacher or curriculum developer. On the other hand, the choice of a given strategy can also be the subject of experimental hypotheses and these considerations then become variables in research studies. For a language teaching analysis, we do not look for a fixed combination of strategies; rather we try to find out whether there is an awareness of the range of instructional options and on what grounds different choices have been made.

Resources

A further and most important policy issue concerns the kinds and numbers of resources to make use of. Curriculum resources which include human resources as well as teaching materials and technological equipment can be considered from various points of view. One of these can be represented by the following scale:

EXTENSIVE ⟵——————————————————⟶ LIMITED
VARIED   SIMPLE

The advantage does not necessarily lie with the extensive and varied option. A rich variety of materials and other resources may of course be stimulating, but it may also be confusing, whereas restricted and simple resources, under certain circumstances, can be much more effective because they are easier to handle.

The resources, chosen by, or given to the teacher, usually provide most of the input, and they can therefore exercise an enormous influence on the way in which the policy is actually implemented. We have considered them last among the policy categories because, ideally, the resources should support or reflect the entire curriculum policy. In actual fact, it is often the other way round: it is the choice of the materials or the programme that often determines (or imposes) not only the content, but also the objectives, the teaching strategies and evaluation procedures.

Evaluation options

The final area of policy decisions concerns evaluation. Some of the possibilities can be illustrated as follows:

FORMATIVE←	→SUMMATIVE
FORMAL←	→INFORMAL
FREQUENT TESTS←	→INFREQUENT TESTS
FREQUENT FEEDBACK←	→INFREQUENT FEEDBACK

In this area, as in the others, much serious thought has been given to the merits of different options. For a language teaching analysis one would look for a rational choice of evaluation procedures which give the student a realistic appraisal of progress, represent a fair judgement, and lead increasingly to self-monitoring and self-assessment. It is in this context, too, that studies on error correction are of special interest (for example, Allwright, 1975; Chaudron, 1977).

Having completed our survey of the middle or policy level of language teaching we now turn to the third or surface level.

The surface level: the language class in action

In classroom observation and the interpretation of teacher talk and student talk we deal with surface-level phenomena, the behavioural manifestations of a) fundamental concepts of language, learning, and teaching, and b) decisions at the second level in the area of curriculum objectives, strategies and evaluation. As was pointed out earlier, ideally, the practice of language teaching at this level should accurately reflect the theoretical positions (level 1) and the policy decisions (level 2) adopted by the teacher; and the observations on classroom activities and classroom talk we record on a classroom observation scheme should offer us clues to the underlying policy decisions and the basic assumptions.

We can see now why we cannot simply borrow observation instruments developed in other fields of education in the expectation that they can be applied to language teaching. We have no reason to believe that the categories they employ apply holos-bolus to language teaching and satisfy us at level 1 and 2. We should not close our minds to what has been produced elsewhere. On the contrary; but we should not accept an observation scheme produced for a different purpose and different circumstances unexamined, without proving that it accords with the criteria and categories we regard as appropriate for language teaching.

In the Modern Language Centre of the Ontario Institute for Studies in Education, in Toronto, Canada, several attempts have been made to devise classroom observation schemes as parts of studies on second language learning and teaching. An early one is in a study of the *Good language learner* with a good deal of background on other observation schemes (Naiman *et al.*, 1978). We have never been entirely satisfied with our efforts in this direction, but the need for improved instruments has been clear to us for a long time. Recently, two schemes were tested by two different research teams. One by Ullmann and Geva (1983) made a deliberate effort to capture behavioural manifestations of some of the content categories and strategies we have described at level 2. The other scheme by Allen, Fröhlich and Spada (1984; see also Fröhlich, Spada and Allen, 1985) is in two parts. Part 1 is a general observation instrument which, like the Ullmann–Geva scheme, tries to focus on a number of useful variables reflecting level 2 policy. But from the point of view of language teaching analysis the second part is particularly interesting. It focuses on two critical teaching strategies, and attempts to differentiate between a more structural and a more communicative orientation in language teaching. A number of behavioural criteria have been worked out in order to substantiate the orientation of a particular language class. This scheme clearly shows the relationship between behavioural indices at level 3 and the underlying strategy at the policy level. (See also Ullman and Geva, 1984.)

Conclusion

In conclusion, I would merely like to reiterate my belief in a combination of a broad basis of theoretical concepts (level 1) on which to build policy directions at the curriculum and classroom level (level 2) and thus to make sense of practical activities as they occur at the behavioural level (level 3) in the daily events of the classroom which can be captured by observation schemes. Such a three-level approach should be helpful to the practitioner who wants to interpret the underlying meaning of his teaching activities. It should be equally useful for empirical research by reminding the researcher that the details of an observation scheme must ultimately be related to underlying policies and fundamental assumptions, if the research wants to avoid being overwhelmed by a mass of unmanageable detail which the foreign language class offers in such profusion.

PART V: EVALUATION

14 Language program evaluation: a synthesis of existing possibilities

James Dean Brown

Introduction

The purpose of this paper is to examine the program evaluation literature in educational psychology with a view to synthesizing that which is most useful and applicable to the special problems of language program evaluation. To that end, various definitions of program evaluation will first be compared; then, the differences and similarities between 'testing', 'measurement' and 'evaluation' will be explored. Historical trends in program evaluation are also discussed with a focus on the product-oriented, static characteristic, process-oriented and decision facilitation approaches which have developed over the past forty years in educational psychology. Three dimensions, specifically applicable to language programs, appear to be dominant in the general literature: formative vs. summative evaluation, product vs. process evaluation and quantitative vs. qualitative evaluation. This is followed by an enumeration of twenty-four different data-gathering procedures which are available to language program evaluators. These procedures are classified into six different categories, which can help the evaluator to select a more limited and practical subset of procedures for use in a specific language program evaluation. The paper concludes by tying together the historical developments, the three dimensions of evaluation theory and the large number of data-gathering procedures through discussion of a model (currently being applied at the University of Hawaii). This model functions as an integral part of the overall process of language curriculum development and maintenance.

Definitions of evaluation

Evaluation is defined in Richards *et al.* (1985) as 'the systematic gathering of information for purposes of making decisions'. This definition is perhaps too broad for the purposes of this paper in that it could equally well be used to define needs analysis. However, it is worth considering the possibility that the difference between needs analysis and program evaluation may be more one of focus than of the actual activities involved.

Another definition supplied by Popham (1975) may help to show how foci can differ even in approaches to program evaluation: 'Systematic educational evaluation consists of a formal assessment of the worth of educational phenomena.' In contrast to Richards *et al.*, this definition may be too restrictive. Certainly, there should be a portion of any program evaluation which focuses on 'formal assessment', but perhaps provision should also be made for a number of informal activities, an issue which will be discussed below. There are indeed forms of evaluation that focus on 'the worth of educational phenomena'; however, there are also types which focus on improving the curriculum. These may be equally constructive and useful, as we will also see.

The definition offered by Worthen and Sanders provides a somewhat broader perspective:

> Evaluation is the determination of the worth of a thing. It includes obtaining information for use in judging the worth of a program, product, procedure, or object, or the potential utility of alternative approaches designed to attain specified objectives.
>
> (1973: 19)

This definition is less restrictive in the sense that, while it still includes the notion of 'the worth of a program' it provides for judging 'the potential utility of alternative approaches'. One problem with this definition, however, is that the goal of evaluation is to 'attain specified objectives'. This too may be unnecessarily limiting because it implies a goal-oriented approach to the evaluation process. While there is certainly room for some goal or product orientation in program evaluation, the processes involved should also be considered for the sake of constantly upgrading and modifying the program to meet new conditions.

It seems, then, that a modified definition is needed to suit the views and purposes expressed in this paper: *evaluation* is the systematic collection and analysis of all relevant information necessary to promote the improvement of a curriculum, and assess its effectiveness and efficiency, as well as the participants' attitudes within the context of the particular institutions involved.

Notice that this definition requires that information not only be gathered but also analyzed, and that both should be done systematically. Note also that there are two purposes: the promotion of improvement as well as the assessment of effectiveness, or 'worth' as Popham put it. Finally, this definition stresses that evaluation is necessarily site-specific in the sense that it must focus on a particular curriculum, and will be affected and bound to the institutions which are linked to the program, whether they be parent-teacher associations, university administration, national or local governments, etc.

Testing, measurement and evaluation

In the interest of clarity, it is important to recognize that the word evaluation is used in a number of different ways. In this paper, the terms testing, measurement and evaluation will be used in very specific ways. *Testing* refers solely to procedures that are based on tests, whether criterion-referenced or norm-referenced in nature. *Measurement* is used more broadly and not only includes testing but also other types of measurements, such as attendance records, questionnaires, teacher ratings of students (or student ratings of teachers), etc. *Evaluation*, an even broader term, includes all kinds of measurements as well as other types of information – some of which may be more qualitative than quantitative in nature. As will be discussed later, qualitative information (for example diaries, meetings, interviews, even conversations over coffee) can be as valuable as data based on testing.

Approaches to program evaluation

Over the years, there have been various approaches proposed for ways to accomplish program evaluation. Generally, they fall into one of four categories: goal attainment approaches, static characteristic approaches, process oriented approaches and decision facilitation approaches. These categories will each be presented in turn and then discussed in terms of how they might best be combined for the purposes of language program evaluation.

Product oriented approaches

Product oriented approaches are those which focus on the goals and instructional objectives of a program with the purpose of determining whether they have been achieved. Chief proponents of this approach include scholars like Tyler, Hammond, and Metfessel and Michael.

Tyler's (1942) view was that programs should be based on clearly defined goals (specified in terms of the students, society and subject matter) and measurable behavioral subjects. The focus of a program evaluation would then be on whether those objectives had been learned. The objectives should be measured at the end of the program with one of two conclusions: if not learned, failure to attain the goals of the program was indicated; if learned, success in meeting the goals was shown. This summary is, of course, an oversimplification. Tyler's thinking was considerably more complex. For instance, the development of goals and objectives involved not only the instructional materials but also the students, the subject matter, societal considerations, philosophy of education and learning philosophy. He also had a rather sophisticated view of what it meant to test those objectives (Tyler, 1951).

In the sixties, Hammond described a product-oriented approach which specified considerably more detail. He advocated that five steps be taken in evaluation: i) identifying precisely what is to be evaluated; ii) defining the descriptive variables; iii) stating objectives in behavioral terms; iv) assessing the behavior described in the objectives; and v) analyzing the results and determining the effectiveness of the program (1973: 168).

Metfessel and Michael (1967) also advocated the product orientation, but they detailed the steps involved with much more precision:

1 Direct and indirect involvement of the total school community;
2 formation of a cohesive model of broad goals and specific objectives;
3 translation of specific objectives into communicable form;
4 instrumentation necessary for furnishing measures allowing inferences about program effectiveness;
5 periodic observations of behaviors;
6 analysis of data given by status and change measures;
7 interpretation of the data relative to specific objectives and broad goals; and
8 recommendations culminating in further implementation, modifications and revisions of broad goals and specific objectives.

Such detailed steps might lead us to think of the approach advocated by Metfessel and Michael (and, in fact, Hammond's as well) as somehow process-oriented like those that will be described below. However, we need only consider the degree to which points 2, 3, 7 and 8 above are concerned exclusively with product (in the form of specific objectives) to see that this approach as well as the two others above are product-oriented approaches.

Static characteristic approaches

Static characteristic approaches are one type of what Worthen and Sanders (1973) term 'professional judgment' evaluations. The static characteristic version of evaluation is conducted by outside experts in order to determine the effectiveness of a particular program. Typically, this would force a program to pull together its records and clean up its facilities in anticipation of the arrival of a team of experts. The experts would then visit the facility to examine those records as well as static characteristics (for example, the number of library books and language lab tapes, the number of Master's degrees and Ph.D.s among the staff, the adequacy of the physical plant, parking facilities, etc.) in order to formulate a report based on their observations. The necessity for this type of evaluation was, and still is, closely linked to *institutional accreditation*: a process whereby an association of institutions will set up criteria, make site visits, and formulate evaluation reports that judge the value of the institution as to whether it should be accredited as a member institution in good standing (see National Study of Secondary Evaluation, 1960). A general problem with this static characteristic approach is pointed to by Popham:

> A major reason for the diminishing interest in accreditation conceptions of evaluation is the recognition of their almost total reliance on intrinsic rather than extrinsic factors. Although there is some intuitive support for the proposition that these process factors are associated with the final outcomes of an instructional sequence, the scarcity of empirical evidence to confirm the relationship has created growing dissatisfaction with the accreditation approach among educators.
>
> (1975: 25)

Process-oriented approaches

A notable shift to *process-oriented approaches* began with the realization that meeting program goals and objectives was indeed important but that evaluation procedures could also be utilized to facilitate curriculum change and improvement. Notable among the advocates of these approaches were Scriven and Stake.

Scriven's (1967) contributions included a dramatic new set of foci for program evaluations. Some of the most important of these are as follows:

1 He originated the distinction between formative and summative evaluation.
2 He emphasized the importance of evaluating not only if the goals had been met but also if the goals themselves were worthy.
3 He advocated *goal free evaluation*, i.e., the evaluators should not only limit themselves to studying the expected goals of the program but also consider the possibility that there were unexpected outcomes which should be recognized and studied.

Notice the degree to which product, in the form of goals, is deemphasized here in favor of process in the forms of formative and goal free evaluation.

Stake is best known for the *Countenance model* of evaluation. The basic elements of this model (Stake, 1967a) begin with a rationale, then focus on descriptive operations (intents and observations) and end with judgmental operations (standards and judgments) at three different levels: antecedents (prior conditions), transactions (interactions between participants) and outcomes (as in traditional goals but also broader in the sense of transfer of learning to real life).

These distinctions are important because i) Stake revealed that evaluators engage in both pure description and judgmental activities and that they should bear in mind the difference between the two and ii) he pointed to a transaction component which he felt should be dynamic, as opposed to antecedents and outcomes, which are relatively static. Again we find that processes should be involved in the evaluation.

Decision facilitation approaches

Another view of program evaluation is that it should serve the purposes of decision makers, who are usually also the administrators. In these approaches, evaluators are still more wary of making judgments of their own, preferring instead to gather information for the benefit of those in a program who must ultimately make the judgments and decisions. Examples of this approach are the CIPP, CSE and Discrepancy models of evaluation.

CIPP, originated by Stufflebeam *et al.* (1971), is an acronym for Context (rationale for objectives), Input (best utilization of resources for achieving objectives), Process (periodic feedback to decision makers) and Product (measurement and interpretation of attainments during and at the end of a program). As further defined by Stufflebeam, this approach had a new definition for evaluation: 'THE (1 PROCESS) OF (2 DELINEATING), (3 OBTAINING), AND (4 PROVIDING) (5 USEFUL) (6 INFORMATION) FOR (7 JUDGING) (8 DECISION ALTERNATIVES).' Stufflebeam points to four key issues which help to illuminate his views even further:

1 Evaluation is performed in the service of *decision making*, hence, it should provide information which is useful to decision makers.
2 Evaluation is a cyclic, continuing *process* and, therefore, must be implemented through a systematic program.
3 The evaluation process includes the three main steps of delineating, obtaining and providing. These steps provide the basis for a methodology of evaluation.
4 The delineating and providing steps in the evaluation process are *interface* activities requiring collaboration.

The CSE model, which is also known as the UCLA model, is named after the acronym for the Center for the Study of Evaluation at the University of California Los Angeles. Like the CIPP model, this approach is designed to facilitate decision making. Alkin (1969) suggests that evaluations should provide information in five different categories of decisions: systems assessment (the state of the overall system), program planning (*a priori* selection of particular strategies, materials, etc.), program implementation (appropriateness of program implementation relative to intentions and audience), program improvement (changes that might improve the program and help deal with unexpected outcomes) and program certification (the overall value of the program).

The *discrepancy model* is yet another decision facilitation model, due largely to Provus (1971), who offered the following definition of evaluation:

> Program evaluation is the process of 1) defining program standards; 2) determining whether a discrepancy exists between some aspect of program performance and the standards governing that aspect of the program; and 3) using discrepancy information either to change performance or to change program standards.

At first glance, this definition could perhaps seem to be a throwback to the product or goal oriented approaches discussed above. However, a quick look at the five stages delineated by Provus will show that this is a process oriented approach, especially in the 'treatment adjustment' stage:

I   Program description stage
II   Program installation stage
III Treatment adjustment stage [process]
IV   Goal achievement analysis stage
V   Cost-benefit analysis

A closer look at how these five stages are meant to fit together will further indicate the degree to which the model is not only process oriented but also designed to promote decision facilitation:

> Successive reappraisals of program operations and of the program standards from which program operations are derived are generally consequences of the decisions made by program staff on the basis of discrepancy information reported in Stages II, III and IV. If a decision is made to reformulate standards rather than to revise program performance, there are immediate implications for the negotiation of all subsequent evaluation stages.

This last model illustrates the degree to which the evolution of approaches to evaluation has been a healthy and progressive one. Each development has built on what was learned in previous approaches. Product-oriented and static characteristic approaches were improved by the addition of process considerations and these were, in turn, refined by adding decision facilitation dimensions. In other words, there appears to be a great deal language educators can learn from this forty years of development in educational psychology. As we shall see below, the model followed by any particular program may draw on several or all of these traditions.

Dimensions of evaluation

Among the evaluation approaches discussed above, there are certain patterns which can help not only in understanding the similarities and differences between the existing approaches but also in formulating an approach tailored to (and, therefore, most advantageous to) a particular program. These patterns center on three dimensions: formative vs. summative, process vs. product and quantitative vs. qualitative. Such opposing points of view are often considered dichotomies, but they are referred to as 'dimensions' here because our experience at the University of Hawaii indicates that they may be complementary rather than mutually exclusive. We take the stance that our particular program should utilize both points of view in each of the dimensions. In other words, all available perspectives may prove valuable for the evaluation of a given program. How they are utilized in a particular setting will naturally depend on the various educational philosophies of the administrators, teachers and students in the program.

Formative vs. summative

The distinction between formative and summative evaluation is not new in the language program evaluation literature. Indeed, it has been a central issue in a number of papers (Bachman, 1981; Jarvis and Adams, 1979; Long, 1984; and Richards, 1984b). The position is taken here that the difference between formative and summative evaluations hinges on the purposes for information gathering and on the types of decisions that will ultimately evolve from each purpose.

Typically, *formative evaluation* is defined as taking place during the development of a program and its curriculum. The purpose, then, is to gather information that will be used to improve the program. The types of decisions that will result from such evaluation will be relatively small scale and numerous, and will result in modifications and fine tuning of the existing program design. *Summative evaluation*, on the other hand, is often thought of as occurring at the end when a program has been completed. The purpose for gathering the information in this type of evaluation is to determine whether the program was successful and effective. The types of decisions that will result from such analyses will be fairly large scale and may result in sweeping changes (for example, the continued funding of a program or its cancellation).

These are, of course, the extreme expressions of what is likely to occur in actual evaluations; they may simply be two ways of viewing and compiling what is approximately the same information. The view taken in our program is that virtually all evaluation should, in a sense, be formative, i.e., all information should rightfully be used to modify and improve the teaching and learning of language. What sense does it otherwise make to devote the energy and resources necessary to effectively do an evaluation if this does not directly benefit the students and the program as a whole?

There also appears to be a logical fallacy with the extreme version of summative evaluation as expressed above. Typically, language programs are ongoing concerns that do not conveniently end; consequently, a summative evaluation is difficult to perform. This makes the formative version of evaluation more intuitively appealing. Yet from time to time, it is probably healthy to pause and ask the larger kinds of questions usually associated with a summative evaluation format. This may be done in a crisis mode, such as when a program and its staff find themselves having to demonstrate their worth to a funding agency in order to avoid being canceled. Crisis-induced evaluation is not likely to be conducive to clear thinking or very beneficial results (other than the mere survival of the program). Instead, it would probably be more constructive if a program were to draw on both notions of evaluation to work out a schema that can accomplish the program's purpose equally well. Perhaps formative evaluation can (and should) be going on constantly with the purpose of producing information and analyses that will be useful for changing and upgrading the program. It might also be useful to pause occasionally to assess the success, efficiency and effectiveness of the program. This might take the form of a yearly report to a sponsoring/funding agency or of a relatively informal analysis and revision deadline set within the program.

Whatever the form, such summative stock-taking can have several beneficial effects. First, it will allow for a larger focus on the overall issues of success or failure rather than on the smaller implementational issues typically involved in formative evaluation. Second, it can be very revealing and even encouraging to take a look at what has been accomplished from a longer perspective. Even though it is sometimes easy to lose sight of those gains and get lost in the smaller details of delivering instruction, it can be very satisfying to realize that language learning has indeed occurred. This positive aspect can help program administrators and teachers remember that something is being accomplished beyond merely coping with one hourly crisis after another. Third, and politically most important, periodic 'summative' evaluations put a program in an excellent position to respond to crises when, and if, they occur. If the information is regularly marshalled under much less pressure, this will be done with considerably more thought and care. Hence, the program will be in a better position to defend itself against pressures from outside. In short, it appears that both the formative and summative notions of evaluation can be useful within a program. The balance struck will, as always, depend on the conditions in the particular program.

Product vs. process

Another distinction, which seems to propel much of the debate discussed above, is between product evaluation and process evaluation. While the difference between summative and formative evaluation hinges on differences in the purpose for gathering information, the distinction between product and process is based on differences in what information might be considered. *Product evaluation* can be defined as any evaluation which is focused on whether the goals (product) of the program were achieved. *Process evaluation*, on the other hand, centers more on what it is that is going on in a program (process) that helps to arrive at those goals (product). Clearly, this distinction is related to the previous one. Summative evaluations will tend to focus on product because the purpose of gathering the information is to make decisions about whether or not the goals of the program have been accomplished. Conversely, formative evaluations will more often look at process because the purpose for gathering the information is not only to determine if the goals have been met but also to study and improve those processes which were involved. Given the position taken above on formative vs. summative evaluations, it should be clear that we are pursuing the study of both product and process in our program. As will be explained next, this will necessarily include the use of both quantitative and qualitative means for gathering and analyzing evaluation information.

Quantitative vs. qualitative

The last distinction to be discussed here, then, is the one that is often made between quantitative and qualitative approaches. The point here is that there are basically only two different types of data that any evaluation study can rely on.

The first, *quantitative data*, are gathered using those measures which lend themselves to being turned into numbers and statistics. Examples might include test scores, student rankings within their class or simply the number of males and females in a program. Such data are readily available in most language programs and certainly more can always be generated. The important part of using quantitative data in evaluation occurs in the next step wherein attempts are made to sort through the data and make sense of them by finding any existing and useful patterns. This is most often done by using descriptive and inferential statistics. Unfortunately, this area of concern is well beyond the scope of this paper; however, numerous books on the topic are available (see Tuckman, 1978 and Shavelson, 1981 for clear introductions to the most useful of these strategies and statistics; also see Smith, 1970 for a now classic example of this type of study in foreign language education and/or Tucker and Cziko, 1978 for an overview of such studies in bilingual education).

Qualitative data, on the other hand, are generally observations that do not so readily lend themselves to becoming numbers and statistics. Examples might include diary entries made by administrators, teachers or students, records of staff meetings, classroom observations, or even recollections of conversations over coffee. While such data often lack credibility because they do not seem 'scientific', it may turn out that they are more important to the actual decisions made in a program than would at first be apparent. Hence, it would seem irresponsible to belittle these sorts of data. What is advocated here is that qualitative data be used – in a principled and systematic manner – so that the information gained will be as complete and useful as possible (see Cook and Reichardt, 1979; Patton, 1978, 1980; and Willis, 1978 for much more on this).

At the University of Hawaii, we are finding that both quantitative and qualitative data provide valuable information that should be used. Since this was also true of what was said about the formative and summative as well as the process and product distinctions, it is probably clear at this point that this paper is generally arguing for gathering as much information as possible from as many perspectives as reasonable in order to make the evaluation and the resulting decisions as accurate and useful as humanly possible.

Evaluation procedures

All of the approaches and dimensions discussed above are important to know about in the evaluation process because evaluators should decide, at least tentatively, which combination of approaches they wish to use (i.e., whether their evaluation will be summative or formative, process- or product-oriented, and quantitative or qualitative – or all of the above). These distinctions and decisions must eventually lead to determining which measures will be applied to changing elements of a particular language program.

There are numerous procedures available to evaluators for gathering information. Some of these lend themselves to collecting quantitative data and others to qualitative information. Thus the term *procedure* is not only being used here to include measures (as defined earlier), which are useful in gathering quantitative data, but also to encompass methods used in gathering qualitative data, for example, observations, interviews, meetings, etc. Many of the existing procedures are presented in Table 1. The purpose of this section is not to explain each and every one of these procedures (there are fuller descriptions in Brown and Pennington's unpublished MS), but rather to demonstrate that they are only variants of six basic categories, and that even these six categories can be classified into two classes that differ in terms of the relationship between the evaluator(s) and the program participants. It is hoped that these categories and classes will help evaluators to make balanced choices among the many procedures available for the evaluation process. Obviously, it would be absurd to attempt the use of all of the procedures listed in Table 1, but a reasonable selection can be made based on the realization that the measures can be grouped in this manner.

TABLE I. EVALUATOR'S ROLE, CATEGORIES AND PROCEDURES

Evaluator's role	*Categories*	*Procedures*
Outsider looking in	Existing information	– Records analysis – Systems analysis – Literature review – Letter writing
	Tests	– Proficiency – Placement – Diagnostic – Achievement
	Observations	– Case studies – Diary studies – Behavior observation – Interactional analyses – Inventories
Facilitator drawing out information	Interviews	– Individual – Group
	Meetings	– Delphi technique – Advisory – Interest group – Review
	Questionnaires	– Biodata surveys – Opinion surveys – Self-ratings – Judgemental ratings – Q sort

To begin with, notice that Table 1 contains 24 different procedures for gathering evaluation information. Initially, the array of procedures in the column on the right may seem bewildering though closer analysis reveals a simpler pattern. Notice, for instance, that there are four types of testing, each considered a separate procedure in the table. Surely, these forms of testing are related and can be considered as one category of procedures. By similar processes, all of the 24 instruments can be classified into the six categories of procedures shown in the second column of Table 1.

Still further analysis reveals that three of the categories in the second column, i.e., existing records, tests, and observations, leave the evaluator more or less in the position of being an outsider looking in on the program as the evaluation process proceeds. The other three, i.e., interviews, meetings and questionnaires, inevitably seem to draw the evaluator into participating in the process of gathering or drawing out information from the participants in the program. This difference can have important consequences with regard to the way the procedures and the results based on them are viewed by participants and evaluators alike. Let us now turn to the steps whereby all of the information presented so far can be implemented. This should help to tie together the many threads that have been developed here.

Discussion

Step one: a framework

Numerous models for curriculum development have been proposed in the language teaching literature, especially in the area of English for specific purposes, and some of them have included an evaluation component (Perry, 1976; Strevens, 1977; Candlin *et al*, 1978). With a view to establishing evaluation that is an integral and ongoing part of the English Language Institute (ELI) curriculum at the University of Hawaii, we instead adapted the rather elaborate 'systematic approach' model developed by Dick and Carey (1985). Ours is the much simpler version shown in Figure 1.

In a systematic approach to curriculum design such as this, the primary information-gathering and organizational elements include the needs analysis, instructional objectives and testing (Dick and Carey, 1985; Brown and Richards, in preparation). The information and insights gained from these activities can then be analyzed and synthesized in the design of materials and delivery of instruction. The working model for this approach which is presently being used in our program may, at first glance, appear to represent five steps which should be followed linearly. Further examination of the model reveals, however, that all of the elements are interconnected by arrows to each other and to an ongoing process of 'evaluation'.

The arrows and their link to evaluation are meant to imply three

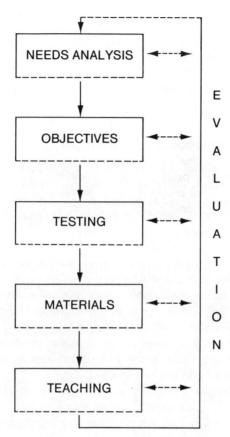

Figure 1   Systematic approach for designing and maintaining language curriculum

things. First, in an ideal situation, curriculum development would start with a thorough needs analysis and then progress through the steps that are shown. However, such an ideal situation is probably very rare. What is much more likely is that a program is already in progress, perhaps even fairly well entrenched, when the curriculum development/revision process is initiated. It may be, therefore, that the starting point is necessarily other than at the needs analysis stage. In fact, it may happen that the needs analysis, formulation of goals and objectives, articulation of test, selection or creation of materials, and delivery of instruction must all occur at about the same time. Second, the process of curriculum development is never finished (unless, of course, a program is canceled). This implies that there should always be provision in the curriculum plan for revision of all of the elements with a view to constantly improving them. Finally, in this model, the ongoing program evaluation is the glue that connects and holds all of the elements together. Without it, there is no cohesion among the elements and, if left in isolation, any one of them may become pointless. In short, the heart of the systematic approach to language curriculum design, as shown here, is evaluation – the part of the model that includes, connects and gives meaning to all of the other elements.

Step two: determining theoretical foci

Keeping the above model in mind, we next needed to make decisions about how the three different dimensions would be handled in the evaluation process. Would it be formative or summative? product or process? quantitative or qualitative? Or, would the evaluation include all of these points of view?

We decided that our evaluation should be *formative* in the sense that it would be ongoing with the purpose of improving all five components of the program. This process will nevertheless be punctuated on a yearly basis by a summative evaluation report to the Graduate Faculty of the Department of ESL. The purpose of these *summative* reports will be to periodically take stock of what has been accomplished each year, to get feedback on the program from professionals in the field, and to involve graduate faculty members in the ELI curriculum as much as possible, given the constraints on their time and energy.

It was also decided that attention should be given to the *processes* going on in the ELI, i.e., the ongoing relationships between students' needs, program goals and course objectives, criterion-referenced and norm-referenced tests, materials, and teaching. Given the particular resources and staffing at our university, we also encourage classroom research (through the Center for Second Language Classroom Research) into process evaluation as defined by Long, 1984, '... the systematic observation of classroom behavior with reference to the theory of (second) language development which underlies the program being evaluated'. In addition, we intend to periodically stop and examine the *product* that is being produced by the program in the form of testing what the students can do at the end of their training, and by determining how they, their ELI teachers, and their major field professors perceive their ESL training in retrospect.

In order to do all of this, both quantitative and qualitative procedures will be used for gathering information. Using quantitative data, we have set up an experiment to discover if our students have learned anything and, if so, how much. As pointed out by Lynch (1986), however, a quantitative study which demonstrates that students who receive a language learning treatment (instruction) significantly outperform a control group who did not receive the treatment is really only showing us that our treatment is *better than nothing*. Of course, the degree to which our treatment is better than nothing may be of interest. We have decided, instead, in favor of a simple pretest–post-test design for each course wherein we will examine improvement within the program rather than comparison to a control group. Such information is being viewed as only one important piece in a puzzle which must include many more pieces – ones which can provide more detail about what is going on in the learning process. Other sources of information of a more qualitative nature (for example, interviews, observations, diaries, etc.) are therefore being included in our evaluation process.

Step three: formulating research questions

Based on the decisions made about the three evaluation dimensions, we have defined useful and practical questions worthy of study. Such questions should logically examine each curriculum component as a potential source of data important to the overall evaluation process. The purpose of gathering all of this information is, of course, to improve these components as well as to more clearly articulate the ways that they work together. One problem that arises is that the amounts and diversity of information which may be included in an evaluation can quickly become overwhelming. Our next task was, therefore, to eliminate less useful information and strike a balance among the information groupings that remained; this necessarily involved a certain amount of selectivity.

Recall that the curriculum components under consideration were needs analysis, objectives, testing, materials, teaching and, of course, the evaluation itself, as shown in Figure 1. Each of these can be viewed from three perspectives: Were they effective? Were they efficient? And what were participants' attitudes toward them? Thus, the process of extracting and synthesizing evaluation information can be viewed as a two-dimensional model as shown in Figure 2.

The first phase in taking control of the scope of the evaluation process was to limit ourselves to one overriding research question for each of the cells shown in Figure 2. The primary questions that we chose to answer are as follows:

A Effective?
1 Which of our original perceptions of the students' *needs*, especially as reflected in the goals and objectives, are being met and which are not?
2 Which of our instructional *objectives*, as reflected in criterion-referenced tests, are being achieved at an acceptable level of performance by the students and which are not?
3 To what degree are the students learning the stated objectives and overall academic English in the three skill areas (reading, listening and

Program components

	Needs	Objectives	Testing	Materials	Teaching
Effective?					
Efficient?					
Attitudes?					

(Left margin label, reading vertically: VIEWPOINTS)

Figure 2   Evaluation components and viewpoints

writing) as measured by the criterion-referenced and norm-referenced *tests* in our program?

4 How effective are the present *materials* in meeting the needs of the students as expressed in the objectives which are measured by the tests?

5 How effective is the *teaching* in the program?

B Efficient?

1 Which of the students' *needs*, as originally perceived, turned out to be necessary when taught, and which turned out to be superfluous, as reflected by performance on the objectives-based criterion-referenced tests?

2 Which *objectives* were necessary and which have previously been learned by the students as indicated by the pretests?

3 How can the criterion-referenced and norm-referenced *tests* be made more efficient, reliable and valid for our purposes?

4 How can *materials* resources be better organized for access by the teachers and students?

5 What types of teacher training can be provided to improve the *teaching* throughout the program?

C Attitudes?

What are the students', teachers' and administrators' attitudes and feelings about the i) students' language learning needs; ii) goals and objectives; iii) criterion-referenced and norm-referenced tests; iv) materials; and v) teaching.

By limiting ourselves to answering these questions during the present academic year, it is hoped that we have narrowed the focus of the evaluation process enough so that it is manageable and practical. There are, of course, numerous other questions that should be answered, and questions will continue to arise as we begin to answer the ones at hand. We will, however, postpone these to be examined in future years because we recognize the need to start the evaluation process with a limited set of research questions.

Step four: selecting procedures

With a relatively small set of research questions stated in writing, our program was then in a position to select the most useful procedures (from Table 1) to answer those questions. Again with a view to limiting the scope of the evaluation process, only two procedures were chosen from each of six categories listed in Table 1. This more limited set is shown in Table 2.

TABLE 2 CATEGORIES, PROCEDURES AND QUESTIONS TO BE ADDRESSED BY EACH

Categories	Procedures	Questions to be addressed
Existing information	– Records analysis – Literature review	A1 B1, B3–B5
Tests	– Placement – Achievement	A3 A1, A2–A4
Observations	– Diary studies – Behavior observation	C1–C5 A5
Interviews	– Individual – Group	C1–C5 C1–C5
Meetings	– Advisory – Interest group	A4, A5, B4, B5 A4, A5, B4, B5
Questionnaires	– Opinion surveys – Judgmental ratings	C1–C5 A4, A5, C1–C5

From the twenty-four available procedures, we have necessarily been very selective. Choosing our procedures as we did, on the basis of Table 1, has helped us to rationally gather a wide variety of information across six categories, while keeping the evaluator fifty per cent in the position of an outsider looking in, and fifty per cent in the role of a participant in the evaluation process. Moreover, each of the procedures, once selected, is serving multiple purposes, as can be seen by examining the diversity and number of questions (in the third column of Table 2) that are being addressed by each procedure. This helps us to consider our central questions from different points of view – all of which must be integrated after the information is gathered in the next step.

Step five: data gathering

Without going into great detail about the data-gathering process, there are three elements that we have found important in keeping the process going: i) marshalling personnel, ii) organization and iii) assigning responsibilities. We were able to marshall personnel by finding release time for three of our teachers (one each for listening, reading and writing) who were already experienced in curriculum development, and by finding funding through grants for two graduate students to help these 'lead' teachers develop, administer and analyze the procedures shown in Table 2. These, or similar strategies, are absolutely necessary for carrying out any project on this scale. Overall organizational issues are being handled by the Director of the ELI with considerable help from the Assistant Director, but responsibilities for each skill area have been delegated to the lead teachers who, in turn, organize the efforts of the teaching staff. Only through the help and cooperation of all the staff, have we been able to plan as far as we have and implement the evaluation process as explained here.

Step six: analysis and synthesis of information

The final step is to analyze and synthesize the sizeable body of information which is being generated by the evaluation process, even with our limited sets of questions and procedures. Again, the staffing and organizational issues discussed in the previous step have proven crucial in carrying out this evaluation process. It is at this point, however, that almost universal interest is expressed within the ELI about the process because, in this step, we are finally able to look at information in a practical and useful manner, and implement change in our perceptions of students' needs, in the course objectives, in the norm-referenced and criterion-referenced tests, in the materials and in the teaching practices in our program. Since this is an ongoing process, it is the last step wherein we can also begin again with step one by formulating new questions for the next year, and looking forward to making continued improvements in the language teaching and learning that we provide to our hundreds of foreign students each year.

Conclusion

Near the beginning of this paper, evaluation was defined as the systematic collection and analysis of all relevant information necessary to promote the improvement of a curriculum and assess its effectiveness and efficiency, as well as the participants' attitudes within the context of the particular institutions involved. The overall purpose of evaluation, it was argued, is to determine the general effectiveness of a program – usually for purposes of improving it, or defending its utility to outside administrators or agencies. This is not a simple issue, but rather a complex of interrelated issues. Evaluation, in fact, should probably be viewed as the drawing together of many sources of information to help examine selected research questions from different points of view, with the goal of forming all of this into a cogent and useful picture of how well the language learning needs of the students are being met. One way to view program evaluation might be that it is a never ending needs analysis, the goal of which is to constantly refine the ideas gathered in the initial needs analysis, such that the program can do an even better job of meeting those needs. All of the components of the curriculum are necessarily involved as sources of information, and each of these must be considered from different points of view. But selectivity and planning are crucial so that the enormous amount of potential information does not become overpowering. In short, evaluation should be the part of a curriculum that includes, connects and gives meaning to all of the other elements in a program.

15 The development and use of criterion-referenced tests of language ability in language program evaluation[1]

Lyle F. Bachman

Introduction

The role of measurement in program evaluation has become increasingly unclear in the past few years, and this is for several reasons. First, evaluators have come to recognize that the processes that take place in a language program are at least as important as the products of the program. That is, what happens in the classroom is of interest not only because of its relationship to program outcomes, but in its own right. Most of these processes, indeed those that are of greatest interest, that take place in the minds of learners, are extremely difficult to measure. A second reason for questioning the role of measurement in program evaluation is the emphasis that many current evaluation theories place on qualitative sources of information, in some cases to the virtual exclusion of quantitative data of any kind. And finally, there are the inadequacies of norm-referenced tests for the purposes of program evaluation and the negative repercussions of their continued use for these purposes.

But rather than causing us to abandon tests as part of language program evaluation, I believe these concerns must lead us to a reorientation in our thinking about the needs for tests and about the types of tests we need. The need to examine the processes of instruction and learning presents a different set of measurement problems from those encountered in measuring outcomes. For example, the use of communication strategies and the amount of comprehensible input a learner obtains are areas of considerable interest not only for second language acquisition research but, it would seem, for language program evaluation as well. These present a challenge to measurement that is both intriguing and formidable, but not, I believe, insurmountable.

In addition to processes, we need to examine the products of the language program. We must pay attention to a wide range of program

1 This is a revised version of a keynote paper presented at the Conference on Trends in Language Programme Evaluation, Bangkok, Thailand, 9–11 December 1986.

outcomes, including the effects of the program on teachers, the school system, and the community. Learner achievement has historically been a major concern of evaluation, and I believe that this will continue to be of prime interest in the future. It is here, of course, that measurement has played the largest role. And while we must not ignore the vital importance of qualitative information about outcomes, such as classroom observation or teacher reports, I agree with Popham (1978) that 'pupil test performance will always play a pivotal role in any approach to evaluation' (p. 4).

The major problems in measuring learner achievement in language program evaluation in the past have, I believe, been twofold: i) the inadequacies of norm-referenced measurement theory and of tests developed within this theory for addressing the needs of program evaluation, and ii) the incompleteness of our definition of language proficiency. This is not to say, however, that these problems must persist. The past decade has seen rapid developments in criterion-referenced testing, so that an emerging measurement technology is now available for application to the needs of language program evaluation (for example, papers in Berk, 1980a, 1984a). This period has also witnessed an expansion in the definition of language proficiency that recognizes both the context – discourse and sociolinguistic – in which language use takes place, and language use as a dynamic negotiation of meaning (for example, Canale and Swain, 1980; Johnson, 1982a; Canale, 1983; Savignon, 1983; Candlin 1986). These developments in criterion-referenced test theory and the broader definition of language ability provide, I believe, the keys to developing language tests that are appropriate to the needs of language program evaluation.

In this paper I will focus on considerations in the development and use of tests of learner outcomes, or achievement, if you will, for purposes of program evaluation. While the measurement of processes is an area that must be addressed, this is ultimately related to our understanding of the developmental process of second language acquisition itself, and consideration of this would take us far beyond the concerns of program evaluation. Similarly, the use of qualitative, that is, non-test information, though essential to evaluation, is beyond the scope of this paper. I will first discuss the needs for measuring outcomes in program evaluation – both formative and summative. I will then present the argument that current language testing practice is inappropriate to these needs. Next, I will outline the fundamental requirements of criterion-referenced tests, and suggest a theoretical framework as a starting point for developing criterion-referenced tests of communicative language ability. Finally, I will repeat a call for a program of research that John Clark and I have outlined elsewhere.

The measurement of learner outcomes for program evaluation

In attempting to delineate the role of tests of learner outcomes in program evaluation, we might begin by considering the range of situations in which evaluation takes place, the types of evaluation decisions that are to be made, and the criteria by which the program will be evaluated. At one end of the range of situations we have contexts in which there is no formal program, but in which there may be some learning and teaching, and in which evaluation might be of interest. If, for example, I were hired as a language tutor by a non-native English speaking student, I might simply arrange to spend some time with him conversing in English. If the student's objective were to attend a college or university in the United States, the evaluation of my effectiveness might come in the form of a TOEFL score. If this were unacceptably low, it would probably terminate my career as a TOEFL preparation coach, irrespective of how interesting I might be as a conversationalist. (It is also possible, of course, that I might succeed despite the fact that I bored my student to tears.) If, on the other hand, the student were more interested in making friends with a native English speaker than in studying in the United States, his TOEFL score might not even be considered relevant to evaluating our interaction.

Formative and summative evaluation

Most of us, however, are concerned with evaluation in the more complex context of a formal instructional program. And here, we find a great deal of variety not only in types of programs, but in the types of decisions to be made. In some situations, we may be interested in identifying ways to improve an on-going program, to upgrade the *status quo*, so to speak, at minimal cost, while in others we may be committed to developing the best 'new and improved' program possible, irrespective of cost. In situations such as these, we will be primarily concerned with what Scriven (1967) has called *formative evaluation*, which is essentially evaluation for the purpose of improving instruction. Formative evaluation takes place during the development of a program, and its major concerns are to determine what the results of the program are, and to diagnose areas of strength and weakness in order to improve instruction. In other situations, we may need to find out whether a new textbook, set of materials, or teaching technique is better than that currently used, or we may need to choose among two or more competing curricula. In contexts such as these, we will be concerned with *summative evaluation*, which typically takes place after the program is complete, and provides information that is relevant to deciding whether or not to adopt a new program. Formative and summative evaluation can thus be distinguished in terms of the types of decisions to which they are addressed (course improvement vs. adoption) and the point at which they typically take place (during a program vs. after the completion of the program).

Objectives-based and program-free evaluation

The criteria by which the program is to be evaluated are also relevant to the measurement of learner outcomes. The primary question is whether we will limit our evaluation to the stated instructional objectives, or whether we will also look at unstated and unexpected outcomes. Here, we can refer to the distinction that Scriven (1974) has made between objectives-based evaluation and so-called 'goal-free', or program-free evaluation. Traditionally, both formative and summative evaluation have focused on examining the extent to which the program has attained its stated objectives. As Scriven has pointed out, however, the problems with this are twofold: i) it ignores potentially important outcomes, both positive and negative, that program developers have not included, either inadvertently or by choice, and ii) it thus introduces bias into the evaluation, in the sense that it looks only at those outcomes which are valued and for which there is a high probability of success. In advocating program-free evaluation, Scriven argues for considering the broader educational and social context in which programs take place, and looking not only for unanticipated outcomes, but also at the consequences of achieving the stated objectives.

My favorite illustration of the failure to fully consider the consequences of achieving one's objectives comes from a curriculum research and development program in which I was involved several years ago. This was a program to develop an English language arts program for elementary school children in a country where English is a foreign language. (I should also mention that the school system in this country was very traditional and quite authoritarian in its structure and administration.) In addition to promoting the development of skills in English, our program aimed at developing attitudes and skills to promote self-directed study, which we felt would be useful in both the students' English class and in their subject matter classes. After the first year of the program, it was clear that both the language skills and self-direction objectives were succeeding beyond our expectations at one of our demonstration schools. Our flush of success, however, soon turned to the blush of chagrin, when this group of self-directed elementary school children marched *en masse* into the principal's office to protest the assignment of their teacher to another class! We had failed to consider the possibility that self-direction could generalize from study habits to social action.

The implication of program-free evaluation for formative evaluation is that we should be concerned with improving the program so that it not only achieves its stated objectives, but is also consistent with the broader goals of the education system and society. Similarly, in summative evaluation we should compare outcomes of competing programs not only in terms of their stated objectives, but also with reference to educational and societal values.

While there is considerable variation in the types of programs we evaluate and in the types of decisions to be made, the kinds of information about learner outcomes that are needed for all these contexts and decisions are quite similar. If we accept the principle of program-free evaluation, there are two types of information about learner outcomes that are essential to both formative and summative evaluation: i) detailed information related to students' achievement of stated instructional objectives (both cognitive and affective), and ii) information related to possible outcomes that are not included as instructional objectives.

The first problem in measurement, then, is to identify the two types of outcomes to be measured. In formative evaluation, identifying instructional objectives is relatively unproblematic. This is also the case for summative evaluation, even though we may be dealing with differing sets of objectives. What is particularly problematic for summative evaluation, however, is the identification of the broader set of possible outcomes, from which the sets of instructional objectives are presumably drawn. The relationships between instructional objectives and possible outcomes in summative evaluation can be illustrated as in Figure 1:

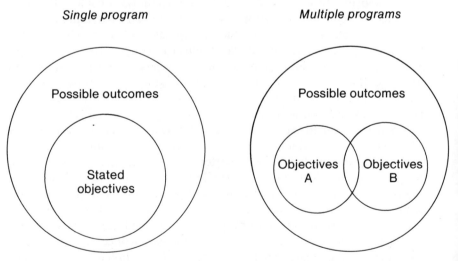

Figure 1   Stated objectives and possible outcomes in summative evaluation

To illustrate these relationships, first consider the evaluation of an English program for individuals whose primary use of English will be to pass an examination that will admit them to a higher level of education. Suppose the instructional objectives of this program were primarily in the areas of grammar and vocabulary. We might find that students in this program perform well on tests of grammar and vocabulary, and that the majority of students who successfully complete this program also obtain high examination scores and subsequent admission to higher education. On the basis of this information, we could say that the program is successful in meeting its objectives. But would we, as program-free evaluators, be satisfied that the program is producing students who are proficient in English? If the developers of the program argue that this is totally irrelevant to the purposes of the program, we might just as easily ask why the program is called 'English', rather than, say, 'test preparation'.

The problem is not different, but is simply multiplied, in the case of two or more competing programs. Suppose, for example, we were asked to compare a course based on a structural syllabus with one based on a functional syllabus, each of which was very successful in meeting its objectives. Here, the impossibility of choosing either as the 'better' program without recourse to a broader set of outcomes is clear. This is because of the distinctiveness of the objectives, and because few of us would accept knowledge of either structures or functions alone as a complete definition of language proficiency. Unfortunately, for evaluators, at least, the distinction between competing programs is seldom this clear, and we are typically faced with choosing between programs with similar objectives. Here, the problem is not so much that of comparing apples with oranges, as comparing *jonathans* with *macintoshes*. The problem, however, is qualitatively the same: unless the two programs have identical sets of objectives (and processes, I might add), they cannot be reasonably compared except with reference to a broader set of outcomes.

To summarize, for virtually every context and purpose of program evaluation, we need to gather detailed information about learners' achievement of instructional objectives. In formative evaluation we need information that is precise enough to permit revision, or fine-tuning, of the program. In summative evaluation I have argued that we must also gather information about outcomes that are not stated as objectives. In evaluating a single program we must examine not only the effectiveness of the program in achieving its objectives, but also the extent to which the outcomes, both stated and unexpected, are worthwhile in the broader context of the education system and society. In evaluating two programs, we cannot use the objective set of either as a criterion, but must use a framework that ideally includes both.

Norm-referenced and criterion-referenced tests

For the past twenty-five years the dominant measurement approach to the development and use of language tests has been that of norm-referencing. This approach characterizes what Spolsky (1978) has referred to as the 'psychometric-structuralist' period of language testing. The distinguishing characteristic of the norm-referenced approach to testing is that test scores are reported and interpreted with reference to the performance of individuals, either in the same group, or in a 'norm' group. That is, a norm-referenced test score provides information about an individual's relative rank with reference to other individuals who have taken the test. The emphasis in developing norm-referenced tests, therefore, is on maximizing differences among individuals. The quintessential norm-referenced test is the 'standardized test' that has two distinguishing characteristics: i) it is administered in a standard way under uniform conditions and ii) it has been tried out with large groups of individuals, whose scores provide standard 'norms' or reference points for interpreting scores.

The other major approach to measurement, that of criterion-referenced testing, has a much longer history and is alive and well in most classroom testing contexts. Nevertheless, with the exception of Cartier's (1968) seminal article and a recent paper by Hudson and Lynch (1984), this approach has been virtually ignored by language testing researchers and writers of texts on language testing. In contrast to scores on norm-referenced tests, criterion-referenced test scores are reported and interpreted with reference to a specific context domain or criterion of performance. They thus provide information about an individual's mastery of a given content domain, or level of performance. One requirement of criterion-referenced test development and interpretation is the specification of a content or ability domain. Because the domain specification is frequently made in terms of instructional objectives, criterion-referenced tests are sometimes also referred to as 'objectives-based' tests.

The inadequacies of standardized norm-referenced tests for purposes of measuring the achievement of instructional objectives have long been recognized (for example, Glaser, 1963; Popham and Husek, 1969; Millman, 1974; Popham, 1978; Cziko, 1983). To mention just one problem, in the classroom setting we are often interested in knowing whether our students have mastered a given set of learning objectives. Knowing that a given student scored in the 90th percentile on the test will not provide this information, since it might well be that the entire group's performance is below a standard that we would be willing to accept as an indication of mastery. Thus, in most classroom uses, criterion-referenced achievement tests are more appropriate than standardized norm-referenced tests.

While there is no necessary connection between the approach we adopt for developing and using language tests and how we define the abilities measured, over the past twenty-five years we have seen the development of a *de facto* union between the norm-referenced approach and 'language proficiency', as opposed to the criterion-referenced, objectives-based approach and 'language achievement'. And while this distinction may be perfectly serviceable for the varied needs for evaluating individuals, I believe the needs of program evaluation are such that this distinction cannot apply, and that in order to meet these needs we must consider a framework for developing and using criterion-referenced tests of language proficiency.

Inadequacies of norm-referenced tests for formative evaluation

As mentioned above, for the purposes of formative evaluation, we need to gather information about learner outcomes that is detailed enough to guide program revision. A number of evaluation researchers (for example, Weiss, 1972; Millman, 1974; Baker, 1974; Popham, 1978) have argued that standardized tests are unsuitable for this purpose because, in general, they are descriptively inadequate. First, the abilities measured by standardized tests of language proficiency are defined in very general terms, so that they can be interpreted only indirectly with reference to specific instructional objectives. Second, there is the frequent mismatch between instructional objectives and the content of a standardized test. Given the wide variety of contexts in which language is taught around the world and the resultant diversity of instructional objectives, it is unreasonable to expect a single standardized test to measure the objectives of any given program with enough detail to be useful for formative evaluation. A third weakness, mentioned earlier, is that scores on standardized tests provide no information about the degree of mastery of content or skills. And finally, there is the problem of content validity caused by the use of statistical criteria in selecting items for standardized tests. In order to maximize individual differences, only those items that are of medium difficulty and that discriminate well between high and low groups of test takers can be included. What this means is that in the process of developing a standardized test, 'easy' items get weeded out. One of the reasons these items are easy is that they have been included in the instructional objectives, and students have mastered their content. Thus, norm-referenced test development procedures tend to eliminate those items whose content is of the greatest interest for formative evaluation.

Proponents of the criterion-referenced approach to test development and use argue that this approach provides a means of solving the problems associated with norm-referenced tests (for example, Hively *et al.*, 1973; Popham, 1978). First, since criterion-referenced tests are based on the domain of instructional objectives, they can provide direct and detailed information about students' achievement of those objectives. Basing the content of the test on specific objectives also avoids the mismatch between teaching and test content that is often found with standardized tests. Second, criterion-referenced test scores are reported in terms of the relative degree of mastery of the instructional objectives, frequently as a percentage, thus providing useful information for diagnosing both strengths and deficiencies in learning. Finally, because there is no need to maximize inter-individual differences, test items that are too easy or which do not discriminate need not be eliminated.

Inadequacies of norm-referenced tests for summative evaluation

In the context of summative evaluation, where the focus is on deciding whether a given program is sufficiently effective to implement, the evaluator needs to gather information that is relevant to *both* the stated instructional objectives and unexpected outcomes. Here, standardized test scores are inadequate as indicators of the achievement of instructional objectives for the same reasons as given earlier with respect to formative evaluation. As indicators of broader outcomes, however, standardized tests can provide useful information for the summative evaluation of a single program. The two standardized tests of English that have probably been used the most widely for this purpose are the *Test of English as a Foreign Language* (TOEFL, 1987) and the family of tests that have been developed over the years under the auspices of the British Council (Carroll, 1981; Seaton, 1983; Davies, 1984). The primary limitation to this use of standardized tests is the extent to which the program developer or the evaluator is willing to accept the definition of language abilities that informs the test.

It is in the context of summatively evaluating two competing programs that the delineation and measurement of learner outcomes poses the greatest problems. Since we virtually never compare two programs that are identical in their objectives, we are almost always faced with a dilemma in deciding what objectives to cover in the test, and whether to use a criterion- or a norm-referenced approach. The objectives-based solution to this problem is to base the test on both sets of instructional objectives. This can be done either by preparing a separate objectives-based test for each program or by developing a single objectives-based test–that covers the instructional objectives of both programs. This approach has generally proven unsatisfactory because test results reveal, to no one's surprise, that students perform best on measures of those objectives they have been taught, and the test scores thus provide little information that is of use in choosing between the two programs. The norm-referenced approach – giving a standardized test to both groups and then comparing their scores – has also proven unsatisfactory. It may be unfair to both programs, since it evaluates them in terms of a third set of objectives – those of the test – that may or may not be related to the objectives of either program. In addition, the norms to which the test is referenced may be inappropriate to the students in the program.

Criterion-referenced tests of language proficiency

In the remainder of this paper, I will outline briefly what I believe to be a viable approach to developing measures of learner outcomes for use in the evaluation of language programs. This approach is not based on a new theory of measurement, and does not involve a radical departure from current views of the nature of language abilities. On the contrary, it simply involves the combination of the criterion-referenced approach to test development with a current specification of the domain of language proficiency.

In order for criterion-referenced tests to provide information about an individual's relative mastery of a given domain of ability, the content of such tests must be sampled from a well-defined domain of ability (Glaser 1963; Nitko, 1984). An additional requirement, if the results of criterion-referenced tests are to be applicable to the needs of both program-free formative, and summative program evaluation, is that the scores must be referenced to an absolute scale of ability. There are thus two issues to be addressed in developing criterion-referenced tests of language proficiency for use in language program evaluation: i) specifying the ability domain, and ii) defining the end points of ability so as to provide an absolute scale.

Communicative language ability

The evidence from recent language testing research is generally consistent with the hypothesis that language proficiency consists of several distinct abilities that are related to each other or which are related to a higher order, general ability (for example, Bachman and Palmer, 1982; Vollmer and Sang, 1983; Carroll, 1983; Upshur and Homburg, 1983; Oller, 1983). Many language testing researchers are thus focusing their efforts on identifying the various abilities involved in using language to communicate, and are for the most part working within an expanded framework of what I choose to call 'communicative language ability'. I define communicative language ability as consisting of both knowledge, or competence, and skill in implementing, or executing that competence, and my framework of CLA includes three components: language competence, strategic competence and the psychophysiological skills required to implement these abilities in language use. This framework is illustrated in Figure 2.

LANGUAGE COMPETENCE

Language competence can be classified into two types: organizational competence and pragmatic competence. Organizational competence comprises those abilities involved in controlling the formal organization of language for creating or recognizing grammatically correct sentences, comprehending their propositional content, and ordering them to form texts. These abilities are of two types: grammatical and textual. Grammatical competence includes rules of lexis, morphology, and syntax, which govern the choice of words to express specific significations, their forms, and their arrangement in sentences to express propositions. Textual competence includes the knowledge of the conventions of cohesion and rhetorical organization for joining utterances together to form a text.

Pragmatic competence includes those abilities which, *in addition to* organizational competence, are employed in the contextualized performance and interpretation of socially appropriate illocutionary acts in discourse. Pragmatic competence thus includes illocutionary competence, or the knowledge of how to perform illocutionary acts, or language functions, and sociolinguistic competence, or knowledge of the sociolinguistic conventions which govern appropriate language use in a particular culture and in varying situations in that culture.

PSYCHOPHYSIOLOGICAL SKILLS

Language competence may be realized in listening, speaking, reading and writing. These skills can be categorized in terms of mode (receptive, productive) and channel (auditory, visual), and distinguished by the psychophysiological skills that are involved in language use. Thus in the receptive mode (listening, reading) auditory and visual skills are employed, while in the productive mode (speaking, writing), neuromuscular skills (articulatory or digital) are employed.

STRATEGIC COMPETENCE

Communicative language use involves a dynamic interchange between the language user, the discourse, and the context of the situation in which the use occurs. The production of discourse thus requires the ability to

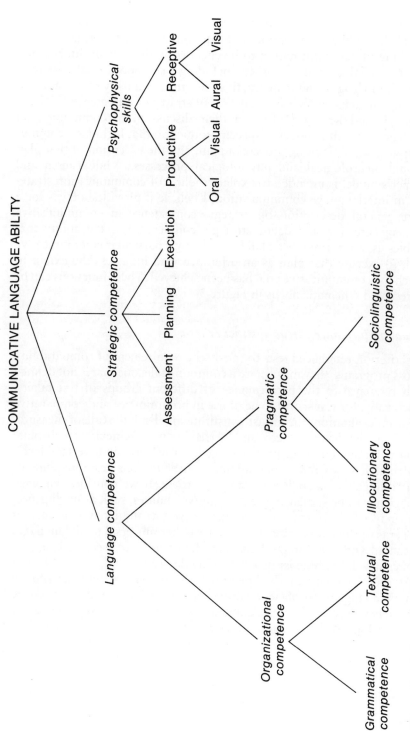

Figure 2   A framework for describing communicative language proficiency

assess the context for information relevant to the communicative goal and to then match information in the discourse to this information. The matching of new information to be encoded with relevant information that is available in the context (including presuppositional and real-world knowledge), and mapping this onto the maximally efficient use of existing language abilites is a function of strategic competence.

Faerch and Kasper (1983), in their discussion of communication strategies, present a model of speech production that includes a communicative goal, a planning process, a plan, and the execution of that plan through neurological and physiological processes. While Faerch and Kasper's model is intended to explain the use of communication strategies in interlanguage communication, I believe it provides a basis for a more general description of strategic competence in communicative language use. I would define strategic competence as the ability that enables us to i) formulate a plan for realizing a particular communicative goal, ii) execute that plan as an utterance, and iii) assess the extent to which the communicative goal has been achieved. These functions can be represented schematically as in Figure 3.

Actual performance versus abstract criteria

For criterion-referenced tests to satisfy the requirement of comparability across programs, they must share a common scale, one that is not defined with reference to the performance of different groups of test takers. Specifically, for test scores to be of use in program-free and comparative program evaluation, they must constitute an absolute scale of measurement, one that has true 'zero' and 'perfect' points. Achieving an absolute scale of foreign language proficiency with true 'zero' and 'perfect' levels is virtually impossible if one attempts to define this scale in terms of actual language use or actual language users. If we consider language proficiency to be similar to other cognitive abilities, such as intelligence, that may not have true zero points, as well as the likely existence of elements of the native language that are either universal to all languages or shared with the foreign language, then true 'zero' second language proficiency does not exist in actual individuals.

At the other end of the spectrum, the individual with absolutely complete language proficiency does not exist. Not only does language proficiency develop diachronically as a function of language change, it also develops in the way that all cognitive abilities constantly develop. And although the language use of native speakers is frequently advocated as a criterion for language proficiency, this is clearly inadequate for several reasons. First, native speakers show considerable variation in proficiency, particularly with regard to abilities such as cohesion, dis-

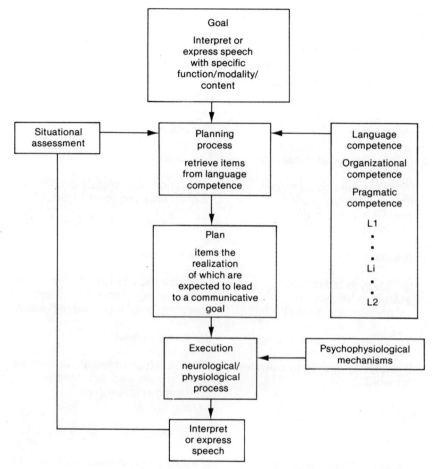

Figure 3   A model of language use (adapted from Faerch and Kasper, 1983)

course organization and sociolinguistic appropriateness. Second, there is the problem of identifying which variety or dialect to adopt as the 'native speaker' criterion. This question, which is often political or social rather than linguistic, is further complicated by the fact that boundaries between language varieties are seldom clearcut (Kachru, 1985). We must also consider differences in usage even within varieties or dialects, as well as differences between 'prescriptive' norms and the norms of actual usage. Finally, the whole concept of 'native speaker' has come to be regarded as little more than an abstraction (for example, Coulmas, 1981; Paikeday, 1985).

Because of these problems, it is virtually impossible to define criterion levels of language proficiency in terms of actual individuals or actual performance. Rather, such levels must be defined abstractly, in terms of the relative presence or absence of the abilities that constitute the domain. To illustrate how levels can be defined abstractly in the context of an oral interview, consider the following scale that Adrian Palmer and I developed a few years ago:

Vocabulary	*Cohesion*
0 *Extremely limited vocabulary*	*No cohesion*
(A few words and formulaic phrases. Not possible to discuss any topic, due to limited vocabulary.)	(Utterances completely disjointed, or discourse too short to judge.)
1 *Small vocabulary*	*Very little cohesion*
(Difficulty in talking with examinee because of vocabulary limitations.)	(Relationships between utterances not adeqately marked; frequent confusing relationship among ideas.)
2 *Vocabulary of moderate size*	*Moderate cohesion*
(Frequently misses or searches for words.)	(Relationships between utterances generally marked; sometimes confusing relationships among ideas.)
3 *Large vocabulary*	*Good cohesion*
(Seldom misses or searches for words.)	(Relationships between utterances well-marked.)
4 *Extensive vocabulary*	*Excellent cohesion*
(Rarely, if ever, misses or searches for words. Almost always uses appropriate word.)	(Uses a variety of appropriate devices; hardly ever confusing relationships among ideas.)

Figure 4   Scales of ability in vocabulary and cohesion (Bachman and Palmer, 1983)

While these scale definitions were designed for measuring fairly broad categories of proficiency, and would need to be specified more precisely to meet the needs of any given program evaluation, they do illustrate the principle of defining scales abstractly, rather than in terms of actual performance or actual speakers.

In summary, I believe that in order to develop tests that are adequate for the uses of language program evaluation, that will yield scores that are comparable across differing sets of instructional objectives, we must begin by i) specifying a domain of communicative language ability that is consistent with current frameworks and ii) defining levels or scales of proficiency abstractly, in terms of relative degrees of ability, and independently of contextual features of language use.

A program of research and development

In a recent paper Bachman and Clark (1987) outline a program of research and development aimed at producing and validating criterion-referenced measures of communicative language ability. This program includes four components, as follows:

1 refining a theoretical model of communicative language ability, with particular attention to defining the specific ability domains in operational terms;
2 developing highly authentic measures of performance, based on the operational definitions of the individual domains of the model, for use as criteria in proficiency testing/development studies;
3 surveying currently available language testing instruments with respect to their degree of congruence with the requirements of a more fully elaborated model, selecting the most promising instruments and validating them against the criterion measures at issue in 2; and
4 developing and validating batteries of new instruments of optimum reliability, validity, and practicality for use in a variety of real-world testing contexts.

Conclusion

In this paper I have discussed the needs and problems of measuring learner outcomes in the evaluation of language programs. I have argued that standardized norm-referenced tests are generally inadequate for these needs, and proposed criterion-referenced tests of language proficiency as a solution. The development of such tests requires a well-specified domain of language proficiency and abstract definitions of proficiency levels. Finally, I have advocated a program of research for developing and validating criterion-referenced tests of language proficiency.

While the solution I have proposed is simple in its conception, its implementation will require a major commitment on the part of language testers, program evaluators, applied linguists, and language teachers. Part of this commitment, I believe, is the realization that the time for armchair model-building is past, and that in order to move forward we must begin the empirical investigation of current models. This commitment will also involve both the recognition that our current models are probably inadequate, and the patience to continue the cyclical process of hypothesis testing and theory revision that will inform our research and development activities. In this regard, the framework of communicative language ability I have described here is not presented as a complete theory, but is intended as a starting point for research and development. And while I believe this framework is specific enough to guide test development and to generate hypotheses for empirical studies, this framework itself is subject to empirical validation, and will in all likelihood change to reflect our growing knowledge.

Much of the discussion in this paper has been at a theoretical level. However, the concerns to which it is addressed are practical. With the current proliferation of techniques and materials for language teaching, the need for program evaluation has never been greater. In the face of claims and counterclaims, choosing the 'best' program has become increasingly problematic, and I believe program evaluation provides the most effective means for examining the validity of these claims. In addition, there is an increasing need for measures of language proficiency for use in research aimed at better understanding the nature of language acquisition and language attrition. As this research has come to examine these processes in the context of the language classroom, the concerns of the language acquisition researcher and the program evaluator are beginning to merge. It is in the arena of classroom-centered research and program evaluation, therefore, that I believe the most pressing issues of measurement are to be found. It is also in this arena that the researcher and the practitioner are most likely to come together to work toward their solution.

16 Mastery decisions in program evaluation[1]

Thom Hudson

While program evaluation may be conducted on a number of levels including administration, teaching and curriculum, this paper focuses more narrowly on the measurement of student performance as the key in evaluation. It addresses the evaluation issue of student mastery or non-mastery of language program objectives. In doing so, it attempts to view in context issues pertaining to i) the nature of evidence to be used for such student evaluation, ii) the need for evaluation to be accountable to program goals, and iii) the appropriate measurement approach to be taken in mastery evaluation. Mastery decision measurement here refers to the attempt to determine whether an examinee has mastered the content he or she has been taught, or has reached a level of competence defined as mastery. It is by no means a new concept. In fact, a normal part of a teacher's job is making decisions concerning student advancement based on performance. The present discussion will focus on the bases for such decisions and the uses of those decisions in program evaluation.

Throughout the discussions which follow, the context of evaluation should always be kept in mind because evaluation always has consequences. Generally, people do not like to be judged, and they tend not to like their products to be judged. While evaluations may be objective, they are never neutral. Further, evaluations will always have audiences, and the original audience seldom remains the sole audience. Peer evaluations made for a teacher trainer have a way of coming to the attention of the program director. An evaluation for the program director has an uncanny way of being quoted later by some funding agency. Nevertheless, I would argue that the aim of facilitating student progress makes continual evaluation an indispensable part of language programs.

The three focal issues noted above lie at the heart of the evaluation of program objectives through student performance, regardless of whether the objectives are stated in behavioral or cognitive terms. First, beliefs about the nature of the evidence to be used in the task of making mastery decisions are basic to whether one believes the outcome decisions to be

1 The author would like to thank Frances Butler, Jean Turner and Fred Davidson for comments on earlier drafts of this paper.

valid. This is a much more prominent issue when decisions result in classifying the student in some way, rather than when they merely rank him or her in relation to peer performance. The second issue, the idea that evaluation should be linked to explicit program goals, may seem on the face of it to be an incontrovertibly laudable notion. However, the process of putting into effect evaluation which is linked to program goals will frequently bring to light disagreements and discrepancies which have not previously been noticed. Third, selection of the appropriate measurement approach must be congruent with the goals of evaluation. The issue of measurement approach is central in that when objectives are identified for inclusion in a program, and thus for proficiency or achievement testing, decisions relating to measurement approaches will change depending upon the theoretical approach taken to program design, evaluation instrument development and score interpretation. In this paper, the application of criterion-referenced measurement (CRM) approaches to assessing student performance in relation to program goals is viewed as inherently tied to program evaluation (cf. Cziko, 1983; Hudson and Lynch, 1984; Oller, 1979; Perkins and Miller, 1984). Further, for the purposes of this paper, measurement is defined as either single administration paper and pencil test results, or cumulative course evaluation stated quantitatively or as observational results.

The nature of data in evaluation

In a discussion of mastery/non-mastery decisions, it is necessary to deal with epistemological and ethical questions of the nature of test scores and the effect of the decisions to be made on the basis of those scores. This is necessary because most researchers and program developers have a healthy scepticism about test scores. The issue is concerned with the basic notions of construct validity in testing situations. As Messick (1980) notes, measured behaviors can represent various constructs to different researchers. For trait psychologists these behaviors represent *signs* of behavior or competence structures, whereas for behavioral psychologists they generally represent *samples* of performance. The importance of this distinction is central to whether one believes that mastery/non-mastery decisions can be validly made on the basis of measurement data. This in turn leads to a questioning of the construct validity of any instruments used. Teachers and program designers will have to specify clearly what the examinee must do to demonstrate that the instructional objectives are met and mastery has been reached.

These two distinctions apply in a practical way to concepts of what the program goals are in that they are often tied to beliefs concerning the nature of language proficiency. In order to point out some of the potential problems associated with the notions of what constitutes data, a specific example will be discussed. This is the relation of testing to the researchers' views of just what language proficiency is and how determination of mastery will address differing views.

The reason much of the discussion centers around the nature of language proficiency is that this directly relates to whether specific language tasks or program objectives can be specified for instruction and measured validly. This in turn relates to the degree to which a test can be used to determine mastery. For example, there have been arguments that all performance in a second or foreign language can be traced to a single underlying 'General Language Proficiency Factor' (Oller, 1976). More recently, this notion of a single factor has been abandoned (Oller, 1983). Many now argue that language competence is divisible into subskills (Bachman and Palmer, 1981) and separate competence types (Canale and Swain, 1980). Obviously, the unitary versus divisible competence issue has important practical implications for testing in terms of whether test results are viewed as *signs* or *samples* of behavior. That is, there is general agreement with a definition which references proficiency to abilities to perform real world tasks however those tasks are defined (Richards, 1985). The key notion, however, is how 'ability to perform' is to be measured. Some who see testing as eliciting *samples* of ability would argue that paper and pencil or other non-'authentic' language tests do not measure much of importance because they have removed the language from its context (Morrow, 1981). For them, mastery would need to be demonstrated in a very different way from how mastery might be demonstrated to those who consider language proficiency to be a *sign* of ability.

The issue of what is meant by proficiency or communicative ability is an essential point to consider in determining how mastery would be defined and what would be tested by a mastery test. Language tests have long aimed at testing an examinee's language proficiency. How they defined this and carried out assessment has been limited both by the theories of language considered to be of import (cf. Spolsky, 1978, for a thorough discussion) and by the currently dominant language teaching methods. The current emphasis on communicative testing has grown from the theories and various instructional methodologies which have emerged to address the concepts of communicative competence. There are currently several competing views which differ in terms of the types of competence they include (cf. Canale and Swain, 1980). The differing views of communicative competence produce differing views as to how language tests can assess the communicative abilities of the examinees, and thus of the program effectiveness. The arguments basically center around the question of the authenticity of the test. The underlying assumptions here relate to considerations of the degree to which the test is an assessment of performance or an assessment of competence, in the weak sense that competence refers to knowledge or ability and perform- ance refers to actual use (Canale and Swain, 1980). The two polar views in terms of communicative testing center around whether the essential purpose of language is interactional communication. That is, Morrow (1981) considers that the role of language testing is to provide proof

> of the candidate's ability to actually use the language, to translate the competence (or lack of it) which he is demonstrating into actual performance 'in ordinary situations', i.e. actually using the language to read, write, speak or listen in ways in contexts which correspond to real life.
>
> (1981: 16)

Canale and Swain (1980) on the other hand, reject the notion that the essential purpose of language is to communicate. In their view,

> there is little reason to view (externally oriented) communication as more essential than other purposes of language such as self-expression, verbal thinking, problem-solving, and creative writing.
>
> (1980: 23)

For Morrow (1981: 16–17), language tests must reflect the following features of language use:

1 Language is used in interaction.
2 Interactions are usually unpredictable.
3 Language has a context.
4 Language is used for a purpose.
5 There is a need to examine performance.
6 Language is authentic, not simplified.
7 Language success is behavior based.

As such, a test of communicative ability would have at least the fol- lowing:

1 It will be criterion-referenced against the operational performance of a set of language tasks.
2 It will be concerned with validating itself against those criteria – concerned with content, construct and predictive validity, not concurrent validity.
3 It will rely on modes of assessment which are not directly quantitative, but which are instead qualitative.
4 Reliability will be subordinate to face validity.

(1981: 17–18)

Taken to the extreme, the requirement for 'authentic' evaluation would disallow testing settings. Other forms of measurement would be needed, indeed only other forms of measurement would be allowed.

Canale and Swain (1980) on the other hand, emphasize that although they consider that the study of communicative competence should center on the relationships and interactions between the grammatical and sociolinguistic systems, certain aspects of each type of competence can be investigated on their own. That is,

> just as there are regularities in a user's knowledge of language use that can be studied independently from grammar itself (e.g. the appropriateness of a speaker's intended meaning in a given sociolinguistic context, regardless of how this meaning is expressed verbally), so there are regularities in a user's knowledge of grammar that can be studied independently from sociolinguistic context (e.g. formal and substantive linguistic universals as discussed by Chomsky 1965).

> (Canale and Swain, 1980)

Here, language or instructional goals could be isolated and tested for specific mastery. They also consider paper and pencil tests to be valid approaches to some types of communicative competence measurement.

In this disagreement we see in part a discrepancy as to whether language measurement provides the evaluator with a *sign* or a *sample*. In ascertaining student mastery or non-mastery the issue will focus on the question, 'Student mastery or non-mastery of what?' This will of course depend upon how carefully and explicitly the program goals are specified. Further, it will involve explicit decisions as to how the student is to demonstrate mastery of those program goals. That is, one approach may rely more heavily on test data while the other may emphasize teacher observation of the candidate.

Accountability of curriculum to program goals

Evaluation of student performance should link proficiency specifications to program design. That is, the information obtained from testing or observation must be oriented in terms of the specific program goals. Hambleton (1983) lists the three common uses of test scores as:

1 Scores obtained from the set of items in a test are used to rank order examinees.
2 Scores are used to make descriptive statements about examinee performance in relation to well-defined domains of content.
3 Scores are used to make mastery/nonmastery decisions in relation to well-defined domains of content.

> (1983: 34)

The first use corresponds to what Cziko (1983) terms the *psychometric* approach to measurement, an approach which has been designed to maximize individual differences such that scores can be interpreted in terms of score comparisons to other members of the group. The second and third correspond to the *edumetric* approach, a test designed to yield scores which are meaningful without reference to the performance of other examinees. While there are practical applications of the first use, such as when only a specified quota of examinees may be selected, the second two uses are of the most direct application in judging the success of an instructional program and in helping to determine areas of the curriculum which need change.

The second and third uses can be linked specifically to explicit student program and course objectives. The second can be linked to diagnostic purposes for the student. The third can be linked to program instructional effectiveness, and can lead to analyses which center around whether the goals are reasonable. Of significance here is that the same test data are used for student evaluation and program evaluation. This leads to accountability of examination results to program goals. By incorporating the dual processes of student evaluation and program evaluation into the same instruments, there is some insurance that the program objectives and curriculum remain the focus of 'all' evaluation in the program.

In linking the mastery instruments to the program content, they will be criterion-referenced. The definition of criterion-referenced test used here is a 'test used to ascertain an individual's status with respect to a well-defined behavioral domain' (Popham, 1978). CRM should be viewed in a context which includes both the model of test construction (Popham, 1978), and a potential numeric score, or standard, used for making mastery/non-mastery decisions (Hudson and Lynch, 1984).

As stated, the items in a criterion-referenced test will sample a 'well defined behavioral domain' (Popham, 1978). This is defined as 'a set of skills of dispositions examinees display when called on to do so in a testing situation' (p. 94). This domain, or criterion, is basically whatever is actually to be measured or tested for. It is linked to the program objectives as stated in the curriculum. It may be a skill or set of skills or knowledge of a specific sort which is defined and described in detail. For instance, it could be the ability to identify the correct grammatical form of a part of speech, to produce topic sentences, or to select from among multiple-choice alternatives the best statement of the main idea for a reading passage which has certain specified characteristics. The key concept is that the criterion behavior be defined in terms of its bounds. Those bounds are the course objectives. To the extent that the specifications used to generate the test items are developed from the curriculum, these bounds will be the course objectives.

It is this process of developing criterion-referenced mastery decision instruments, instruments which are directly accountable to the curriculum, which often brings out differences and disagreements not previously considered to be differences among instructors, administrators and materials developers. This process of explicitly defining how the program goals are to be operationalized can indicate just where disagreements as to the nature of the skill and the nature of the means of assessing that skill lie. Teachers and materials developers are more able to communicate differences in perceptions. All educators involved will be required to articulate their views concerning how the program addresses learning. Although time consuming and occasionally frustrating, this process strengthens the program of instruction by helping to rationalize the relationships of instructional goals and methods.

The process of developing instruments and administering them to students can help to ensure that the program is constantly evaluated. That is, by using the results of mastery decisions, the evaluator can determine the extent to which the program is i) producing the desired results and ii) realistic in its goals. This is not effectively possible when test scores are used to rank students in terms of other students. However, since mastery testing provides information as to whether the examinees have actually reached competence in those areas which the program is designed to teach, the evaluator is able to match the curriculum to the population of students in the program.

Measurement approaches to dependability and standard setting

Decision dependability

When the relevant question is whether an examinee has or has not mastered the course material, a measurement approach which is linked to the dependability of the decisions which are made about examinees is essential. Further, when the relevant question is the degree to which students have mastered the material, a measurement approach should indicate the dependability of the extent to which the instrument has measured the domain of concern. The relative standing of examinees is not of primary concern. The measurement approach to mastery testing is concerned not with *relative* standing, but rather with *absolute* standing with respect to the instructional goal. The distinction here between *absolute* and *relative* is that used in the literature of educational measurement (see Shavelson and Webb, 1981). *Absolute* refers to decisions concerning whether or not a particular skill has been acquired or a particular degree of competency has been reached. *Relative* refers to decisions concerning the rank-ordering of individuals on a particular skill or competency. With mastery testing, we hope to make absolute decisions concerning whether a student is ready for advancement, placement into a particular level, etc. Mastery testing thus requires a measurement approach which is primarily concerned with the consistency of 'absolute' decisions made on the basis of scores.

Regardless of the approach to measurement, reliability is a critical issue. When we use the term reliability we are, in general, referring to consistency of measurement. The general definition for traditional reliability is the proportion of observed score variance that is true score variance – true score variance being the proportion of observed score variance that is without error. Classical reliability is concerned with specifying the variance component for persons (and error) in order to rank individuals for 'relative' judgments and decisions. As a primary concern, these relative judgments are not overly important for mastery testing. Mastery testing will normally take place in instructional settings designed to teach the examinees the course material. If the program is successful, i.e., students master the material, the restriction of range in test scores will result in a reduction of observed score variance. This in turn will lower reliability as estimated by correlation between parallel tests (Allen and Yen, 1979). A CRM approach to reliability is primarily concerned with the consistency of absolute decisions made on the basis of test scores. Many researchers in CRM thus avoid the term 'reliability' in favor of 'dependability' or 'agreement' (Berk, 1980a). This notion of dependability is especially appropriate in that many of the indices used in the CRM approach fall outside of classical test theory assumptions. For example, they do not assume parallel forms and/or they are not defined in terms of the traditional ratio of observed score to true score variance.

These indices which focus on dependability have been classified by Berk (1980a) into three main categories: *threshold-loss agreement*, *squared-error loss agreement*, and *domain score estimation*. The first two indices are concerned with the dependability of mastery/non-mastery classification while the third is concerned chiefly with the internal dependability of the test as a sampling of the domain of interest, i.e., the curricular objectives. The following discussion will briefly summarize the approaches to 'dependability indices'. For a fuller discussion see Berk, 1980a, and Hudson and Lynch, 1984.

Subkoviak (1980) reviews the threshold-loss agreement methods. These all involve calculation of two coefficients $\hat{p}_0$ and $\hat{K}$ (kappa); where $\hat{p}_0$ is the proportion of examinees consistently classified as masters or non-masters (or some other non-overlapping intervals of mastery), and $\hat{K}$ is the proportion of consistent classifications beyond that expected by chance. Thus, $\hat{p}_0$ represents the proportion of decision consistency that occurs for whatever reason on two tests; $\hat{K}$ represents the proportion of decision consistency attributable solely to the test. While always lower than $\hat{p}_0$, $\hat{K}$ tends to be higher if the cut score used to assign mastery/non-mastery is near the mean (assuming a unimodal distribution), whereas $\hat{p}_0$ tends to be lower. Coefficient $\hat{p}_0$ would thus seem more desirable since the closer to the cut score the observed scores become, the less confident we should feel about our mastery/non-mastery decisions.

A second category of CRM agreement indices is squared-error loss, which is based on squared deviations of individual scores from the cut score. Whereas the threshold loss indices focus on consistency of classification, the squared-error loss coefficients deal with consistency of measurement or scores. Unlike the threshold-loss agreement indices, this approach is sensitive to the *degree* of mastery or non-mastery and assumes that the consequences of misclassifying individuals who are at the extreme distances from the cut score are more serious than those for individuals close to the cut score. One of the first indices developed as an estimate of reliability for CRM tests comes under this category. Livingston and Zieky (1982) derived their statistic from NRM/classical test theory by substituting the cut score for the group mean. Brennan (1980) provides an improvement of this statistic by applying *generalizability theory* (see Shavelson and Webb, 1981; Bolus, Hinofotis, and Bailey, 1982). His index, $\Phi(\lambda)$ phi(lambda), is an 'index of dependability' for criterion-referenced or mastery tests, where (λ) equals the cut score.

The final category of CRM approaches to dependability is domain score estimation. Brennan (1980) uses the formula for the generalizability coefficient for absolute decisions as a 'general purpose' estimate of dependability for scores on CRM tests, without reference to a cut score. This coefficient, which he calls phi (Φ) is the ratio of true or *universe score* variance to observed score variance, where universe score variance is observed score variance minus error, and error includes the variance component for items.

Each of these approaches will have differing uses in mastery decisions and program evaluation. Berk (1984b) indicates that, in practical terms, the $\hat{p}_0$ index probably has the greatest utility for classroom and program tests. For placement decisions where degrees of mastery and non-mastery are of interest, $\Phi(\lambda)$ would probably be the most suitable. The domain score estimation Φ can be useful in program evaluation when a standard error statistic must be selected which will reflect the imprecision of the instrument and the sampling error of the examinees.

Standard setting

The value of mastery testing depends on the validity of the standard or cut score. The validity of the mastery decisions is haunted by what Shepard (1984) calls the 'Achilles heel' of standard setting. There is general agreement that the selection of the standard is necessarily an arbitrary selection. However, while Glass (1978) views this arbitrariness as negative, others such as Popham (1978) and Hambleton (1978) point out that arbitrariness need not always be a pejorative term. To them arbitrary judgments may be deliberated and informed decisions rather than blind capricious applications of a number. The key here is that standards in a program be developed over time as experience with the content of the curriculum is gained.

The fundamental problem with standard setting is that it is necessary to take a continuum of ability and establish a dichotomous point above which is designated mastery and below which is designated non-mastery. While some see the mastery paradigm as implying an all or nothing interpretation of learning (Shepard, 1984), when it is used in program evaluation the paradigm may equally be seen as addressing the decision of when a student will benefit more from repeating the course material than by advancing. As discussed above, this is obviously clearer at extreme scores than in the middle. However, with the appropriate methods of establishing the standard as well as appropriate dependability estimates, those involved in program development and evaluation can establish standards which are reasonable and informed. The discussion which follows presents two standard setting methods which focus on test content and criterion group comparisons (cf. Shepard, 1984, for an extensive discussion of standard setting methods).

In utilizing test content for setting score standards, experts typically examine the test items and judge how many of the items must be passed to demonstrate mastery. The decisions are based on how a hypothetical master would perform. Of the content-based methods for establishing standards, the Angoff (1971) procedure is perhaps the most straight-forward (Shepard, 1984). It can be especially useful in evaluations linked to a particular curriculum or program. In this procedure the content expert assigns a probability to each test item. This is the probability that a minimally competent examinee will answer the item correctly. The sum of the probabilities is then used to determine the standard. It is to be expected that raters will have different internalized standards, but the accuracy and consistency of the content experts can be refined over time.

The Angoff or other such content-based methods cannot be used in isolation. There should be some reference to criterion groups of students in order to validate the content evaluations. This approach, or family of approaches, involves identifying masters and non-masters according to some other measure or set of measures. Zieky and Livingston (1977) identified several varieties of the Contrasting Groups method. In this method, judges identify the two groups and the standard is set at the score which best discriminates between the two groups. The two groups might also be made up of instructed and non-instructed groups of students (Berk, 1976). In practice there will always be overlap between the two groups. The two classifications will have been made on different measures and each of those measures has its own error component. Thus, decisions must be made regarding what to do with the overlap of the two groups. The test users can decide to use the median score of the borderline group (Livingston and Zieky, 1982), they can take the score at which there is the least overlap of the criterion groups, or they can use still some other method for examination of the borderline group to decide which standard to select.

If this procedure of identifying mastery and non-mastery groups has been utilized in the item analysis and test construction process, much of the problem of overlap can be addressed in advance. Additionally, test items can be selected which produce a 'reasonable' standard. In an actual program, a test which has a passing standard of 35 per cent or 95 per cent would not seem appropriate, regardless of how well the standard separates masters from non-masters. The standard should appear valid to those who are not testing specialists.

Conclusions

Clearly the application of mastery/non-mastery measurement to program evaluation is problematic and interpretation of its results requires numerous caveats. The discussion above has indicated that when carried out systematically it will raise issues of how we know what we know, how we view what we teach, and how we measure what we want to classify. Mastery/non-mastery testing is clearly not as exact as we would like. However, what it lacks in exactness it makes up for in comprehensibility of evaluation. As a source of information it can be an important tool in program evaluation.

17 Tailoring the evaluation to fit the context

Warwick B. Elley

The ideal programme evaluation is often characterised as a tightly controlled experiment assisted by carefully chosen compliant principals, properly trained co-operative teachers and large representative samples of willing students, randomly assigned to operationally defined treatments. The task of assessment may be facilitated by the ready availability of valid objective tests of all relevant outcomes, which lend themselves to multivariate statistical analyses of results – all supplemented and enriched by masterful ethnographic studies, whose observations are highly reliable and replete with insight.

In the real world, unfortunately, things are different. Samples are biased or unmatched, school principals are unco-operative, teachers defect, or take maternity leave, pupils move out of the district, or fall ill, contamination occurs between experimental and control groups, and tests prove too difficult or too easy for students. These and other unexpected stumbling blocks require the resourceful evaluator of a language programme to consider alternative ways of assessing the merits of new programmes, and to make informed judgements about which hallowed principles are essential, which are desirable, what might be feasible under the circumstances, and what is to be avoided at all costs.

In an effort to help disentangle, and to provoke discussion on such matters, this paper will outline various decision points in typical evaluation exercises, and make suggestions for coping with planned and unplanned contingencies.

Who should undertake the evaluation?

We will assume that the new language programme is at an advanced stage of development and that formative evaluation has already brought about required improvements. We will assume, further, that the need for a formal evaluation has been accepted – as a basis for changing – or confirming – new policy, or some such respectable motive.

Ideally, the evaluator should be independent of the curriculum development team, so that no vested interests are involved, or perceived to be involved. The enthusiast who initiates a new programme and breathes life and structure into it over a lengthy time span is rarely able to be dispassionate about its limitations. Evaluators need to be impartial. If, as is sometimes the case, nobody is at hand who is neutral, willing and competent to undertake the evaluation, then it is important to organise a committee of people to discuss the plans at each stage, and to ensure that at least the data collection and analysis stages are undertaken by neutral researchers, rather than the developer.

How important is the information to be gained from the evaluation?

An early priority in any evaluation is to clarify the purpose of the exercise. For instance, if the results are likely to influence the adoption of an innovative curriculum in thousands of classrooms – with costly implications for teacher retraining, materials production and public relations, then the evaluators should insist on large representative samples, ample time for developing a battery of suitable tests, and opportunities to probe teacher and pupil reactions in a range of sub-groups of the population on a variety of dimensions. Merely observing a few classrooms, and consulting a biased sample of teachers, is not good enough.

On the other hand, if the programme covers only a small unit, requires minimal changes in teachers, is confined to a small group of students, or is unlikely to have implications for policy, then the time and effort expended should be tailored accordingly. The researcher who conducts costly national surveys of thousands of students to obtain precise estimates of the readability and benefits of a new resource book which may or may not be used in a small number of classrooms, can justly be accused of employing a sledgehammer to crack a nut. In other words, effort should be expended where it is most likely to lead to major decisions.

What are the aims of the programme?

A question too often left unasked by evaluators is that concerned with the precise aims – the intended outcomes of the new programme. Non-specific aims such as 'improvements in English language competence', or 'better literacy levels of all students' may be sufficient to satisfy interested parents, and many teachers. The evaluator, however, needs to pin the developers down, to have them explain what this programme is expected to do that alternative programmes would not do as well. A list of objectives, rated for priority, with specific examples, is desirable, but all too rarely found.

To illustrate, a new English syllabus may produce impressive gains in children's word recognition and vocabulary knowledge, while having no measurable impact on their reading comprehension (see Mezynski, 1983) – and perhaps a harmful effect on attitudes. In another instance of excessive vagueness, the study of formal English grammar in school has long been promoted as a means of assisting first-language users to understand and use their language. A closer analysis of this justification led to the claim that grammar is primarily intended to improve children's ability to write fluent English prose. The fact that it apparently has no such effect was not confidently established until the question was put in this precise fashion, and careful evaluations made of children's writing, done under varied conditions of regular systematic study of grammar compared with no grammar at all. (See Harris, 1962; Elley *et al.*, 1979; Hartwell, 1985.) If grammar promoters change their justification – to a preparation for learning other languages, or to enrich one's understanding of a major human activity (for example, Kitzhaber, 1970), then the shape of the evaluation – and no doubt of the teaching – would change accordingly.

It is not uncommon for the oral objectives of a language course to be skirted over lightly, or neglected entirely by evaluators. Foreknowledge of such likely omissions can, of course, induce some teachers to pay more attention to the written objectives, and so produce distorted findings in an evaluation which focuses only on these. Some evaluators will no doubt ignore such charges, and point to the evidence that language modes develop in parallel, especially amongst ESL students. It is true that correlations amongst reading, writing, listening, and speaking skills are always positive and often high, but one cannot use such evidence about individuals to compare groups following different courses. A writing programme that stresses accuracy in mechanics may enhance some aspects of student writing, but it would probably have quite different incidental effects on oral language development and attitudes to language than a more liberal programme which encouraged inventive spelling, creative writing and vivid imagery. And one cannot argue that high correlations observed under one style of teaching will be maintained under another.

Thus, evaluators should determine precise aims, and use them to guide test development and analysis. If, for some reason, no such aims are obtainable, a meticulous analysis of lesson plans, exercises, or review tests is a second best alternative. Conclusions drawn from such sources would still be best checked out with teachers or others familiar with the course.

What sort of design?

Traditionally, the experimental group with matched control group design has been widely used, and in the author's opinion has much to recommend it. If the pupils studying the new programme do not learn more than a comparable control group in the same period, then serious questions need to be asked.

Sometimes, however, the new programme has no counterpart for comparison, or no suitable schools are available for this purpose. In this case a pre-test–post-test comparison (before and after the new programme is taught) is usually preferred, provided the evaluator can obtain a frame of reference to evaluate the size of the gains observed between the two tests. Merely knowing that the new programme produced in Year 4 pupils an increase in reading score from (say) 30 per cent to 45 per cent on the same test after a full school year may be evaluated as creditable or disappointing, depending on whether the average Year 4 pupil improves by 10 per cent or by 20 per cent on such a measure over the same time period. A good index of such an expected gain can be obtained by testing children of adjacent grade groups at the pre-test stage. If Year 4 children, at the beginning of the year, average 30 per cent and Year 5 children in the same schools average 40 per cent, then a year's growth is reckoned at approximately 10 per cent for children at this stage under these conditions. Thus, an observed gain of 15 per cent in the programme group can be readily interpreted as better than expectation.

Another popular design is to survey a large representative sample of a complete year group in a country, or self-contained region, before the new programme is introduced, in order to establish a baseline. Then, once the programme or policy has been introduced and the initial 'growing pains' are overcome, the same survey could be mounted with the same tests in the same schools, perhaps two or three years later, in order to identify any upward or downward shifts. If no other systematic changes in the pupils' environment have occurred to influence the results, we can then attribute such shifts to the new programme. (See, for example Freyberg, 1964.) Large-scale surveys of this sort enable the evaluator to discount the effect of particular teachers, and to study the influence of the programme on specific sub-groups – such as slow children, rural schools or ethnic minorities.

Often the new programme will show up well because of an artificial 'Hawthorne Effect'. Students who know they are part of a novel experiment will naturally try harder. This effect can be overcome somewhat by not informing students about the purpose of the project, or by telling control groups that they too are part of it. Another useful strategy is to provide the control groups with new materials in their course and to give the teachers an additional refresher course. The writer has found too that if the project goes on for several months, the novelty wears off, and the pupils take it all for granted.

How large a sample?

In an imaginary homogeneous school system, where all pupils were similar in ability, all teachers equally competent, and all home influences uniform in their effects, a single classroom would be sufficient to evaluate a new language programme. In reality, however, it is necessary to choose a sample which is large enough to show how a cross-section of teachers will handle the programme with a cross-section of students, under typical learning conditions.

Normally the number and choice of schools involves a trade-off between need for regular travel and communication between schools on the one hand and the need for wide representation on the other.

Just occasionally the population is small enough that every school can be included in the sample, as in the case of the island of Niue, in the South Pacific, where the author was able to interview and test every Grade 4 pupil in the six primary schools in the whole island (Elley, 1980). On the other hand, an assessment of the Grade 6 programme of Indonesia, with a grade population of over a million students, and incomplete statistics on rolls, required the evaluators to design an elaborate three-stage sampling procedure, with schools drawn from all parts of that very diverse country (Moegradi *et al.*, 1977).

In between such extremes is the more common case, which requires practical decisions about size of sample, and the method of selection.

The number of schools and pupils to include in an evaluation is influenced by several factors. First is the homogeneity of the population in the kinds of skills and attitudes being assessed. Sometimes they are very homogeneous – as in the Fiji Book Flood (Elley and Mangubhai, 1983), where all eight selected schools were small rural, and devoid of books or libraries; all teachers were second language speakers of English, and trained to use a particular programme; and pupils had virtually no contact with English outside the school. Not surprisingly, the average and spread of attainment levels in English in all schools were similar, so that a sample of eight classrooms at each of two levels, in eight schools chosen at random in a restricted, readily accessible rural area (plus four control schools) was considered sufficient to enable the researchers to generalise to most of the remaining 600 small primary schools in the nation. With more diversity, a larger sample, drawn in such a way as to represent that diversity, would have been necessary.

A second factor to consider is the extent to which teacher variability – in enthusiasm or ability – can affect the programme to be evaluated. If the course is largely 'teacher proof' – as in T.V. instruction, programmed learning, computer-aided instruction, or SRA Kits – then a small sample is likely to tell the same story as an extensive one. However, if teacher competence or interest is crucial to the outcome of the programme, then a sufficiently large number of classrooms must be included to demonstrate effects with all kinds of teachers. A programme that works well with only very able and committed teachers, while leaving pupils of average teachers worse off, is better avoided, or greatly modified. Certainly, it is important to go well beyond the special laboratory or experimental school, often linked to a university or teachers' college, with handpicked teachers and able youngsters. The merits of many a new curriculum have been grossly distorted by such injudicious practice.

A third factor, which will increase the required sample size, is the need to study sub-groups within the sample – sexes, language groups, ethnic minorities, and the like. To draw conclusions about small sub-groups one must either select a huge sample, or increase the proportion of members in such groups, remembering to reduce their influence by weighting when generalising about the total group.

There is, of course, no magic number in making decisions about sample size. The IEA surveys of achievement in reading, literature, ESL, and other subjects, have normally been conducted with at least 100 schools in the relevant grade level for each country. Such a number allows sub-group comparisons and would be desirable for large-scale, important non-experimental surveys. However, when the design involves matched contrast groups and the quality of the teaching is not expected to be a major source of variance, then eight or ten classrooms may be sufficient to identify the important trends. If the teacher has little or no role to play, and the unit of analysis is the individual student, then three or four classrooms, representing all ethnic and socio-economic groups would normally be enough. All of these suggestions could be modified of course, if the evaluation is charged with producing pin-point precision.

How is the sample chosen?

For large-scale national or regional surveys, schools would best be selected by a stratified random sample procedure. With smaller-scale experimental, or quasi-experimental evaluations a 'judgement' sample, selected to represent a range of socio-economic, ethnic, regional, and/or school-type factors would be preferred. Often the selection of schools presents no problem, as the new course may be suitable for, or being adopted by only a small number of classrooms. In other cases, travel costs, over-use of particular schools, or other administrative influences may narrow the choice.

If the evaluator is faced with choosing, say, ten from a potential pool of many relatively homogeneous schools, then some form of randomisation may help. In a recent evaluation the author listed all schools in a district ranked by socio-economic status, then grouped adjacent schools into sets of five. From each set two schools were selected at random, and the school to receive the experimental course was chosen at random from these two (at the appropriate grade level). The other school became a member of the control group. If only three or four pairs of schools had been chosen this way, we would not have trusted the laws of chance to produce well-matched groups under these conditions, and would have delayed assigning schools to groups until some form of pretesting had been done.

Once selected, the schools should be approached, politely, to seek co-operation. If administrative authority cannot be brought to bear to convince reluctant principals, then weight might be added to the persuasiveness of the approach by reference to professional responsibility, to the cost and importance of the programme, to the potential benefits for the school – and to the assurance of confidentiality. If all this fails, a substitute school should be selected from the same set, preferably chosen beforehand. Should this approach fail also, a third school should be tried, and if this proves unsuccessful then the evaluator might be wise to abandon the project and take a training course in sales promotion.

Occasionally, the curriculum developers will have already selected the schools for the new programme, and allowed the evaluator no choice. One useful strategy for this case is to survey all pupils in these schools, on an achievement test of language skills which are related to the course outcomes, and to identify another larger set of schools with similar student composition to those of the first set. The students in the relevant grade levels of the second set are also tested, and classes chosen from them in such a way as to match the first set in average achievement overall. If recent national examination results are available, in relevant subjects, then much of this effort can be short-circuited.

Another complication occurs if the developers have chosen schools which have no potential counterpart for controls. Perhaps all schools throughout the country have decided to or been told to adopt the new programme. One solution then is to survey the students in all schools at the next highest grade level – i.e. those who have not yet taken the new course. Then wait until the next cohort (who now proceed to take the course), reach the same age and stage of schooling, and assess their competence on the same tests. If we can accept the assumption that adjacent cohorts are similar in ability – which is a safe assumption for a set of about five or more classes (other things being equal) then any mean differences favouring the second group would reflect well on the new programme.

What kinds of measuring devices?

If the major aims of the programme are to improve achievement levels, as they usually are, then group achievement tests will need to be used; if the objectives focus more on attitudes or interests, then suitable attitude scales, or observation techniques or diary reports will be more appropriate. Testing of oral language, of course, will require individual interviewing, and much more time.

Most language programmes aim at improved skills in some or all of the four modes of reading, writing, speaking, and listening. While an improvement in one mode often produces a similar gain in others, this is not always the case. Therefore a wise evaluator will select or prepare tests of each mode which forms part of the programme objectives. Sometimes there are standardised tests of reading and listening available which can be used or adapted for the occasion. More often evaluators are forced to develop their own instruments, tailor-made to fit the objectives, the culture and the ability levels of the students.

Common problems with available standardised tests of achievement are:

1 They are widely used and frequently too familiar in some schools.
2 They are often unsuitable culturally, by virtue of language or assumed background knowledge.
3 The skills measured do not match those of the new programme.
4 They are too easy or too difficult for the pupils at the beginning or end of the programme.
5 They are too costly or time-consuming for the purpose.

If new tests are to be constructed, they should normally be designed specifically to fit the objectives of the new programme. Where another programme is being used for contrast, with different objectives, these too should be assessed. If funds and time permit, it is also preferable to include some way of assessing any unintended outcomes. Measures of interest, attitude scales, interviews with teachers and/or randomly selected pupils, and systematic classroom observations can all throw light on such outcomes.

Test construction is an art which can be acquired by regular practice, by learning the common pitfalls, by study of high quality standardised tests, by seeking help from critical editors, and by exercising a little imagination.

Once the aims of the course are clarified, careful decisions need to be made on the following matters:

1 The weighting to be assigned each skill or concept. This is often best done in consultation with developers and teachers.

2 The source of suitable passages, sentences, topics. Frequently they will be written from scratch, or adapted from other tests, newspapers, magazines, children's books, encyclopedias, travel brochures, advertisements, official forms etc.
3 The kinds of question-type: discrete-point or integrative, i.e. objective tests which assess one point at a time, such as multiple-choice and matching items, or tests of the students' internalised grammar, such as essay, cloze, dictation, oral repetition, picture matching, etc.
4 The length of the test, bearing in mind the age of the children, the importance of the skills assessed, the need for high reliability, etc.
5 Whether to have different students in a class take different but parallel forms of each test (matrix sampling) or to have all students take all questions.
6 How to trial the questions on comparable groups of students.

Much has been written on the virtues and weaknesses of different kinds of test items. For assessing the ability to write fluent prose, there is no substitute for an open-ended or relatively unstructured essay, report or paragraph. When testing vocabulary or comprehension, the author usually favours multiple-choice questions of four options (only one of which is correct), always provided there is time and expertise available to develop them properly. Cloze tests, in which students complete the blanks where words have been systematically omitted from prose passages, are easier to prepare for most teachers, and usually just as reliable. Some test specialists now recommend that the first letter of the missing word, or the number of letters in the word, be provided for the student. Many textbooks are available with sound advice about and examples of these procedures, so they will not be developed further at this point.

Writing and improving the items

After writing a set of questions, a wise test constructor will set aside his or her first drafts and return to them with a fresh perspective in the following days. Each question should be re-examined thoroughly for ambiguities, relevance, difficulty levels, and fairness, by the writer and by others who know the subject well, or are familiar with the common pitfalls of testing.

Next it is usually advisable to trial the test on a sample of students similar in ability to the target groups, in order to identify further weaknesses and check out difficulty levels, reliability, and time limits. Ideally, a sample of 100 or more students is desirable for the trial run, but if this is not feasible, a single class can provide useful information on most of these aspects. If even this is impossible, a sample of students in the grades above and below the target grade is often helpful. While a published standardised test and three-hour examination will aim for reliability indices of 0.9 or better, a test which is intended only for evaluating group performance can be quite adequate with reliability indices of 0.7–0.8 or thereabouts. In the writer's experience an objective test of reading or listening comprehension which contains 30 to 35 questions of suitable difficulty levels – with facility indices between 30 per cent and 80 per cent – and respectable discrimination indices – will be sensitive enough to detect any systematic differences of consequence. Tests which depend on unseen paragraphs to be read or listened to should normally include a range of six or seven short passages on various topics, rather than one or two long ones, as present research has shown clearly that students' knowledge about the topic of a passage is a major influence on comprehension. The same recommendations apply to cloze passages. Younger children need shorter tests and passages, of course.

Tests containing discrete sentences, as in spelling, or syntax, or vocabulary, should likewise contain about 30 or more questions. If vocabulary test items are presented in the context of a suitable sentence or phrase, as is desirable, it is important to ensure that the content does not provide a clue to the answer, for example,

> The *handsome* salesman was popular with the ladies.
> A good-looking
> B ugly
> C reliable
> D dishonest

For this item, shrewd students who did not know the answer could infer that good-looking salesmen were more likely to be popular than ugly ones. Such reasoning would improve students' chances of guessing the answer. Of course, if the test aims to assess inference skills, this feature would become a virtue.

Are pre-tests advisable?

Some textbooks advocate the use of pre-tests, on the grounds that they ensure that the evaluator has a clear indication of the students' baseline levels of knowledge and skill at the outset. Others contend that a pre-test is hazardous, as it sensitises the students to the important concepts, and provides them with practice which helps in the final evaluation.

For evaluating language programmes, the author recommends the use of a pre-test in most cases, but not necessarily the same test as is used at the end of the project. Thus, if the programme focuses on literacy skills, then any good test of reading comprehension is likely to serve the purpose of equating groups, and/or provide data for adjusting scores when the groups are not well matched. In addition, it may well show the evaluator how suitable the programme materials are likely to be, and whether there are pupils who have already mastered the skills to be taught, or are likely to be out of their depth. A cloze pre-test, made up of several prose passages drawn from materials in the programme, could make a direct contribution in the latter case. Dictation and vocabulary tests are also considered sensitive measures for equating groups.

Administering the tests

Careful thought should always be given to the timing of the evaluation. If the programme covers a full year, then the pre-tests should be given as early as possible in the school year – or even before the end of the previous year, while the post-tests should be given as close to the end of the current school year as possible. Practical difficulties such as delays in class formation or use of unprepared teachers at the beginning of the year, or frequent absences, external examinations, or school picnics at the end of the year, should be taken into account in planning, and regular communication maintained with school principals on such issues.

Tests should be printed, collated and sorted well beforehand, and instructions given to test administrators about how to motivate the students, what to tell them, what time limits are allowed, and how their answers should be recorded and changed – if desired. Where novel kinds of test items are included, directions to students should be clear-cut and examples provided. It is advisable to have the test supervisor read them aloud to students, while they follow and listen. Time should be allowed for questions, and the test supervisor should walk around, checking to see that instructions are properly followed.

If matrix sampling is used, and this is usually recommended, then papers should be sorted on a rotation basis beforehand. Where there are (say) three parallel forms of each test then they are best distributed in sequence – A, B, C, A, B, C, etc. around the class so that no student sits next to another student answering the same paper. Such an arrangement reduces the possibility of cheating, while providing for a wider coverage of skills tested in the same time – an important virtue in language testing. The fact that individual students' scores are not comparable is not relevant, as the evaluator requires only group data for drawing conclusions.

Timetabling the tests to accommodate teachers' and pupils' daily programmes often requires negotiation and compromise. Ideally, all students in one school should take the tests at the same time, or at least in adjacent periods – to avoid leakage about test questions. Other desirable objectives are to have all tests administered in the mornings, in quiet conditions, in spacious classrooms, with good lighting, and under optimum conditions of motivation. If these desiderata are not always possible, at least it is important that both experimental and control groups are equally favoured in these respects.

If individual interviews are required for oral discussion or testing, they should be prearranged at a convenient time for the schools, and a suitable quiet spot decided on before testing begins. As these are very time-consuming sessions, it is advisable to select only a random sample of each class, or at least to use matrix sampling and ask different questions of different pupils. The author has found it useful to alternate between two completely different oral tests in such interviews. Pupil 1 takes Test A, Pupil 2 Test B, and Pupil 3 Test A again, etc. This form of alternation within classes is preferable to giving all one class Test A and another Test B, as the results will reflect the influence of a larger range of teachers. Where possible, oral tests should be taped to allow for later marking and for reliability checks.

Marking the tests

Objective marking (or scoring) is normally straightforward, but should be spot-checked for accuracy. Many reports exist of inaccurate markings, by teachers (for example Chapman *et al.*, 1985). In case of an unsuspected fault in the marking key, the author has found it helpful to examine the wrong answers of the first six high-scoring students in the first set marked. This precaution should help identify any such problem before the remainder are marked. In the light of research on the question of penalising wrong 'guesses' in objective questions, and the extra work and doubtful assumptions involved in doing so, this practice is not recommended. Students should be informed of this before testing commences.

If cloze tests are used, decisions will be required on whether to penalise spelling (don't!) and whether to allow near-synonyms for the right answers. Studies by the author and others show correlations over 0.95 between the two scoring systems – i.e. exact replacements only or allowing for synonyms, so the former is usually preferred. However, a wrong answer which is synonymous with, or of the same form class (part of speech) as the target word is usually indicative of greater proficiency than a wild guess, and may well provide the evaluator with helpful information. The final decision will depend, then, on the time available and the overall purpose of the exercise. If some synonyms are permitted they should be listed and agreed on by markers, after the first set of papers is marked.

Essays, paragraph answers and oral language tapes are best marked by (paid) experienced language teachers, after discussion of criteria, and marking schemes, close study of several specimens, and practice and feedback on a range of sample essays. As such marking is notoriously unreliable, it is wise to plan for double-marking in those cases, and, to arrange this in such a way that the second marker does not know the mark given by the first. Three markers provide only marginal improvement over two.

Monitoring the instruction

In spite of thorough in-service training, a few teachers will probably not enter into the spirit of the new programme. Some may ignore it altogether. Therefore, an astute evaluator will seek evidence that the new materials are being used, that students are producing the required work, and that lessons are being taught as planned. As Beeby points out, teachers have a remarkable capacity for continuing to teach their usual programme under a new label (Beeby, 1979).

Monitoring may be accomplished by spontaneous visits, planned classroom observations, collection of student work, interviewing with teachers, principal, pupils. Those involved in the initial teacher training may do this as an extension of their training function. Sometimes teachers may be rated on a three-point scale, according to how faithfully they appear to be implementing the programme, and the pupil results analysed in relation to such a rating. In this way, more specific information may be obtained on the effects of particular teacher practices and attitudes. It is clearly misleading to evaluate the pupils' growth on the assumption that they took one programme when they were in fact following another.

While it may be beyond the evaluator's means to monitor the control groups in the same way, it is advisable to try. The author once discovered in an experiment on the effects of story reading to Fijian pupils, that one control group teacher was reading stories to her class, a very unusual practice at that time. Not surprisingly, the reading tests of her class were clearly deviant from the remaining control group classes.

Sometimes the teachers (or students) in the control groups will have casual contact with those following the experimental programme, and deliberately change their course to adopt some of its principles. For instance, a new language programme in Singapore, which the writer has had close contact with, was adopted and evaluated in 90 classrooms. After encouraging comments in newspapers, and before objective data were obtained, the rumour was spread that the programme was both successful and enjoyable. Not surprisingly, perhaps, while visiting control group schools, the writer discovered several teachers had meticulously prepared their own 'Blown-up Books' for the new programme, at considerable expense, and were teaching in similar vein to the experimental groups. The moral should be clear. Experimental and control groups should be kept apart when possible, and some monitoring undertaken to check on the possibilities of such 'contamination'.

Analysis of results

Many aspects of collating and processing of results could be discussed at this point, but space limitations must restrict us to a few. One problem, often overlooked in a two-group contrast design is the loss of cases through pupil illness, transfer, or unusable test results. Sometimes a teacher is transferred, or unco-operative, resulting in the loss of a whole class. The effect of such 'mortality' on any pre-test equating of groups should be checked after marking is complete, for these omissions do often cause a bias in the results. Sometimes, it is worth a second visit to a school to pick up cases of pupil absence; otherwise it may be necessary to adjust the results for lack of comparability.

Of course it is often the case that groups are not equated anyway. The professional approach to this problem is usually to adjust post-test scores using analysis of covariance. This method is outlined in most respectable textbooks on educational or psychological statistics. Another procedure which the author has found relatively straightforward is a comparison of residual scores after a regression analysis. The researcher predicts all students' post-test scores on the basis of their pre-test scores, using a regression equation derived from results for all students. Each student's actual post-test score is then subtracted from his/her predicted score to produce a 'residual'. Then the residuals of experimental and control groups are compared on a t-test or an analysis of variance. In one large evaluation study where this method was adopted, the results were compared with those obtained from a less complex, but less defensible procedure – merely dropping students at random from the lower quartile of the less able group until pre-test means were matched. In the event, the results for both analyses were virtually identical. (See Elley and Mangubhai 1983.) The particular method chosen will normally be dictated by the availability of computer facilities and programmes. If the matching of groups is not too far out, the results obtained by each procedure are likely to be very similar. The method which is least reputable, in comparing unmatched groups, is a straight comparison of mean gain scores. The assumption that progress at one point in an interval scale is equivalent to the same quantity of progress at a higher or lower point on that scale is rarely justified, and the situation is therefore best avoided.

'Ceiling effects' in the tests used give rise to another problem. Sometimes the brighter students in a project will score so near the top of the mark scale (the 'ceiling') on the pre-test that it is virtually impossible for them to show as much gain in the qualities measured as students who start from a lower base. If Mary starts at 85 per cent and improves to 95 per cent on the post-test, her level of improvement is not readily comparable with that of John, who moved from 50 per cent to 80 per cent on the same test.

The pre-test results should provide warning of this problem, so that an alert evaluator will add more difficult items for the post-test. If it is not recognised until too late, and the results are likely to be biased as a result, the researcher can either omit those students from the analysis – after identification in a scattergram – or report the findings with and without their results. The problem will be most serious where there are unequal numbers of such students in experimental and control groups, or where analyses are to be undertaken comparing bright and slower pupils.

Evaluations are often improved by analysis of sub-groups. Whereas an overall comparison of means may show little difference between experimental and control groups, a closer examination may well reveal that boys improved while girls did not, or less able students caught up on the gifted. More important, a breakdown of results by class may show that certain teachers who followed the new programme faithfully achieved different results from those who did not. Perhaps the new programme is more effective with females, or experienced teachers, or graduates, or teachers with particular language background or personality type. Likewise, an analysis of test scores by sub-test, or item by item, may well show differential gains and losses which were masked in the first analysis. Such revelations often provide the most valuable part of an evaluation, as they offer clues to developers about where improvement might be feasible, and to decision makers about the likelihood of further benefits once these improvements are made.

Any comparison of high and low ability groups must be handled with care, due to the artificial tendency of students' scores at the extremes of the distribution to regress towards the mean of the group on re-testing – at the post-test stage. Thus, if students are grouped into (say) four quarters by ability on the basis of pre-test scores, the means of the highest and lowest groups will drift towards the overall mean without any treatment at all, due to this statistical regression. Evaluations of remedial programmes with slow readers often show more flattering outcomes because of this phenomenon.

Conclusion

Much more could be written about less common contingencies in programme evaluations. Clearly, the rigour of scientific procedure must often be moderated with pragmatic considerations – for human subjects rarely conform exactly as predicted or according to the dictates of researchers. Nevertheless, administrators do need to make decisions – often costly ones – and the results of a well-controlled, independent, quasi-experimental study are usually more dependable than the starry-eyed views of those who develop the curriculum, or of a handful of unrepresentative teachers, especially if there are sceptical Treasury officers to convince. Furthermore, a careful study of patterns in the results of particular groups, of observations made in certain classrooms, and of interviews with judiciously selected teachers, can produce important incidental benefits which may lead the developers to further improvement, and researchers to new hypotheses.

Whether the evaluators should be held responsible for recommending the programmes they evaluate is much debated. The current writer believes they should play some part in decision making, as they do possess expert information. After all the potential for misunderstanding of research findings by administrators is considerable – especially where there are acknowledged limitations and qualifications. However, the decision should rarely be restricted to the evaluator, as other considerations such as cost of materials, disruption of schools, retraining of teachers and revision of curricula, not to mention political considerations, will usually help sway the decision process.

Evaluation is a demanding but professional challenge. Nevertheless, if the quality of our educational programmes is to be enhanced, and we are to avoid following the misleading bandwagons of the past, it is an essential part of the enterprise of education.

Bibliography

Agard, F. B. and H. B. Dunkel. 1948. *An investigation of second language teaching*. Boston: Ginn and Company.

Ager, D. 1985. Language learning – an intellectual challenge? *British Journal of Language Teaching 23* (1): 11–22.

Alatis, J. E. (Ed.) 1978. *International dimensions of bilingual education*. Washington, D.C.: Georgetown University Press.

Alatis, J. E., H. B. Altman, and P. M. Alatis. (Eds.) 1981. *The second language classroom: directions for the 1980s*. Oxford: Oxford University Press.

Alatis, J. E., H. H. Stern, and P. Strevens. (Eds.) 1983. *Applied linguistics and the preparation of second language teachers; toward a rationale*. Washington, D.C.: Georgetown University Press.

Alcorso, C. and M. Kalantsis. 1985. The learning process and being a learner. In the AMEP report to the Committee of Review of the Adult Migrant Education Program, Department of Immigration and Ethnic Affairs, Canberra.

Alderson, J. C. and A. Hughes. (Eds.) 1981. Issues in language testing. *ELT documents 111*. London: The British Council.

Alkin, M. C. 1969. Evaluation theory development. *Evaluation Comment 2* (1).

Allen, J. P. B. 1983. A three-level curriculum model for second-language education. *Canadian Modern Language Review 40* (1): 23–43.

Allen, J. P. B., G. Barker, and M. Canale. 1985. Strategy-oriented activities in language learning materials development. Presentation at the TESOL Convention, New York.

Allen, J. P. B., J. Howard, and R. Ullmann. 1984. Module making research. In Allen and Swain 83–98.

Allen, M. J. and W. M. Yen. 1979. *Introduction to measurement theory*. Monterey: Brooks/Cole.

Allen, P., M. Fröhlich, and N. Spada. 1984. The communicative orientation of language teaching: an observation scheme. In Handscombe, Orem, and Taylor 231–52.

Allen, P. and M. Swain. (Eds.) 1984. Language issues and education policies: exploring Canada's multilingual resources. *ELT Documents 119*. Oxford: Pergamon Press.

Allen, W. and N. Spada. 1983. Designing a communicative syllabus in the People's Republic of China. In Jordan 132–45.

Allwright, R. L. 1972. Prescription and description in the training of language teachers. In Quistgaard, Schwarts, and Spang Hanssen 150–66.

Allwright, R. L. 1975. Problems in the study of the language teacher's treatment of learner error. In Burt and Dulay 96–109.

Allwright, R. L. 1982. Perceiving and pursuing learners' needs. In Geddes and Sturtridge 24–31.

Allwright, R. L. 1983a. The nature and function of the syllabus in language learning and teaching. Unpublished mimeo. Department of Linguistics and Modern English Language, University of Lancaster.

Allwright, R. L. 1983b. Classroom-centred research on language teaching and learning: a brief historical overview. *TESOL Quarterly 17* (2): 191–204.

Allwright, R. L. 1986. Making sense of instruction: what's the problem? *Papers in Applied Linguistics, PALM: University of Michigan 1* (2): 1–10.

Altman, H. B. and C. V. James. (Eds.) 1980. *Foreign language teaching: meeting individual needs.* Oxford: Pergamon Press.

Angoff, W. H. 1971. Scales, norms, and equivalent scores. In Thorndike 508–600.

Anthony, E. M. 1963. Approach, method, and technique. *English Language Teaching Journal 17* (2): 63–7.

Apple, M. W. 1979. *Ideology and curriculum.* London: Routledge and Kegan Paul.

Apple, M. 1981. Reproduction, contestation and curriculum: an essay in self criticism. *Interchange 12* (2/3): 27–47.

Asher, J. J. 1966. The learning strategy of the total physical response: a review. *Modern Language Journal 50* (2): 79–84.

Asher, J. J. 1972. Children's first language as a model for second language learning. *Modern Language Journal 56* (3): 133–9.

Asher, J. J., J. A. Kusudo, and R. de la Torre. 1974. Learning a second language through commands: the second field test. *Modern Language Journal 58* (1–2): 24–32.

Au, K. and C. Jordan. 1981. Teaching reading to Hawaiian children: finding a culturally appropriate solution. In Trueba, Guthrie, and Au 139–52.

Auerbach, E. R. and D. Burgess. 1985. The hidden curriculum of survival ESL. *TESOL Quarterly 19* (3): 475–95.

Baalen, T. van. 1983. Giving learners rules: a study into the effect of grammatical instruction with varying degrees of explicitness. *Interlanguage Studies Bulletin 7* (1): 71–100.

Bach, E. and R. T. Harms (Eds.) 1968. *Universals in linguistic theory.* New York: Holt, Rinehart and Winston.

Bachman, L. F. 1981. Formative evaluation in specific purpose program development. In Mackay and Palmer 106–16.

Bachman, L. F. forthcoming. *Fundamental considerations in language testing.* Reading, Mass.: Addison-Wesley.

Bachman, L. F. and J. L. D. Clark. 1987. The measurement of foreign/second language proficiency. *Annals of the American Association of Political and Social Sciences 490.*

Bachman, L. F. and A. S. Palmer. 1981. The construct validation of the FSI oral interview. *Language Learning 31* (1): 67–86.

Bachman, L. F. and A. S. Palmer. 1982. The construct validation of some components of communicative proficiency. *TESOL Quarterly 16* (4): 449–65.

Bachman, L. F. and A. S. Palmer. 1983. *Oral interview test of communicative proficiency in English.* Photocopy.

Bachman, L. F. and S. J. Savignon. 1986. The evaluation of communicative language proficiency: a critique of the ACTFL oral interview. *Modern Language Journal 70* (4): 380–90.

Baker, E. 1974. Formative evaluation of instruction. In Popham (1974): 533–85.

Baldegger, M., M. Muller, and G. Schneider. 1980. *Kontaktschwelle deutsch als Fremdsprache.* Strasbourg: Council of Europe.

Barmada, W. 1983. Ten English language centres in the Arab world: an investigation into their 'macro ESP/ELT problems'. M.Sc. dissertation. Birmingham: The University of Aston.

Barrett, R. P. (Ed.) 1982. *The administration of intensive English language programs.* Washington, D.C.: National Association for Foreign Student Affairs.

Bassano, S. 1986. Helping learners adapt to unfamiliar methods. *English Language Teaching Journal 40* (1): 13–19.

Beeby, C. E. 1979. *Assessment of Indonesian education: a guide in planning.* Wellington: New Zealand Council for Education Research in association with Oxford University Press: 136.

Bem, S. L. and D. L. Bem. 1973. Does sex-biased job advertising 'aid and abet' sex discrimination? *Journal of Applied Psychology 3* (1): 6–18.

Bennett, N., C. Desforges, A. Cockburn, and B. Wilkinson. 1984. *The quality of pupil learning experiences.* London: Lawrence Erlbaum Associates.

Beretta, A. and A. Davies. 1985. Evaluation of the Bangalore project. *English Language Teaching Journal 39* (2): 121–7.

Berk, R. A. 1976. Determination of optimal cutting scores in criterion-referenced measurement. *The Journal of Experimental Education 45* (2): 4–9.

Berk, R. A. (Ed.) 1980a. *Criterion-referenced measurement: the state of the art.* Baltimore: John Hopkins University Press.

Berk, R. A. 1980b. A consumers' guide to criterion-referenced test reliability. *Journal of Educational Measurement 17* (4): 323–49.

Berk, R. A. (Ed.) 1984a. *A guide to criterion-referenced test construction.* Baltimore: John Hopkins University Press.

Berk, R. A. 1984b. Selecting the index of reliability. In Berk, 1984a: 231–66.

Berliner, D. C. 1984. Making the right changes in preservice teacher education. *Phi Delta Kappan 66* (2): 94–6.

Berne, E. 1964. *Games people play.* New York: Grove Press.

Bernstein, B. 1971. On the classification and framing of educational knowledge. In Young 1971.

Berwick, R. 1978. Beyond Chinatown: the English language needs of Vancouver's Chinese Community. *TESL Talk 9*: 13–20.

Berwick, R. 1984a. Child's play for adult learners: simulations in company language training. *Language Training 5* (1): 6–8.

Berwick, R. 1984b. The normative bases of needs assessment in applied linguistics: a critical re-examination. *JALT Journal 1*: 147–68.

Bhatia, V. K. 1986. Specialist discipline and the ESP curriculum. In Tickoo: 47–63.

Birckbichler, D. W. and A. C. Omaggio. 1978. Diagnosing and responding to individual learner needs. *Modern Language Journal 62* (7): 336–45.

Bloom, B. 1972. Innocence in education. *School Review 80* (3): 333–52.

Bolus, R. E., F. B. Hinofotis, and K. M. Bailey. 1982. An introduction to generalizability theory in second language research. *Language Learning 32*: 245–58.

Bosco, F. J. and R. J. Di Pietro. 1970. Instructional strategies: their psychological and linguistic bases. *IRAL 8* (1): 1–19.

Bourdieu, P. and J.-C. Passeron. 1977. *Reproduction in education, society and culture.* Beverly Hills, Calif: Sage.

Bowers, R. 1980a. The individual learner in the general class. In Altman and James: 66–80.

Bowers, R. 1980b. War stories and romances: interchanging experience in ELT. *ELT Documents special – Projects in Materials Design*: 71–81.

Bowers, R. 1983. Project planning and performance. *ELT Documents 116*: 99–120.

Bradshaw, J. 1974. The concept of social need. *Ekistics 37* (220): 184–7.

Breen, M. P. 1984. Process syllabuses for the language classroom. In Brumfit 1984: 47–60.

Breen, M. P. 1985a. Authenticity in the language classroom. *Applied Linguistics* 6 (1): 60–70.

Breen, M. P. 1985b. The social context for language learning – a neglected situation? *Studies in Second Language Acquisition 7* (2): 135–58.

Breen, M. P. 1987a. Learner contributions to task design. *Lancaster Practical Papers in English Language Education 7.* Englewood Cliffs N.J.: Prentice Hall.

Breen, M. P. 1987b. Contemporary paradigms in syllabus design. Part 2. *Language Teaching 20* (2). Cambridge: Cambridge University Press.

Breen, M. P. and C. N. Candlin. 1980. The essentials of a communicative curriculum in language teaching. *Applied Linguistics 1* (2): 89–112.

Breen, M. P. and C. N. Candlin. Forthcoming. Which materials? A consumer's and designer's guide. In Sheldon.

Brennan, R. L. 1980. Applications of generalizability theory. In Berk, 1980a: 186–232.

Brindley, G. P. 1984. *Needs analysis and objective setting in the adult migrant education program.* Sydney, N.S.W.: Adult Migrant Education Service.

Brink, A., H. Mullins, B. Pedler, and H. Reade. 1985. *Let's try to do it better.* Adelaide: South Australian Adult Migrant Education Service.

British Council. 1978. Report on the Dunford House seminar ESP course design. London: The British Council.

Britten, D. 1985. Teacher training in ELT (Part 1). *Language teaching 18* (2): 112–28.

Brock, C. A. 1986. The effects of referential questions on ESL classroom discourse. *TESOL Quarterly 20* (1): 47–59.

Brophy, J. E. 1979. Teacher behavior and its effects. *Journal of Educational Psychology 71* (6): 733–50.

Brophy, J. E. and T. L. Good. Forthcoming. Teacher behavior and student achievement. In Wittrock.

Broudy, H. S. 1956. Teaching – craft or profession? *The Educational Forum,* January, 1956: 175–84.

Broughton, G. (Ed.) 1968. *Success with English. The Penguin Course. Teacher's Handbook 1.* London: Penguin Books.

Brown, A. L. and J. D. Day. 1983. Macrorules for summarizing texts: the development of expertise. *Journal of Verbal Learning and Verbal Behaviour* 22 (1): 1–14.

Brown, H. C., C. A. Yorio, and R. H. Crymes (Eds.) 1977. *On TESOL '77.* Washington, D.C.: TESOL.

Brown, J. D. and M. C. Pennington. Developing effective evaluation systems for language programs. University of Hawaii at Manoa. Unpublished manuscript.

Brown, J. D. and J. C. Richards. In preparation. The language teaching matrix: An introduction to curriculum development in language teaching. University of Hawaii at Manoa.

Brumfit, C. J. 1978. 'Communicative' language teaching: an assessment. In Strevens: 33–44.

Brumfit, C. J. 1979. 'Communicative' language teaching: an educational perspective. In Brumfit and Johnson: 183–91.

Brumfit, C. J. (Ed.) 1983. Language teaching projects for the third world. *ELT Documents 116.* Oxford: Pergamon Press.

Brumfit, C. J. (Ed.) 1984. General English syllabus design: curriculum and syllabus design for the general English classroom. *ELT Documents 118.* Oxford: Pergamon Press.

Brumfit, C. J. and K. Johnson (Eds.) 1979. *The communicative approach to language teaching.* Oxford: Oxford University Press.

Bruner, J. S. 1960/1977. *The process of education.* Mass: Harvard University Press.

Buckingham, T. and W. C. Pech. 1976. An experience approach to teaching composition. *TESOL Quarterly 10* (1): 55–65.

Burstall, C., M. Jamieson, S. Cohen, and M. Hargreaves. 1974. *Primary French in the balance.* Windsor: NFER Publishing Company.

Burt, M. K. and H. C. Dulay (Eds.) 1975. *On TESOL '75.* Washington, D.C.: TESOL.

Bushman, R. W. and H. S. Madsen. 1976. A description and evaluation of suggestopedia – a new teaching methodology. In Fanselow and Crymes: 29–39.

Butler, J. and L. Bartlett. 1986. The active voice of teachers: curriculum planning in the AMEP. *Prospect 2* (1): 13–28.

Byrne, D. 1981. Integrating skills. In Johnson and Morrow: 108–14.

Canale, M. 1983. On some dimensions of language proficiency. In Oller, 1983b: 333–42.

Canale, M. and M. Swain. 1980. Theoretical bases of communicative approaches to second language teaching and testing. *Applied Linguistics 1* (1): 1–47.

Candlin, C. N. 1984a. Applying a systems approach to curriculum innovation in the public sector. In Read: 151–79.

Candlin, C. N. 1984b. Syllabus design as a critical process. In Brumfit, 1984: 29–46.

Candlin, C. N. 1986. Explaining communicative competence limits of testability? In Stansfield: 38–57.

Candlin, C. N., C. J. Bruton, and J. L. Leather. 1974. Doctor–patient communication skills. *Working Papers 1* (4). University of Lancaster.

Candlin, C. N., J. M. Kirkwood, and H. M. Moore. 1978. Study skills in English: theoretical issues and practical problems. In Mackay and Mountford, 1978a: 190–219.

Candlin, C. N., J. H. Leather, and C. J. Bruton. 1976. Doctors in casualty: applying communicative competence to components of specialist course design. *IRAL 14* (3): 245–72.

Carrier, M. 1983. Computer assisted needs analysis. *Language Training 4* (4): 3–5.

Carroll, B. J. 1981. Specifications for an English language testing service. In Alderson and Hughes: 66–110.

Carroll, D. 1980. An evaluation model for the Bangalore project. *Regional Institute of English Bulletin* 4 (1): iv–xvii.

Carroll, J. B. 1963. Research on teaching foreign languages. In Gage, 1963: 1060–100.

Carroll, J. B. 1975. *The teaching of French as a foreign language in eight countries.* New York: John Wiley and Sons.

Carroll, J. B. 1983. Psychometric theory and language testing. In Oller, 1983b: 80–107.

Cartier, F. 1968. Criterion-referenced testing of language skills. *TESOL Quarterly* 2 (1): 27–32.

Casey, J. B. 1968. The effectiveness of two methods of teaching English as a foreign language in some Finnish secondary schools. Unpublished report. University of Helsinki.

Chambers, F. 1980. A re-evaluation of needs analysis in ESP. *The ESP Journal* 1 (1): 25–33.

Chapman, J. W., R. St George, and R. Ibell. 1985. Error rate differences in teacher marking of the progressive achievement tests. *New Zealand Journal of Educational Studies* 20 (2): 165–9.

Charles, D. 1984. The use of case studies in business English. In James: 24–33.

Chastain, K. D. and F. J. Weerdehoff. 1968. A methodological study comparing the audio-lingual habit theory and the cognitive code-learning theory. *Modern Language Journal* 52 (5): 268–79.

Chaudron, C. 1977. A descriptive model of discourse in the corrective treatment of learners' errors. *Language Learning* 27: 29–46.

Chaudron, C. 1983. Languages for specific purposes. Review article. *Journal of Pragmatics* 7 (6): 713–26.

Christison, M. A. and K. J. Krahnke. 1986. Student perceptions of academic language study. *TESOL Quarterly* 20 (1): 61–81.

Clark, J. L. D. 1969. The Pennsylvania project and the 'audio-lingual versus traditional' question. *Modern Language Journal* 53 (6): 388–96.

Clark, J. L. 1986. Curriculum renewal in school foreign language learning: an overview. *Australian Review of Applied Linguistics* 9 (1): 14–42.

Coffing, R. T. and T. E. Hutchinson. 1974. Needs analysis methodology: a prescriptive set of rules and procedures for identifying, defining and measuring needs. Paper presented at Annual Meeting of the American Educational Research Association. Chicago. April, 1974.

Cohen, A. M. and R. D. Smith. 1976. *The critical incident in growth groups: theory and technique.* La Jolla, Calif: University Associates, Inc.

Cook, V. J. 1983. What should language teaching be about? *English Language Teaching Journal* 37 (3): 229–34.

Cook, T. D. and C. S. Reichardt (Eds.) 1979. *Qualitative and quantitative methods in evaluation research.* Beverly Hills, Calif: Sage.

Corder, S. P. 1977. Language teaching and learning: a social encounter. In Brown, Yorio, and Crymes: 1–13.

Corder, S. P. 1981. *Error analysis and interlanguage.* Oxford: Oxford University Press.

Coste, D. 1983. General presentation and comments. In Council of Europe, 1983b: 3–32.

Coste, D., J. Courtillon, V. Ferenczi, M. Martins-Baltar, and E. Papo. 1976. *Un niveau-seuil*. Strasbourg: Council of Europe.

Coulmas, F. (Ed.) 1981. *A Festschrift for native speaker*. The Hague: Mouton.

Council of Europe. 1981. *Modern languages programme 1971–1981: Report presented by CDCC project group 4*. Strasbourg: Council for Cultural Co-operation of the Council of Europe.

Council of Europe. 1983a. *Across the threshold towards multilingual Europe – vive le multilinguisme européen*. Strasbourg: Council for Cultural Co-operation of the Council of Europe.

Council of Europe. 1983b. *Contributions to a renewal of language learning and teaching: some current work in Europe*. Strasbourg: Council of Europe.

C.R.E.D.I.F. 1962. *Voix et images de France*. Paris: Didier.

C.R.E.D.I.F. 1967. *Bonjour Line. Teachers Book*. Commentaries and teaching methods by H. Gross and B. Mason. London: Harrap.

C.R.E.D.I.F. 1970. *Voix et images de France, deuxième partie*. Leçons de transition, introduction générale, fasicule 1 (édition experimentale). Paris: Didier.

C.R.E.D.I.F. 1972. *De vive voix. Guide pédagogique*. Paris: Didier.

Criper, C. and A. Davies. Forthcoming. Edinburgh ELTS validation project. Project report. ELTS Research paper 1. University of Cambridge Local Examinations Syndicate.

Crocker, A. 1984. Method as input and product of LSP course design. In Swales and Mustafa: 129–50.

Crombie, W. 1985a. *Discourse and language learning: a relational approach to syllabus design*. Oxford: Oxford University Press.

Crombie, W. 1985b. *Process and relation in discourse and language learning*. Oxford: Oxford University Press.

Cronbach, L. J., S. R. Ambron, S. M. Dornbusch, R. D. Hess, R. C. Hornik, D. C. Phillips, D. F. Walker, and S. S. Weiner. 1980. *Toward reform of program evaluation: aims, methods, and institutional arrangements*. San Francisco: Jossey-Bass.

Cziko, G. A. 1983. Psychometric and edumetric approaches to language testing. In Oller, 1983b: 289–307.

Dalkey, N. C. 1969. *The delphi method: an experimental study of group opinion*. Santa Monica, Calif: Rand Corporation.

Dam, L. 1982. *Beginning English: an experiment in learning and teaching*. Danmarks Laererhojskole: Copenhagen.

Darling-Hammond, L., A. E. Wise, and S. R. Pease. 1983. Teacher evaluation in the organizational context: a review of the literature. *Review of Educational Research* 53 (3): 285–328.

Das, B. K. (Ed.) 1985. *Communicative language teaching*. Singapore: RELC. Singapore University Press.

Davies, A. 1981. Review of Munby 1978. (q.v.). *TESOL Quarterly* 15 (3): 332–6.

Davies, A. 1984. Validating three tests of English language proficiency. *Language Testing* 1 (1): 50–69.

Dewey, J. 1938. *Experience and education*. New York: Collier Macmillan.

Dick, W. and L. Carey. 1978. *The systematic design of instruction*. Glenview: Scott Foresman. 2nd ed. 1985.

Dinsmore, D. 1985. Waiting for Godot in the EFL classroom. *English Language Teaching Journal* 39 (4): 225–34.

Donmall, B. G. (Ed.) 1985. *Language awareness*. National Council for Language in Education Papers and Reports 6. London: Centre for Information on Language Teaching and Research.

Downes, P. J. 1985. Language awareness in a child development course – a case study. In Donmall: 65–70.

Dowsett, G. and J. Shaw. 1986. Teachers' evaluation activities: some ideas from the National Course Reporting Study. *Prospect 2* (1).

Drobnic, K. 1978. Mistakes and modification in course design: an EST case history. In Todd-Trimble, Trimble, and Drobnic: 313–21.

Drury, J. 1983. The introduction of service English courses in ESL tertiary institutions in Africa. *ELT Documents 116*: 121–34.

Dubin, F. and E. Olshtain. 1986. *Course design*. Cambridge: Cambridge University Press.

Dudley-Evans, T. and J. Swales. 1980. Study modes and students from the Middle East. *ELT Documents 109*: 91–103.

Duff, P. A. 1985. Another look at interlanguage talk: taking task to task. *Working Papers 4* (2) University of Hawaii at Manoa, Department of English as a Second Language: 1–62.

Educational Testing Service 1980. Construct validity in psychological measurement: proceedings of a colloquium on theory and application in education and employment. *ERIC* Ed 201642.

Eisner, E. W. 1984. Can educational research inform educational practice? *Phi Delta Kappan 65* (7): 447–52.

Eisner, E. W. 1985. *The educational imagination: on the design and evaluation of school programs*. New York: Macmillan.

van Ek, J. A. 1975. *The threshold level*. Strasbourg: Council of Europe.

van Ek, J. A. 1977. *The threshold level for modern language learning in schools*. London: Longman.

van Ek, J. A. 1980. *Threshold level English in a European unit/credit system for modern language learning by adults*. Oxford: Pergamon Press.

van Ek, J. A. and L. G. Alexander. 1980. *Threshold level English*. Oxford: Pergamon Press.

van Ek, J. A., L. G. Alexander, and M. A. Fitzpatrick. 1977. *Waystage English*. Oxford: Pergamon Press.

van Ek, J. A., and J. L. M. Trim. 1984. *Across the threshold*. Oxford: Pergamon Press.

von Elek, T. and M. Oskarsson. 1973. *Teaching foreign language grammar to adults: a comparative study*. Stockholm: Almqvist and Wiksell.

Elias, J. L. and S. Merriam. 1980. *Philosophical foundations of adult education*. New York: Association Press.

Elley, W. B. 1980. A comparison of content-interest and structuralist reading programmes in Niue primary schools. *New Zealand Journal of Educational Studies 15* (1): 39–53.

Elley, W. B., I. H. Barham, H. Lamb, and M. Wyllie. 1979. *The role of grammar in a secondary school curriculum*. Wellington: New Zealand Council for Educational Research.

Elley, W. B. and F. Mangubhai. 1983. The impact of reading on second language learning. *Reading Research Quarterly 19* (1): 53–67.

Eskey, D. 1982. Faculty. In Barrett: 39–44.

Faerch, C. and G. Kasper, 1983a. Plans and strategies in foreign language communication. In Faerch and Kasper, 1983b: 20–60.

Faerch, C. and G. Kasper (Eds.) 1983b. *Strategies in interlanguage communication.* London: Longman.

Fanselow, J. F. 1977. An approach to competency-based teacher education in second language teaching. In Fanselow and Light (Eds.): 129–39.

Fanselow, J. F. and R. H. Crymes (Eds.) 1976. *On TESOL '76.* Washington, D.C.: TESOL.

Fanselow, J. F. and R. L. Light (Eds.) 1977. *Bilingual, ESOL and foreign language teacher preparation: models, practices, issues.* Washington, D.C.: TESOL.

Fenstermacher, G. D. 1978. A philosophical consideration of recent research on teacher effectiveness. In Shulman: 157–85.

Findley, C. A. and L. A. Nathan. 1980. Functional language objectives in a competency based ESL curriculum. *TESOL Quarterly 14* (2): 221–31.

Fink, S. R. 1972. Dialog memorization in introductory language instruction. A comparison of three different strategies. In Quistgaard, Schwarts, and Spang-Hanssen: 273–89.

Finocchiaro, M. and M. Bonomo. 1973. *The foreign language learner: a guide for teachers.* New York: Regents.

Finocchiaro, M. and C. J. Brumfit. 1983. *The functional notional approach.* Oxford: Oxford University Press.

Flanagan, J. C. 1954. The critical incident technique. *Psychological Bulletin 51* (4): 327–58.

Frank, C., M. Rinvolucri, and M. Berer. 1982. *Challenge to think.* Oxford: Oxford University Press.

Frankel, M. A. 1983. Designing a pre-EAP reading course: practical problems. In Jordan: 119–31.

Freedman, E. S. 1971. The road from Pennsylvania – where next in language teaching experimentation? *Audio-Visual Language Journal 9* (1): 33–8.

Freedman, E. S. 1976. Experimentation into foreign language teaching methodology. *System 4* (1): 12–28.

Freedman, E. S. 1979. Valid research into foreign language teaching – two recent projects. *System 7* (3): 187–99.

Freedman, E. S. 1982. Experimentation into foreign language teaching methodology: the research findings. *System 10* (2): 119–33.

Freeman, D. 1982. Observing teachers: three approaches to in-service training and development. *TESOL Quarterly 16* (1): 21–8.

Freire, P. 1970. *Pedagogy of the oppressed.* New York: Herder and Herder and London: Penguin Books.

Freire, P. 1972. *Cultural action for freedom.* London: Penguin Books.

Freudenstein, R., J. Beneke, and H. Ponisch. 1981. *Language incorporated: teaching foreign languages in industry.* Oxford: Pergamon Press.

Freyberg, P. S. 1964. A comparison of two approaches to the teaching of spelling. *British Journal of Educational Psychology 34* (2): 178–86.

Fries, C. C. and A. C. Fries. 1961. *Foundations for English teaching.* Tokyo: Kenkyusha.

Fröhlich, M., N. Spada, and P. Allen. 1985. Differences in the communicative orientation of L2 classrooms. *TESOL Quarterly 19* (1): 27–57.

Fullan, M. 1982. *The meaning of educational change.* Ontario: Ontario Institute for Studies in Education Press.

Gabrielsen, G. 1986. Pupil initiative and teacher accountability. In Stolen.

Gage, N. L. (Ed.) 1963. *Handbook of research on teaching.* Chicago: Rand McNally.

Gage, N. L. 1978. *The scientific basis of the art of teaching.* New York: Teachers College Press.

Gage, N. L. 1984. What do we know about teaching effectiveness? *Phi Delta Kappan 66* (2): 87–93.

Gary, J. O. 1975. Delayed oral practice in initial stages of second language learning. In Burt and Dulay: 89–95.

Gass, S. M. and C. G. Madden (Eds.) 1985. *Input in second language acquisition.* Rowley, Mass: Newbury House.

Gass, S. M. and E. M. Varonis. 1985. Task variation and nonnative/nonnative negotiation of meaning. In Gass and Madden: 149–61.

Gattegno, C. 1972. *Teaching foreign languages in schools: the silent way.* New York: Educational Solutions.

Gebhard, J. G. 1984. Models of supervision: choices. *TESOL Quarterly 18* (3): 501–14.

Geddes, M. and G. Sturtridge (Eds.) 1982. *Individualisation.* London: Modern English Publications.

Geertz, C. 1983. *Local knowledge: further essays in interpretive anthropology.* New York: Basic Books.

Gibbons, J. P. 1980. A shape for language learning units. *The English Bulletin 7* (3): 44–7.

Gibbons, J. 1982. Coping with authentic texts. *Modern English Teacher 9:* 3–4.

Gibbons, J. P. 1984. Sequencing in language syllabus design. In Read: 272–80.

Gibbons, J. and J. Evans. 1983. Coping with the coursebook. *World Language English 2* (4): 237–44.

Gingras, R. C. (Ed.) 1978. *Second language acquisition and foreign language teaching.* Arlington, Virginia: Center for Applied Linguistics.

Giroux, H. 1983. Theories of reproduction and resistance in the new sociology of education: a critical analysis. *Harvard Educational Review 53* (3): 257–93.

Glaser, R. 1963. Instructional technology and the measurement of learning outcomes: some questions. *American Psychologist 18:* 519–21.

Glass, G. V. (Ed.) 1976. *Evaluation studies review annual.* (Vol. 1) Beverly Hills, Calif: Sage.

Glass, G. V. 1978. Standards and criteria. *Journal of Educational Measurement 15* (4): 237–61.

Good, T. L. and D. A. Grouws. 1977. Teaching effects: a process-product study in fourth-grade mathematics classrooms. *Journal of Teacher Education 28* (3): 49–54.

Good, T. L. and D. A. Grouws. 1979. The Missouri mathematics effectiveness project: an experimental study in fourth-grade classrooms. *Journal of Educational Psychology 71* (3): 355–62.

Gordon, D. 1984. The image of science, technological consciousness and the hidden curriculum. *Curriculum Inquiry 14* (4).

Green, P. S. (Ed.) 1975. *The language laboratory in school.* Edinburgh: Oliver and Boyd.

Griffith, W. S. 1978. Educational needs: definition, assessment and utilization. *School Review 86* (2): 382–94.

Guba, E. G. and Y. S. Lincoln. 1981. *Effective evaluation.* San Francisco: Jossey-Bass.

Hall, G. E. and S. F. Loucks. 1977. A developmental model for determining whether the treatment is actually implemented. *American Educational Research Journal 14* (3): 263–76.

Halliday, M. A. K., A. McIntosh, and P. D. Strevens. 1964. *The linguistic sciences and language teaching.* London: Longman.

Hambleton, R. K. 1978. On the use of cut-off scores with criterion-referenced tests in instructional settings. *Journal of Educational Measurement 15* (4): 277–90.

Hambleton, R. K. 1980. Test score validity and standard-setting methods. In Berk, 1980a: 80–123.

Hambleton, R. K. 1983. Application of item response models to criterion-referenced assessment. *Applied Psychological Measurement 7* (1): 33–44.

Hammerly, H. 1982. *Synthesis in second language teaching: an introduction to linguistics.* Burnaby, B.C.: Second Language Publications.

Hammond, R. L., 1973. Evaluation at the local level. In Worthen and Sanders: 157–70.

Hancock, C. R. 1977. CBTE/PBTE and the modern-day Jonahs. In Fanselow and Light: 124–8.

Handscombe, J., R. A. Orem, and B. P. Taylor (Eds.) 1984. *On TESOL '83.* Washington, D.C.: TESOL.

Hansen, J. and C. Stansfield. 1981. The relationship of field dependent-independent cognitive styles to foreign language achievement. *Language Learning 31* (2): 349–67.

Harding, E. and A. Tealby. 1981. Counselling for language learning at the University of Cambridge: progress report on an experiment. *Mélanges Pedagogiques*: 95–120.

Harlow, L. L., W. F. Smith, and A. Garfinkel. 1980. Student-perceived communication needs: infrastructure of the functional/notional syllabus. *Foreign Language Annals 13* (1): 11–22.

Harris, R. J. 1962. An experimental inquiry into the functions and value of formal grammar in the teaching of English. Ph.D. Dissertation. University of London.

Hartwell, P. 1985. Grammar, grammars, and the teaching of grammar. *College English 47* (2): 105–27.

Hawkes, N. 1983. Some aspects of communicative course design. In Johnson and Porter: 89–103.

Hawkey, R. 1980. Needs analysis and syllabus design for specific purposes. In Altman and James: 81–93.

Hawkey, R. 1983. Programme development for learners of English for vocational purposes. In Richterich, 1983: 79–87.

Hawkey, R. 1984. From needs to materials via constraints: some general considerations and Zimbabwean experience. In Read: 112–32.

Hawkins, E. 1981. *Modern languages in the curriculum.* Cambridge: Cambridge University Press.

Hawkins, E. (Ed.) 1984. *Awareness of language: an introduction.* Cambridge: Cambridge University Press.

Hawkins, L. E. 1971. Immediate versus delayed presentation of foreign language script. *Modern Language Journal 55* (5): 280–90.

Haycraft, J. 1983. The pre-beginner phase. *English Language Teaching Journal 37* (1): 48–51.

Hencley, S. P. and J. R. Yates (Eds.) 1974. *Futurism in education: methodologies.* Berkeley, Calif.: McCutchan Publishing Company.

Herrington, A. J. 1985. Writing in academic settings: a study of the contexts for writing in two college chemical engineering courses. *Research in the Teaching of English 19* (4): 331–59.

Higgs, T. V. (Ed.) 1984. *Teaching for proficiency, the organizing principle.* Lincolnwood, Illinois: National Textbook Company.

Hiragama-Grant, G. and M. Sedgwick. 1978. E.S.P. syllabus design processes in retrospect. In Todd-Trimble, Trimble, and Drobnic: 322–36.

Hively, W., G. Maxwell, G. Rabehl, D. Sension and S. Lundlin. 1973. *Domain-referenced curriculum evaluation: a technical handbook and case study from the Minnemast Project.* CSE Monograph Series in Evaluation, Vol. 1. Los Angeles: Center for the Study of Evaluation, UCLA.

Hoadley-Maidment, E. 1983. Methodology for the identification of language learning needs of immigrant learners of English through mother-tongue interviews. In Richterich, 1983: 39–51.

Holec, H. 1980. Learner-centered communicative language teaching: needs analysis revisited. *Studies in Second Language Acquisition 3* (1): 26–33.

Holliday, A. 1984. Research into classroom culture and necessary input into syllabus design. In Swales and Mustafa: 29–51.

Holliday, A. and T. Cooke. 1982. An ecological approach to ESP. In Waters: 123–43.

Holmes, D. H. 1977. Adult English as a second language: demographic study and needs assessment of Spanish speaking students. Doctoral dissertation. University of Southern California.

Holt, J. 1976. *Instead of education.* Harmondsworth: Penguin Books.

Horowitz, D., 1986a. Process, not product: less than meets the eye. *TESOL Quarterly 20* (1): 141–4.

Horowitz, D. 1986b. What professors actually require: academic tasks for the ESL classroom. *TESOL Quarterly 20* (3): 445–62.

Hudson, T. and B. Lynch. 1984. A criterion-referenced measurement approach to ESL achievement testing. *Language Testing 1* (2): 171–201.

Hughes, A. and D. Porter (Eds.) 1983. *Current developments in language testing.* London: Academic Press.

Hutchinson, T. and A. Waters. 1984. How Communicative is ESP? *English Language Teaching Journal 38* (2): 108–13.

Hutchinson, T. and A. Waters. 1987. *English for specific purposes.* Cambridge: Cambridge University Press.

Ingram, D. E. 1982. Developing a language programme. *RELC Journal 13* (1): 64–86.

Ingram, D. E. 1984. *Australian second language proficiency ratings.* Canberra: Commonwealth Department of Immigration.

Jackson, P. 1968. *Life in classrooms.* New York: Holt, Rinehart and Winston.

James, G. (Ed.) 1984. The ESP classroom. *Linguistic Studies 7.* Exeter University.

Jarvis, G. and S. Adams. 1979. *Evaluating a second language program.* Washington, D.C.: Center for Applied Linguistics.

Johns, T. F. 1981. Some problems of a world-wide profession. *ELT Documents 112*: 16–22.

Johnson, F. C. 1973. *English as a second language: an individualised approach.* Brisbane: Jacaranda.

Johnson, K. 1979. Communicative approaches and communicative processes. In Brumfit and Johnson, 192–238.

Johnson, K. 1982a. Some communicative processes. In Johnson, 1982b: 147–55.

Johnson, K. (Ed.) 1982b. *Communicative syllabus design and methodology.* Oxford: Pergamon Press.

Johnson, K. and K. Morrow (Eds.) 1981. *Communication in the classroom.* Harlow: Longman.

Johnson, K. and D. Porter (Eds.) 1983. *Perspectives in communicative language teaching.* London: Academic Press.

Johnson, R. K. 1981. On syllabuses, and on being communicative. *The English Bulletin (Hong Kong) vii* (4): 52–60.

Johnson, S. M. 1980. Performance-based staff layoffs in the public schools: implementation and outcomes. *Harvard Educational Review 50* (2): 214–33.

Johnston, M. 1985. Second language acquisition research in the adult migrant education program. *Prospect 1* (1): 19–46.

Jordan, R. (Ed.) 1983. *Case studies in ELT.* London: Collins.

Jupp, T. C. and S. Hodlin. 1975. *Industrial English – an example of theory and practice in functional language teaching.* London: Heinemann.

Kachru, B. 1985. Standards, codification and sociolinguistic realism: the English language in the outer circle. In Quirk and Widdowson: 11–30.

Kaplan, R. B. (Ed.) 1984. *Annual Review of Applied Linguistics.* Vol. 5. Cambridge: Cambridge University Press.

Kaufman, R. A. 1972. *Educational system planning.* Englewood Cliffs, N.J.: Prentice Hall.

Keating, R. F. 1963. *A study of the effectiveness of language laboratories.* New York: Institute of Administrative Research, Teacher's College, Columbia University.

Kiparsky, P. 1968. Linguistic universals and linguistic change. In Bach and Harms: 171–202.

Kirk, E. T. 1978. A critical analysis of teacher evaluation instruments in use in Alabama school systems. Doctoral dissertation. Auburn University.

Kitzhaber, A. R. (Ed.) 1970. *The Oregon curriculum: a sequential program in English.* New York: Holt, Rinehart and Winston.

Knapp, M. S. 1982. *Toward the study of teacher evaluation as an organizational process: a review of current research and practice.* Menlo Park, CA: Educational and Human Services Research Center, SRI International.

Knowles, M. S. 1970. *The modern practice of adult education: andragogy versus pedagogy.* New York: Association Press.

Krashen, S. D. 1981. *Second language acquisition and second language learning.* Oxford: Pergamon Press.

Krashen, S. D. 1982. *Principles and practice in second language acquisition.* Oxford: Pergmon Press.

Krashen, S. D. and H. W. Seliger. 1975. The essential contributions of formal instruction in adult second language learning. *TESOL Quarterly 9* (2): 173–83.

Krashen, S. D. and T. D. Terrell. 1983. *The natural approach: language acquisition in the classroom.* San Francisco: Alemany Press.

Lado, R. 1961. *Language testing: the construction and use of foreign language tests.* London: Longman.

LaForge, P. G. 1983. *Counseling and culture in second language acquisition.* Oxford: Pergamon Press.

Larsen-Freeman, D. (Ed.) 1980. *Discourse analysis in second language research.* Rowley, MA: Newbury House.

Larsen-Freeman, D. 1983. Training teachers or educating a teacher. In Alatis, Stern, and Strevens: 264–74.

Larson, P., E. L. Judd, and D. S. Messerschmitt (Eds.) 1985. *On TESOL '84.* Washington: TESOL.

Lawrence, M. S. 1972. *Writing as a thinking process.* Ann Arbor: University of Michigan Press.

Lawson, K. H. 1979. *Philosophical concepts and values in adult education.* Revised edition. Milton Keynes: The Open University Press.

Lee, R. R. 1977. Performance criteria for teachers: design of a model for innovation. In Fanselow and Light: 140–7.

Levin, L. 1972. *Comparative studies in foreign-language teaching.* Stockholm: Almqvist and Wiksell.

Lewis, A. C. 1982. *Evaluating educational personnel.* Arlington, VA: American Association of School Administrators.

Lilley, A. D. 1984. The establishment of an independent inter-faculty ESP centre. In Swales and Mustafa: 184–96.

Lim, K. B. 1968. Prompting vs. confirmation, pictures vs. translation, and other variables in children's learning of grammar in a second language. Unpublished thesis. Harvard University.

Lindquist, E. F. (Ed.) 1951. *Educational measurement.* Washington, D.C.: American Council on Education.

Linstone, H. A. and M. Turoff. 1975. *The Delphi methodology: techniques and applications.* Reading, Mass.: Addison-Wesley.

Liskin-Gasparro, J. E. 1984. The ACTFL proficiency guidelines: a historical perspective. In Higgs: 11–42.

Littlejohn, A. 1985. Learner choice in language study. *English Language Teaching Journal 39* (4): 253–61.

Livingston, S. A. and M. J. Zieky. 1982. *Passing scores: a manual for setting standards of performance on educational and occupational tests.* Princeton, N.J.: Educational Testing Service.

Long, M. H. 1980. Inside the 'black box': methodological issues in classroom research on language learning. *Language Learning 30* (1): 1–42.

Long, M. H. 1983. Native speaker/non-native speaker conversation and the negotiation of comprehensible input. *Applied Linguistics 4* (2): 126–41.

Long, M. H. 1984. Process and product in ESL program evaluation. *TESOL Quarterly 18* (3): 409–25.

Long, M. H. and G. Crookes. 1986. Intervention points in second language classroom processes. Paper presented at RELC Regional Seminar. Singapore 21–26 April 1986.

Long, M. H. and P. A. Porter. 1985. Group work, interlanguage talk, and second language acquisition. *TESOL Quarterly 19* (2): 207–28.

Long, M. H. and C. Sato. 1983. Classroom foreigner talk discourse: forms and functions of teachers' questions. In Seliger and Long: 268–86.

Low, G. D. 1986. Storylines and other developing contexts in use-of-language test design. *Indian Journal of Applied Linguistics special edition on language testing 12* (1–2): 15–38.

Low, G. D. 1987. The need for a multi-perspective approach to the evaluation of foreign language teaching materials. *Evaluation and research in education 1*: 19–29.

Low, G. D. In press. On teaching metaphor. *Applied Linguistics*.

Low, G. D. and I. Lau. 1983. The discourse-task syllabus: a design option for high surrender value courses for adult beginners. *Language Learning and Communication 2*: 295–309.

Lugton, R. C. and C. H. Heinle (Eds.) 1971. *Toward a cognitive approach to second-language acquisition*. Philadelphia: The Center for Curriculum Development. 31–52.

Lynch, B. 1986. Evaluating a program inside and out. Paper presented at the 20th annual TESOL Convention. Anaheim, California, 3–9 March 1986

Mackay, R. 1978. Identifying the nature of learners' needs. In Mackay and Mountford, 1978a: 21–37.

Mackay, R. and M. Bosquet. 1981. LSP curriculum development: from policy to practice. In Mackay and Palmer: 1–28.

Mackay, R. and A. Mountford (Eds.) 1978a. *English for specific purposes: a case study approach*. London: Longman.

Mackay, R. and A. J. Mountford. 1978b. The teaching of English for special purposes: theory and practice. In Mackay and Mountford, 1978a: 2–20.

Mackay, R. and J. D. Palmer (Eds.) 1981. *Languages for specific purposes: program design and evaluation*. Rowley, Mass.: Newbury House.

Mackey, W. F. 1965. *Language teaching analysis*. London: Longman.

Mager, R. F. 1962. *Preparing instructional objectives*. Palo Alto, CA: Fearon. 2nd ed. 1975.

Maley, A. 1984. Constraints-based syllabuses. In Read: 90–111.

Maley, A. 1985. On chalk and cheese, babies and bathwater and squared circles: can traditional and communicative approaches be reconciled? In Larson, Judd, and Messerschmitt: 159–69.

Markee, N. 1986a. Towards an appropriate technology model of communicative course design. Issues and definitions. (Mimeo)

Markee, N. 1986b. The relevance of sociopolitical factors to communicative course design. *The ESP Journal 5* (1): 3–16.

Marti-Viano, M. and V. Orquin. 1982. Identifying our students' strategies for learning English as a foreign language. *Modern English Teacher 9* (4): 38–41.

McDonagh, J. 1984. *ESP in perspective*. London: Collins.

McKinnon, K. R. 1965. An experimental study of the learning of syntax in second language learning. Unpublished doctoral dissertation. Harvard University.

Mead, R. G. Jr. (Ed.) 1983. *Foreign languages: key links in the chain of learning*. Middlebury: Northeast Conference.

Medley, D. M. 1982. Teacher effectiveness. In Mitzel, Vol. 4: 1894–903.

Messick, S. 1980. Constructs and their vicissitudes in educational and psychological measurement. In *Educational Testing Services 1980*: 93–106.

Metfessel, N. S. and W. B. Michael. 1967. A paradigm involving multiple criterion measures for the evaluation of the effectiveness of school programs. *Educational and Psychological Measurement 27* (2): 931–43.

Mezynski, K. 1983. Issues concerning the acquisition of knowledge: effects of vocabulary training on reading comprehension. *Review of Educational Research 53* (2): 253–79.

Miller, J. P. 1976. *Humanizing the classroom: models of teaching in affective education.* New York: Praeger.

Millman, J. 1974. Criterion-referenced measurement. In Popham, 1974: 309–97.

Mitchell, R., B. Parkinson, and R. Johnston. 1981. *The foreign language classroom – an observational study.* Stirling: Stirling University.

Mitzel, H. E. (Ed.) 1982. *Encyclopedia of educational research.* 5th ed. New York: The Free Press.

Moegradi, M. C. and W. B. Elley. 1979. Evaluation of achievement in the Indonesian education system. *Evaluation in Education 2* (4): 281–351.

Mohan, B. 1978. Facets of the ESL curriculum. Unpublished mimeo. University of British Columbia, Division of Language Education, Vancouver, B.C.

Monette, M. L. 1977. The concept of educational need: an analysis of selected literature. *Adult Education (Washington) 27* (2): 116–27.

Monette, M. L. 1979a. Need assessment: a critique of philosophical assumptions. *Adult Education (Washington) 29* (2): 83–95.

Monette, M. L. 1979b. Paulo Freire and other unheard voices. *Religious Education 74* (5): 543–54.

Morrow, K. 1981. Communicative language testing: revolution or evolution. In Alderson and Hughes: 9–25.

Moskowitz, G. 1978. *Caring and sharing in the foreign language class.* Rowley, Mass: Newbury House.

Mueller, T. H. 1971. The effectiveness of two learning models: the audio-lingual habit theory and the cognitive code-learning theory. In Pimsleur and Quinn: 113–22.

Munby, J. 1978. *Communicative syllabus design.* Cambridge: Cambridge University Press.

Munby, J. 1984. Communicative syllabus design: principles and problems. In Read: 55–67.

Murphy-O'Dwyer, L. M. 1985. Diary studies as a method for evaluating teacher training. *Lancaster Practical Papers in English Language Education 7*: 97–128.

Naiman, N., M. Fröhlich, H. H. Stern, and A. Todesco. 1978. The good language learner. *Research in Education Series 7.* Toronto: Ontario Institute for Studies in Education.

National Centre for Industrial Language Training (NCILT) 1980. Increasing student autonomy in industrial language training. *NCILT working paper 14.* Southall, Middlesex: NCILT.

National Study of Secondary Evaluation. 1960. *Evaluation criteria.* Washington, D.C.

Nilsen, A. P. 1977. Sexism in children's books and elementary classroom materials. In Nilsen *et al.*: 161–79.

Nilsen, A. P., H. Bosmajian, H. L. Gershuny, and J. P. Stanly (Eds.): *Sexism and language.* Urbana, Ill: National Council of Teachers of English.

Nitko, A. J. 1984. Defining the criterion-referenced test. In Berk, 1984a: 8–28.

Nunan, D. 1985. *Language teaching course design: trends and issues*. Adelaide: National Curriculum Resource Centre.

Nunan, D. 1986a. Can the language classroom ever be truly communicative? Distinguished Scholar Series, University of the Pacific, Stockton, California.

Nunan, D. 1986b. Communicative language teaching: the learner's view. Paper presented at RELC Regional Seminar, Singapore. 21–26 April 1986.

Nunan, D. 1988. *The learner-centred curriculum: a study in second language teaching*. Cambridge: Cambridge University Press.

Nunan, D. and G. Brindley. 1986. A practical framework for learner-centred curriculum development. Paper presented at 20th annual TESOL Convention. Anaheim, California, 3–9 March 1986.

Nuttall, C. 1982. *Teaching reading skills in a foreign language*. London: Heinemann.

Oller, J. W. Jr. 1976. Evidence for a general language proficiency factor: an expectancy grammar. *Die Neuren Sprachen 76*: 165–74.

Oller, J. W. Jr. 1979. *Language tests at school*. London: Longman.

Oller, J. W. Jr. 1983a. A consensus for the eighties? In Oller, 1983b. 351–6.

Oller, J. W. Jr. (Ed.) 1983b. *Issues in language testing research*. Rowley, Mass: Newbury House.

Oller, J. W., K. Prapphal, and M. Byler. 1982. Measuring affective factors in language learning. *RELC Occasional Papers 19*. Singapore: Regional English Language Centre.

Oller, J. W. Jr. and P. A. Richard-Amato (Eds.) 1983. *Methods that work: a smorgasbord of ideas for language teachers*. Rowley, Mass: Newbury House.

Olsson, M. 1973. Learning grammar: an experiment. *English Language Teaching Journal 27* (3): 266–9.

O'Neill, R. *et al.* 1976. *Kernel Lessons intermediate*. Harlow: Longman.

Paikeday, Thomas M. 1985. *The native speaker is dead!* Toronto: Paikeday.

Pal, A. 1982. An applied psycholinguistic experiment in remedial teaching of English grammar. *IRAL 20* (2), 152–60.

Palmer, J. D. 1981a. Discourse analysis. In Mackay and Palmer: 74–91.

Palmer, J. D. 1981b. Register research design. In Mackay and Palmer: 64–73.

Palmer, M. and D. Byrne. 1982. *Track (Book 1)*. Harlow: Longman.

Parish, R. and R. Arrends. 1983. Why innovative programs are discontinued. *Educational Leadership 40* (4): 62–5.

Parlett, M. R. and D. Hamilton. 1972. Evaluation as illumination. A new approach to the study of innovatory programmes. *Occasional paper 9*. Centre for Research in Educational Sciences: University of Edinburgh.

Parlett, M. R. and D. Hamilton. 1976. Evaluation as illumination: a new approach to the study of innovatory programs. In Glass, 1976: 140–57.

Patton, M. Q. 1978. *Utilization-focused evaluation*. Beverly Hills, Calif: Sage.

Patton, M. Q. 1980. *Qualitative evaluation methods*. Beverly Hills, Calif: Sage.

Pennington, M. C. 1985a. Effective administration of an ESL program. In Larson, Judd, and Messerschmitt: 301–16.

Pennington, M. C. 1985b. Review of the teacher/learner interaction series: Three videotapes for ESL teacher-training workshops. *TESOL Quarterly 19* (2): 353–6.

Pennington, M. C. 1986. Teacher preparation for multicultural instruction. Paper presented at the 20th annual TESOL Convention. Anaheim, California. 3–9 March 1986.

Perkins, K. and L. D. Miller. 1984. Comparative analyses of English as a second language reading comprehension data. *Language Testing 1* (1): 21–32.

Perry, F. A. 1976. The systems approach to basic English language training in the Canadian armed forces. *System 4* (3): 178–81.

Phillips, J. K. (Ed.) 1981. *Action for the '80s: a political, professional, and public program for foreign language education*. Skokie, Ill: National Textbook Company.

Pimsleur, P. and T. Quinn (Eds.) 1971. *The psychology of second language learning*. Cambridge: Cambridge University Press.

Politzer, R. L. 1968. The role and place of the explanation in the pattern drill. *IRAL 6* (4): 315–31.

Popham, W. J. (Ed.) 1974. *Evaluation in education: current applications*. Berkeley, Calif: McCutchan.

Popham, W. J. 1975. *Educational evaluation*. Englewood Cliffs, N.J.: Prentice Hall.

Popham, W. J. 1978. *Criterion-referenced measurement*. Englewood Cliffs N.J.: Prentice Hall.

Popham, W. J. and T. R. Husek. 1969. Implications of criterion-referenced measurement. *Journal of Educational Measurement 6*, 1–9.

Popper, K. 1972. *Objective knowledge*. Oxford: Oxford University Press.

Porreca, K. L. 1984. Sexism in current ESL textbooks. *TESOL Quarterly 18* (4): 705–24.

Postman, N. and C. Weingartner. 1969. *Teaching as a subversive activity*. Harmondsworth: Penguin Books.

Postovsky, V. A. 1974. Effects of delay in oral practice at the beginning of second language learning. *Modern Language Journal 58* (5–6): 229–39.

Potts, P. 1984. The role of evaluation in a communicative curriculum and some consequences for materials design. *Lancaster Practical Papers in English Language Education 6*. Oxford: Pergamon Press.

Prabhu, N. 1984. Procedural syllabus. In Read: 272–80.

Pratt, D. 1980. *Curriculum, design, and development*. New York: Harcourt, Brace, Jovanovich.

Provus, M. M. 1971. *Discrepancy evaluation for educational program improvement and assessment*. Berkeley, Calif: McCutchan Publishing.

Quinn, T. J. 1984. Functional approaches in language pedagogy. In Kaplan: 60–80.

Quirk, R. and H. G. Widdowson (Eds.) 1985. *English in the world*. Cambridge: Cambridge University Press.

Qvistgaard, J., H. Schwarts, and H. Spang-Hanssen (Eds.) 1972. *Proceedings of the third International Congress of Applied Linguistics*. Copenhagen: AILA, Heidelberg: Julius Groos Verlag. ED074796.

Raths, J. 1982. Evaluation of teachers. In Mitzel: 611–17.

Rea, P. M. 1983. Evaluation of educational projects, with special reference to English language education. In Brumfit, 1983: 85–98.

Read, J. (Ed.) 1984. Trends in language syllabus design. *Anthology Series 13*, Singapore. SEAMEO Regional Language Centre.

Redfern, G. B. 1980. *Evaluating teachers and administrators: a performance objectives approach*. Boulder, Colo: Westview Press.

Reiss, M. A. 1981. Helping the unsuccessful language learner. *Modern Language Journal 65* (2): 121–8.

Richards, J. C. 1984a The secret life of methods. *TESOL Quarterly 18* (1): 7–23.
Richards, J. C. 1984b Language curriculum development. *RELC Journal 15* (1): 1–29.
Richards, J. C. 1985. Planning for proficiency. *Catesol Occasional Papers 11*: 16–30.
Richards, J. C., J. Platt, and H. Weber. 1985. *Longman dictionary of applied linguistics*. Harlow: Longman.
Richards, J. C. and T. Rodgers. 1982. Method: approach, design, and procedure. *TESOL Quarterly 16* (2): 153–68.
Richards, J. C. and T. S. Rodgers. 1986. *Approaches and methods in language teaching: a description and analysis*. Cambridge: Cambridge University Press.
Richterich, R. 1975. The analysis of language needs: illusion-pretext-necessity. *Education and Culture 28*: 9–14.
Richterich, R. 1979. Identifying language needs as a means of determining educational objectives with the learners. In *A European unit/credit system for modern language learning by adults*. Report of the Ludwigshafen Symposium (1979) Council of Europe: 71–5.
Richterich, R., 1980. A model for the definition of language needs of adults. In Trim, Richterich, van Ek, and Wilkins: 31–62.
Richterich, R. (Ed.) 1983. *Case studies in identifying language needs*. Oxford: Pergamon Press.
Richterich, R. and J. L. Chancerel (Eds.) 1980. *Identifying the needs of adults learning a foreign language*. Oxford: Pergamon Press.
Rivers, W. M. 1981. *Teaching foreign-language skills*. Chicago: University of Chicago Press.
Rivers, W. M. and B. J. Melvin. 1981. Language learners as individuals: discovering their needs, wants, and learning styles. In Alatis, Altman, and Alatis: 79–93.
Roberts, C. 1982. Needs analysis for ESP programmes. *Language Learning and Communication 1* (1): 105–20.
Roberts, J. 1982. Recent developments in ELT, parts 1 and 11. *Language Teaching 15* (2): 94–110 and *15* (3): 174–94.
Rodgers, T. S. 1980. Materials development: in prospect. *ELT Documents special – Projects in Materials Design*. London: The British Council: 164–71.
Rodgers, T. S. 1984. Communicative syllabus design and implementation: reflection on a decade of experience. In Read: 28–51.
Rogers, A. J. 1976. Malaysia: a case study. Implementation of the new English curriculum in forms four and five. Technical paper. Kuala Lumpur, Malaysia: Ministry of Education.
Rogers, C. R. 1969. *Freedom to learn; a view of what education might become*. Columbus: Charles E. Merrill.
Robinson, P. 1980. *ESP (English for specific purposes)*. Oxford: Pergamon Press.
Rosenshine, B. U. and N. Furst. 1973. The use of direct observation to study teaching. In Travers: 122–83.
Rubin, J. and I. Thompson. 1982. *How to be a more successful language learner*. Boston: Heinle and Heinle.
Savignon, S. J. 1972. *Communicative competence: an experiment in foreign-language teaching*. Philadelphia: The Center for Curriculum Development, Inc.

Savignon, S. J. 1983. *Communicative competence: theory and classroom practice*. Reading, Mass.: Addison-Wesley.

Savignon, S. J. and M. S. Berns (Eds.) Forthcoming. *Initiatives in communicative language teaching*. Volume 2. Reading, Mass: Addison-Wesley.

Saylor, J. G. and W. M. Alexander. 1974. *Planning curriculum for schools*. New York: Holt, Rinehart and Winston.

Schaffarzick, J. and D. Hampson (Eds.) 1975. *Strategies for curriculum development*. Berkeley, Calif: McCutchan.

Scherer, G. A. C. and M. Wertheimer. 1964. *A psycholinguistic experiment in foreign-language teaching*. New York: McGraw Hill.

Schmidt, M. F. 1981. Needs assessment in English for specific purposes: the case study. In Selinker, Tarone and Hanzeli: 199–210.

Schroder, K. 1981. Methods of exploring language needs in industry. In Freudenstein, Beneke, and Ponisch, 43–54.

Schumann, J. H. 1978. The acculturation model for second-language acquisition. In Gingras: 27–50.

Schutz, N. W. and B. L. Derwing. 1981. The problem of needs assessment in English for specific purposes: some theoretical and practical considerations. In Mackay and Palmer: 29–44.

Scriven, M. 1967. The methodology of educational evaluation. In Tyler, Gagné, and Scriven: 39–83.

Scriven, M. 1974. Evaluation perspectives and procedures. In Popham, 1974: 3–93.

Seaton, I. 1983. The English Language Testing Service (ELTS): two issues in the design of the new 'non-academic module'. In Hughes and Porter: 129–39.

Seliger, H. W. 1975. Inductive method and deductive method in language teaching: a re-examination. *IRAL 13* (1): 1–18.

Seliger, H. W. and M. H. Long (Eds.) 1983. *Classroom oriented research in second language acquisition*. Rowley, Mass.: Newbury House.

Selinker, L., E. Tarone, and U. Hanzeli (Eds.) 1981. *English for academic and technical purposes: studies in honor of Louis Trimble*. Rowley, Mass: Newbury House.

Shavelson, R. 1976. What is *the* basic teaching skill? *Journal of Teacher Education 14* (2): 144–51.

Shavelson, R. J. 1981. *Statistical reasoning for the behavioral sciences*. Boston: Allyn and Bacon.

Shavelson, R. J., J. H. Block, and M. M. Ravitch. 1972. Criterion-referenced testing: comments on reliability. *Journal of Educational Measurement 9* (2): 133–7.

Shavelson, R. J. and P. Stern. 1981. Research on teachers' pedagogical thoughts, judgements, decisions and behavior. *Review of Educational Research 5* (4): 455–98.

Shavelson, R. J. and N. M. Webb. 1981. Generalizability theory: 1973–1980. *British Journal of Mathematical and Statistical Psychology 34* (2): 133–66.

Shaw, A. M. 1977. Foreign language syllabus development: some recent approaches. *Language Teaching and Linguistics Abstracts 10* (4): 217–33.

Shaw, P. A. 1982. Ad hoc needs analysis. *Modern English Teacher 10* (1): 12–14.

Sheldon, L. (Ed.) Forthcoming. Textbook and materials evaluation. *ELT Documents*. Oxford: Pergamon Press.

Shepard, L. A. 1984. Setting performance standards. In Berk, 1984a: 169–98.

Short, E. C. 1983. The forms and use of alternative curriculum development strategies. *Curriculum Inquiry 13* (1): 43–64.

Shulman, L. S. (Ed.) 1978. *Review of research in education.* Vol. 6. Itasca, Illinois: Peacock.

Sinclair, J. McH., and R. M. Coulthard. 1974. *Towards an analysis of discourse.* London: Oxford University Press.

Sjoberg, K. and B. Trope. 1969. The value of external direction and individual discovery in learning situations: the learning of a grammatical rule. *Scandinavian Journal Of Educational Research 13* (4): 233–40.

Smith, B. O. 1969. *Teachers for the real world.* Washington, D.C.: American Association of Colleges for Teacher Education Yearbook: 27–50.

Smith, P. D. Jr. 1970. *A comparison of the cognitive and audiolingual approaches to foreign language instruction. The Pennsylvania foreign language project.* Philadelphia: The Center for Curriculum Development Inc.

Spolsky, B. 1978a. Introduction: linguists and language testers. In Spolsky 1978b.

Spolsky, B. (Ed.) 1978b. *Advances in language testing.* Arlington, Virginia: Center for Applied Linguistics: v–x.

St. Pierre, R. G. 1979. The role of multiple analyses in quasi-experimental evaluations. *Education Evaluation and Policy Analysis 1* (6): 29–35.

Stake, R. E. 1967a. The countenance of educational evaluation. *Teachers' College Record 68* (7): 523–40.

Stake, R. E. 1967b. Towards a technology for the evaluation of educational programs. In Tyler, Gagné and Scriven: 1–12.

Stansfield, C. W. (Ed.) 1986. Towards communicative competence testing. *Proceedings of the second TOEFL invitational conference.* Princeton, New Jersey: Educational Testing Service.

Stenhouse, L. 1975. *An introduction to curriculum research and development.* London: Heinemann.

Stern, H. H. 1980. Directions in foreign language curriculum development. In *Proceedings of the National Conference on Professional Priorities.* ACTFL Materials Centre: 12–17.

Stern, H. H. 1981. Communicative language teaching and learning: towards a synthesis. In Alatis, Altman, and Alatis: 131–48.

Stern, H. H., 1982a. French core programs across Canada: how can we improve them? *Canadian Modern Language Review/Revue canadienne des langues vivantes 39* (1): 34–47.

Stern, H. H. 1982b. *Issues in early core French: a selective and preliminary review of the literature 1975–1981.* Toronto: Board of Education for the City of Toronto.

Stern, H. H. 1983a. *Fundamental concepts of language teaching.* Oxford: Oxford University Press.

Stern, H. H., 1983b. Toward a multidimensional foreign language curriculum. In Mead: 120–46.

Stern, H. H., 1985. The time factor and compact course development. *TESL Canada Journal 3* (1): 13–27.

Stern, H. H. and J. Cummins. 1981. Language teaching/learning research: a Canadian perspective on status and directions. In Phillips: 195–248.

Stevick, E. W. 1971. *Adapting and writing language lessons.* Washington, D.C.: Foreign Service Institute, United States Department of State.

Stevick, E. W. 1976. *Memory, meaning and method. Some psychological perspectives on language learning.* Rowley, Mass: Newbury House.

Stevick, E. W. 1980. *Teaching languages: a way and ways.* Rowley, Mass: Newbury House.

Stolen, L. (Ed.) 1986. *Extended report of the Council of Europe seminar Lillehammer.* Informasjonssentret for Sprakpedagogik. Oslo.

Strain, J. E. 1986. Design-procedure versus method-technique. *System 14* (3): 287–94.

Strevens, P. 1974. Some basic principles of teacher training. *English Language Teaching Journal 29* (1): 19–27.

Strevens, P. 1977. *New orientations in the teaching of English.* Oxford: Oxford University Press.

Strevens, P. (Ed.) 1978. *In honour of A. S. Hornby.* Oxford: Oxford University Press.

Stubbs, M. 1976. *Language, schools and classrooms.* London: Methuen.

Stufflebeam, D. L. 1974. Alternative approaches to educational evaluation: a self-study guide for educators. In Popham, 1974: 97–143.

Stufflebeam, D. L., W. J. Foley, W. J. Gephart, E. G. Guba, R. L. Hammond, H. O. Merriman, and M. M. Provus. 1971. *Educational evaluation and decision making.* Itasca, Ill: F. E. Peacock.

Stufflebeam, D. L., C. H. McCormick, R. O. Brinkerhoff, and C. O. Nelson. 1985. *Conducting educational needs assessments.* Boston: Kluwer-Nijhoff Publishing.

Subkoviak, M. J. 1980. Decision-consistency approaches. In Berk, 1980a: 129–85.

Swales, J. 1980. 'The educational environment and its relevance to ESP programme design. *ELT Documents special – Projects in Materials Design*: 61–70.

Swales, J. 1984. A review of ESP in the Arab world 1977–1983: trends, developments and retrenchments. In Swales and Mustafa: 9–21.

Swales, J. 1985a. ESP – The heart of the matter or the end of the affair? In Quirk and Widdowson: 212–23.

Swales, J. 1985b. *Episodes in ESP.* Oxford: Pergamon Press.

Swales, J. and H. Mustafa (Eds.) 1984. *English for specific purposes in the Arab World.* Birmingham: The University of Aston.

Taba, H. 1962. *Curriculum development; theory and practice.* New York: Harcourt, Brace and World.

Taylor, B. P. 1982. Curriculum design and the selection of teaching materials. In Barrett: 45–50.

Test of English as a Foreign Language. 1987. *TOEFL test and score manual.* Princeton, N.J.: Educational Testing Service.

Thiele, A. and G. Scheibner-Herzig. 1983. Listening comprehension training in teaching English to beginners. *System 11* (3): 277–86.

Thorndike, R. L. (Ed.) 1971. *Educational measurement.* Washington, D.C.: American Council on Education. 2nd ed.

Tickoo, M. L. (Ed.) 1986. *Language across the curriculum.* Singapore: RELC.

Todd-Trimble, M., L. Trimble, and K. Drobnic (Eds.) 1978. *English for specific purposes/science and technology.* Corvallis: Oregon State University Press.

Tongue, R. and J. Gibbons. 1982. Structural syllabuses and the young beginner. *Applied Linguistics 3* (1): 60–9.

Torrey, J. W. 1969. The learning of grammatical patterns. *Journal of Verbal Learning and Verbal Behaviour 8* (3): 360–8.

Tough, A. 1971. *The adult's learning projects.* Toronto: Ontario Institute for Studies in Education.

Travers, R. M. W. (Ed.) 1973. *Second handbook of research on teaching.* Chicago: Rand McNally.

Trim, J. L. M. 1980. The place of needs analysis in the Council of Europe modern languages project. In Altman and James: 46–65.

Trim, J. L. M., R. Richterich, J. A. van Ek, and D. A. Wilkins (Eds.) 1980. *Systems development in adult language learning.* Oxford: Pergamon Press.

Trimby, M. J. 1979. Needs assessment models: a comparison. *Educational Technology 19* (12): 24–8.

Trueba, H. T., G. P. Guthrie, and K. Au (Eds.) 1981. *Culture and the bilingual classroom.* Rowley, Mass: Newbury House.

Tucker, G. R. and G. A. Cziko. 1978. The role of evaluation in bilingual education. In Alatis: 423–46.

Tucker, G. R., W. E. Lambert, and A. Rigault. 1969. Students' acquisitions of French gender distinctions: a pilot investigation. *IRAL 7* (1): 51–5.

Tuckman, B. W. 1978. *Conducting educational research.* New York: Harcourt, Brace, Jovanovich. 2nd ed.

Tyler, R. W. 1942. General statement on evaluation. *Journal of Educational Research 35* (7): 492–501.

Tyler, R. W. 1949. *Basic principles of curriculum and instruction.* Chicago: University of Chicago Press.

Tyler, R. W. 1951. The functions of measurement in improving instruction. In Lindquist: 47–67.

Tyler, R. W., R. M. Gagné, and M. Scriven (Eds.) 1967. *Perspectives of curriculum evaluation.* Chicago: Rand McNally.

Ullmann, R. 1982. A broadened curriculum framework for second languages. *English Language Teaching Journal 36* (4): 255–62.

Ullman, R. and E. Geva. 1983. TALOS: The target language observation scheme. Mimeo. Toronto: Modern Language Centre, Ontario Institute for Studies in Education.

Ullmann, R. and E. Geva. 1984. Approaches to observation in second language classes. In Allen and Swain: 113–28.

Upshur, J. A. and T. J. Homburg. 1983. Some relations among language tests at successive ability levels. In Oller, 1983b: 188–201.

Vollmer, H. J. and F. Sang. 1983. Competing hypotheses about second language ability: a plea for caution. In Oller 1983b: 29–75.

Wagner, M. J. and G. Tilney. 1983. The effect of 'superlearning techniques' on the vocabulary acquisition and alpha brainwave production of language learners. *TESOL Quarterly 17* (1): 5–17.

Walker, D. F. 1971. A naturalistic model for curriculum development. *School Review 80* (1): 51–65.

Warheit, G. J., J. M. Buhl, and R. A. Bell. 1978. A critique of social indicators analysis and key informants surveys as needs assessment methods. *Evaluation and Program Planning 1,* 239–47.

Waters, A. (Ed.) 1982. *Issues in ESP.* Oxford: Pergamon Press.

Weatherman R. and K. Swenson. 1974. Delphi technique. In Hencley and Yates: 97–114.

Weiss, C. H. 1972. *Evaluation research: methods for assessing program effectiveness.* Englewood Cliffs, N.J.: Prentice-Hall.

West, M. 1953. *A general service list of English words.* London: Longman.

Wickrama, O. U. W. 1982. Linguistic features of commercial law texts and their pedagogical implications. M.Sc. Thesis. Birmingham: University of Aston.

Widdowson, H. G. 1981a. Les fins et les moyens d'un enseignement de l'anglais en vue d'objectifs specifiques. (Teaching English for special purposes: objectives and approaches) *Etudes de Linguistique Appliquée 43*: 8–21.

Widdowson, H. G. 1981b. English for specific purposes: criteria for course design. In Selinker, Tarone, and Hanzell (Eds.): 1–11.

Widdowson, H. G. 1983. *Learning purpose and language use.* Oxford: Oxford University Press.

Widdowson, H. G. (Ed.) 1984a. *Explorations in applied linguistics 2.* Oxford: Oxford University Press.

Widdowson, H. G. 1984b. Criteria for course design. In Widdowson, 1984a: 177–88.

Wilkins, D. A. 1976. *Notional syllabuses.* Oxford: Oxford University Press.

Willing, K. 1985a. *Learning styles in adult migrant education.* Sydney: New South Wales Adult Migrant Education Service.

Willing, K. 1985b. *Helping adults develop their learning strategies.* Sydney: Adult Migrant Education Service.

Willis, G. (Ed.) 1978. *Qualitative evaluation.* Berkeley, Calif: McCutchan.

Willis, J. D. 1985. Theory and methodology: do we do what we are knowing? In Das.

Wingard, P. 1983. Training English lecturers in an overseas university. In Jordan: 244–55.

Winitz, H. (Ed.) 1981. *The comprehension approach to foreign language instruction.* Rowley, Mass: Newbury House.

Witkin, B. R. 1977. Needs assessment kits, models and tools. *Educational Technology 17* (11): 5–18.

Wittrock, M. E. (Ed.) Forthcoming. *Handbook of research on teaching.* 3rd ed.

Wohl, M. 1967. Classroom experiment to measure the relative efficiency of two different linguistic models in their application to the teaching of English as a foreign language. Unpublished report. Michigan University.

Worthen, B. R. and J. R. Sanders. 1973. *Educational evaluation: theory and practice.* Worthington, Ohio: C. A. Jones Publishing Company.

Xiem, N. V. 1969. The role of explanation in the teaching of the grammar of a foreign language: an experimental study of two techniques. Unpublished thesis. University of California, Los Angeles.

Yalden, J. 1983. *The communicative syllabus: evolution, design, and implementation.* Oxford: Pergamon Press.

Yalden, J. 1987. *Principles of course design for language teaching.* Cambridge: Cambridge University Press.

Young, M. F. D. (Ed.) 1971. *Knowledge and control.* London: Collier-Macmillan.

Young, R. 1980. Modular course design. *ELT Documents special – Projects in Materials Design.* London: The British Council: 222–31.

Zieky, M. J. and S. A. Livingston. 1977. *Basic skills assessment. Manual for setting standards on the basic skills assessment tests.* Princeton, N.J.: Educational Testing Service.

Index